Exploring Hypertext Programming:

Writing Knowledge Representation and Problem-Solving Programs

The Advanced Programming Technology Series

Exploring Hypertext Programming:
Writing Knowledge Representation and Problem-Solving Programs
by Safaa H. Hashim

Exploring Natural Language Processing:
Writing BASIC Programs that Understand English
by David Leithauser

Exploring the Geometry of Nature:
Computer Modeling of Chaos, Fractals, Cellular
Automata and Neural Networks
by Edward Rietman

Exploring Hypertext Programming:

Writing Knowledge Representation and Problem-Solving Programs

Safaa H. Hashim

Notices

IBM, IBM PC, and **PC DOS** are registered trademarks of International Business Machines Inc.

Turbo Prolog is a trademark of Borland International.

Turbo Prolog Toolbox is a trademark of Borland International.

MS DOS is a registered trademark of Microsoft Corporation.

HyperCard is a registered trademark of Apple Computers Inc.

MicroIBIS is a registered trademark of BlueSoft Inc.

Windcrest books are published by Windcrest Books, an imprint of TAB BOOKS. The name "Windcrest" is a registered trademark of TAB BOOKS.

Published by **Windcrest Books**
FIRST EDITION/FIRST PRINTING

Library of Congress Cataloging-in-Publication Data

Hashim, Safaa H.
Exploring hypertext programming : writing knowledge representation and problem-solving programs / by Safaa H. Hashim.
p. cm.
ISBN 0-8306-3208-5
1. Hypertext systems. I. Title.
QA76.76.H94H38 1990 89-70482
005.75'4—dc20 CIP

TAB BOOKS offers software for sale. For information and a catalog, please contact TAB Software Department, Blue Ridge Summit, PA 17294-0850.

Questions regarding the content of this book should be addressed to:

Windcrest Books
Imprint of TAB BOOKS
Blue Ridge Summit, PA 17294-0850

Director of Acquisitions: Ron Powers
Book Editor: David Harter
Production: Katherine Brown

I dedicate this book to my father Hussien Hashim Al-Mali.

Contents

APPENDICES

Acknowledgments

Throughout this project I was fortunate to have the love and support of Maria Elizabeth De Castro, Leah Redil, and their family. I am heavily indebted to Maria for her help in editing most of the chapters in this book. Also I would like to thank Borland International, especially Mike Floyde and Nan Borreson for helping me out with many questions and requests on Borland products. From the College of Environmental Design at the University of California in Berkeley I would like to thank my advisers, professor Horst Rittel and professor J. P. Protzen, for the interesting discussions on Issue Based Information Systems. And last, but not least, I can't forget the support and encouragement of my friends, Haider Taha, Basil Al-Ubadi Abdul-Aziz Al-Shaye, Nabel Kamal, and Adeeb Nori. I would like to thank Jeff Conklin and the staff at the software technology program at MCC.

Introduction

"Deep in the heart of everyone,
There is a wide frontier,
A vast expanse to overcome,
Beset with toil and fear.

There is no smooth and easy path,
Each one must find their way,
And prove their merit traveling on
With faith, from day to day."

—A poem titled PIONEERS by Dovie A. Owens

The frontier is the ever-increasing amount of information that we can create, manipulate, and store in computers. The pioneers are those who think up new ideas that make the storage and retrieval of information faster, easier, affordable, and—more important—interesting. One such idea is Hypertext.

The first pioneer was Vannevar Bush, president Franklin D. Roosevelt's science adviser. In 1945, in an article titled "As We May Think" in the "Atlantic Monthly" Bush proposed a machine, called "Memex." His idea is that the Memex would improve the quality of human thinking by providing quick access to huge databases of information. He proposed the Memex to help keep track of the increasing amount of our knowledge in science and technology. His main concern was the evolution process of knowledge in a society. His Memex is not only for storing and retrieving large amounts of knowledge. He wanted it to help researchers in retrieving multiple views of the same body of knowledge. Eventually researchers using the Memex would create new knowledge that would extend the Memex:

"Much needs to occur, however, between the collection of data and observations, the extraction of parallel material from the existing record, and the final insertion of new material into the general body of the common record. For mature thought there is no mechanical substitute. But creative thought and essentially repetitive thought are very different things. For the latter there are, and may be, powerful mechanical aids."

Five years later, these lines inspired a second pioneer, Doug Engelbart, who at the time was in graduate school at the University of California at Berkeley. In 1962, while at the Stanford Research Institute (SRI), Engelbart outlined his ideas on what he called "augmentation," as in "augmenting human intellect." In 1968 Engelbart finished his work on a system he called NLS (oN Line System) which included a mouse, multiple windows, electronic mail, and teleconferencing capabilities. In 1978 Tymshare of Cupertino, California, bought NLS from SRI and renamed it "Augment." Augment is now marketed by McDonnell-Douglas as a commercial network system. Augment has facilities for editing text and graphics and it can manage complex databases. Augment allows the setup of links between different documents. Users of Augment can expand and contract mouse-sensitive areas on the screen to reveal additional levels. It is true that capability to hide pieces of information on different levels supports selective viewing, but you soon get overwhelmed when trying to extract one particular piece. To deal with this problem Augment designers used the idea of viewing filters. Filters let you selectively control the format, content, and scope of information displayed on the screen.

Bush's article in the *Atlantic Monthly* inspired a third pioneer, Ted Nelson. As Engelbart was developing his "Augment" system, Ted Nelson was working on a system that would change the way we read and write using computers. Nelson coined the term "hypertext" to describe what he calls the "writing of tomorrow." His task was not an easy one. At that time there were no computer screens—computers were mainly scientific machines programmed by feeding them punch cards. Nelson's motivation for creating hypertext systems is his search for appropriate systems to help keep track of all the "things" that one might want to understand and master. His hypertext system would have a large database of the world's literature as building blocks. Using his system, which he calls "Xanadu," one can browse randomly and create new literary documents by combining complete, or fragments of, existing blocks. The resulting new document doesn't exist as a separate item. What exists is just the structure—i.e., network of nodes and links—which is the result of accumulated changes made to the original building blocks. To retrieve the resulting document, the system uses the structure as a blueprint to reassemble the new document from the original source building blocks.

As you can see, the work of these three pioneers is not about how we present information, rather it is about how we use information. The hypertext way of presenting information is just a tool that makes it easier to understand, and generate information. In this sense, we can consider hypertext as a knowledge representation technique. To take this one step further, we can use hypertext as the basis for knowledge-based systems, which in Artificial Intelligence are known as "expert systems."

In this book I would like to explore with you the programming of hypertext based knowledge systems. My programming language of choice is Turbo Prolog. Turbo Prolog is an efficient and affordable compiler for the popular logic programming language Prolog. The book is in three parts. In PART ONE I discuss the elements of hypertext, their meaning and how to program them. In PART TWO I use the elements of hypertext from PART ONE to build a complete file-based hypertext system which I call ET—i.e., Extended Text. In the last chapter of PART TWO, in Chapter 8, I will discuss the basics for constructing external databases. In PART THREE, armed with the programming techniques learned in PARTS ONE and TWO, you explore the programming of a hypertext system for computer-based cooperative work and problem solving, which I call MicroIBIS (Micro Issue Based Information System).

Part One

The Elements of Hypertext

1

Hypertext: The Basics

"Science is facts. Just as houses are made of stones, so is science made of facts. But a pile of stones is not a house and a collection of facts is not necessarily science."

—Henri Poincare; (1854 – 1912) French scientist

This chapter will define hypertext and will discuss its basic elements: What does the term "hypertext" mean? What are the differences between hypertext and presenting text (printed matter) and database systems. Also discussed will be some of the advantages and disadvantages of using hypertext.

Also in this chapter, you will find some Turbo Prolog programming examples—the language used in this book. Prolog, in its declarative style, will help us represent hypertext concepts in a compact and logical form. This chapter requires basic knowledge of Turbo Prolog programming (at least the first three chapters of the Turbo Prolog user manual. Without any further delays, let's start talking hyper.

WHAT HYPERTEXT MEANS

Ted Nelson, the hypertext guru and the author of "Xanadu," believed in the effect of words in publicizing new ideas and concepts. He wanted a short word that is easy to remember, with one syllable being the word "text" or "write." After seeing movies of Ivan Sutherland and others, showing their pioneering work on interactive graphics, he realized what this would mean if it were applied to text. In his article "To Strike the Lighting, Hyper Age, February – March, 1988," he explains how he wanted to publicize and inform everyone about "the new writing of tomorrow." First, he tried using words like: linktext, jumptext, non-sequential text, and zapwrite; but once he thought of "hypertext," he knew it was the perfect word for it!

Webster's dictionary defines hyper as a prefix—the first part of a composite word—which means "over," "above," and "excessive." In science and mathematics, it means "generalized" or "extended." It is similar to hyper in hyperspace, hyper-dimensional, hyper-cube, hyper-sphere.

Thus, the word hyper in "hypertext" would give "text" an extended or generalized form. In hypertext, the information is not presented in a single layer of text. It is a multilayered environment. What you see on the computer screen is only one layer; but there is "more" than what you see.

Now that you know what hypertext means, let's discuss its basic elements.

BASIC ELEMENTS OF HYPERTEXT

In essence, hypertext can be described as these two types: "chunks of textual information" and "links" (references) between these chunks. Think of a textual chunk as a building in a city. To go from one building to another, you use streets. Links are the streets of hypertext—you use them to go from one chunk of text to another.

It doesn't seem much, does it? In fact, according to this definition, any book or newspaper article will easily qualify as a hypertext system. After all, you can say that in any book: its paragraphs, its sections, its chapters, and its parts are all linked to one another. They follow each other, explicitly (on the book pages), and implicitly through the plot of the book (introduction, pro and con arguments, and conclusion). Most of the time, you will find references within the text to footnote explanations and figures or tables. So, what's the difference?

The major difference is that books or articles are linear (also called sequential or serial). When you read a book, there is one line or one sequence to follow—and it never changes. A book has only one plot. While in a hypertext document, you can jump anywhere in the text by following a link. FIGURE 1-1 shows a sketch for this concept.

Here is a question for you: Can you think of a manual hypertext-like system that is not a computer system? To make it easier for you, here is a hint: You use this system when you are trying to find something in a library.

You most probably guessed it right. Yes, it is the library card catalogue. The key element in the card catalogue is the notecard. Soon after the invention of the card catalogue in the middle 1800's, libraries became a place for exploration of knowledge rather than just a place for storing books. These cards opened a whole new way for capturing a vast amount of knowledge (saved in thousands of books) in one catalogue of index cards.

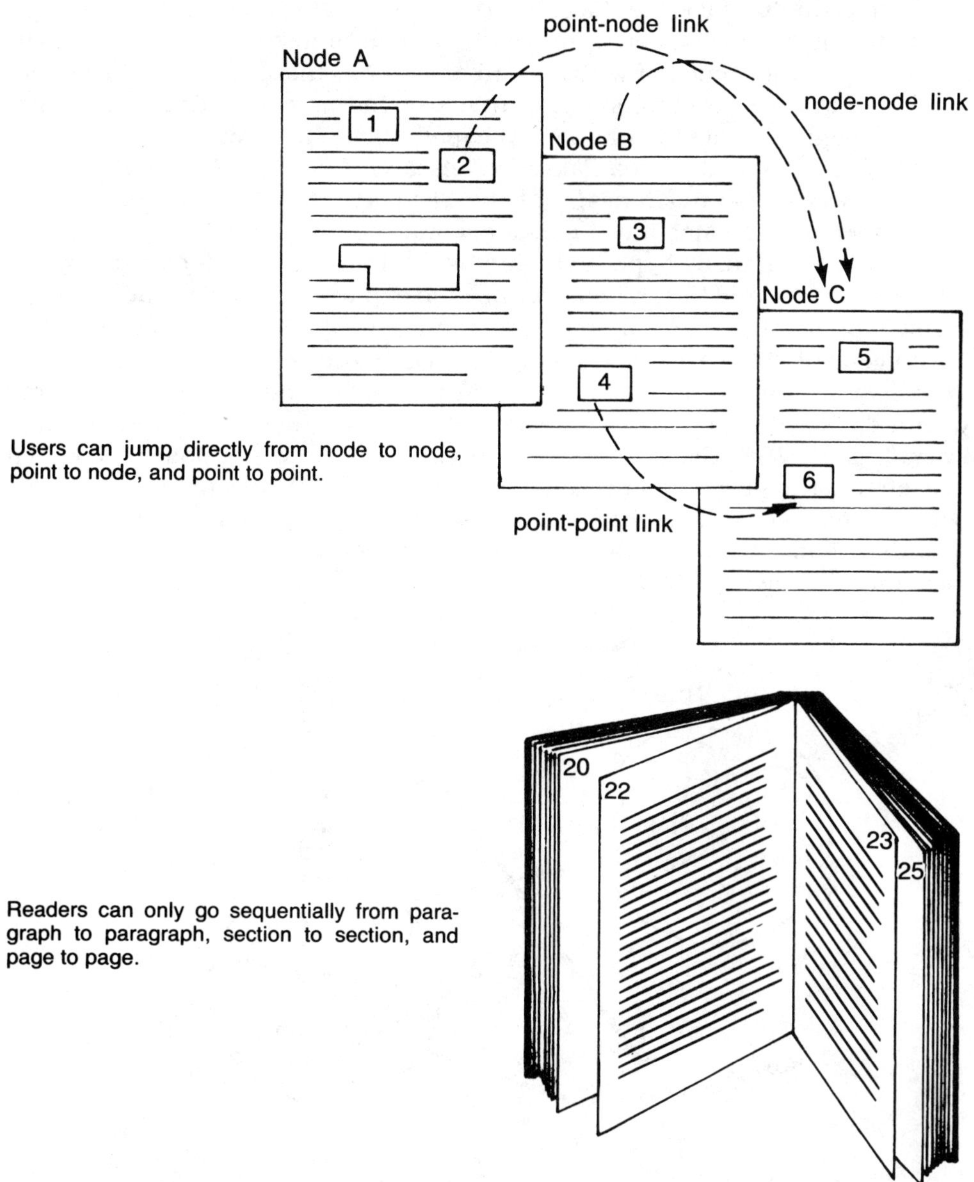

Fig. 1-1. Comparing a hypertext document to a printed document.

Here is a typical scenario of what normally happens when you go to a library. You have a particular topic in mind and you go to the subject index catalogue; you look for the drawer with the letter that matches the first letter of your topic; you then open the drawer and look for a card with your selected book title; you write the book name and catalogue number on a piece of paper; and then go to the stacks, and look for the book. When you find the book, and realize that it is not what you want, you then scan some of the books next to it; and soon you will come out with a number of books that can cover your topic.

There are two existing systems that use the notecard idea—and metaphor—to communicate their hypertext capabilities. These systems are: "NoteCard" of Xerox PARC (Xerox Palo Alto Research Center), which operates on Xerox D series Lisp machines; and the "HyperCard" of Apple Computers, which operates on a Macintosh personal computer.

Clearly, then, many hypertext systems echo the card catalogue analogy. It is the experience and the joy of searching and exploring books in a library, that many hypertext designers are trying to capture in a computer system.

In general, "hypertext system" is referred to as a computer-based system. When you deal with chunks of text in the computer, you are actually dealing with a database organized as a network. FIGURE 1-2 shows a sketch of a network. In a network, the system saves text in "nodes." These nodes are linked to each other to give the network its distinctive form. *Nodes* are relationships between nodes and are represented as either complete files or database records in a file. *Links*, on the other hand, are pointers whose values are the locations of nodes.

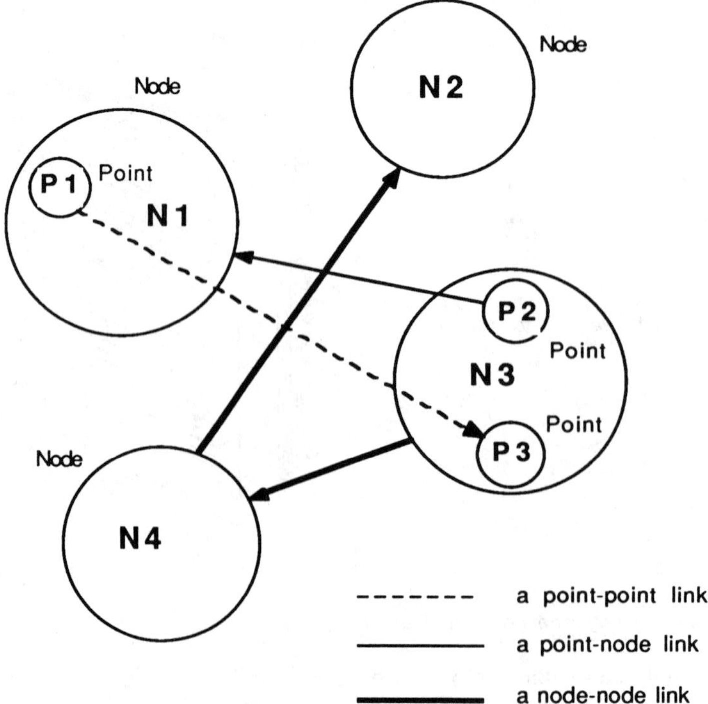

Fig. 1-2. The concept of hypertext as a network.

NODES, POINTS, AND LINKS

The conclusion is that hypertext is a network of nodes and links; but how about connecting only a part of the text in a node (not the whole node) to another node. This implies that the node itself is made of chunks of text. In general, there are two types of text in a node:

1) Text linked to other chunks of text; or to other nodes in the database file; this kind of text is called a "point."
2) Non-linked text, which is simply called "regular text."

By this, a hypertext document is defined as a network of:

1) Chunks of text: nodes or points.
2) Links.

So, how can these elements be used in building a hypertext system?

First, you need a programming language—one that is powerful, robust, and capable of satisfying your current and future needs.

Second, you need to know more about the network in practical terms. What do nodes really mean when coded in a program? Are they database records? Are they lists of symbols? How about points—how do you implement them? Do you use a field in a database record as a point? Do you use an entry in array as a point? Do you use an element of a list as a point? Now, how about links? Can you use pointers (as in C or Pascal), or a relation (as in Prolog), or a function (as in LISP)?

Third: Is the actual coding of a hypertext system in a program?

The rest of this chapter will cover the first two points and part of the third point. From Chapter 2 and on, I will do more hypertext programming and say less about the theory of hypertext. Without any more delays, let's deal with the first point—choosing a programming language.

WRITING HYPERTEXT PROGRAMS IN TURBO PROLOG

You might ask why I am using Turbo Prolog and not any other programming language. Because the advantages are overwhelming.

With Turbo Prolog you can combine both artificial intelligence and hypertext in one program. The reasons are:

- Turbo Prolog is a powerful AI programming language. You can develop an expert system that saves its knowledge in a hypertext network. To answer a question, to satisfy a goal, and to diagnose a problem, it only needs to follow the links. Conditions in a rule are satisfied when there are links to *factual nodes*—nodes that contain facts.

- Turbo Prolog is a relational programming language. Hypertext links are themselves relations. In this case, a list of relations is used to represent a hypertext network. You can use these relations to query the network when searching for information.
- Version two of Turbo Prolog has two sets of database predicates:

  Internal database predicates are: "assert," "asserta," "assertz," "retract," "retracta," "retractz," "consult," and "save." For a large database, the random access memory (RAM) requirements for these predicates can easily exceed the capacity of your computer. The external database predicates in version two solve this problem. In Chapters 2, 3, and 4, internal database predicates are used in hypertext programs.

  External database predicates are composed of an external collection of chained terms. These chained terms give you direct access to data that is not a part of your Prolog program. You can store the external database in any one of three locations: in file, in memory, or in EMS—extended memory system. The external database supports B+ trees, which provide fast data retrieval and the ability to sort quickly. In PART TWO, you will learn how to use these predicates in programming your hypertext system.

To move swiftly along links (between points and nodes) you need windows, menus, special effects, and many other user-interface tools. Turbo Prolog and its TOOLBOX have these and more:

- Turbo Prolog has extensive windowing capabilities.
- Turbo Prolog TOOLBOX has several menu-building programs.
- Turbo Prolog provides advanced graphic and sound predicates that you can use to extend hypertext to hypermedia.

RELATING THE ELEMENTS OF HYPERTEXT TO TURBO PROLOG

Now that you have a programming language, how do you relate it to the three elements of hypertext—nodes, points and links. I will talk, in some detail, about each one of these elements; but first, ready your Turbo Prolog for programming. With each element that is discussed, I will define its "domains" declarations. Also, sample programs will explain how these elements work together in generating extended text—hypertext.

NODES

A node is a chunk of text that you can break down into smaller chunks that are called "regions." A *region* (source or destination) is a set of contiguous characters that is displayed, in some way, as being a single unit. An example of a region is a paragraph. A paragraph is a chunk of text that you can break down into sentences. A node in itself is a region—a chunk of text.

One Idea per Node

"The important thing involved is, of course, ideas. The whole purpose of paragraphing is to separate ideas, to give each one its own setting so that it can be fully and clearly developed without interference from others."—Lucile Vaughan Payne, *The Lively Art of Writing.*

In hypertext, thoughts are organized in a network. To communicate these thoughts to others, you use a chain of ideas. If you put only one idea in a node, then by tracing a path in the network, you can retrieve a chain of ideas. This way, hypertext can serve as a powerful writing and problem-solving tool; but unlike the paragraph, a node is a separate unit. It doesn't need to relate to its neighbors.

Node Size—Not Too Big and Not Too Small

"Resist the temptation to make everything bigger and more gorgeous when you need strong communication."—Frank Thomas and Ollie Johnston; in Paul Heckel's *The Elements of Friendly Software Design.*

"One Idea per Node" should serve as a good measure for the size of your nodes. If you have many small sized nodes, this will increase the degree of organization of information in your system. Consequently, you will get a large network that causes delay in retrieving links. On the other hand, few large-sized nodes will minimize delay; but this might cost you the "One Idea per Node" principle.

Nodes in Turbo Prolog

In Turbo, you can represent a node in many ways. I will show you three ways to do that.

1) You can use a compound object—a term—to represent a node; for example:

```
DOMAINS
    TEXT = text(STRING)
    ID   = SYMBOL
    NODE = node(ID)

DATABASE
has_text(NODE,TEXT)
```

Here, a node has an identification number ID, which is a symbolic name. (You can supply your own ID numbers for each node you add; or you can write Turbo rules to automatically generate a new ID number when adding a new node.) Notice the compound object NODE; it is a "unary relation"—a term with one argument.

2) Also, you can define a node as a database fact. Remember that in Turbo Prolog, database facts are declared in a separate database section. Look at this code:

```
DOMAINS
      TEXT  = text(STRING)
      ID    = SYMBOL
DATABASE
   node(ID,TEXT)
```

3) In Turbo Prolog version 2.00, you can use Turbo's external database predicates. I will discuss this approach in PART TWO; but to give you the flavor of this approach, enter and run this piece of code:

```
DOMAINS
   db_selector = hyperdb
   node = node(STRING)
GOAL
   db_creat(hyperdb,"filename.hyp",in_memory)
   chain_insertz(hyperdb,nodes_chain,node,
      node("I like the late night time."),ID),
   readln(_),
   ref_term(hyperdb,node,ID,node(STRING)),
   write("node contents= ",STRING).
```

The built-in predicate "chain_insertz" inserts a node in the database file "filename.hyp". It will generate an ID number for the node node("I like the late night"). I use this ID in the built-in predicate "ref_term" to access the text ("STRING") of the node.

In general, all information of a hypertext system is in nodes. Nodes are like the rooms of a building. In a building, you need corridors or hallways to go from one room to another. The links in a hypertext system are like the hallways. You use them to go from one node to another.

LINKS

Links are "relations" which act as glue between the different nodes. Basically, there are three types of links: node-node, point-node, and point-point links. The simplest form of linking is the node-node link.

In Turbo Prolog you can represent the linking relation as a predicate. For example, the relation "link(Node,Node)" represents a node-node link. The program declaration for this relation will then be:

```
DOMAINS
   ID    = SYMBOL
   TEXT  = STRING
   NODE  = node(ID)
```

```
PREDICATES
    link(NODE,NODE)
    has_text(NODE,TEXT)
```

This is fine as a representation, but how does it work in a program? Let's write a program which uses this declaration to generate a hypertext output. Take a look at the program in FIG. 1-3. The main predicate in this program is "hypertext(NODE,TEXT)". It has the flow pattern (i,o)—meaning, you supply the node and it gives you back the hypertext. The best way to study the program is by running it. If you want to see how "hypertext" generates its output, put the "trace" compiler directive at the top of the program.

Fig. 1-3. Hypertext program with only nodes and links.

```
DOMAINS
 ID = SYMBOL
 TEXT = STRING
 NODE = node(ID)

PREDICATES
 hypertext(NODE,TEXT)
   hypertext1(NODE,TEXT,TEXT)
 link(NODE,NODE)
 has_text(NODE,TEXT)

CLAUSES

/* ********************** has_text ********************** */

 has_text(node(n1), "I like the late night time.").
 has_text(node(n2), "The night is the only time I can do my work.").
 has_text(node(n3), "I usually stay up to 3 or 4 am. each day.").
 has_text(node(n4), "The day time I spend it at school.").

/* ************************* link ********************** */
 link(node(n1),node(n2)).
 link(node(n2),node(n3)).
 link(node(n2),node(n4)).
 link(node(n3),node(n4)).

 /* ********************* hypertext ******************** */

/* Hypertext is any possible text in NODE only,
   or text of NODE and the nodes linked to NODE */

/* hypertext is the text in node NODE */

 hypertext(NODE,TEXT) :-
   has_text(NODE,TEXT).

/* hypertext is the text in NODE and all
   nodes linked to NODE */

 hypertext(NODE,TEXT) :-
   has_text(NODE,STR),
   link(NODE,NODE1),
   hypertext1(NODE1,STR,TEXT).

/* ************************ hypertext1 **************** */
```

(Fig. 1-3. continued)

```
  hypertext1(NODE,STR1,TEXT) :-
    link(NODE,NODE2),
    has_text(NODE2,STR2),
    concat(STR1,STR2,STR),
    hypertext1(NODE2,STR,TEXT).

  hypertext1(NODE,STR,TEXT) :-
    has_text(NODE,STR1),
    concat(STR,STR1,TEXT).

/* ************************ END END END **************** */
```

Run the program and give this goal:

```
hypertext(node(n1),HYPERTEXT)
```

Notice how the "hypertext" uses: First, the predicate "has_text" to retrieve the text of "node1"; second, the "link" predicate to find out which node is linked to "node(n1)"; and third, the recursive predicate "hypertext1" to retrieve and glue the text of all nodes linked directly or indirectly, to "node1".

I will talk more about how Turbo Prolog generates all possible "hypertext" solutions when I introduce "points" in the next section.

In some hypertext systems, there are no points—just nodes and links. A good example is an on-line help system. It only provides out-links from the entire node; this form is fine for a browsing system, but is inadequate for authoring applications, in which the references need to be placed within the text. At this point, this is all you need to know about nodes. Now, it is time to know more about points.

POINTS

A *point* is part of a node that is linked to another node or point. Basically, there are three kinds of links:

1) link a point to a node,
2) link a point to another in the same node,
3) link a point in a node to another point in a different node.

In general, you can make a point the source or the destination of a link. (An example of a system where points are allowed to be sources and destinations of links is the Tektronix Neptune system.) In FIG. 1-2, the sketch of a hypertext network, notice the point-node and point-point links.

In Turbo Prolog, you can represent points as compound objects. Take a look at the following domains and predicates declarations:

```
DOMAINS
    ID        = SYMBOL
    TEXT      = txt(STRING)
    NODE      = n(ID)
```

```
    POINT    = p(ID)
    ELEMENT  = p(ID); txt(STRING)
    ELEMENTS = ELEMENT*

PREDICATES
  nn_link(NODE,NODE)
  pn_link(POINT,NODE)
  pp_link(POINT,POINT)
  has_elements(NODE,ELEMENTS)
  has_text(POINT,TEXT)
```

Here, the contents of the node is a list of elements. An element is either a string of regular text—the compound object txt(STRING)—or a point—the compound object p(ID). Also, notice the three link predicates. From top to bottom, they are: node-node, point-node, and point-point link predicates.

The program in FIG. 1-4 uses nodes, points, and links to generate all possible hypertext network paths.

Fig. 1-4. Hypertext program with nodes, points, and links.

```
DOMAINS
  ID       = SYMBOL
  TEXT     = txt(STRING)
  NODE     = n(ID)
  POINT    = p(ID)
  ELEMENT  = p(ID); txt(STRING)
  ELEMENTS = ELEMENT*

PREDICATES
  hypertext(NODE,TEXT)
    hypertext1(NODE,TEXT,TEXT)
      hypertext2(NODE,ELEMENTS,TEXT,TEXT)

/* links: node-node and point-node */

  nn_link(NODE,NODE)
  pn_link(POINT,NODE)

/* contents of node and point objects */

  has_elements(NODE,ELEMENTS)
  has_text(POINT,TEXT)

GOAL
  hypertext(n(n1),HYPERTEXT).

CLAUSES

/* contents of node objects */

 has_elements(n(n1),[txt("I like the "),p(p1),txt("in my place. ")]).
 has_elements(n(n2),[txt("The night is the only time I can do my work. ")]).
 has_elements(n(n3), [txt("I usually stay up to 3 or 4 am. each day. ")]).
 has_elements(n(n4), [txt("The day time I spend it at "),p(p2)]).
 has_elements(n(n5), [txt(", after midnight, when it is very quite, ")]).
 has_elements(n(n6), [txt("--University of California at Berkeley. ")]).

/* contents of point objects */
```

(**Fig. 1-4.** continued)

```
has_text(p(p1), txt("late night time ") ).
has_text(p(p2), txt("school") ).

/* node-node links */

nn_link(n(n1),n(n2)).
nn_link(n(n2),n(n3)).
nn_link(n(n2),n(n4)).
nn_link(n(n3),n(n4)).

/* point-node links */

pn_link(p(p1),n(n5)).
pn_link(p(p2),n(n6)).

/* Gnerating the hypertext "TEXT" of a given node "NODE" */

hypertext(NODE,TEXT):-
  hypertext1(NODE,txt(""),TEXT).

hypertext1(NODE,txt(OldTXT),txt(NewTXT)):-
  has_elements(NODE,ELEMENTS),
  hypertext2(NODE,ELEMENTS,txt(""),txt(TempTXT)),
  concat(OldTXT,TempTXT,NewTXT).

hypertext1(NODE,txt(OldTXT),TEXT):-
  has_elements(NODE,ELEMENTS),
  hypertext2(NODE,ELEMENTS,txt(""),txt(TempTXT)),
  concat(OldTXT,TempTXT,TXT1),
  nn_link(NODE,NODE1),
  hypertext1(NODE1,txt(TXT1),TEXT).

hypertext2(_,[],TEXT,TEXT).

hypertext2(NODE,[txt(TXT)|Rest],txt(OldTXT),TEXT):-
  concat(OldTXT,TXT,TempTXT),
  hypertext2(NODE,Rest,txt(TempTXT),TEXT).

hypertext2(NODE,[p(P)|Rest],txt(OldTXT),TEXT):-
  has_text(p(P),txt(PointTXT)),
  concat(OldTXT,PointTXT,TXT1),
  pn_link(p(P),NODE1),
  hypertext1(NODE1,txt(TXT1),txt(TempTXT)),
  hypertext2(NODE,Rest,txt(TempTXT),TEXT).

/* ********************** END END END ****************** */
```

FIGURE 1-5 shows the hypertext network for this program. When you load and run the program, Turbo will give you all possible hypertext outputs starting from the node n1. Try a different goal where the input node is n2 instead of n1. This will give a different set of paths in the network. How does Turbo Prolog generate all the possible paths in a network? It's the backtracking feature of Prolog.

This program, in fact, shows an interesting combination between Prolog features and hypertext. One of these features is the "backtracking." After you run the program, Turbo will execute the goal:

```
hypertext(node(n1),HYPERTEXT),
```

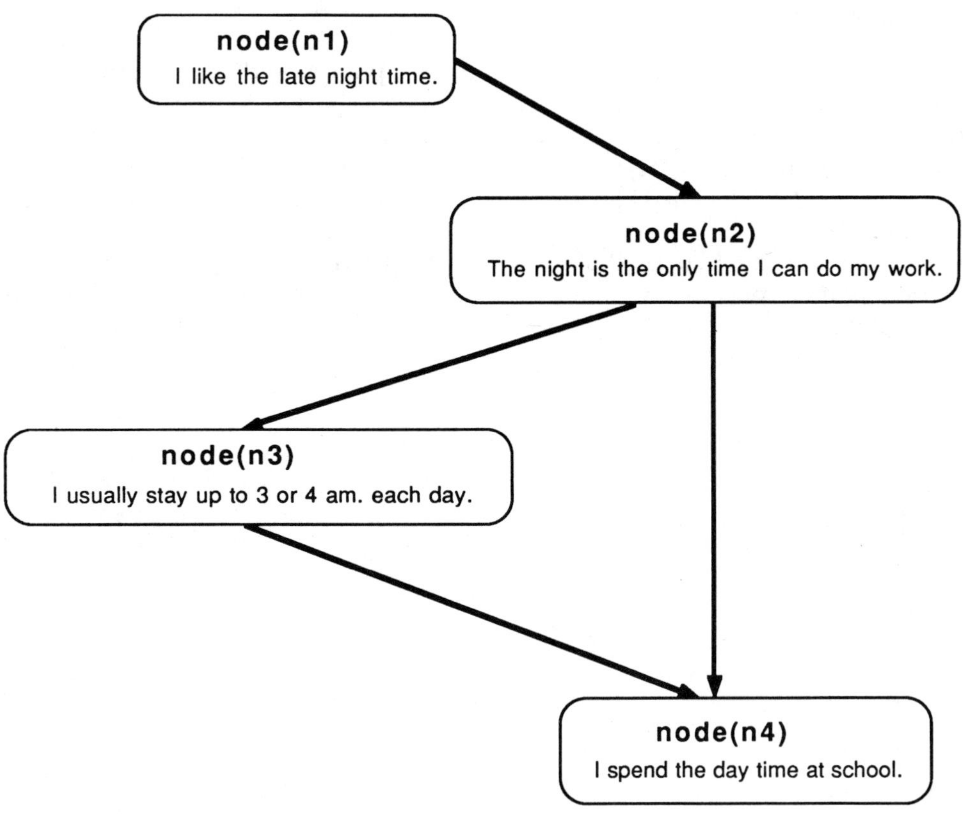

Fig. 1-5. Hypertext network for the program in Fig. 1-4.

The first goal will generate all alternative values for "HYPERTEXT." Every "HYPERTEXT" value represents a different path in the hypertext network. Every time Turbo finishes tracing a path, it backtracks one step to generate a different path. It keeps doing this until it exhausts all alternative answers:

HYPERTEXT = I like the late night time.
HYPERTEXT = I like the late night time. I usually stay up to 3 or 4 a.m. each day. The day time I spend it at school.
HYPERTEXT = I like the late night time. I usually stay up to 3 or 4 a.m. each day.
HYPERTEXT = I like the late night time. The day time I spend it at school.
HYPERTEXT = I like the late night time. The night is the only time I can do my work.
5 Solutions

The "backtracking" feature of Prolog is only one of the techniques that you can use to write AI-based hypertext systems. In this book, I take advantage of Turbo's AI features in building hypertext systems.

HYPERTEXT FILES

A hypertext file is a database with nodes, points, and links as records in the database. Each hypertext file represents a separate network. Vendors of hypertext systems may use different terminology for identifying hypertext files. For example, in the HyperCard system for the Macintosh, a file is called a stack and nodes are called cards. In this book I use "file" to represent a hypertext network.

In the ultimate hypertext system, files are themselves parts of a meta-network. In a meta-network, you can link one file—a hypertext network—to nodes and points in a different file.

2

Hypertext Programming in Turbo Prolog

"A user expects that his programs be no more complicated to understand than the task they are doing for him."

—*Paul Heckel; "The Elements of Friendly Software Design"*

Chapter 1 listed three major steps you need to know before writing hypertext programs. These steps are:

1) Choosing an appropriate programming language—I chose Turbo Prolog.
2) Knowing more about representing a hypertext network in the programming language of your choice. For example, in Turbo Prolog you can either use the internal or the external (built-in) database predicates.
3) The actual coding of the hypertext system in a program.

In this chapter, and in Chapter 3, you will learn step 3—that is, how to write hypertext programs in Turbo. You will write programs that let you view and expand the hypertext network. These are a few simple, but powerful programs. They are simple because I use only basic—non-advanced—prolog programming. Yet, they are advanced enough to use them in building complete hypertext systems. In short, I will follow Albert Einstein's advice: "Make things as simple as possible—but not simpler."

The first part of any Turbo program is the declaration part. These are the "domains," the "predicates," and the "database" sections.

DECLARING THE NETWORK

The simplest hypertext system is one with nodes saved in separate files. This is implemented by declaring a node as a compound object:

```
DOMAINS
  FILENAME = STRING
  NODE = node(FILENAME)
```

The compound object "node(FILENAME)" helps you to pass nodes as arguments to a predicate. For example, you can pass nodes to these relations:

```
    nnlink(NODE,NODE)  /* a node-node link  */
    pnlink(POINT,NODE) /* a point-node link */
```

Notice the "point" object in the "pnlink"—meaning, you need to declare point objects. One possibility is to declare a point as a compound object with one argument. The argument of a point object is a string representing the hypertext. In general, a complete declaration of the hypertext network should look something like this:

```
DOMAINS
  FILENAME = STRING
  NODE = node(FILENAME)
  POINT = point(STRING)
DATABASE
  nnlink(NODE,NODE)
  pnlink(POINT,NODE)
  pplink(POINT,POINT)
  node(NODE)
  point(STRING)
```

You need the database section to save the configuration of the network to an external file. This means that your hypertext system is built from three types of files:

- The hypertext program. This is a set of one or more Turbo Prolog programs—files with the ".pro" extension.
- The hypertext network configuration file—a file with the ".net" extension.
- Files with the text for the nodes—these are files with the ".hyp" extension.

It's show time. For example, FIG. 2-1 shows the main program. This program needs another module for extracting a hypertext point from a node. This additional module is listed in FIG. 2-2. In FIG. 2-3 is a list of facts representing a sample network configuration file. FIGURE 2-4 contains the text of five sample nodes. When trying the example, remember to save the text for each of the five nodes in a separate file. You can name these files as node1.hyp, node2.hyp, node3.hyp, node4.hyp, and node5.hyp.

Fig. 2-1. A simple hypertext viewing program.

```
/* ******************** PROGRAM WINDOWS ****************** */
PREDICATES
  blankwindow
  editwindow

CLAUSES
% blankwindow
blankwindow :- makewindow(1,7,0,"",0,0,25,80).

% edit window
editwindow :- makewindow(2,15,112,"HyperText",3,0,21,80).

/* ********************** UTILITY PREDICATES ************ */

DOMAINS
  STRINGLIST = STRING*

PREDICATES
  write_list(STRINGLIST)
  nondeterm repeat

CLAUSES
  repeat.
  repeat:-repeat.

  write_list([]).
  write_list([H|T]):-
        write(H),
        write_list(T).

/* ******************** HYPERTEXT PREDICATES ************ */

DOMAINS
  FILENAME = STRING
  NODE = node(FILENAME)
  POINT= point(STRING)

DATABASE - hypdb
  pnLINK(POINT,NODE)

include "fig2-2.pro" % collects a hypertext-point contents

PREDICATES

  hyperEDIT(STRING)
    hyperSTATUS(STRING,INTEGER,INTEGER)
    % findHYPERtext in file "find-h.pro"
      getTARGETnode(STRINGLIST,STRING)

CLAUSES

/* ****************************************************** */
/* ********************** hyperEDIT ********************* */
/* ****************************************************** */

/* Edit the contents of a node */

hyperEDIT(FILEname) :-
   repeat,
   file_str(FILEname,INstr),
   MSG="End editing (ESC),  Follow hyper link (F10) ",
   edit(INstr,OUTstr,"NODE EDITOR",FILEname,MSG,
        1,"H-Help.txt",1,1,1,1,Pos,ReturnStatus),
```

(**Fig. 2-1**. continued)

```
   hyperSTATUS(OUTstr,Pos,ReturnStatus).

/* ****************************************************** */
/* ****************** hyperSTATUS *********************** */
/* ****************************************************** */

/*

If RetrunStatus = 0, edit was terminated with an F10,
Then (execute) these steps to follow point-node link

   - Display destinations (files) of point-node links
   - Pick One file "F" and enter it at the prompt
   - hyperEDIT "F"

*/

/* ********************* hyperSTATUS ******************* */

/* When ReturnStatus = 0, edit was terminated with an F10 */

hyperSTATUS(FILEstr,POS,0):-    /* ,fkey(1)):- */
   findHyperText(FILEstr,Pos,Htext),
   Htext <> "",
   findall(Tnode,pnlink(point(Htext),node(Tnode)),NODElist),
   getTARGETnode(NODElist,TARGETnode),
   TARGETnode <> "",
   hyperEDIT(TARGETnode), !, fail.

hyperSTATUS(_,_,0):-
   makewindow(3,15,16,"Message",17,0,6,50),
   write("No hypertext point was selected." ),
   write("\n Or hypertext-point has no links."),
   write("\nPress return to continue"),
   repeat,
     inkey(_),
   removewindow,
   !, fail.

/*
COMMENT ON THE USE OF   "!, fail"--cut and fail--
combination in the first clause of "hyperSTATUS:"

   We use fail to ensure that the user comes back to
   the source node after investigating a destination
   node. Usually you press F10 to go to a link destination
   (via menu). After you finish your work at the
   destination node you press ESC. This ends editing, and
   brings you back to the place after "hyperOPTION" above.
   You pass the cut and the predicate fails. The fail
   makes sure that the "repeat" loop in hyperEDIT will
   start the editor again in the source node.
*/

/* When ReturnStatus = 1, edit was terminated with an ESC */

hyperSTATUS(_,_,1).


/* ****************** getTARGETnode ******************* */

getTARGETnode(Tlist,Tnode):-
   makewindow(4,31,112,"Target Node",8,10,8,60),
```

(**Fig. 2-1.** continued)

```
    write_list(Tlist),
    write("\n\nEnter one of the above list nodes: "),
    readln(Tnode),
    removewindow.

/* ******************************************************* */
/* ******************** END OF CODE ********************* */
/* ******************************************************* */
GOAL

retractall(pnlink(_,_)),

consult("fig2-3.net",hypdb), % load the network configuration

/*
Or instead of consulting the file "fig2-3.net" you can
directly assert the database facts to the memory:

assert(pnlink(point("Vannevar Bush"),node("node4.hyp"))),
assert(pnlink(point("Douglas Engelbart"),node("node3.hyp"))),
assert(pnlink(point("Ted Nelson"),node("node2.hyp"))),
save("fig2-3.net",hypdb),
*/

blankwindow,
editwindow,

hyperEDIT("node1.hyp"),

removewindow, % removing the editwindow
removewindow. % removing the blankwindow

/* ************** END OF MAIN PROGRAM ****************** */
```

Fig. 2-2. The predicate "findHyperText"

```
% File name: find-h.pro
/* ****************************************************** */
/* ******************** findHyperText ***************** */
/* ****************************************************** */

PREDICATES
    findHyperText(STRING,INTEGER,STRING)
        findStart(STRING,INTEGER,INTEGER)
            findStart1(STRING,INTEGER,INTEGER)
        findHyperText1(STRING,STRING,STRING)

CLAUSES
/* Given a string "String" and a position (integer) in
   that string "Pos", "findHyperText" finds the hypertext
   region pointed at by the user.

   A hypertext region has a starting and ending label:
   Starting label = "{"
   Ending label   = "}"
*/


findHyperText(String,Pos,HyperStr):-
    findStart(String,Pos,Spos),
    frontstr(Spos,String,_,String1),
    findHyperText1(String1,"",HyperStr).
```

(**Fig. 2-2.** continued)

```
/* ******************** findStart & findStart1 *********** */

findStart(String,Pos,StartPos):-
   frontstr(Pos,String,String1,_),
   findStart1(String1,Pos,StartPos).

findStart1(String,Pos,Pos):-
   StartLabelPos=Pos-1,
   frontstr(StartLabelPos,String,_,StartLabel),
   StartLabel="{", !.

findStart1(String,Pos,StartPos):-
   NewPos=Pos-1,
   frontstr(NewPos,String,FrontString,_),
   findStart1(FrontString,NewPos,StartPos).

/* ****************** findHyperText1 ********************** */

findHyperText1(Str,HyperStr,HyperStr):-
   fronttoken(Str,"}",_), !.

findHyperText1(Str,Hstr,HyperStr):-
   frontchar(Str,' ',Rest),
   concat(Hstr," ",Htemp),
   findHyperText1(Rest,Htemp,HyperStr), !.

findHyperText1(Str,Hstr,HyperStr):-
   frontchar(Str,'\n',Rest),
   concat(Hstr,"\n",Htemp),
   findHyperText1(Rest,Htemp,HyperStr), !.

findHyperText1(Str,Hstr,HyperStr):-
   fronttoken(Str,Htoken,Rest),
concat(Hstr,Htoken,Htemp),
   findHyperText1(Rest,Htemp,HyperStr).

/* ++++++++++++++++++++++++ END END END ++++++++++++++++ */
```

Fig. 2-3. A network configuration file.

```
pnlink(point("Vannevar Bush"),node("node4.hyp"))
pnlink(point("Douglas Engelbart"),node("node3.hyp"))
pnlink(point("Ted Nelson"),node("node2.hyp"))
```

Fig. 2-4. The text for five sample nodes.

```
File "node1.hyp" contains the string:

" The three most known figures in the history of hypertext
are {Vannevar Bush}, {Douglas Engelbart}, and {Ted
Nelson}."


File "node2.hyp" contains the string:

"  Ted Nelson, coined the terms HYPERTEXT and HYPERMEDIA.
His interest was in what he calls the 'The writing of the
future.' At the same time that {Douglas Engelbart} was
```

(**Fig. 2-4.** continued)

```
working on his AUGMENT system, Nelson was working on his
XANADU system."


File "node3.hyp" contains the string:

"   NLS, for oN Line System, was the first hypertext
system. It was built by Douglas Engelbart, who was
influenced by {Bush's ideas}. Engelbart, in 1963, wrote an
article titled 'A conceptual Framework for the
Augmentation of Man's Intellect.'"


File "node4.hyp" contains the string:

"   {Vannevar Bush}  is credited with first describing
hypertext in his 1945 article "As We May Think. Bush
called his system Memex."


File "node5.hyp" contains the string:

"    Vannevar Bush was president Franklin D. Roosevelt's
Science Advisor. His famous article As We May Think,
appeared in the ATLANTIC in 1945.
```

To run the program in FIG. 2-1, you need to have these files:

fig2-1.pro, node2.hyp,
fig2-2.pro, node3.hyp,
fig2-3.net, node4.hyp, and
node1.hyp, node5.hyp

in the same directory. Load the file "fig2-1.pro", and look at the goal section at the end of the program:

```
GOAL
  retractall(pnlink(_,_)), % clear the memory from facts
  consult("fig2-3.net",hypdb), % load network configuration
  blankwindow, % a blank window over the whole screen
  editwindow, % a window for the Turbo Prolog editor
  hyperEDIT("node1.hyp"), % start by loading node1 in editor
  removewindow, % removing the editwindow
  removewindow. % removing the blankwindow
```

First, I clear the memory from all previous, if any, "pnlink" facts. Next, I load the network configuration facts. In this example, the network is configured with point-node links only. After I set up the right configuration, I am ready for some special effects. A blank window to form the background of the system comes first. The editor window is next. The goal "hyperEDIT" calls the Turbo editor and activates the network through a hotkey—in this case it is F10. When you are done exploring the network, you press the ESC key to exit "hyper-EDIT"; and of course, you have to remove the two windows that were created earlier before returning to Turbo environment.

EDITING NODES AND POINTS WITH THE TURBO PROLOG EDITOR

The word "text" in hypertext is a strong indication of what it is about. Other than the help system version of hypertext (systems for on-line help), a text editor is a must. A hypertext editor is not just any editor. There are certain features that make an editor a hypertext editor. Here is a list of some of these features:

- You can control what, where, and how text is displayed in the editor from your program. For instance, you might choose to highlight the points, put a box around them, or mark them with special symbols. In this "hyperEDIT" predicate, you will mark a hypertext region by including it between two braces ("{" and "}"). We will talk about this in the next section (marking a hypertext point with "{" and "}").
- You can create mouse-sensitive areas. For example, the mouse icon can change in special areas of the editor to reflect the type of points or links. In this case, you can't have this feature in "hyperEDIT." Our "hyperEDIT" uses the built-in "edit" predicate for all editing purposes. Turbo Prolog doesn't support a mouse interface to "edit."
- To view or create a link, you can place the cursor in the hypertext point. Then, by clicking the mouse, or pressing a hotkey, you will cause the system to find the referenced node or point and to immediately open a new window for it on the screen. In "hyperEDIT" you use the arrow keys to move the cursor into a hypertext point. Then by pressing F10, you get a list of all target nodes. Picking a target node will cause "hyperEDIT" to display the node in a new window.

In Turbo Prolog, you can have some of these features when you use the "edit" predicate of version 2.00. It has this declaration:

```
edit(INstr,OUTstr,HeadStr,HeadStr2,Msg,Pos,
  HelpFileName,EditMode,Indent,Insert,TextMode,
  ReturnPosition,ReturnStatus)
```

with the flow pattern of:

edit(i,o,i,i,i,i,i,i,i,o,o)

You can read more about this predicate in the Turbo Prolog manual; but to use "edit" as part of a hypertext editor, I need to explain some of its arguments:

INstr—is the string loaded in the editor.
Msg—is the message displayed at the bottom line of the editor, at the time of entry, to remind the user of his options.
OUTstr—is the returned edited string.
Pos—is the cursor position when you first enter the editor.
ReturnPosition—is the cursor position in OutPutStr that you get when you exit the editor.

ReturnStatus—is the editor return status. There are two possible return status codes. If you exit the editor with F10, your return status is 0. Otherwise, if you use ESC to exit, your return status is 1.

For now, the most important thing to know is how you mark points in a node; and how you use a special key (F10 or ESC) to extract the string of a point. First, let's talk about marking hypertext points.

Marking a Hypertext Point with "{" and "}"

To mark a chunk of text in a node as a point, you need some visual effects. It would be better if you could change the color attribute of the text field, or enclose the text in a box; but unfortunately you can't do this in the Turbo Prolog editor—simply because you have no control from outside of the editor on the text fields attributes. So, you have to use delimiters to signal the start and end of hypertext. For example, the text in node1 has three points, each is marked with two opposite braces:

The three most known figures in the history of hypertext are {Vannevar Bush}, {Douglas Engelbart}, and {Ted Nelson}.

To pick a point, you put the cursor anywhere between "{" and "}" then press the pick-hypertext hotkey. In Turbo Prolog editor, there are only two possibilities.

- You use the F10 key as the pick-hypertext key, and you use the ESC key as the exit-the-editor key
- You use the ESC key as the pick-hypertext key, and you use the F10 key as the exit-the-editor key

In the programs, I will use the first alternative. Okay, you placed the cursor under the hypertext and pressed the F10 key, but how can you extract the hypertext from the "OUTstr." The predicate "findHyperText" in FIG. 2-2 does this trick.

EXTRACTING HYPERTEXT WITH THE "findHyperText" PREDICATE

To show you how "findHyperText" works, first of all you need to see how it is activated. First, you are in "hyperEDIT" editing a node; and you want to explore a hypertext point in that node. So, you put the cursor at the point, and press F10. Let's stop here, and take a look at the code for "hyperEDIT."

```
/* hyperEDIT */
  hyperEDIT(FILEname) :-
    repeat,
    file_str(FILEname,INstr),
```

```
    MSG="End editing (ESC), Follow hyper link (F10) ",
    INpos = 1,
    edit(INstr,OUTstr,"NODE EDITOR",FILEname,MSG,
       INpos,"H-Help.txt",1,1,1,1,OUTpos,ReturnStatus),
  hyperSTATUS(OUTstr,OUTpos,ReturnStatus).
```

Once you have pressed F10, "edit" will succeed, and binds: "OUTstr," "OUTpos," and "ReturnStatus." These, in turn, are passed to the predicate "hyperSTATUS." Basically, you should have two major "hyperSTATUS" clauses; one for each possible return status value of "ReturnStatus." Our immediate concern is when ReturnStatus equals zero—edit was terminated with an F10. So, our next stop is the first "hyperSTATUS" clause in FIG. 2-1. Here is the code for "hyperSTATUS":

```
hyperSTATUS(OUTstr,OUTpos,0):-
   findHyperText(OUTstr,OUTpos,Hypertext),
   Htext <> "",
   findall(Tnode,pnlink(point(Htext),node(Tnode)),NODElist),
   getTARGETnode(NODElist,TARGETnode),
   TARGETnode <> "",
   hyperEDIT(TARGETnode), !, fail.
```

As you can see, "findHyperText" takes "OUTstr" and "OUTpos"—generated by "edit"—as its input, and gives "HyperText" as its output. The program for "findHyperText" is in a separate file (see FIG. 2-2). Here is the code for the main predicate in the program:

```
findHyperText(String,Pos,HyperStr):-
   findStart(String,Pos,Spos),
   frontstr(Spos,String,_,String1),
   findHyperText1(String1,"",HyperStr).
```

The first subgoal, "findStart," finds the starting position of the hypertext point. Then, you use the built-in "frontstr" to cut the original string "String" into two halves at the "Spos" position. This way, you will have the hypertext point at the front of the second half—at the front of "String1"; and, finally, "findHyperText1" isolates the hypertext point and binds it to the variable "HyperStr."

Now you know how to extract the text of a hypertext point. All you need to do is to find all the links associated with it. So get back to "hyperSTATUS." In "hyperSTATUS" you do this by using "findall" to generate a list of all the nodes linked to our point; and "getTARGETnode" helps you choose a node to review. FIGURE 2-5 shows the "hyperEDIT" window with the cursor at a hypertext point, and you are about to press the F10 key.

In FIG. 2-6 you can see how target nodes are listed; and you are prompted to enter your choice. The node you choose should not be empty. Now, you have

```
                              HyperText
NODE EDITOR  Line 1     Col 2     node1.hyp  Indent  Insert  Text mode
The three most known figures in the history of hypertext
  are {Vannevar Bush}, {Douglas Engelbart}, and {Ted Nelson}.

End editing (ESC),  Follow hyper link (F10)
```

Fig. 2-5. The main window of "hyperEDIT"

```
                              HyperText
NODE EDITOR  Line 2     Col 11    node1.hyp  Indent  Insert  Text mode
The three most known figures in the history of hypertext
  are {Vannevar Bush}, {Douglas Engelbart}, and {Ted Nelson}.

                    Target Node
          node4.hyp

          Enter your target node: _

F2-Save  F3-Load  F6-Switch  F9-Compile                      Alt-X-Exit
```

Fig. 2-6. Selecting a node from a list of target nodes.

the name of the target node, and you want to view it in the editor. What do you do? Simply call "hyperEDIT" and voilà! You have the target node in the main window. Remember, it all started by calling "hyperEDIT" in the GOAL section of the main program.

So far, you went from one node to another through a hypertext point in the first node. Once you are done with the second node, how do you get back to the first node? In the next section, I will show you how I did this in the program of FIG. 2-1.

MOVING BACK AND FORTH BETWEEN NODES AND POINTS

In writing your hypertext system, you should consider the navigation issue. It is very easy to get lost in the network. You need to give the users of your system a hand in finding their way around. You need to provide some navigation tools. Some of these tools are:

- a button, a menu entry, or a hotkey, to take you back to the node of origin—this is the first node you loaded when entering the hypertext system. It is also known as the "home node."
- a button, a menu entry, or a hotkey, to activate a link.
- a button, a menu entry, or a hotkey, to end inspection of the current node, and takes you back to the previous node. In this case I use ESC to do this.
- a network map, to locate your current position in the network. Also, it will make it easier for you to move between the different nodes in the network. I will write network-map programs in PART TWO, when I build a complete hypertext browsing system.

In the program of FIG. 2-1, you activate a link with F10. Once you are done with your target node, you press ESC to get back to the source node. How did I do it? Let me give you a hint—by backtracking.

Take a look at the last two subgoals of "hyperSTATUS." These are the cut and fail combination (! and fail). They cause the "hyperSTATUS" subgoal in "hyperEDIT" to fail. When "hyperSTATUS" fails, Turbo will backtrack to "edit;" and, "edit" in turn, will load back the source node in the main window. Notice that when you are back in the source node, the cursor is at the top of the node. This is not the same position when you left. It would be much easier if you come back to the same place where you left—especially if your work in the node isn't done yet. In Chapter 3, I will show you how to get back to where you left, when I expand the program of FIG. 2-1 to handle more operations on links.

3

Operating on Points, Nodes, and Links

> "Operationism holds that the meaning of a term is fully and exclusively determined by its operational definition. Thus, Bridgman says: The concept of length is therefore fixed when the operations by which length is measured are fixed: that is, the concept of length involves as much as and nothing more than the set of operations by which length is determined. In general, we mean by any concept nothing more than a set of operations; the concept is synonymous with the corresponding set of operations."
>
> —*Carl G. Hempel; Philosophy of Natural Science.*

Let's say you have a hypertext network. Whether you use hypertext for information retrieval or for problem solving, sooner or later you will need to update its network.

If you are using hypertext for information retrieval, you will need to add or delete information. Also, if you are using hypertext for problem solving, you will need to add or delete partial solutions. In problem solving systems, often you break down the problem into manageable parts. Most of the times your definition of the problem changes. To modify a problem definition you will need to add or delete parts of the representation. Also, most problem solving approaches use subgoals to reach the goal—the solution. To reach its goal, a problem solving system automatically generates new (to be tested) subgoals and deletes old (already been tested and failed) ones. So, how do you update the hypertext network?

Updating a hypertext network includes one or more of these operations:

- adding nodes, points, and links
- deleting nodes, points, and links
- changing nodes, points, and links

Before you update the network, you will finish what you have started in Chapter 2. In Chapter 2, you saw a point-node link viewing program (see FIG. 2-1). In the next section, you will see the program extended to view node-node, point-node, and point-point links.

VIEWING NODE-NODE, POINT-NODE, AND POINT-POINT LINKS

In the viewing program of Chapter 2 (see FIG. 2-1), you can only view point-node links. When viewing a link, press the hotkey and the program will list all nodes linked to that point, but how do you handle the viewing of node-node, point-node, and point-point links all at once? You can do this either by using three hotkeys, or by using a menu of three options.

The hypertext editor—"hyperEDIT"—uses the built-in "edit" predicate. In "edit," only you can use one hotkey—ESC or F10. Still, you can program "hyperEDIT" so that it can recognize three hotkeys, but this will make things more complicated. So, I'll use the menu approach. In Chapter 4, I will talk about the differences between using hotkeys and menus in executing hypertext operations. If you want to know about the advantages and disadvantages of both approaches, refer to "Hotkeys vs. Menus" in Chapter 4.

The Turbo Prolog TOOLBOX has five different menu predicates that you can use in your programs. The basic menu predicate in the TOOLBOX is "menu." The declaration for this predicate is:

```
menu(PosRow,PosCol,Wattr,Fattr,ItemList,Title,InitItem,
 ChoiceCode)
```

If you are not familiar with "menu," you can refer to the TOOLBOX manual for instructions. What concerns us most in this declaration are the arguments "ItemList," "Title," "InitItem," and "ChoiceCode." In the hypertext viewing program, you use this form of "menu":

```
menu(0,30,15,112,["view a Node-node link",
                  "view a Point-node link",
                  "view a pOint-point link"],
"VIEW A LINK",1,Choice)
```

When you execute a "menu" goal, it displays a window of three options. The cursor will be on the first option—"View a Node-node link." When you choose an option, "menu" will bind "Choice" to the number of that option. It is the job of your hypertext program to relate the returned value of "Choice" to a link-viewing action, but how do you get to the "VIEW A LINK" menu from "hyperEDIT" after you press F10? Also, after you pick an option, how do you view the destination of the link? The best way to show you how to do this is through a sample program. The sample program is in FIG. 3-1. In the next two sections I will describe this program and how to operate it.

The program in FIG. 3-1 is a modified version of the program in FIG. 2-1. The differences are: in "hyperEDIT" predicate, in the database declaration section, and in the user-interface. To increase the clarity of the program, I use the "include" directive. With "include" I can distribute the program in several files with one file serving as the main program. To run the whole program I include all the files in the main program. Turbo Prolog includes the files in the main program at run time. In the next section, I will show you how to put the database section and the user-interface in "include" files.

Fig. 3-1. Viewing N-N, P-N and P-P links.

```
include "tdoms.pro"   % TOOLBOX text domains declarations
include "tpreds.pro"  % TOOLBOX text predicates declaration
include "menu.pro"    % TOOLBOX menu program
include "fig3-2.pro"  % domains and database declarations
include "fig3-3.pro"  % general utility predicates
include "fig3-4.pro"  % user-interface predicates
include "fig2-2.pro"  % finding a hypertext point

PREDICATES

  hyperEDIT(STRING,INTEGER)
    hyperSTATUS(STRING,STRING,INTEGER,INTEGER)
     % findHYPERtext in file "find-h.pro"
      hyperOPTION(STRING,STRING,INTEGER,INTEGER)
        searchPOINT(STRING,STRING,STRING,INTEGER)
          searchPOINT1(STRING,STRING,STRING,INTEGER)

CLAUSES

/* ****************************************************** */
/* ********************** hyperEDIT ******************** */
/* ****************************************************** */

/* Edit the contents of a node */

hyperEDIT(FILEname,InitPos) :-
   repeat,
     file_str(FILEname,INstr),
     MSG="End editing (ESC),  Follow hyper link (F10) ",
     edit(INstr,OUTstr,"NODE EDITOR",FILEname,MSG,
          InitPos,"H-Help.txt",1,1,1,1,Pos,ReturnStatus),
     hyperSTATUS(FILEname,OUTstr,Pos,ReturnStatus).


/* ****************************************************** */
/* ***************** hyperSTATUS ********************** */
/* ****************************************************** */

/* If RetrunStatus = 0, edit was terminated with an F10,
   Then (execute) these actions are true:
```

(**Fig. 3-1.** continued)

```
   display hypertext-menu with the options:

      A. View node-node link

      - Display destinations (files) of node-node links
      - Pick One file "F" or hit ESC
      - hyperEDIT "F" (with input cursor position = 1)

      B. View point-node link

      - Display destinations (files) of point-node links
      - Pick One file "F" or hit ESC
      - hyperEDIT "F" (with input cursor position = 1)

      C. View point-point link

      - Display destination nodes (files) of point-node links
      - Pick One node (file) "F" or hit ESC
      - hyperEDIT "F" (with cursor on destination point)

*/

/* ********************* hyperSTATUS ******************** */

/* When ReturnStatus = 0, edit was terminated with an F10 */

hyperSTATUS(FILEname,FILEstr,POS,0):-
  menu(0,30,15,112,["view a Node-node link",
                    "view a Point-node link",
                    "view a pOint-point link"],
       "VIEW A LINK",1,Choice),
  hyperOPTION(FILEname,FILEstr,POS,Choice), !, fail.


/*
COMMENT ON THE USE OF   "!, fail"--cut and fail--
combination in the first clause of "hyperSTATUS:"

   I use fail to ensure that the user comes back to
   the source node after investigating a destination
   node. Usually you press F10 to go to a link destination
   (via menu). After you finish your work at the
   destination node you presses ESC. This ends editing, and
   brings you back to the place after "hyperOPTION" above.
   You pass the cut and the predicate fails. The fail
   makes sure that the "repeat" loop in hyperEDIT will
   start the editor again in the source node. */


/* When ReturnStatus = 1, edit was terminated with an ESC */

hyperSTATUS(_,_,_,1).

/* ********************** hyperOPTION ****************** */

% View a node-node link

hyperOPTION(FILEname,_,_,1):-
  findall(Tnode,nnlink(node(FILEname),node(Tnode)),NODElist),
  menu(0,30,15,112,NODElist,"NODE-NODE LINK",1,NODEchoice),
  nth_member(NODElist,NODEchoice,TARGETnode),
  hyperEDIT(TARGETnode,1), !.
hyperOPTION(_,_,_,1).
```

(**Fig. 3-1.** continued)

```
% View a point-node link

hyperOPTION(Fname,FILEstr,POS,2):-
   findHyperText(FILEstr,Pos,Htext),
   Htext <> "",
   findall(Tnode,
           pnlink(point(Htext),node(Fname),node(Tnode)),
           NODElist),
   menu(0,30,15,112,NODElist,"POINT-NODE LINK",1,NODEchoice),
   nth_member(NODElist,NODEchoice,TARGETnode),
   hyperEDIT(TARGETnode,1), !.

hyperOPTION(_,_,_,2):-
   msg(17,0,"Hypertext point was not selected." ).

% View a point-point link

hyperOPTION(Fname,FILEstr,Pos,3):-
   findHyperText(FILEstr,Pos,Htxt),
   Htxt <> "",
   findall(Tnode,
           ppLINK(point(Htxt),node(Fname),_,node(Tnode)),
           NODElist),
   menu(0,30,15,112,NODElist,"POINT-POINT LINK",1,NODEchoice),
   nth_member(NODElist,NODEchoice,TARGETnode),
   ppLINK(point(Htxt),node(Fname),point(Ttxt),node(TARGETnode)),
   file_str(TARGETnode,STR),
   searchPOINT(Ttxt,STR,"",TPos),
   hyperEDIT(TARGETnode,TPos), !.

hyperOPTION(_,_,_,3):-
   msg(17,0,"Hypertext point was not selected." ).


/* ************************ searchPOINT **************** */

searchPOINT(Hstr,Str,Nstr,Pos):-
  fronttoken(Hstr,Tok,Hstr1),
  fronttoken(Str,Tok,Str1),
  concat(Nstr,Tok,Nstr1),
  searchPOINT1(Hstr1,Str1,Nstr1,Pos), !.

searchPOINT(Hstr,Str,Nstr,Pos):-
  fronttoken(Str,Tok,Str1),
  concat(Nstr,Tok,Nstr1),
  searchPOINT(Hstr,Str1,Nstr1,Pos).

searchPOINT1("",_,Nstr,Pos):-
  str_len(Nstr,Pos), !.

searchPOINT1(Hstr,Str,Nstr,Pos):-
  fronttoken(Hstr,Tok,Hstr1),
  fronttoken(Str,Tok,Str1),
  concat(Nstr,Tok,Nstr1),
  searchPOINT1(Hstr1,Str1,Nstr1,Pos).

/* ******************** END OF CODE ******************** */

GOAL
retractall(nnlink(_,_)),
retractall(pnlink(_,_,_)),
retractall(pplink(_,_,_,_)),
```

(**Fig. 3-1.** continued)

```
consult("fig3-5.net",hypdb),

blankwindow,
editwindow,
hyperEDIT("node1.hyp",1),
removewindow,
removewindow.

/* ********************* END END END ******************** */
```

The Viewing-Program "include" Files

In this book, I build hypertext systems as collections of Turbo Prolog programs. For example, I consider the program in FIG. 3-1 as the main hypertext program. This program needs other supporting programs to supply non-hypertext related predicates. The program declarations and the user-interface are in separate files. To make the main program operational, I need to include these files in it. Notice the "include" statements at the top of the program:

```
include "tdoms.pro"  % TOOLBOX text domains declarations
include "tpreds.pro" % TOOLBOX text predicates declaration
include "menu.pro"   % TOOLBOX menu program
include "fig2-3.pro" % domains and database declarations
include "fig3-3.pro" % general utility predicates
include "fig3-4.pro" % user-interface predicates
include "fig2-2.pro" % finding a hypertext point
```

The program declarations are in the "domain-h.pro" module in FIG. 3-2. Take a look at the database section labeled "hypdb."

Fig. 3-2. The include module "domain-h.pro"

```
/* ************************************************************ */
/* DOMAIN AND DATABASE DECLARATIONS                             */
/* ************************************************************ */

DOMAINS
  FILENAME = STRING
  NODE = node(FILENAME)
  POINT= point(STRING)

DATABASE - hypdb
  nnlink(NODE,NODE)
  pnlink(POINT,NODE,NODE)
  pplink(POINT,NODE,POINT,NODE)

/* ********************** END END END ****************** */
```

In this section, I have predicate declarations for the links: nnlink, pnlink, and pplink. Network configuration files—files with the ".net" extension—contain nothing but nnlink, pnlink, and pplink database facts.

Another important include module is the "utility.pro," in FIG. 3-3. This module contains general Turbo Prolog predicates that I use with different programs.

Fig. 3-3. The include module "utility.pro"

```
/* ****************************************************** */
/* UTILITY PREDICATES                                     */
/* ****************************************************** */

/*
DOMAINS
    STRINGLIST= STRING*
*/

PREDICATES
  nth_member(STRINGLIST,INTEGER,STRING)

CLAUSES

/* ********************** nth_member ******************** */
  nth_member([],_,""):-!.
  nth_member([H|_],1,H):- !.
  nth_member([_|T],N,MEMBER):-
    M=N-1,
    nth_member(T,M,MEMBER).
```

I distributed the user-interface of the program between four "include" modules. I borrowed three modules from the TOOLBOX, but to use the TOOLBOX "menu.pro" module, I need two other modules: "tdoms.pro" (domains declarations) and "tpreds.pro" (TOOLBOX utility predicates). The fourth module is "user-h.pro" in FIG. 3-4.

In "user-h.pro" are two window-making predicates, "blankwindow" and "editwindow," and a predicate for displaying messages—"msg." Each window-making predicate has one subgoal: the built-in "makewindow" predicate. In "blankwindow" you create a window that covers the whole screen to act as a background. In "editwindow" you create your hypertext major window. This is the window where you load and edit hypertext nodes. The message predicate "msg" which has three arguments, has the flow pattern: (i,i,i). For example, to display the message "Current node has no links" in the window positions of row 20 and column 0, I give the goal:

```
msg(20,0,"Current node has no links.")
```

"msg" will display the message string in a window titled "Message" at the lower left corner of the screen. What "msg" does (after it displays your message) is to wait for you to press any key before it removes the message window. In Chapter 4, I will discuss how "msg" works.

Fig. 3-4. The include module "user-h.pro"

```
/* ******************************************************* */
/* USER INTERFACE PREDICATES                               */
/* ******************************************************* */

PREDICATES

blankwindow
editwindow
msg(INTEGER,INTEGER,STRING)

CLAUSES

/* ******************** SYSTEM WINDOWS ****************** */

% blank window
blankwindow :- makewindow(1,7,0,"",0,0,25,80).

% edit window
editwindow :-
  makewindow(2,15,112, "", 3,0,21,80).

/* *********************** msg ************************** */

msg(R,C,Str):-
   makewindow(10,22,112,"Message",R,C,3,40),
   window_str(Str),
   repeat,
      inkey(_),   % repeat waiting for a key to be pressed.
   !,
   removewindow.

/* +++++++++++++++++++++++++++++++++++++++++++++++++++++++ */
```

Building Your Own Network Configuration File

To operate the hypertext viewing program, you need two kinds of hypertext files:

1) Node files—files with the ".hyp" extension, and
2) Network configuration files—files with the ".net" extension.

You must have one or more node files, and at least one configuration file. Also, these files should be in the same directory path of the main program. You can see a sample network configuration in FIG. 3-5. Notice in the program in FIG. 3-1 that I consult the file "fig3-5.net" in the goal section. A network configuration contains the "nnlink," "pnlink," and "pplink" database facts. You can build your own network configuration file in two ways by using:

- the Turbo Prolog editor.
- the built-in "assert," "save," and "consult" predicates to create and load a configuration file.

To use the second approach, you need to:

1) assert your "link" facts to Turbo's knowledge base.
2) use the built-in "save" predicate to save the knowledge base to a file.
3) consult the configuration file using "consult."

Notice that in Turbo Prolog version 2, the built-in predicates ("assert," "save," and "consult") have two forms. For example, there are these two forms for "assert":

- A one-argument form: assert(<fact>). For example, to assert an "nnlink" using this form you can give the goal:

  ```
  assert(nnlink(node("node3.hyp"),node("node5.hyp")))
  ```

- A two-arguments form: assert(<fact>,DatabaseName). For example, you can use "hypdb" as a name for a database section. To assert the same "nnlink" declared in the "hypdb" database section, I use:

  ```
  assert(nnlink(node("node3.hyp"),node("node5.hyp")),hypdb)
  ```

In the program I use the second approach. When you assert, retract, save, or consult database facts, remember to use the second form. Now you have all you need to know about the files that make the hypertext system. It is time for some action. In the next section I will show you how to run the program.

NOTE! Some of you might not have access to Turbo Prolog. Others don't like, or don't have the time, to type in the code for the examples of this chapter. If this applies to you, I recommend that you order the companion program diskettes. One of these diskettes contain executable versions of FIG. 3-1, FIG. 3-8, and FIG. 3-13 of this chapter, along with the required network configuration and hypertext files. You can use the companion diskette offer, at the end of the book, to order the program diskettes.

Running the Complete Viewing Program

Load and run the main program, in FIG. 3-1. The first thing the program does is to load the network configuration file in FIG. 3-5.

Fig. 3-5. A network configuration for the program in Fig. 3-1.

```
nnlink(node("node3.hyp"),node("node5.hyp"))
nnlink(node("node2.hyp"),node("node3.hyp"))
nnlink(node("node1.hyp"),node("node2.hyp"))
pnlink(point("Ted Nelson"),node("node1.hyp"),node("node2.hyp"))
pnlink(point("Douglas Engelbart"),node("node1.hyp"),node("node3.hyp"))
pnlink(point("Douglas Engelbart"),node("node2.hyp"),node("node3.hyp"))
pnlink(point("Vannevar Bush"),node("node1.hyp"),node("node5.hyp"))
pnlink(point("Bush's ideas"),node("node3.hyp"),node("node4.hyp"))
pplink(point("Bush's ideas"),node("node3.hyp"),point("Vannevar
            Bush"),node("node1.hyp"))
```

After it does that, it displays the root node in the hypertext editor (see FIG. 3-6).

Then, to view a node-node link, you press F10 to get the "VIEW A LINK" menu (see FIG. 3-7).

From this menu, pick the "view a Node-node link" option. You will get another menu, but this time with all the destination nodes listed as options (see FIG. 3-8).

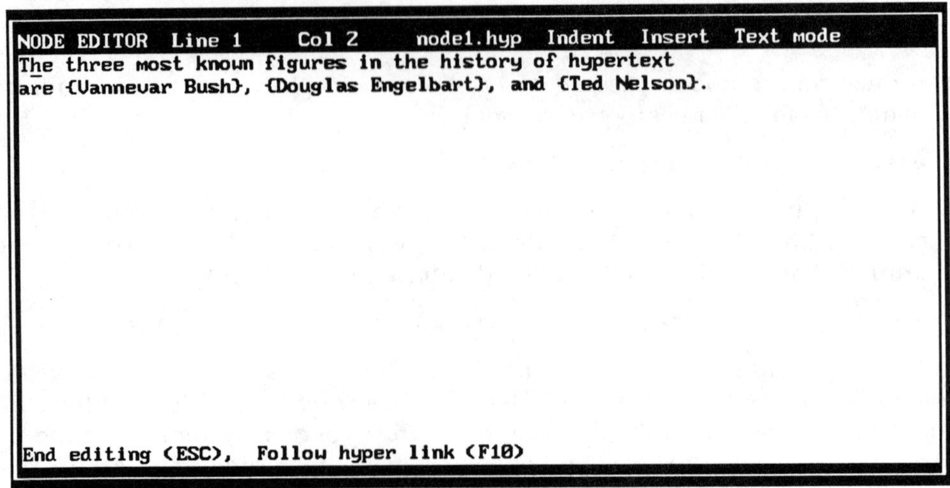

Fig. 3-6. Displaying the root node in the hypertext editor.

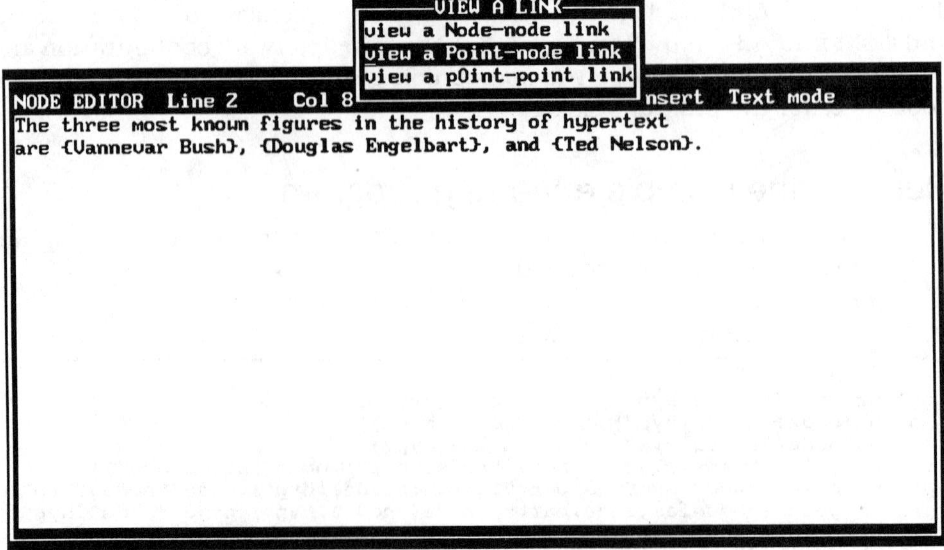

Fig. 3-7. Activating the "VIEW A LINK" menu.

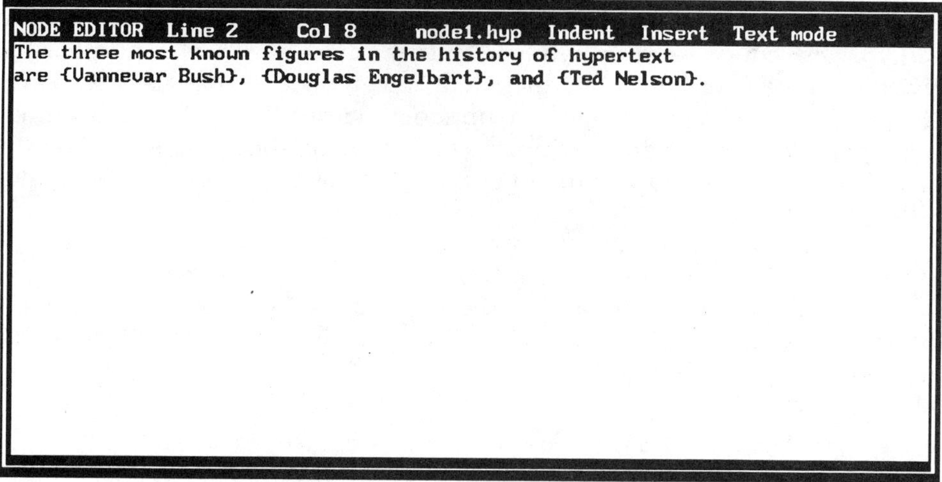

Fig. 3-8. Listing all destination nodes in a menu.

Pick one of the destination nodes. The system will load this node in the main window and puts you in "hyperEDIT" mode.

As for viewing point-node and point-point links, first pick a hypertext source point in the current node. As you did in Chapter 2 (see FIG. 2-1), put the cursor between "{" and "}" and press F10. The system will display the "Link-Viewing" menu and you can either pick the "view a Point-node link" option, or the "view a pOint-point link" option.

HYPERTEXT BROWSING SYSTEMS vs. AUTHORING SYSTEMS

In a hypertext browsing system, you can only read what is there. Whether it is a document, a help system, a user manual, or an electronic newsletter, it is a closed system. While in hypertext authoring systems, you can read, add to, delete from, and change what is there. In other words, a browsing system is a read-only system; but an authoring system is a read-and-write system.

In terms of the hypertext network of browsing systems, the network is static—you can't add to it, delete from it, or change it. While in authoring systems, the network is dynamic—you can add to it, delete from it, or change it.

The program in FIG. 3-1 is a good example of a browsing system. This program can be modified to make it an authoring system. For the rest of the chapter, I will do exactly this. Starting from the next section, I will show you how to modify this program into an authoring system. I will modify it so you can add, delete, and change links. Let's start with the "add a link" feature.

ADDING LINKS

In the viewing program, I use a hotkey to get to the "VIEW A LINK" operation menu. Now I have an additional operation—"Add a link" operation, but the hypertext editor can use only one hotkey, and I have two operations. To solve the conflict, I use the other approach. You guessed it; I can use a "menu." When I press F10, I get a menu of two options: "View a link" and "Add a link." Each option will lead to another menu. For example, the "Add a link" option will lead to an "ADD A LINK" menu of three options: "add a Node-node link," "add a Point-node link," and "add a Point-point link."

The new version of our program is in FIG. 3-9. This program uses an extended user-interface utility predicate from FIG. 3-10. The program in FIG. 3-9 uses an additional user-interface predicate from the TOOLBOX called "read-filename" (see FIG. 3-10). I will talk about this in a minute, but first I'll show you the modifications I made.

Fig. 3-9. A program for viewing and adding links

```
include "fig3-2.pro"   % domains and database declarations

/* ************** Turbo Prolog TOOLBOX programs ********* */

include "tdoms.pro"       % TOOLBOX text domains declarations
include "tpreds.pro"      % TOOLBOX text predicates declaration

DATABASE
  insmode
  lineinpstate(STRING,COL)
  lineinpflag

% required Turbo Prolog TOOLBOX modules

% "filename" predicate is in the TOOLBOX's "filename.pro"
% "filename.pro" requires "lineinp.pro"
% "lineinput" predicate is in the TOOLBOX's "lineinp.pro"

include "lineinp.pro"     % TOOLBOX line input predicate
include "filename.pro"    % TOOLBOX file name input predicate
include "menu.pro"        % TOOLBOX menu program
include "status.pro"      % TOOLBOX status line program

/* ***************** hypertext modules ****************** */

include "fig3-3.pro"     % general utility predicates
include "fig3-9.pro"      %  user-interface predicates
include "fig2-2.pro"      % finding a hypertext point

/* ***************** general predicates section ********* */

PREDICATES

  hyperEDIT(STRING,INTEGER,INTEGER)
    hyperSTATUS(STRING,STRING,INTEGER,INTEGER)
    % findHYPERtext in file "find-h.pro"
      linkOPTION(STRING,STRING,INTEGER,INTEGER)
        viewOPTION(STRING,STRING,INTEGER,INTEGER)
          searchPOINT(STRING,STRING,STRING,STRING,INTEGER)
            searchPOINT1(STRING,STRING,STRING,STRING,INTEGER)
        addOPTION(STRING,STRING,INTEGER,INTEGER)
```

(**Fig. 3-9.** continued)

```
/* ******************* clauses section ****************** */

CLAUSES

/* **************************************************** */
/* ********************** hyperEDIT ******************** */
/* **************************************************** */

/* Edit the contents of a hypertext node. In this version
   of hypertext, a node is a file in the current disk
   directory. */

hyperEDIT(FILEname,InPos,OutPos) :-
   repeat,
     file_str(FILEname,INstr),
     MSG="End editing (ESC),  Follow hyper link (F10) ",
     edit(INstr,OUTstr,"NODE EDITOR",FILEname,MSG,
          InPos,"H-Help.txt",1,1,1,1,OutPos,ReturnStatus),
     hyperSTATUS(FILEname,OUTstr,OutPos,ReturnStatus).

/* **************************************************** */
/* ***************** hyperSTATUS ********************** */
/* **************************************************** */

hyperSTATUS(Fname,Fstr,Pos,0):-
  menu(0,35,15,112,["View a link",
                    "Add a link"],
       "LINK OPERATIONS",1,Choice),
  linkOPTION(Fname,Fstr,Pos,Choice), !, fail.

/* When ReturnStatus = 1, edit was terminated with an ESC */

% Ask if user wants to save changes to file.

hyperSTATUS(Fname,Fstr,_,1):-
   cursor(R,_), Row=R+2,
   lineinput(Row,35,30,15,112,
             "Save changes to file (y/n): ","",ANS),
   upper_lower(ANS1,ANS),
   ANS1 = "Y",
   file_str(Fname,Fstr), !.

% Exit editor without saving the changes.

hyperSTATUS(_,_,_,1).

/* ************************ linkOPTION ***************** */

linkOPTION(Fname,Fstr,Pos,1):-
  menu(0,15,15,112,["view a Node-node link",
                    "view a Point-node link",
                    "view a pOint-point link"],
       "VIEW A LINK",1,Choice),
  viewOPTION(Fname,Fstr,Pos,Choice), !.

linkOPTION(_,_,_,1). % return with no action

linkOPTION(Fname,Fstr,Pos,2):-
  menu(0,55,15,112,["add a Node-node link",
                    "add a Point-node link",
                    "add a pOint-point link"],
       "ADD A LINK",1,Choice),
  addOPTION(Fname,Fstr,Pos,Choice), !.

linkOPTION(_,_,_,2). % return with no action
```

(**Fig. 3-9.** continued)

```
/* ********************** viewOPTION ******************** */

viewOPTION(FILEname,_,_,1):-
  findall(Tnode,nnlink(node(FILEname),node(Tnode)),NODElist),
  menu(0,30,15,112,NODElist,"NODE-NODE LINK",1,NODEchoice),
  nth_member(NODElist,NODEchoice,TARGETnode),
  hyperEDIT(TARGETnode,1,_), !.
viewOPTION(_,_,_,1).

viewOPTION(Fname,FILEstr,POS,2):-
   findHyperText(FILEstr,Pos,Htext),
   Htext <> "",
   findall(Tnode,
           pnlink(point(Htext),node(Fname),node(Tnode)),
           NODElist),
   menu(0,30,15,112,NODElist,"POINT-NODE LINK",1,NODEchoice),
   nth_member(NODElist,NODEchoice,TARGETnode),
   hyperEDIT(TARGETnode,1,_), !.

viewOPTION(_,_,_,2):-
   msg(17,0,"Hypertext point was not selected." ).


viewOPTION(Fname,FILEstr,Pos,3):-
   findHyperText(FILEstr,Pos,Htxt),
   Htxt <> "",
   findall(Tnode,
           ppLINK(point(Htxt),node(Fname),_,node(Tnode)),
           NODElist),
   menu(0,30,15,112,NODElist,"POINT-POINT LINK",1,NODEchoice),
   nth_member(NODElist,NODEchoice,TARGETnode),
   ppLINK(point(Htxt),node(Fname),point(Ttxt),node(TARGETnode) ),
   file_str(TARGETnode,STR),
   searchPOINT(Ttxt,STR,"",TPos),
   hyperEDIT(TARGETnode,TPos,_), !.

viewOPTION(_,_,_,3):-
   msg(17,0,"Hypertext point was not selected." ).

/* ************************ addOPTION ***************** */

% Adding a node-node link.

addOPTION(Fname1,_,_,1):-
  cursor(R,_), Row=R+2,
  readfilename(Row,35,15,112,hyp,"",Fname2),
  assert(nnlink(node(Fname1),node(Fname2))), !.

addOPTION(_,_,_,1).  % return with no action


% Adding a point-node link.

addOPTION(Fname,Fstr,Pos,2):-
  cursor(R,_), Row=R+2,
  readfilename(Row,35,15,112,hyp,"",Fname2),
  findHyperText(Fstr,Pos,Htxt),
  assert(pnlink(point(Htxt),node(Fname),node(Fname2))), !.

addOPTION(_,_,_,2).  % return with no action

% Adding a point-point link.

addOPTION(Fname,Fstr1,Pos1,3):-
```

(**Fig. 3-9.** continued)

```
  cursor(R,_), Row=R+2,
  readfilename(Row,35,15,112,hyp,"",Fname2),
  hyperEDIT(Fname2,1,Pos2),
  file_str(Fname2,Fstr2),
  findHyperText(Fstr1,Pos1,Htxt1),
  findHyperText(Fstr2,Pos2,Htxt2),
  assert(pplink(point(Htxt1),node(Fname),point(Htxt2),node(Fname2))),
  !.

addOPTION(_,_,_,3).  % return with no action

/* ************************ searchPOINT **************** */

searchPOINT(Hstr,Str,Nstr,Pos):-
  fronttoken(Hstr,Tok,Hstr1),
  fronttoken(Str,Tok,Str1),
  concat(Nstr,Tok,Nstr1),
  searchPOINT1(Hstr1,Str1,Nstr1,Pos), !.

searchPOINT(Hstr,Str,Nstr,Pos):-
  fronttoken(Str,Tok,Str1),
  concat(Nstr,Tok,Nstr1),
  searchPOINT(Hstr,Str1,Nstr1,Pos).

searchPOINT1("",_,Nstr,Pos):-
  str_len(Nstr,Pos), !.

searchPOINT1(Hstr,Str,Nstr,Pos):-
  fronttoken(Hstr,Tok,Hstr1),
  fronttoken(Str,Tok,Str1),
  concat(Nstr,Tok,Nstr1),
  searchPOINT1(Hstr1,Str1,Nstr1,Pos).

/* ************************* END END END *************** */

GOAL

% retract all previous database facts (old configuration)

retractall(nnlink(_,_)),
retractall(pnlink(_,_,_)),
retractall(pplink(_,_,_,_)),

% asserting the network configuration knowledge-base

consult("fig3-5.net", hypdb),

% displaying system windows

blankwindow,
editwindow,

% initiating the hypertext system by editing the root node

hyperEDIT("node1.hyp",1,_),

% before exiting the program remove the system windows

removewindow,
removewindow.
```

Fig. 3-10. An extended user-interface module.

```
/* ******************************************************** */
/* USER INTERFACE PREDICATES                                */
/* ******************************************************** */

PREDICATES

blankwindow
editwindow
dirwindow
statusline
msg(INTEGER,INTEGER,STRING)
textSCREEN

CLAUSES

/* ******************** SYSTEM WINDOWS ****************** */

% blank window
blankwindow :- makewindow(1,7,0,"",0,0,25,80).

% edit window
editwindow :-
  makewindow(2,15,112,"",3,0,21,80).

% directory window
dirwindow :-
  cursor(R,C), Row=R+1,
  makewindow(3,15,112,"Directory",Row,C,8,45).

% main status line
statusline:-
  makestatus(112,
"F1-Help F2-Save F3-Load F4-Replace F5-Zoom F7-Xcopy F8-Xedit F10-Htext ESC-
End").

/* ********************** msg ************************** */

msg(R,C,Str):-
   makewindow(10,22,112,"Message",R,C,3,40),
   window_str(Str),
   repeat,
      inkey(_),  % repeat waiting for a key to be pressed.
   !,
   removewindow.

/* ********************** textSCREEN ****************** */
% display the system version information.

textSCREEN:-
  makewindow(11,112,15,"",7,10,9,60),
  write("\t\t\t  ET 1.0"),
  write("\n\t\t A Hypertext Authoring System"),
  write("\n\t\t\t    by "),
  write("\n\t\t       Safaa H. Hashim"),
  write("\n\n In 'Exploring Hypertext Programming: writing "),
  write("knowledge\n representation and problem solving "),
  write("programs'. TAB BOOKS"),
  repeat,
    inkey(_),  % repeat waiting for a key to be pressed.
  !,
  removewindow.

/* ******************************************************** */
```

(**Fig. 3-10.** continued)

```
/* ******************** changeDIR *********************** */
/* ***************************************************** */

PREDICATES
  changeDIR(INTEGER,INTEGER,INTEGER,INTEGER)
  changeDISK(STRING)
  pathNAME(STRING)

CLAUSES

changeDIR(ROW,COL,WATTR,FATTR):-
  disk(DISK),
  lineinput_repeat(ROW,COL,45,WATTR,FATTR,"Directory: ",DISK,NEWDISK),
  changeDISK(NEWDISK),!,
  removewindow.
changeDIR(_,_,_,_).

changeDISK(DISK):-
  pathNAME(DISK),
  disk(DISK),!.
changeDISK(_):-
  msg(17,1,"error in directory name."), % in "user-h.pro"
  fail.

pathNAME(DISK):-
  fronttoken(DISK,_,Str),
  fronttoken(Str,":",Str1),
  fronttoken(Str1,"\\",_).

/* *********************** END END END ***************** */
```

You start your journey from "hyperEDIT." It is the same good old "hyperEDIT." The last subgoal in "hyperEDIT" is "hyperSTATUS." In "hyperEDIT," when you press F10, Turbo will bind the last argument of the "hyperSTATUS" subgoal to 0. To prove the subgoal, Turbo tries the first clause of "hyperSTATUS" in the program:

```
hyperSTATUS(Fname,Fstr,Pos,0):-
  menu(0,35,15,112,["View a link",
                    "Add a link"],
      "LINK OPERATIONS",1,Choice),
  linkOPTION(Fname,Fstr,Pos,Choice), !, fail.
```

In this clause, menu displays a list of two options (see FIG. 3-11). Turbo then passes your choice to "linkOPTION."

In "linkOPTION" you have four clauses. If you choose to view links, Turbo will try the first two clauses. Otherwise, if you choose to add links, it will try the last two clauses. Here are the two clauses responsible for adding links:

```
linkOPTION(Fname,Fstr,Pos,2):-
  menu(0,55,15,112,["add a Node-node link",
                    "add a Point-node link",
                    "add a pOint-point link"],
      "ADD A LINK",1,Choice),
  addOPTION(Fname,Fstr,Pos,Choice), !.
  linkOPTION(_,_,_,2). % return with no action
```

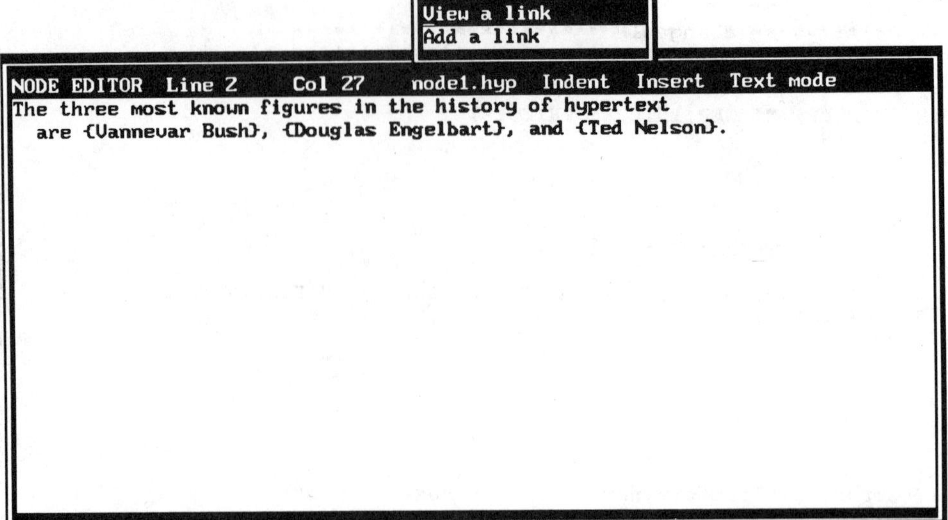

Fig. 3-11. The LINK OPERATIONS menu.

When you pick the second option, "menu" will bind "Choice" to the integer 2. The next subgoal is "linkOPTION." The last argument in "linkOPTION" is "Choice," which is now bound to 2. When Turbo tries to satisfy this subgoal, it finds two matching clauses:

```
linkOPTION(Fname,Fstr,Pos,2):-
  menu(0,55,15,112,["add a Node-node link",
                    "add a Point-node link",
                    "add a pOint-point link"],
      "ADD A LINK",1,Choice),
  addOPTION(Fname,Fstr,Pos,Choice),!.
linkOPTION(_,_,_,2). % user pressed ESC
                     % or addOPTION failed
```

Turbo tries the first clause first. This will cause the display of a menu with three options (see FIG. 3-12). Each option corresponds to a link type. Notice that I am using the same programming technique I used in "hyperSTATUS." The first subgoal is "menu," which binds "Choice" to either 1, 2, or 3 depending on the option you pick. Then Turbo passes the value of "Choice" to the last subgoal: the "addOPTION" predicate. If Choice is 1 (you want to add an "nnlink"), Turbo will try to match the "addOPTION" subgoal with one of these two clauses:

```
addOPTION(Fname1,_,_,1):-
    cursor(R,_), Row=R+2,
    readfilename(Row,35,15,112,hyp,"",Fname2),
    assert(nnlink(node(Fname1),node(Fname2))), !.
```

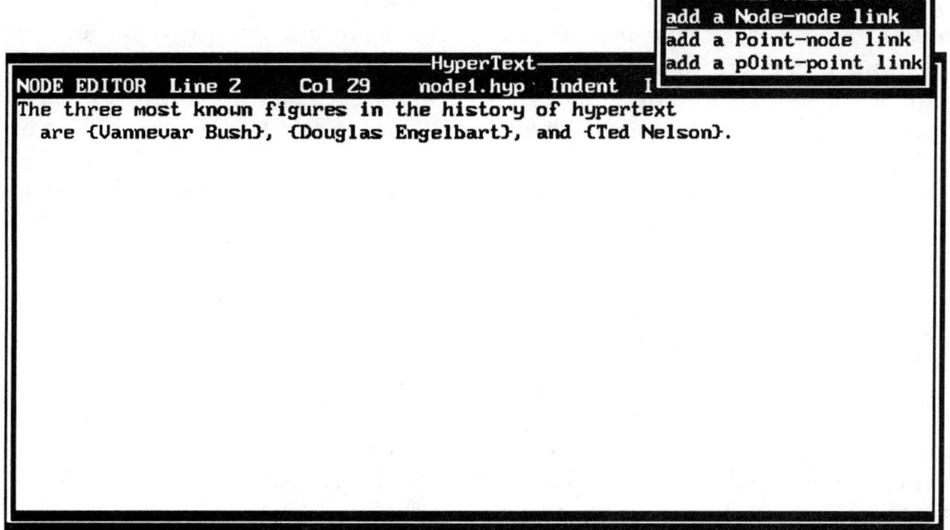

Fig. 3-12. The ADD A LINK menu.

```
addOPTION(_,_,_,1):-
  msg(17,0,"Error in adding a node-node link").
```

but if Choice is 2 (you want to add a "pnlink"), Turbo will try matching "addOPTION" subgoal with one of these two clauses:

```
addOPTION(SN,Fstr,Pos,2):-
    cursor(R,_), Row=R+2,
    readfilename(Row,35,15,112,hyp,"",TN),
    findHyperText(Fstr,Pos,Htxt),
    assert(pnlink(point(Htxt),node(SN),node(TN))), !.
  addOPTION(_,_,_,2):-
   msg(17,0,"Error in adding a point-node link").
```

Otherwise, if Choice is 3 (you want to add a "pplink"), Turbo will try matching "addOPTION" subgoal with one of these two clauses:

```
addOPTION(SN,Fstr1,Pos1,3):-
    cursor(R,_), Row=R+2,
    readfilename(Row,35,15,112,hyp,"",TN),
    hyperEDIT(TN,1,Pos2),
    file_str(TN,Fstr2),
    findHyperText(Fstr1,Pos1,Htxt1),
    findHyperText(Fstr2,Pos2,Htxt2),
    assert(pplink(point(Htxt1),node(SN),point(Htxt2),
node(TN))),!.
  addOPTION(_,_,_,3):-
   msg(17,0,"Error in adding a point-point link").
```

That's all for programming the "Add a link" operation. Simple, isn't it? Remember, however, that my approach is just one possible way. You can try designing and coding your own program for the "Add a link" operation. Also, comparing your code to mine will give you a better understanding of the problems involved. As Mark Twain once said: "The harder I work, the better my luck gets."

So the more you try my programs or write your own programs, the better your programming will be. Now I want to tell you about a new TOOLBOX predicate in my program. The predicate is "filename."

The TOOLBOX Predicate "readfilename"

I use "readfilename" to prompt users to input a filename. If the file is not in the current directory path, you should supply the path. Also, if you don't know the file name it will help us find it. You simply press ENTER and it will display a box menu (another TOOLBOX menu predicate) of files in the current directory. Here is the declaration form for "readfilename":

```
readfilename(ROW,COL,WATTR,FATTR,EXTENSION,OLDFILENAME,
NEWFILENAME)
```

It returns NEWFILENAME as its output. OLDFILENAME is a default filename, and EXTENSION is a default file extension. This predicate is in the TOOLBOX file "filename.pro." To use it, you must include this file in your program; but that's not all. "readfilename" uses "lineinp" as a subgoal. This subgoal displays a prompt message and reads the user input, but "lineinp" is a module by itself. "lineinp.pro" is included before "filename.pro."

In the next chapter I will explain how to use "filename" as part of the user-interface in hypertext systems. For now, let's move on to the next operation: deleting links.

DELETING LINKS

When you design an authoring system, you want to have a dynamic network of nodes, points, and links. In a dynamic network, you might add a link between two nodes at one time. As you continue developing the network, you might need to delete the link, change its source, change its destination, or change both its source and destination. In this section, I talk about deleting links. I will program a "Delete a link" hypertext operation.

Unlike the viewing and adding operations, deleting links is a little bit more complex. Take a look at the examples in FIG. 3-13. In the examples, I show an "nnlink" that I want to delete. The source of the link is the node "S." The target of the link is the node "T." In the figure, there are five possible cases for "T." For each case there are two states. One before the link is deleted, and one after the link is deleted.

In the "A" case, the link between "T" and "S" is the only tie between "T" and the network. When you delete this link, you will also isolate "T." So what do you do with "T"?

- You can program the system so it can ask the user if they still want to keep "T." If not, the system will automatically delete "T."
- You delete the isolated "T" without asking the user.

In this case, the program asks before it deletes the link. This approach has the advantage of keeping the node for future reference. Also, this way you can use the combination of the delete and add links operations to change link destination. Major disadvantages are:

- You run the risk of having too many isolated links.
- If you have many isolated nodes, you might overload the system when your hypertext system is completely loaded in memory.
- You might lose track of the contents of many isolated links. This will make it harder to search for a node that has what you need.

In this case, where nodes are separate files on disk, you have no problem. Keeping non-linked nodes on disk will not affect the system's performance, but you need to have some browsing or text search capability in your hypertext system. One way of doing this is to have a temporary gate to DOS—a DOS shell. Once in DOS, you can search for a part or all text—hypertext point—that you need for reference. You get the filename that contains the text. When done, you exit the DOS shell and return to the hypertext system. Here you can re-link those isolated, non-linked nodes when and where you find it necessary to do so.

As for the other four cases: B, C, D, and E in FIG. 3-13, the decision to delete a link is much more complex than that in "A." For example, in the case of "B," after you delete the "S"-"T" link, you will have an isolated cluster of three nodes. Should you just delete "T" and link the other two nodes directly to "S" or should you delete the whole cluster? The decision is yours. It also depends on the type of application you are writing, and the flexibility you want to have in your system.

In FIG. 3-13, in all the cases except that of "A," the target node "T" had extra links other than the deleted link. In this case, I will only delete nodes in situations similar to that of "A," but only after confirmation by the user. Other than that, I will delete the link and keep the node. Now I'll show you how to write the "Delete a link" operation. Equally important is the integration of this operation in your hypertext system.

A Program for Viewing, Adding, and Deleting Links

The new program (the one with the "Delete a link" operation) is a modified version of the program in FIG. 3-9. The complete code for this new version of the program is in FIG. 3-14.

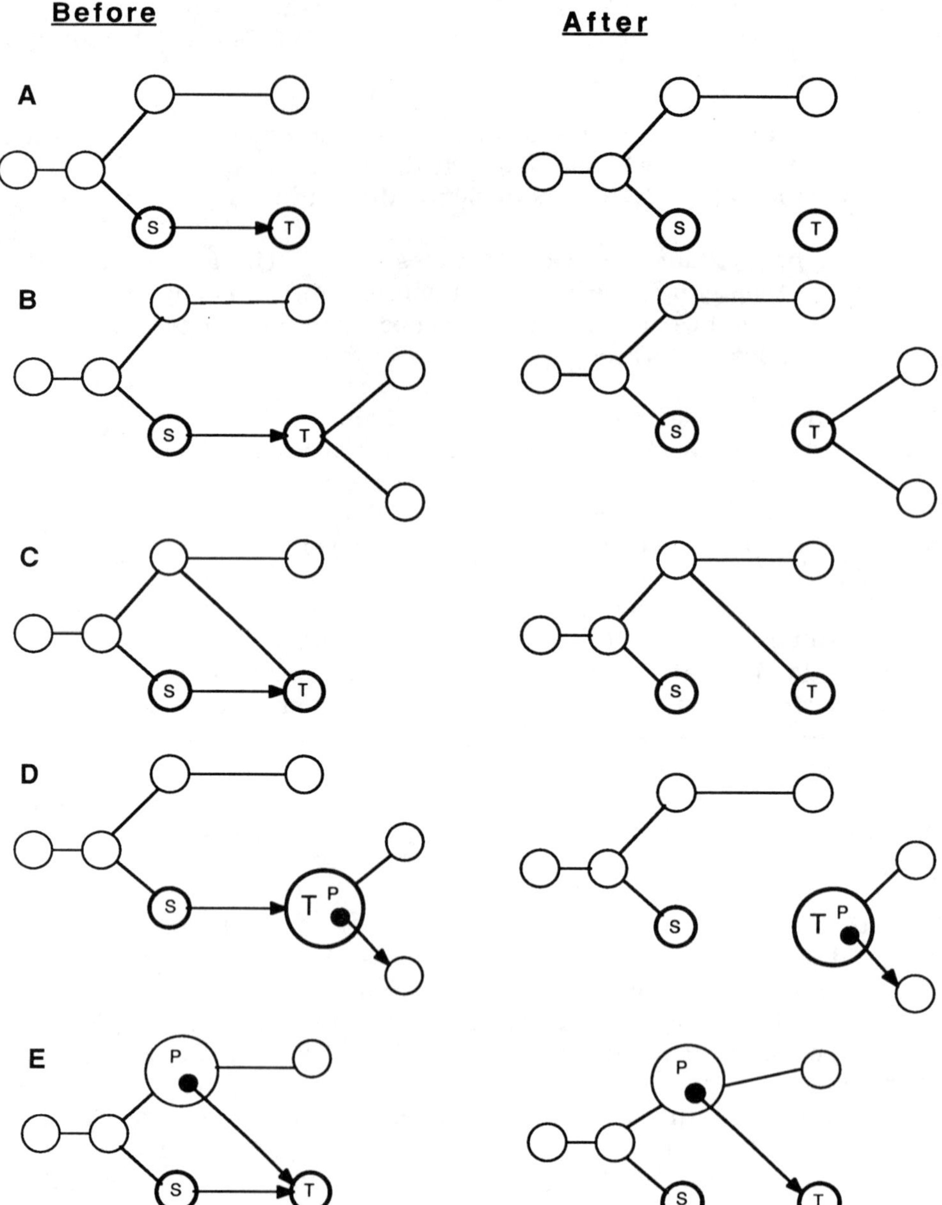

Fig. 3-13. Deleting a link from the hypertext network.

The "Delete a link" operation is not the only new thing in this program. Also used is the menu predicate "boxmenu" which is in the Turbo Prolog TOOLBOX "boxmenu.pro" program. "boxmenu" is used to display the list of target nodes of a particular link. In Chapter 4, I will tell you more on how to do this. Now concentrate on the "Delete a link" operation.

Fig. 3-14. A program to view, add, and delete links.

```
include "fig3-2.pro"   % domains and database declarations

/* ************** Turbo Prolog TOOLBOX programs ********* */

include "tdoms.pro"      % TOOLBOX text domains declarations
include "tpreds.pro"     % TOOLBOX text predicates declaration

DATABASE
  insmode
  lineinpstate(STRING,COL)
  lineinpflag

% required Turbo Prolog TOOLBOX modules

% "filename" predicate is in the TOOLBOX's "filename.pro"
% "filename.pro" requires "lineinp.pro"
% "lineinput" predicate is in the TOOLBOX's "lineinp.pro"

include "lineinp.pro"    % TOOLBOX line input predicate
include "filename.pro"   % TOOLBOX file name input predicate
include "menu.pro"       % TOOLBOX menu program
include "boxmenu.pro"    % TOOLBOX menu program
include "status.pro"     % TOOLBOX status line program

/* ***************** hypertext modules ****************** */

include "fig3-3.pro"     % general utility predicates
include "fig3-9.pro"     % user-interface predicates
include "fig2-2.pro"     % finding a hypertext point

/* ***************** general predicates section ********* */

PREDICATES

  hyperEDIT(STRING,INTEGER,INTEGER)
    hyperSTATUS(STRING,STRING,INTEGER,INTEGER)
    % findHYPERtext in file "find-h.pro"
      linkOPTION(STRING,STRING,INTEGER,INTEGER)
        viewOPTION(STRING,STRING,INTEGER,INTEGER)
          searchPOINT(STRING,STRING,STRING,INTEGER)
            searchPOINT1(STRING,STRING,STRING,INTEGER)
        addOPTION(STRING,STRING,INTEGER,INTEGER)
        deleteOPTION(STRING,STRING,INTEGER,INTEGER)
          del_nnlink(STRING,STRING)
          del_pnlink(STRING,STRING)
          del_pplink(STRING,STRING)
            del_node(STRING)

/* ******************* clauses section ****************** */

CLAUSES

/* ******************************************************* */
/* ********************** hyperEDIT ********************* */
/* ******************************************************* */

/* Edit the contents of a hypertext node. In this version
   of hypertext, a node is a file in the current disk
   directory. */

hyperEDIT(FILEname,InPos,OutPos) :-
   repeat,
     file_str(FILEname,INstr),
```

(**Fig. 3-14.** continued)

```
     MSG="End editing (ESC),  Follow hyper link (F10) ",
     edit(INstr,OUTstr,"NODE EDITOR",FILEname,MSG,
          InPos,"H-Help.txt",1,1,1,1,OutPos,ReturnStatus),
     hyperSTATUS(FILEname,OUTstr,OutPos,ReturnStatus).

/* ***************************************************** */
/* ****************** hyperSTATUS *********************** */
/* ***************************************************** */

/* When ReturnStatus = 0, edit was terminated with an F10 */

hyperSTATUS(Fname,Fstr,Pos,0):-
  menu(0,35,15,112,["View a link",
                    "Add a link",
                    "Delete a link"],
       "LINK OPERATIONS",1,Choice),
  linkOPTION(Fname,Fstr,Pos,Choice), !, fail.

/* When ReturnStatus = 1, edit was terminated with an ESC */
% Ask if user wants to save changes to file.

hyperSTATUS(Fname,Fstr,_,1):-
   cursor(R,_), Row=R+2,
   lineinput(Row,35,30,15,112,
             "Save changes to file (y/n): ","",ANS),
   upper_lower(ANS1,ANS),
   ANS1 = "Y",
   file_str(Fname,Fstr), !.

% Exit editor without saving the changes.

hyperSTATUS(_,_,_,1).

/* ************************ linkOPTION ***************** */

% the VIEW A LINK option

linkOPTION(Fname,Fstr,Pos,1):-
  menu(0,10,15,112,["view a Node-node link",
                    "view a Point-node link",
                    "view a pOint-point link"],
       "VIEW A LINK",1,Choice),
  viewOPTION(Fname,Fstr,Pos,Choice), !.

linkOPTION(_,_,_,1). % return with no action

% the ADD A LINK option

linkOPTION(Fname,Fstr,Pos,2):-
  menu(0,35,15,112,["add a Node-node link",
                    "add a Point-node link",
                    "add a pOint-point link"],
       "ADD A LINK",1,Choice),
  addOPTION(Fname,Fstr,Pos,Choice), !.

linkOPTION(_,_,_,2). % return with no action

% the DELETE A LINK option

linkOPTION(Fname,Fstr,Pos,3):-
  menu(0,55,15,112,["delete a Node-node link",
                    "delete a Point-node link",
                    "delete a pOint-point link"],
       "DELETE A LINK",1,Choice),
```

(**Fig. 3-14.** continued)

```
  deleteOPTION(Fname,Fstr,Pos,Choice), !.

linkOPTION(_,_,_,3). % return with no action

/* ********************** viewOPTION ******************** */

viewOPTION(S,_,_,1):-
  findall(T,nnlink(node(S),node(T)),Tlist),
  cursor(R,C), Row=R+1, Col=C+1,
  boxmenu(Row,Col,4,45,15,112,Tlist,
         "NODE-NODE LINK",1,Nchoice), Nchoice <> 0,
  nth_member(Tlist,Nchoice,TN),
  hyperEDIT(TN,1,_), !.
viewOPTION(_,_,_,1).

viewOPTION(_,FILEstr,POS,2):-
  findHyperText(FILEstr,Pos,SP),
  SP <> "",
  findall(T,pnlink(point(SP),_,node(T)),Tlist),
  cursor(R,C), Row=R+1, Col=C+1,
  boxmenu(Row,Col,4,45,15,112,Tlist,
         "POINT-NODE LINK",1,Nchoice), Nchoice <> 0,
  nth_member(Tlist,Nchoice,TN),
  hyperEDIT(TN,1,_), !.

viewOPTION(_,_,_,2).

viewOPTION(_,FILEstr,Pos,3):-
  findHyperText(FILEstr,Pos,Htxt),
  Htxt <> "",
  findall(T,pplink(point(Htxt),_,_,node(T)),Tlist),
  cursor(R,C), Row=R+1, Col=C+1,
  boxmenu(Row,Col,4,45,15,112,Tlist,
         "POINT-POINT LINK",1,Nchoice),
  Nchoice <> 0,
  nth_member(Tlist,Nchoice,TN),
  pplink(point(Htxt),_,point(Ttxt),node(TN)),
  file_str(TN,STR),
  searchPOINT(Ttxt,STR,"",TPos),
  hyperEDIT(TN,TPos,_), !.

viewOPTION(_,_,_,3).

/* ************************* addOPTION ***************** */

% Adding a node-node link.

addOPTION(Fname1,_,_,1):-
  cursor(R,_), Row=R+2,
  readfilename(Row,35,15,112,hyp,"",Fname2),
  assert(nnlink(node(Fname1),node(Fname2))), !.

addOPTION(_,_,_,1).  % return with no action

% Adding a point-node link.

addOPTION(FILEname,Fstr,Pos,2):-
  cursor(R,_), Row=R+2,
  readfilename(Row,35,15,112,hyp,"",Fname2),
  findHyperText(Fstr,Pos,Htxt),
  assert(pnlink(point(Htxt),node(FILEname),node(Fname2))),
  !.

addOPTION(_,_,_,2).  % return with no action
```

(**Fig. 3-14.** continued)

```
% Adding a point-point link.

addOPTION(FILEname,Fstr1,Pos1,3):-
  cursor(R,_), Row=R+2,
  readfilename(Row,35,15,112,hyp,"",Fname2),
  hyperEDIT(Fname2,1,Pos2),
  file_str(Fname2,Fstr2),
  findHyperText(Fstr1,Pos1,Htxt1),
  findHyperText(Fstr2,Pos2,Htxt2),
  assert(pplink(point(Htxt1),node(FILEname),point(Htxt2),
               node(Fname2))),!.

addOPTION(_,_,_,3).  % return with no action

/* ********************* deleteOPTION ******************* */

% delete a nnlink

deleteOPTION(SN,_,_,1):-
  findall(T,nnlink(node(SN),node(T)),Tlist),
  cursor(R,C), Row=R+1, Col=C+1,
  boxmenu(Row,Col,4,45,15,112,Tlist,
          "NODE-NODE LINK",1,Nchoice), Nchoice <> 0,
  nth_member(Tlist,Nchoice,TN),
  retract(nnlink(node(SN),node(TN)),hypdb),
  del_nnlink(SN,TN), !.

deleteOPTION(_,_,_,1).

% delete a pnlink

deleteOPTION(SN,Fstr,Pos,2):-
  findHyperText(Fstr,Pos,SP),
  SP <> "",
  findall(T,pnlink(point(SP),node(SN),node(T)),Tlist),
  cursor(R,C), Row=R+1, Col=C+1,
  boxmenu(Row,Col,4,45,15,112,Tlist,
          "NODE-NODE LINK",1,Nchoice),
  nth_member(Tlist,Nchoice,TN),
  retract(pnlink(point(SP),node(SN),node(TN)),hypdb),
  del_pnlink(SN,TN), !.

deleteOPTION(_,_,_,2).

% delete a pplink

deleteOPTION(SN,Fstr,Pos,3):-
  findHyperText(Fstr,Pos,SP),
  SP <> "",
  findall(T,pplink(point(SP),node(SN),point(TP),node(T)),Tlist),
  cursor(R,C), Row=R+1, Col=C+1,
  boxmenu(Row,Col,4,45,15,112,Tlist,
          "NODE-NODE LINK",1,Nchoice),
  nth_member(Tlist,Nchoice,TN),
  retract(pplink(point(SP),node(SN),point(TP),node(TN)),hypdb),
  del_pplink(SN,TN), !.

deleteOPTION(_,_,_,3).

/* ************************** del_nnlink *************** */

% target node TN is linked only to SN
del_nnlink(SN,TN):-
  findall(SN1,nnlink(node(SN1),node(TN)),L1), L1=[SN],
  findall(TN1,nnlink(node(TN),node(TN1)),L2), L2=[],
```

(**Fig. 3-14.** continued)

```
  findall(SN1,pnlink(_,node(SN1),node(TN)),L3), L3=[],
  findall(TN1,pnlink(_,node(TN),node(TN1)),L4), L4=[],
  findall(SN1,pplink(_,node(SN1),_,node(TN)),L5), L5=[],
  findall(TN1,pplink(_,node(TN),_,node(TN1)),L6), L6=[],
  del_node(TN). % ask user before deleting target node

/* ************************ del_pnlink ***************** */

% target node TN is linked only to a point in SN

del_pnlink(SN,TN):-
  findall(SN1,pnlink(_,node(SN1),node(TN)),L1), L1=[SN],
  findall(SN1,nnlink(node(SN1),node(TN)),L2), L2=[],
  findall(TN1,nnlink(node(TN),node(TN1)),L3), L3=[],
  findall(TN1,pnlink(_,node(TN),node(TN1)),L4), L4=[],
  findall(SN1,pplink(_,node(SN1),_,node(TN)),L5), L5=[],
  findall(TN1,pplink(_,node(TN),_,node(TN1)),L6), L6=[],
  del_node(TN). % ask user before deleting target node

/* ************************ del_pplink ***************** */

% target TN only has a point linked to a point in SN

del_pplink(SN,TN):-
  findall(SN1,pplink(_,node(SN1),_,node(TN)),L1), L1=[SN],
  findall(SN1,nnlink(node(SN1),node(TN)),L2), L2=[],
  findall(TN1,nnlink(node(TN),node(TN1)),L3), L3=[],
  findall(TN1,pnlink(_,node(TN),node(TN1)),L4), L4=[],
  findall(SN1,pnlink(_,node(SN1),node(TN)),L5), L5=[],
  findall(TN1,pplink(_,node(TN),_,node(TN1)),L6), L6=[],
  del_node(TN). % ask user before deleting target node

/* *********************** del_node ******************** */

% ask the user if he wants to delete TN which is an isolated
% node in the hypertext network.

del_node(TN):-
  cursor(R,C), ROW = R+1,
  concat(TN," is not linked, delete (y/n): ",TXT),
  lineinput(ROW,C,45,15,112,TXT,"",ANS),
  upper_lower(ANS1,ANS),
  ANS1="Y",
  deletefile(TN), !.

del_node(_).    % else return without deleting TN.

/* ************************ searchPOINT ***************** */

searchPOINT(Hstr,Str,Nstr,Pos):-
  fronttoken(Hstr,Tok,Hstr1),
  fronttoken(Str,Tok,Str1),
  concat(Nstr,Tok,Nstr1),
  searchPOINT1(Hstr1,Str1,Nstr1,Pos), !.

searchPOINT(Hstr,Str,Nstr,Pos):-
  fronttoken(Str,Tok,Str1),
  concat(Nstr,Tok,Nstr1),
  searchPOINT(Hstr,Str1,Nstr1,Pos).

searchPOINT1("",_,Nstr,Pos):-
  str_len(Nstr,Pos), !.

searchPOINT1(Hstr,Str,Nstr,Pos):-
  fronttoken(Hstr,Tok,Hstr1),
```

(**Fig. 3-14.** continued)

```
    fronttoken(Str,Tok,Str1),
    concat(Nstr,Tok,Nstr1),
    searchPOINT1(Hstr1,Str1,Nstr1,Pos).

/* ************************* END END END **************** */

GOAL

% retract all previous database facts (old configuration)

retractall(nnlink(_,_)),
retractall(pnlink(_,_,_)),
retractall(pplink(_,_,_,_)),

% asserting the network configuration knowledge-base

assert(nnlink(node("node1.hyp"),
              node("node2.hyp"))),
assert(nnlink(node("node2.hyp"),
              node("node3.hyp"))),
assert(nnlink(node("node3.hyp"),
              node("node5.hyp"))),
assert(pnlink(point("Bush's ideas"),
              node("node3.hyp"),
              node("node4.hyp"))),
assert(pnlink(point("Vannevar Bush"),
              node("node1.hyp"),
              node("node5.hyp"))),
assert(pnlink(point("Douglas Engelbart"),
              node("node1.hyp"),
              node("node3.hyp"))),
assert(pnlink(point("Ted Nelson"),
              node("node1.hyp"),
              node("node2.hyp"))),
assert(pplink(point("Bush's ideas"),
              node("node3.hyp"),
              point("Vannevar Bush"),
              node("node1.hyp"))),

% displaying system windows

blankwindow,
editwindow,

% initiating the hypertext system by editing the root node

hyperEDIT("node1.hyp",1,_),

% before exiting the program remove the system windows

removewindow,
removewindow.
```

Load and run the program in FIG. 3-14, but before you do this, make sure that you have all "include" files in the same directory. The first thing you will see is the root node loaded in "hyperEDIT." When you press F10, the main menu appears with three options (see FIG. 3-15).

When you choose the "Delete a link" option, "hyperEDIT" passes control to "deleteOPTION." This predicate has six clauses: two for deleting an "nnlink," two for deleting a "pnlink," and two for deleting a "pplink." I will

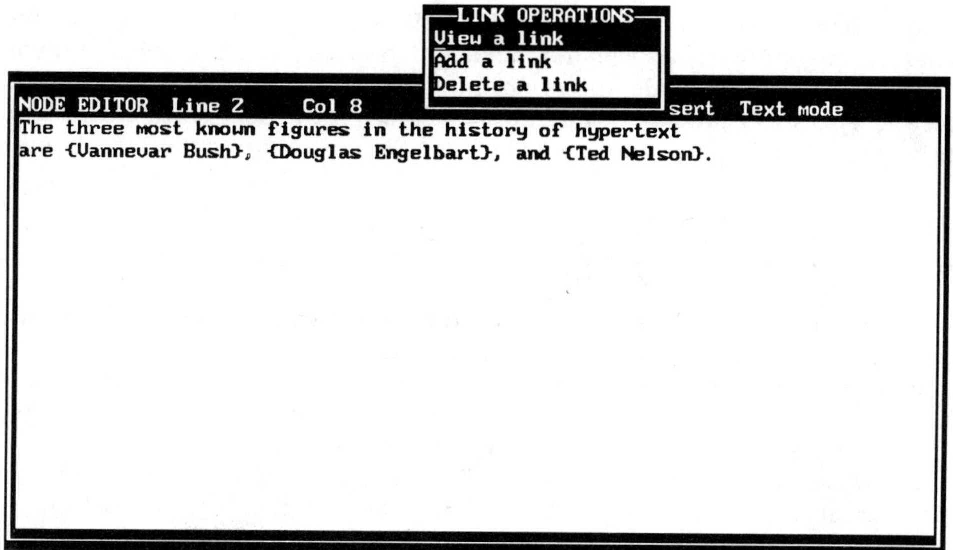

Fig. 3-15. Main menu with view, add, and delete options.

show you how the program deletes an "nnlink." The same thing will apply equally to "pnlink" and "pplink."

When you choose to delete an "nnlink," the program passes control to the first two clauses of "deleteOPTION":

```
deleteOPTION(SN,_,_,1):-
   findall(T,nnlink(node(SN),node(T)),Tlist),
   cursor(R,C), Row=R+1, Col=C+1,
   boxmenu(Row,Col,4,45,15,112,Tlist,"NODE-NODE LINK",
          1,Nchoice),
   Nchoice <> 0, nth_member(Tlist,Nchoice,TN), X=SN, Y=TN,
   retract(nnlink(node(X),node(Y)),hypdb),
   del_nnlink(X,Y), !.
deleteOPTION(_,_,_,1).
```

In the first clause, "findall" finds the list of all target nodes. Next, "boxmenu" displays this list so that you can choose one node. Then, "retract" deletes the link. The last subgoal is "del_nnlink," which checks if, after deleting the link, the target node is an isolated node:

```
del_nnlink(SN,TN):-
  findall(SN1,nnlink(node(SN1),node(TN)),L1), L1=[SN],
  findall(TN1,nnlink(node(TN),node(TN1)),L2), L2=[ ],
  findall(SN1,pnlink(_,node(SN1),node(TN)),L3), L3=[ ],
  findall(TN1,pnlink(_,node(TN),node(TN1)),L4), L4=[ ],
  findall(SN1,pplink(_,node(SN1),_,node(TN)),L5), L5=[ ],
  findall(TN1,pplink(_,node(TN),_,node(TN1)),L6), L6=[ ],
  del_node(TN). % ask user before deleting target node
```

It does that by using a series of "findall" subgoals. If all these subgoals are true, the target node is an isolated node, which means you can delete it if you want to. To delete the node, the program uses "del_node." In "del-node" you use the TOOLBOX predicate "lineinput" to prompt the user for confirmation. If the answer is yes, the program deletes the file representing the target node.

CHANGING THE SOURCE AND DESTINATION OF A LINK

So far, three operations to help us edit the hypertext network have been built. To complete the set, you need to add the "Change a link" operation. What I will do in this section is go over the design of this operation. I will leave the actual writing of code for you as an exercise. What you need to do is take the program in FIG. 3-14 and add the "Change a link" operation.

Now assume you are in "hyperEDIT" and want to change an "nnlink" of the current source node. You press F10, and you get a menu of four options:

- View a link
- Add a link
- Delete a link
- Change a link

Say you choose the last option. The system will respond with a menu of two options:

- change Source node
- change Destination node

As soon as you choose one, the system will ask you for the name and type of the replacement. If you are changing the source node to a different source node, you must supply the new source node. Once you do that, the system will retract the old "nnlink" and assert a new one. You might like to change the source node to a source point. Here the system first asks for the name of the node of that point. After you supply the name, it will bring the node into "edit." Select or create the point and press F10 to select it. The rest is the same. The system will retract the old "nnlink" and add a new "pnlink."

The next step is to build the code for changing "pnlinks" and "pplinks." To do this, you use the same logic in changing "nnlinks."

Another idea is to use a combination of "Delete a link" and "Add a link" operations. You can use this combination to change link destinations. There is an efficient and a less efficient way to do the same thing. I will stop here to end this chapter and give you a break. In the next chapter I will again discuss the user-interface.

4

Designing a Hypertext User-Interface

"Let every eye negotiate for itself, and trust no agent."

—*William Shakespeare*

These words from Shakespeare said it all. The purpose of this chapter is to show you how to build an easy-to-use user-interface for your hypertext programs—a user-interface which communicates with you through your eyes rather than your memory—WYSIWYG (What You See Is What You Get). This kind of user-interface is becoming the standard on many computer systems. It was first developed at Xerox PARC. It became very popular after its use in Apple Macintosh computers. On the IBM-PC, the most common application of the WYSIWYG idea is in the MicroSoft Windows-2.0 and Windows-386 programs. For the IBM Personal System 2 (PS/2), there is the Presentation Manager. There are many other implementations of WYSIWYG and more yet to come.

Today, for many hypertext system designers, a WYSIWYG user-interface is a must—simply because it is the closest thing to the natural way of reading and writing of text. With WYSIWYG you don't need to remember or learn a new set of commands when you use different applications. Also, you don't need extensive training or reading of manuals before you can start using a hypertext program. A WYSIWYG approach is what many user-interface specialists call a "direct manipulation" interface approach. Ben Shneiderman, the author of "Designing the User Interface: Strategies for Effective Human-

Computer Interaction," classify user-interfaces in terms of their interaction styles. He lists these three categories:

- menu selection systems,
- command languages, and
- direct manipulation.

DOS, and UNIX operating systems use "command language" as an interface style. On the other hand, Apple's Macintosh, Microsoft's Windows, and IBM's Presentation Manager use direct manipulation. A system that uses the "menu selection" is Borland's Integrated Programming Environment for Turbo Prolog, Turbo C, Turbo Basic, and Turbo Pascal. Most of Borland language products have tools that help build menu-based user-interface systems. Because I am using Turbo Prolog, a Borland product, it makes more sense to use the "menu selection" approach in our programs.

My focus in this chapter will be on two major topics:

1) Using Turbo Prolog's TOOLBOX in designing the user-interface, and
2) Major considerations in designing the user-interface.

To design a manageable and reusable user-interface, you must break the task into functional parts. You consider these parts as tools, or "widgets," which you can use to create complex applications. They ensure a consistent user-interface across applications. A set of such tools is usually referred to as a toolkit or toolbox. Today, there are many commercial toolboxes for most programming languages. In this case I will use Turbo Prolog's TOOLBOX from Borland International. In the next sections, I will use some of the TOOLBOX predicates to write user-interface programs. Next, I will discuss programming techniques for creating an efficient user-interface.

Also, I will discuss two major considerations in the programming of a user-interface. First is comparing the use of hotkeys with that of menus. I will analyze which technique is best for what. Second is the design of a permissive user-interface. The idea here is to build a flexible interface—one that won't break down when you make mistakes.

USING TURBO PROLOG'S TOOLBOX IN DESIGNING THE USER-INTERFACE

The TOOLBOX provide tools that simplify many time-consuming programming tasks. The TOOLBOX has 80 tools that you can use in your programs. Also, it has 40 examples to show you how you can use the tools in your applications. The TOOLBOX has predicates to help:

- user-interface design and construction,
- screen-layout design tools,
- business graphics images,

- communication with remote devices,
- importing files from other systems, and
- generating language parsers.

In this chapter, I will deal with the first two set of tools. I will give a review of some of the predicates available to you in each set of these tools. Also, I will complement the discussion with some examples to show you how to use these predicates. To run the examples on your Turbo Prolog system, you need to know about tool domain and predicate declarations.

Declaring Tool Domains and Predicates

Borland built the tool predicates as independent modules. So to use the "menu" predicate, all you need is the "menu.pro"program; but as with any Turbo Prolog predicate, tool predicates must have domain and predicate declarations. What you can do is define domain and predicate declarations for the tool predicates you use in your main program. You can integrate the declarations of the tool predicates with the other predicates of your program, but I don't recommend such integration. I prefer that you declare tool predicates separately. This way you need not worry about accidentally changing tool predicates. You must put tool domain and predicate declarations at the top of your program. Nonetheless, declarations could be anywhere in your program given that their declarations appear before any call to these predicates. A simpler approach is to have two separate declaration files—one for all tool domains and one for tool predicates. Then, you can use the "include" directive to include these files in your application programs. Don't worry, you don't need to create these two files. Your Turbo Prolog TOOLBOX comes with two such files. These are "TDOMS.PRO" and "TPREDS.PRO."

In "TDOMS.PRO," you will find all the domain declarations you need for using tool predicates. In "TPREDS.PRO," you will find all predicate declarations for tool predicates. As I said, to use these two files, all you need is to include:

```
include "tdmos.pro"
include "tpreds.pro"
```

at the top of your program. Now, some tool predicates require the use of some "database" facts. Database facts are predicates which you can assert, retract, or consult, but you must first declare these facts in a special database section. So, if a tool predicate requires a database fact, you must declare this fact in a database in your application program. An example of these database facts are those required by the "lineinput" tool predicates in the "lineinp.pro" program. I used "lineinput" in Chapter Three (see FIG. 3-9). You will see this database section:

```
DATABASE
    insmode
    lineinpstate(STRING,COL)
    lineinpflag
```

Done with the basics of using tool predicates, you can start with the first set of tools: user-interface tool predicates.

USER-INTERFACE TOOLS

These tools should help you write most of the user-interface for your applications. It includes predicates for different types of menus, text input-lines, filename input-lines, status-lines, context-sensitive help and some Basic Input/Output (BIOS) calls. There are more than 20 predicates in the user-interface tools section of the TOOLBOX. In this book, I will cover only the tool predicates that I use in the programs. These predicates will include: one filename-input tool and different menu tools, line-input tools, and status-line tools. You noticed that I already used some of these predicates in Chapter 3, but I will use these predicates most extensively in PART TWO and PART THREE, when I discuss complete hypertext systems. For a complete review and use of tool predicates, refer to the TOOLBOX User Guide and Reference Manual. Now, to start with, I will talk about creating menus.

Menu Tools

The TOOLBOX offers a full range of menu predicates. These include: simple menus, box menus, line menus, pull-down menus, and tree menus. Let's discuss some of these predicates.

Simple Menus: The "menu" Tool Predicate. The file "menu.pro" has three menu predicates, "menu," "menu_leave," and "menu_mult." In this book I will only need "menu" combined with other non-simple menus. For this reason, I will not talk about "menu_leave" and "menu_mult" here. I will leave it up to you to look up these two predicates in the TOOLBOX user guide, but to give you an overview, here is a summary of what each predicate is all about:

- "menu": This is a simple menu predicate.
- "menu_leave": which creates a pop-up menu similar to that of "menu," but it won't remove the menu window after you made your choice.
- "menu_mult": again, this predicate will create a pop-up menu similar to that of "menu," but unlike "menu" and "menu_leave," it can return a list of all the selections you made from the menu.

As for "menu," I already discussed it in Chapter 3. I'll review it once more. The form your "menu" goal should be:

```
menu(Row,Col,Wattr,Fattr,ItemList,Title,InitItem,ChoiceCode)
```

Its flow pattern is: (i,i,i,i,i,i,o), and its eight arguments are:

- Row and Col are, respectively, the row and column positions of the upper left-hand corner of the menu window on the text screen.

- Wattr and Fattr are, respectively, the color-attribute values for the window area and its frame. To generate a menu window without frame, you should give "Fattr" the value zero.
- ItemList is a list of items to choose from. Each item must have a STRING domain.
- Title is the heading of the menu which would appear in the menu's window frame. The Title must be of STRING domain.
- InitItem is an integer number referring to the location of the selection bar when Turbo first displays the menu. For example, if InitItem is 1, when Turbo executes menu, the selection bar will be on the first item of the menu.
- ChoiceCode is an integer number returned by menu referring to our menu selection. For example, if ChoiceCode is 3, this means the third item was chosen from the menu.

Take a look at the example of "menu" in FIG. 4-1. It is a direct forward application, so I need say no more.

Box Menus: The "boxmenu" Tool Predicate. In a box menu, Turbo displays the items in more than one column. This is especially useful when you want to display a menu of a large number of items. For example, you might use a box menu to choose from a list of all files in a directory. If you were to do this with "menu," and you have more than 25 files, you won't be able to see all the filenames at once. You have to scroll down the menu to see the rest of them. While with "boxmenu," Turbo will display filenames in multiple rows and columns. To choose a particular item, you use the arrow keys to move up,

Fig. 4-1. An example of "menu"

```
% "tdoms.pro", "tpreds.pro" and "menu.pro" must be in the %current directory,
or you supply their directory path like %this:
%
% include "c:\\toolbox\\tdoms.pro"
% include "c:\\toolbox\\tpreds.pro"
% include "c:\\toolbox\\menu.pro"

include "tdoms.pro"
include "tpreds.pro"
include "menu.pro"

PREDICATES
  translate(INTEGER,STRING)

CLAUSES
  translate(1,"view a Node-node link").
  translate(2,"view a Point-node link").
  translate(3,"view a pOint-point link").

GOAL
  menu(0,30,15,112,["view a Node-node link",
                    "view a Point-node link",
                    "view a pOint-point link"],
       "VIEW A LINK",1,Choice),
  translate(Choice,Item),
  write("You want to [",Item,"].").
```

down, left, or right. The form and flow pattern of "boxmenu" is similar to that of "menu," except for two additional arguments:

```
boxmenu(Row,Col,NoOfRows,NoOfCols,Wattr,Fattr,ItemList,
        Title,InitItem,ChoiceCode)
```

flow pattern: (i,i,i,i,i,i,i,i,i,o).

The two additional arguments are: NoOfRows and NoOfCols. These two arguments, respectively, define the number of rows and columns of the box menu window. To try "boxmenu" use the example of FIG. 4-2.

Fig. 4-2. An example of "boxmenu"

```
include "c:\\toolbox\\tdoms.pro"
include "c:\\toolbox\\tpreds.pro"
include "c:\\toolbox\\boxmenu.pro"

PREDICATES
  translate(INTEGER,STRING)

GOAL

  boxmenu(0,0,5,20,6,4,["First","Second","Third"],"Choose one",1,X),
  translate(X,CHOICE),
  write("You chose the [",CHOICE,"] item.").

CLAUSES
  translate(1,"First").
  translate(2,"Second").
  translate(3,"Third").
```

Line Menu: The "linemenu" Tool Predicate. When you execute a "linemenu" goal, Turbo generates a menu on a single line. The form of a "linemenu" goal is the following:

```
linemenu(Row,Wattr,Fattr,ItemList,Choice)
```

As for the five attributes, here are their descriptions:

- Row, is the row on which you want to display the line menu.
- Wattr, is the screen color attributes of the menu window.
- Fattr, is the color attributes of the menu window frame.
- ItemList, is the list of items in the menu.
- Choice, "linemenu" instantiate this variable to an integer number representing your choice from the menu.

For an example using "linemenu" see FIG. 4-3. In this listing I use "linemenu" with "menu" to create a pull-down menu.

Pull-down Menu: The "pulldown" Tool Predicate. In FIG. 4-3, I showed you how to make a pull-down menu using "linemenu" and "menu," but our "pldwn" predicate is a very simple one. The TOOLBOX has a much advanced pull-down menu predicate—it is in the "pulldown.pro" file. The "pulldown"

Fig. 4-3. Using "linemenu" and "menu" to create a pull-down menu.

```
/* ************************************************************
Note: To make this program work properly do the following
      change to the TOOLBOX file "linemenu.pro"

      In the predicate "linemenu" change the last two
      subgoals so they can be as the following:


      CHOICE=ENDCOL.
      % removewindow.

      Commenting "removewindow" will keep the line menu
      on the screen while we activate the regular menu
      predicate.
********************************************************** */

include "c:\\toolbox\\tdoms.pro"
include "c:\\toolbox\\tpreds.pro"
include "c:\\toolbox\\linemenu.pro"
include "c:\\toolbox\\menu.pro"

DOMAINS
  grp = grp(STRING,STRINGLIST)
  grps = grp*

PREDICATES
  pldwn(ATTR,ATTR,grps,INTEGER,INTEGER)
    getLineMenu(grps,STRINGLIST)
    GetMenuHeader(INTEGER,STRINGLIST,STRING)
    GetMenuList(STRING,grps,STRINGLIST)
    count(STRINGLIST,INTEGER,INTEGER)
    getCol(INTEGER,INTEGER,INTEGER)


CLAUSES

  pldwn(Wattr,Fattr,Groups,MainChoice,SubChoice):-
    repeat,
      getLineMenu(Groups,LineOptions),
      linemenu(0,Wattr,Fattr,LineOptions,MainChoice),
      GetMenuHeader(MainChoice,LineOptions,Header),
      count(LineOptions,0,COUNT),
      getCol(COUNT,MainChoice,Col),
      GetMenuList(Header,Groups,List),
      menu(2,Col,Wattr,Fattr,List,"",1,SubChoice),
      fail.

/* ************************* count ********************* */


  count([],C,C).
  count([_|T],InitNum,NewNum):-
    MidNum=InitNum+1,
    count(T,MidNum,NewNum).

/* ************************* getCol ******************** */

  getCol(Count,Num,Col):-
    Len=80/Count,
    Col=(Num-1)*Len.

/* ********************** getLineMenu ****************** */

getLineMenu([],[]).
```

(**Fig. 4-3.** continued)

```
getLineMenu([grp(Header,_)|T1],[Header|T2]):-
  getLineMenu(T1,T2).

/* ********************** getMenuHeader ***************** */

getMenuHeader(1,[Header|_],Header).
getMenuHeader(Num,[_|T],Header):-
  Num1=Num-1,
  getMenuHeader(Num1,T,Header).

/* ********************** getMenuList ******************* */

getMenuList(Header,[grp(Header,List)|_],List).
getMenuList(Header,[_|T],List):-
  getMenuList(Header,T,List).

/* ********************* END END END END **************** */

GOAL
  makewindow(1,0,0,"",0,0,25,80),
  pldwn(15,112,[grp("Nodes",["Load","New","Save"]),
                grp("Edit",[]),
                grp("Links",["Add","Delete","Change"]),
                grp("Setup",["Colors","Windows"])], C1,C2).
```

tool predicate has this form:

```
pulldown(Attr,MenuList,Choice,SubChoice)
```

Where:

- Attr is the color attribute of windows and their frames in a pull-down menu.
- MenuList is the list of choices in the menu. It is a list of "curtain" compound objects. A curtain object has the following form:

  ```
  curtain(Column,Header,CurtainMenuList)
  ```

Where "Column" is the column of the upper-left-hand corner of a submenu. When you first execute the pull-down menu, a line menu appears at the top of the display. When you choose a "Header," you get the "curtainMenuList" under that header.

- Choice is an integer number representing the choice of a certain curtain.
- SubChoice is an integer number representing your choice from the menulist under that curtain.

A simple example of using "pulldown" is this:

```
include "tdoms.pro"
include "tpreds.pro"
include "pulldown,pro"

GOAL
  pulldown(7, [ curtain(5,"Files",["Load","New","Save"]),
```

```
curtain(15,"Edit",[ ]),
curtain(25,"Run",[ ]),
curtain(35,"Test","[0Proto.","Applic."]),
curtain(45,"Quit",[ ]) ],
    Choice,SubChoice).
```

To respond to a user-selection from the pull-down menu, you need clauses for the "pdwaction" predicate. For example, to respond to a user choice from the above pull-down menu, you must at least have these corresponding "pdwaction" clauses:

```
pdwaction(1,1):- ... % load a file
pdwaction(1,2):- ... % create new file
pdwaction(1,3):- ... % save current file
pdwaction(2,0):- ... % edit current file
pdwaction(3,0):- ... % execute the current file
pdwaction(4,1):- ... % test prototype
pdwaction(4,2):- ... % test application
pdwaction(5,0):- ... % quit system
```

Tree Menu: The "treemenu" Tool Predicate. This predicate creates a tree-like menu. It is very useful as a navigation tool in a tree-like data structure. This is not a tree in the botanical sense of the word, but one of a more abstract nature. A very well-known example of a tree structure is the family tree. There are two kinds of family tree: "ancestor tree" and "descendant tree." In the "ancestor tree" you start with an individual and work back through parents, grandparents, and so on. In the descendent tree, on the other hand, you work forward through children, grandchildren, and so on. You encounter tree-structures in the organizational charts of most companies, institutions, and universities. Also, you can break down most of the complex machines and systems into a tree-structure of parts and operations.

A tree is a hierarchical arrangement of data. A tree structure has a root node—the starting or main node. You can consider the rest of the nodes in the tree as the root's offspring, or the offspring of an offspring, and so on. You can usually visualize tree-structures as "upside down" hierarchy, with the root at the top, and the rest of the tree spread out below.

In hypertext, you can use trees for storing and retrieving text. So tree menus could prove very helpful visualizing and accessing the text. The TOOLBOX predicate "treemenu," in the file "tree.pro," allows you to create a tree menu. To use "treemenu" in your program, you must at least have the following "include" and declaration statements:

```
include "tdoms.pro"

  DOMAINS
    SELECTOR = INTEGER
    TREE = tree(STRING,SELECTOR,TREELIST)
    TREELIST = TREE*
```

```
DATABASE
  treewindow(ROW,COL,ROW,COL,ROW,COL)
  treechoice(SELECTOR)

include "tpreds.pro"
include "status.pro"
include "tree.pro"
```

For an example on using "treemenu," take a look at FIG. 4-4. The program in FIG. 4-4 displays the simple tree menu of FIG. 4-5.

An important part of the tree-menu is the logical representation of the tree itself. The TOOLBOX uses a recursive object definition to represent the tree structure. So a tree is a compound object which, among other things, includes a list of sub-trees. Here is the domain declarations for the "tree" object:

```
DOMAINS
  SELECTOR= INTEGER
  TREE = tree(STRING,SELECTOR,TREELIST)
  TREELIST = TREE*
```

Fig. 4-4. Using the "treemenu" tool predicate.

```
include "c:\\toolbox\\tdoms.pro"

DOMAINS
  SELECTOR=INTEGER
  TREE = tree(STRING,SELECTOR,TREELIST)
  TREELIST = TREE*

DATABASE
  treewindow(ROW,COL)
  treechoice(SELECTOR)

include "c:\\toolbox\\tpreds.pro"
include "c:\\toolbox\\status.pro"
include "c:\\toolbox\\tree.pro"

CLAUSES
  treeaction(_):-
    cursor(R,C),
    makewindow(1,112,15,"",R,C,2,10),
    write("Text on the node"),
    readln(_),
    removewindow.

GOAL

  treemenu(right,
           tree("Francis",1,
                 [tree("Josie",2,[tree("Martinez",3,[]),
                                  tree("Dodge-Colt",4,[])
                                 ]),
                  tree("San Francisco",5,[]),
                  tree("Antoich",6,[]),
                  tree("Honda",7,[]),
                  tree("Allen",8,[tree("12",9,[])])
                 ]),Choice).
```

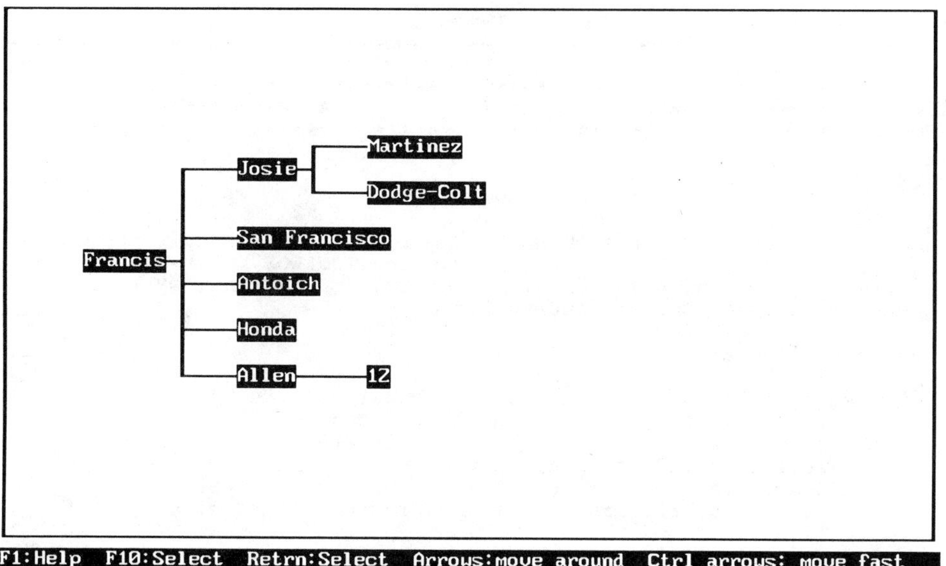

Fig. 4-5. Tree menu created by the program in Fig. 4-4.

To display a tree-menu, all you have to do is to represent your options as "tree" objects, and pass them to "treemenu." Take a look at the "tree" object in the GOAL section of FIG. 4-4. When Turbo executes this goal, you will get the tree-menu in FIG. 4-5.

Probably you have noticed the tiny "clauses" section, which has only one clause. This is because you need to have at least one clause for the predicate "treeaction" so the program can work. To move around in the menu-window, use the arrow keys. When you select from the menu, place the cursor on the option and press F10, or the ENTER key. In FIG. 4-4, I use "treeaction" to display a window with some text on the current node. You can use "treeaction" to fire a regular menu of options under each node. An example of this approach is in the "Xtree.pro" demo program in the TOOLBOX user guide.

Let's go back to the tree-menu in FIG. 4-5. When I wrote the code for this menu, I had in mind certain relationships between the nodes. The kind of relationships you have in mind are not obvious. It would be better if you can express these relationships directly in the tree-menu. One way to do this is by writing relationship names on the links. To carry out this idea, you need to modify the "tree.pro" file. In FIG. 4-6 you will find a modified version of "tree-.pro"—I call this version "tree2.pro" (I used Portions of "tree.pro" in my "tree-2.pro" with permission from Borland International). Later in Chapter 9, you will use "tree2.pro" in MicroIBIS. MicroIBIS is a hypertext-based problem solving system. In PART TWO (Chapter 9-13) I discuss the theory and design of MicroIBIS.

In this version, notice that I extended the domain declaration of "tree." In the new declaration "tree" has four, instead of three, arguments. The additional argument—i.e., the first one—is a relationship name which has a

Fig. 4-6. A modified version of "treemenu" predicate.

```
/* ******************************************************** */
/* ****************** File Name: tree2.pro ************* */
/* ******************************************************** */

/*
                              Treemenu (V.2)

(modified version of the TURBO PROLOG TOOLBOX TREE MENU)
(Based on treemenu in "tree.pro" from the TOOLBOX, parts of
 tree.pro was used by permission from BORLAND INTERNATIONAL.
 Copyright 1986, Borland International)

modifications are in:

1. predicate "listsum" is now tail recursive (more efficient).
2. Arrows pointing to parent nodes are added.
3. the arcs between nodes are labeled with relation names
   to facilitate this tree definition.
4. predicate draw_right is now tail recursive, the
   draw_rightlist appears at the end of draw_right, not in
   the middle.
5. a new predicate "writetext1" was added for writing labels.

*/
/* ******************************************************** */
/*
include "tdoms.pro"

DOMAINS
  SELECTOR=INTEGER
  TREE = tree(STRING,STRING,SELECTOR,TREELIST)
  TREELIST = TREE*

DATABASE
  treewindow(ROW,COL)
  treechoice(SELECTOR)
*/

DOMAINS
  ROWLIST=ROW*
  COLLIST=COL*

PREDICATES
  treemenu(SYMBOL,TREE,SELECTOR)
  treeaction(SELECTOR)
  f10action(SELECTOR)

  draw(symbol,TREE)

writetext(ROW,COL,INTEGER,STRING,SELECTOR)
writetext1(ROW,COL,STRING,COL)
treeline_ver(ROW,ROW,COL)
treeline_ver1(ROW,ROW,COL)
treeline_hor(COL,COL,ROW)
treeline_hor1(COL,COL,ROW)
scr_ch(ROW,COL,CHAR)

lastinlist(ROW,ROWLIST)
lastinlist(COL,COLLIST)
listsum(ROWLIST,ROW,ROW)
listsum(COLLIST,COL,COL)
treekeyact(KEY)
just(ROW,COL)
just1(ROW,COL,ROW,COL)
```

(**Fig. 4-6.** continued)

```
    just2(ROW,COL)
    nodelistlen(ROWLIST,INTEGER)
    nodelistlen(COLLIST,INTEGER)
    remove_treechoice
    newupdate(DBASEDOM)
    treedrop(INTEGER,STRING,STRING)


 CLAUSES

 /* ********************* treeline_ver ****************** */

 /* draw vertical lines connecting elements in the tree */
   treeline_ver(R1,R2,C):-
         treewindow(STROW,STCOL),           /* find the starting position */
         makewindow(_,_,_,_,_,_,ROWS,COLS), /* returns the tree windows size */
         C>=STCOL, C<STCOL+COLS-2, R1<STROW+ROWS-2,
         R2>=STROW, SLROW=STROW+ROWS-2,
         max(STROW,R1,STROW1), min(R2,SLROW,SLROW1),
         CC=C-STCOL, RR1=STROW1-STROW, RR2=SLROW1-STROW,
         treeline_ver1(RR1,RR2,CC),fail.
   treeline_ver(_,_,_).

 /* ******************** treeline_ver1 ****************** */

   treeline_ver1(R1,R2,C):-
         R2>R1, R=R1+1,
         scr_char(R1,C,'°'),
         treeline_ver1(R,R2,C).

 /* ********************** treeline_hor **************** */

 /* draw horizontal lines connecting elements in the tree */
   treeline_hor(C1,C2,R):-
         treewindow(STROW,STCOL), makewindow(_,_,_,_,_,_,ROWS,COLS),
         SLCOL=STCOL+COLS-2,
         R>=STROW, R<STROW+ROWS-2, C1<SLCOL, C2>STCOL,
         max(STCOL,C1,STCOL1), min(C2,SLCOL,SLCOL1),
         RR=R-STROW, CC1=STCOL1-STCOL, CC2=SLCOL1-STCOL,
         treeline_hor1(CC1,CC2,RR),fail.
   treeline_hor(_,_,_).

 /* ********************** treeline_hor1 **************** */

   treeline_hor1(C1,C2,R):-
         C2>C1, C=C1+1,
         scr_char(R,C1,'á'),
         treeline_hor1(C,C2,R).

 /* ************************* scr_ch ******************** */

 /* write a character in a tree window  */
   scr_ch(R,C,CH):-
         treewindow(STROW,STCOL), makewindow(_,_,_,_,_,_,ROWS,COLS),
         R>=STROW, R<STROW+ROWS-2, C>=STCOL, C<STCOL+COLS-2, !,
         RR=R-STROW, CC=C-STCOL,
         scr_char(RR,CC,CH).
   scr_ch(_,_,_).

 /* ************************* treedrop ****************** */

   treedrop(0,TEXT,TEXT):-!.
   treedrop(N,TEXT,TEXT1):-frontstr(N,TEXT,_,TEXT1).

 /* ************************* writetext ***************** */
```

(Fig. 4-6. continued)

```
   writetext(ROW,COL,ATTR,TEXT,SELECT):-
         str_len(TEXT,LEN),
         treewindow(STROW,STCOL), makewindow(_,_,_,_,_,_,ROWS,COLS),
         ROW>=STROW, ROW<STROW+ROWS-2, COL<STCOL+COLS-2, COL+LEN>STCOL,
         REALROW=ROW-STROW,
         RSTART=COL-STCOL,
         REND=RSTART+LEN,
         VST=STCOL-STCOL, VEND=VST+COLS-2,
         max(RSTART,VST,RSTART1), min(REND,VEND,REND1),
         REALLEN=REND1-RSTART1,
         DROP=RSTART1-RSTART,
         treedrop(DROP,TEXT,TEXT1),
         field_str(REALROW,RSTART1,REALLEN,TEXT1),
         field_attr(REALROW,RSTART1,REALLEN,ATTR),
         cursor(R,C),
         R=REALROW,
         C>=RSTART1, C<RSTART1+REALLEN,     !,
         field_attr(R,RSTART1,REALLEN,31),
         assert(treechoice(SELECT)).
   writetext(_,_,_,_,_).

 /* ************************** writetext1 **************** */

 writetext1(ROW,COL,TEXT,COLAFTERTEXT):-
   str_len(TEXT,LEN),
   COLAFTERTEXT=COL+LEN,
   treewindow(STROW,STCOL), makewindow(_,_,_,_,_,_,ROWS,COLS),
   ROW>=STROW, ROW<STROW+ROWS-2, COL<STCOL+COLS-2, COL+LEN>STCOL,
   REALROW=ROW-STROW,


   RSTART=COL-STCOL,
   REND=RSTART+LEN,
   VEND=COLS-2,
   max(RSTART,0,RSTART1), min(REND,VEND,REND1),
   REALLEN=REND1-RSTART1,
   DROP=RSTART1-RSTART,
   treedrop(DROP,TEXT,TEXT1),
   field_str(REALROW,RSTART1,REALLEN,TEXT1), !.

 writetext1(_,C,_,C).

 /* **************************** listsum ***************** */

   listsum([],S,S):-!.
   listsum([H|T],OS,NS):-TS=OS+H,listsum(T,TS,NS).

 /* ********************** lastinlist ******************* */

   lastinlist(RMAX,[RMAX]) :- !.
   lastinlist(RMAX,[_|T]) :- lastinlist(RMAX,T).

 /* ********************* nodelistlen ******************* */

   nodelistlen([],0):-!.
   nodelistlen([_|T],N):-
         nodelistlen(T,X),
         N=X+1.

 /* ********************** newupdate ******************** */

   newupdate(_):-retract(treewindow(_,_)),fail.
   newupdate(X):-assert(X).

 /* ************************ just *********************** */
```

(**Fig. 4-6.** continued)

```
/* Cursor window control */
  just(R,C):-
        cursor(ROW,COL),        /* current cursor pos */
        RR=ROW+R, CC=COL+C,
        makewindow(_,_,_,_,_,_,ROWS,COLS),
        ROWSS=ROWS-3, COLSS=COLS-3,
        just1(RR,CC,ROWSS,COLSS).

/* ************************ just1 *********************** */

/* move cursor and control windows */
  just1(R,C,_,_):-R<0,!,cursor(0,C),just2(R,0).
  just1(R,C,_,_):-C<0,!,cursor(R,0),just2(0,C).
  just1(R,C,ROWS,_):-R>ROWS,!,cursor(ROWS,C),DR=R-ROWS,just2(DR,0).
  just1(R,C,_,COLS):-C>COLS,!,cursor(R,COLS),DC=C-COLS,just2(0,DC).
  just1(R,C,_,_):-cursor(R,C),fail.

/* ************************* just2 ********************** */

/* scroll tree in window with cursor and update tree position */
  just2(DR,DC):-
        scroll(DR,DC),  /* scroll is a Turbo Prolog standard predicate */
        treewindow(R,C),!,
        CC=C+DC, RR=R+DR,
        newupdate(treewindow(RR,CC)),
        fail.

/* *********************** treekeyact ****************** */

/* Tree input key action */
  treekeyact(right)      :-just(0,1).
  treekeyact(ctrlright)  :-just(0,5).
  treekeyact(left)       :-just(0,-1).
  treekeyact(ctrlleft)   :-just(0,-5).
  treekeyact(up)         :-just(-1,0).
  treekeyact(pgup)       :-just(-5,0).
  treekeyact(down)       :-just(1,0).
  treekeyact(pgdn)       :-just(5,0).
  treekeyact(ctrlhome)   :-treewindow(R,C),!,RR=-R,CC=-C,just2(RR,CC).
  treekeyact(end)        :-cursor(_,C),makewindow(_,_,_,_,_,_,_,COLS),
                           DC=COLS-3-C,just(0,DC).
  treekeyact(home)       :-cursor(_,C),DC=-C,just(0,DC).
  treekeyact(cr)         :-treechoice(CHOICE), !, treeaction(CHOICE).
  treekeyact(esc).

/* ******************************************************
@@@ F10 is a hypertext hotkey that displays hypertext
   operations menu
****************************************************** */
  treekeyact(fkey(10))  :-
    treechoice(CHOICE), !,
    f10action(CHOICE). % f10action is a hotkey action


/*treekeyact(fkey(1)):-help.  If helpsystem is used */

/*treekeyact(fkey(5)):- resizing the tree-window */

/* ******************** remove_treechoice ************** */

  remove_treechoice:- retract(treechoice(_)), fail.
  remove_treechoice.

/* ***************************************************** */
/* ***********************draw_right ******************* */
```

(**Fig. 4-6.** continued)

```
/* ****************************************************** */
/* @@@ This is a modified version of draw_right */

PREDICATES
  draw_right(TREE,ROW,ROW,COL,COL,COL,COL,ROW)
  draw_rightlist(STRING,STRING,SELECTOR,TREELIST,
                 STRINGLIST,STRINGLIST,
                 ROWLIST,ROWLIST,
                 ROW,ROW,
                 COL,COL,COL,COL,ROW)

 connect_nodesright(STRINGLIST,ROW,COL,INTEGER,COL,COL,ROWLIST)
 con_nodesright(STRINGLIST,ROW,COL,ROW,ROW,COL,COL,ROWLIST)
 cornerright(ROW,ROW,ROW,ROW,CHAR)
 check_lastright(ROW,COL,ROWLIST)

CLAUSES

draw_right(_,_,_,_,_,_,_,_):-
  keypressed, !,
  readkey(KEY),
  treekeyact(KEY),
  fail.

draw_right(tree("root",NAME,SELECT,[]),
           CURROW,NEWCURROW,
           _,CURCOL,CURCOL,_,RESROW):- !,
  NEWCURROW=CURROW+2,
  RESROW=NEWCURROW,
  writetext(RESROW,CURCOL,112,NAME,SELECT).

draw_right(tree(RELATION,NAME,SELECT,[]),
           CURROW,NEWCURROW,
           _,CURCOL,CURCOL,COLSTEP,RESROW):- !,
  NEWCURROW=CURROW+2,
  str_len(RELATION,LEN),
  CURCOL1=CURCOL+LEN+COLSTEP,
  RESROW=NEWCURROW,
  writetext(RESROW,CURCOL1,112,NAME,SELECT).

draw_right(tree("root",NAME,SELECT,TREELIST),
           CURROW,NEWCURROW,
           LASTNAMECOL,NEXTNAMECOL,CURCOL,COLSTEP,RESROW):- !,
  draw_rightlist("",NAME,SELECT,TREELIST,
                 [],_,
                 [],_,
                 CURROW,NEWCURROW,
                 LASTNAMECOL,NEXTNAMECOL,CURCOL,COLSTEP,RESROW).

draw_right(tree(RELATION,NAME,SELECT,TREELIST),
           CURROW,NEWCURROW,
           LASTNAMECOL,NEXTNAMECOL,CURCOL,COLSTEP,RESROW):-
  draw_rightlist(RELATION,NAME,SELECT,TREELIST,
                 [],_,
                 [],_,
                 CURROW,NEWCURROW,
                 LASTNAMECOL,NEXTNAMECOL,CURCOL,COLSTEP,RESROW).

/* ************************ draw_rightlist ************** */

draw_rightlist(RELATION,NAME,SELECT,[],
               RELlist,RELlist,
               NodeRowList,NodeRowList,
               CurRow,CurRow,
               NEXTNAMECOL,NEXTNAMECOL,CURCOL,COLSTEP,RESROW):-
```

(**Fig. 4-6.** continued)

```
    str_len(NAME,NAMELEN),
    str_len(RELATION,RELLEN),
    CURCOL1=CURCOL+1+NAMELEN+COLSTEP+COLSTEP+RELLEN,
    CURCOL2=CURCOL+COLSTEP+RELLEN,
    nodelistlen(NODEROWLIST,LEN),
    listsum(NODEROWLIST,0,SUM),
    RESROW=SUM div LEN,
    COLAFTERarrow=1+CURCOL2+NAMELEN,
    COLAFTERdash=2+CURCOL2+NAMELEN,
    COLAFTERname=CURCOL2+NAMELEN,
    connect_nodesright(RELlist,RESROW,COLAFTERdash,
                    LEN,CURCOL1,COLSTEP,NODEROWLIST),
    writetext(RESROW,CURCOL2,112,NAME,SELECT),
    scr_ch(RESROW,COLAFTERname,'<'),
    scr_ch(RESROW,COLAFTERarrow,'á'),
    check_lastright(RESROW,COLAFTERdash,NODEROWLIST), !.

  draw_rightlist(RELATION,NAME,SELECT,[H|T],
                RELlist,ResRELlist,
                NodeRowList,ResNodeRowList,
                CurRow,CurRow2,
                LNCOL,LNCOL2,CURCOL,COLSTEP,RESROW):-
    H=tree(Rel,_,_,_),
    str_len(NAME,NAMELEN),
    str_len(RELATION,RELLEN),
    CURCOL1=CURCOL+1+NAMELEN+COLSTEP+COLSTEP+RELLEN,
    draw_right(H,CurRow,CurRow1,LNCOL,LNCOL1,CURCOL1,COLSTEP,Noderow),
    draw_rightlist(RELATION,NAME,SELECT,T,
                  [Rel|RELlist],ResRELlist,
                  [Noderow|NodeRowList],ResNodeRowList,
                  CurRow1,CurRow2,
                  LNCOL1,LNCOL2,CURCOL,COLSTEP,RESROW).

  /* ********************* check_lastright *************** */

  check_lastright(ROW,_,[ROW|_]):-!.

  check_lastright(ROW,COL,[_|LIST]):-!,
    check_lastright(ROW,COL,LIST).

  check_lastright(ROW,COL,_):-
    scr_ch(ROW,COL,'Ç').

  /* ***************** connect_nodesright *************** */

  connect_nodesright([REL],ROW,COL,1,COL1,COLSTEP,_) :-!,
    treeline_hor(COL,COL1,ROW),
    writetext1(ROW,COL1,REL,COL2),
    COL3=COL2+COLSTEP,
    treeline_hor(COL2,COL3,ROW).

  connect_nodesright(Rlist,ROW,COL,_,COL1,COLSTEP,[RMAX|L]):-
    lastinlist(RMIN,[RMAX|L]),
    con_nodesright(Rlist,ROW,COL,RMIN,RMAX,COL1,COLSTEP,[RMAX|L]).

  con_nodesright(_,_,_,_,_,_,_,[]).
  con_nodesright(_,_,COL,_,_,_,_,[R1,R2|_]):-
    R22=R2+1,
    treeline_ver(R22,R1,COL), fail.

  con_nodesright([Hrel|Trel],ROW,COL,RMIN,RMAX,COL1,COLSTEP,[ROW1|T]):-
    CC=COL+1,
    treeline_hor(CC,COL1,ROW1),
    writetext1(ROW1,COL1,Hrel,COL2),
    COL3=COL2+COLSTEP,
    treeline_hor(COL2,COL3,ROW1),
```

(**Fig. 4-6.** continued)

```
   cornerright(ROW,RMIN,RMAX,ROW1,CORNCHAR),
   scr_ch(ROW1,COL,CORNCHAR),
   con_nodesright(Trel,ROW,COL,RMIN,RMAX,COL1,COLSTEP,T).

/* ********************** cornerright ****************** */

cornerright(RMIN,RMIN,_,RMIN,'ô') :- !.

cornerright(RMAX,_,RMAX,RMAX,'ê') :- !.

cornerright(_,RMIN,_,RMIN,'ö') :- !.

cornerright(_,_,RMAX,RMAX,'â') :- !.

cornerright(RMIDT,_,_,RMIDT,'é') :- !.

cornerright(_,_,_,_,'û').


/* ************************** draw ********************** */

/* draw a tree in the selected direction */

  draw(right,TREE):-
    draw_right(TREE,0,_,0,_,0,3,_).

/* ************************ treemenu ****************** */

/* @@@@@ modified version @@@@@ */
/* treemenu constructs and displays a box diagram of a tree structure */

treemenu(DIRECTION,TREE,CHOICE) :-
/* if this makewindow is commented out the tree will be
drawn in the currently active window */
  makewindow(81,66,23,"",0,0,24,80),
  makestatus(112,"F1:Help  F10:Select  Retrn:Select  Arrows:move around  Ctrl
arrows: move fast"),
  newupdate(treewindow(0,0)),
  repeat,
    remove_treechoice,
    draw(DIRECTION,TREE),
    readkey(KEY),
    treekeyact(KEY), !,
  removestatus,
  not(KEY=esc),
  treechoice(CHOICE),!.

/* ****************** END END END *********************** */
```

STRING domain. Let's take a look at the new version of "tree":

```
DOMAINS
   SELECTOR= INTEGER
   TREE = tree(STRING,STRING,SELECTOR,TREELIST)
   TREELIST = TREE*
```

Now, when you execute a "treemenu" goal, Turbo will write the relationship names on the links between the nodes. An example using the modified "treemenu" predicate in "tree2.pro" is our program in FIG. 4-7.

Fig. 4-7. Using "treemenu" from "tree2.pro" of Fig. 4-6.

```
include "c:\\toolbox\\tdoms.pro"

DOMAINS
  SELECTOR=INTEGER
  TREE = tree(STRING,STRING,SELECTOR,TREELIST)
  TREELIST = TREE*

DATABASE
  treewindow(ROW,COL)
  treechoice(SELECTOR)

include "c:\\toolbox\\tpreds.pro"
include "c:\\toolbox\\status.pro"
include "c:\\toolbox\\tree2.pro"   % tree2.pro is in Fig. 4-6

CLAUSES
  treeaction(_). % clauses matched by Turbo when you press ENTER
  f10action(_).  % clauses matched by Turbo when you press F10

GOAL

  treemenu(right,
           tree("root","Francis",1,
                 [tree("wife_of","Josie",2,
                        [tree("working_address_of","Martinez",3,[]),
                         tree("car_of","Dodge-Colt",4,[])
                                ]),
                  tree("working_address_of","San Francisco",5,[]),
                  tree("home_address_of","Antoich",6,[]),
                  tree("car_of","Honda",7,[]),
                  tree("son_of","Allen",8,
                       [tree("age_of","12",9,[])])
                 ]),Choice).
```

To try "tree2.pro," first: copy the program in a file in your current directory. Then load and run the program in FIG. 4-7. As a result, you will get the screen in FIG. 4-8. Compare the tree menus of FIG. 4-5 and FIG. 4-8. What do you think now? FIGURE 4-8 is more informative, isn't it?

If you have not noticed, the "tree.pro" and "tree2.pro" both display a status-line at the bottom of the screen. The status-line reminds you of the command keys you need while in the tree-menu window. To create a status-line, I use the tool predicate "makestatus." I will not go into further details on using the status-line tool predicates. I recommend that you take a look at "Chapter Two" in the TOOLBOX user guide.

User-Input Tools

These predicates are used to prompt for input in a given screen field. The TOOLBOX has two kinds of user-input predicates: one for reading general input-lines, and one for reading filenames.

Reading an input_line: The "lineinp.pro" Tool. For reading input-lines, the TOOLBOX offers three predicates:

```
lineinput
```

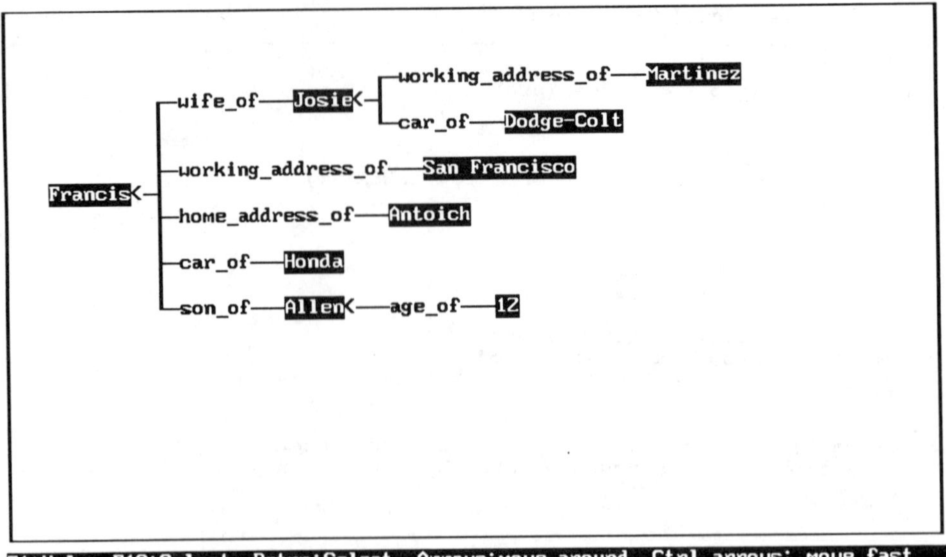

Fig. 4-8. A tree-menu created by the program in Fig. 4-7.

```
lineinput_leave
lineinput_repeat
```

These predicates have the same form. For example, "lineinput" has this form:

```
lineinput(Row,Col,Len,Wattr,Fattr,Prompt,BeforeStr,AfterStr)
```

"Prompt," "BeforeStr," and "AfterStr" are strings. When you execute "lineinput," Turbo displays the prompt "Prompt" with the default text "BeforeStr," but if you change the default text, "lineinput" will instantiate "AfterStr" to your input. The "lineinput_leave" predicate does the same thing as "lineinput" with one exception; it leaves the input field on the screen after you have completed entering your input. As for "lineinput_repeat," when used in combination with "fail," it allows you to input several texts in the same field.

Reading a Filename: The "filename.pro" Tool. In most applications, you will need to operate on files (loading, creating, saving, or copying text in files). To operate on files, you will need a subprogram or procedure to read filenames. A typical read-filename procedure could prompt you with a message such as "Enter name of file?", and wait for input. Of course, you can do this with the built-in "readln" predicate, but what you need is more than reading a line of input. For example, you might like to have the system prompt you with a default filename. Then, if you accept the default name, the system would do nothing. Another possibility is to use wild card matching characters in the filename. The program must list all the matching filenames in a menu so that you can pick the one you want. In short, you need a complete standalone utility procedure to read filenames. The TOOLBOX predicate "readfilename" in "filename.pro" is such a procedure.

To use "readfilename" you must first include the following declarations and files:

```
include "c:\\toolbox\\tdoms.pro"
DATABASE
  insmode
  lineinpstate(STRING,COL)
  lineinpflag
include "c:\\toolbox\\tpreds.pro"
include "c:\\toolbox\\lineinp.pro"
include "c:\\toolbox\\filename.pro"
```

As you can see, "filename.pro" needs "lineinp.pro," which in turn requires the special DATABASE section. To see "readfilename" in action: first, enter and execute the above programs and declarations. Then try the following goal:

```
GOAL
  makewindow(1,7,7," ",0,0,25,80),
  readfilename(15,10,7,7,pro,"work.pro",NewName),
  write("\n the file name you chose is >> ",NewName),
  readln(_).
```

Reading Filenames Using File Masks: The "bios.pro" Tool. Another useful filename-related tool predicate is "findmatch in the "bios.pro" file. What "findmatch" does is to search a directory for filenames that match a given string mask. If the search is successful, it returns all available matching-file information. The form of "findmatch" is this:

```
findmatch(SearchFileSpec,SearchAttr,MatchFileName,MFAttr,
         MFHour,MFMin,MFYear,MFDay,MFSize)
```

You supply the DOS file specification in the "SearchFileSpec" and the search attribute "SearchAttr." The predicate on its part will return:

- the matching filename in "MatchFileName,"
- the matching file attribute in "MFAttr,"
- the matching file creation time in "MFHour," MFMin," "MFYear," "MFMonth," and "MFDay," and
- the matching file size in "MFSize."

As an exercise, use "findmatch" and "readfilename" in a program to retrieve a list of all files matching a given file mask.

PUTTING IT ALL TOGETHER

In this section, I will build a complete user-interface shell for a hypothetical hypertext application. In building the shell, I will use many of the user-interface tool predicates from the previous sections. The program starts by including the related TOOLBOX programs. Then, it will include our utility user-interface predicate from FIG. 3-9. The main predicate in the program is "default hyperMAIN." Take a look at the complete program in FIG. 4-9, and its major screen in FIG. 4-10.

The first thing "hyperMAIN" does is to display the system's main items. These include:

- a blank window to cover the whole screen,
- the editor window,
- the status-line, and
- the pull-down menu.

For every option on the pull-down menu there is a matching "pdwaction" clause. At present the shell is an empty one, but with proper functions assigned to the different "pdwaction" clauses, you can build a workable hypertext application. This is exactly what I will do in PART TWO of this book. I will use this user-interface shell to build an authoring hypertext system, which I call "ET."

Fig. 4-9. A user-interface shell for hypertext systems.

```
include "fig3-2.pro"    % domains and database declarations

/* ****************************************************** */
/* ************** Turbo Prolog TOOLBOX programs ********* */
/* ****************************************************** */
include "c:\\toolbox\\tdoms.pro"   % TOOLBOX text domains declarations
include "c:\\toolbox\\tpreds.pro"  % TOOLBOX text predicates declaration

DATABASE
% pulldown predicates
  pdwstate(ROW,COL,SYMBOL,ROW,COL)

% line input predicates
  insmode
  lineinpstate(STRING,COL)
  lineinpflag

% required Turbo Prolog TOOLBOX modules

% "filename" predicate is in the TOOLBOX's "filename.pro"
% "filename.pro" requires "lineinp.pro"
% "lineinput" predicate is in the TOOLBOX's "lineinp.pro"

include "c:\\toolbox\\status.pro"    % TOOLBOX status line predicate
include "c:\\toolbox\\pulldown.pro"  % TOOLBOX pulldown menu predicate
include "c:\\toolbox\\lineinp.pro"   % TOOLBOX line input predicate
include "c:\\toolbox\\filename.pro"  % TOOLBOX file name input predicate
include "c:\\toolbox\\menu.pro"      % TOOLBOX menu program
include "c:\\toolbox\\boxmenu.pro"   % TOOLBOX menu program


/* ****************************************************** */
/* ********************** hyperMAIN ********************* */
/* ****************************************************** */

/* ******* Hypertext user-interface module ************** */
```

(**Fig. 4-9.** continued)

```
include "fig3-9.pro"     % user-interface predicates

/* ***************** hyperMAIN predicates *************** */

PREDICATES
  hyperMAIN

CLAUSES

/*
          1         2         3         4         5         6         7
01234567890123456789012345678901234567890123456789012345678901234567890123456
*/

  hyperMAIN:-
    blankwindow,
    textSCREEN,
    editwindow,
    statusline,
    pulldown(112,[ curtain(7,"Nodes",["Load ",
                               "New node",
                               "Save",
                               "Write to",
                               "Directory",
                               "Change dir.",
                               "Operating system"
                              ]),
                 curtain(27,"Edit",[]),
                 curtain(47,"Configure",["Load network",
                                  "Delete network",
                                  "Write to",
                                  "Save network"
                                 ]),
                 curtain(67,"Quit",[])
                ],
                _,_),
    removewindow,
    removewindow.

/* ****************************************************** */
/* *********************** pdwaction ******************* */
% the pulldown menu actions.

/* *************  1. NODES MENU ACTIONS ***************** */

% 1.1 Load a node file (file with extension ".hyp")
 pdwaction(1,1):-
   shiftwindow(OLD),
   cursor(Row,_),
   readfilename(Row,35,15,112,hyp,"",Fname),
   shiftwindow(2), clearwindow,
   write("\n The system will load file > ", Fname),
   shiftwindow(OLD).

% 1.2 Creat a new node
 pdwaction(1,2):-
   shiftwindow(OLD),
   shiftwindow(2), clearwindow,
   write("\n The system will create the file work.hyp"),
   shiftwindow(OLD).

% 1.3 Save current node
pdwaction(1,3):-
   shiftwindow(OLD),
   shiftwindow(2), clearwindow,
```

(**Fig. 4-9.** continued)

```
    write("\n The system will save the current file."),
    shiftwindow(OLD).

% 1.4 Write current node to another file
pdwaction(1,4):-
  shiftwindow(OLD),
  cursor(Row,Col), R=Row+1,
  readfilename(R,Col,15,112,hyp,"",Fname),
  shiftwindow(2), clearwindow,
  write("\n The system will save current node into the file > ",Fname),
  shiftwindow(OLD).

% 1.5 list current directory
pdwaction(1,5):-
  shiftwindow(OLD),
  disk(PATH),
  dirwindow,
  dir(PATH,"*.hyp ",_,1,1,1),
  removewindow,
  shiftwindow(OLD), !.

% if user presses ESC, then the action succeeds

pdwaction(1,5):-
 removewindow.        % remove dirwindow

% 1.6 Change current directory path
pdwaction(1,6):-
  cursor(Row,Col),
  makewindow(_,_,_,_,RO,CO,_,_),
  Row1=RO+Row, Col1=CO+Col,
  changeDIR(Row1,Col1,15,112). % in "user-h.pro"

% 1.7 A DOS shell

pdwaction(1,7):- system("").

/* ************** 2. EDIT CURRENTLY LOADED NODE ********* */

pdwaction(2,0):-
  shiftwindow(OLD),
  shiftwindow(2), clearwindow,
  write("\n The system will edit the current node (file)."),
  shiftwindow(OLD).

/* ********** 3. NETWORK CONFIGURATION OPTIONS ********** */

% 3.1 Load a configuration file, a file with ".net" ext.

pdwaction(3,1):-
  shiftwindow(OLD),
  cursor(R,_), Row=R+1,
  readfilename(Row,35,15,112,net,"",Fname),
  shiftwindow(2), clearwindow,
  write("\n The system will consult network config. file > ",Fname),
  shiftwindow(OLD).

% 3.2 Delete the currently active network configuration

pdwaction(3,2):-
  shiftwindow(OLD),
  shiftwindow(2), clearwindow,
  write("\n The system will delete current network config. facts."),
  shiftwindow(OLD).
```

(**Fig. 4-9.** continued)

```
% 3.3 Write current config. facts to a given file

pdwaction(3,3):-
  shiftwindow(OLD),
  cursor(Row,_), R=Row+1,
  readfilename(R,35,15,112,net,"",Fname),
  shiftwindow(2), clearwindow,
  write("\n The system will write current config. to file > ",Fname),
  shiftwindow(OLD).

% 3.4 Save current config. facts to current config. file.

pdwaction(3,4):-
  shiftwindow(OLD),
  shiftwindow(2), clearwindow,
  write("\n The system will save current config."),
  shiftwindow(OLD).

/* *************** 4. QUIT HYPERTEXT ******************** */

pdwaction(4,0):- !, fail.

pdwaction(_,_).


/* ************************* END END END **************** */

GOAL
hyperMAIN
```

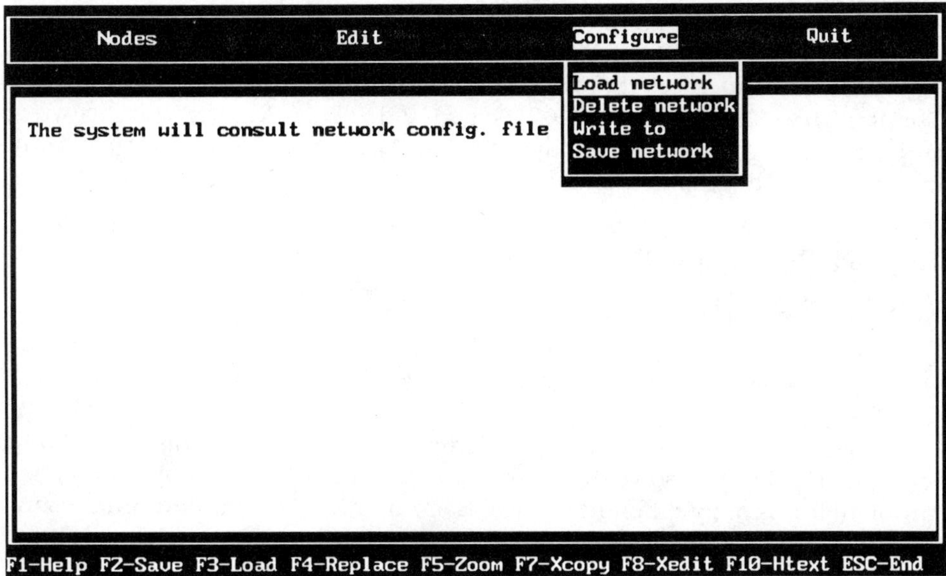

Fig. 4-10. The main screen of a user-interface shell.

SCREEN-LAYOUT TOOLS

These tools allow you to design screen layouts. A screen layout is a set of text-fields. Some of these fields could be input fields, to elicit input from the user. Other fields could be output fields—i.e., to display output to the user. Still, some fields can act both as input and output fields. Usually I use combinations of both input and output in a single screen layout. One possible application of screen layout tools is for designing information filling forms, such as those used in banks and government agencies. Another application for screen layout tools is the dialogue box. You use a dialogue box for three purposes:

- to elicit information from the user,
- to display information for the user, and
- to allow the user to change the existing information.

Without going into details, I'll talk about an application of dialogue boxes. In PART THREE, I will talk about writing a hypertext-based problem solving system I call MicroIBIS. MicroIBIS allows a group of people to work on solving a specific problem. Each participant in the problem solving process enters his comments in a separate node. To know who said what and when, you need to associate nodes with names and dates. To do this, each hypertext node will have its own dialogue box. When you want to create a node, first, MicroIBIS will fire a dialogue box. This dialogue box will have several fields for you to fill. If you want, you can leave some or all of these fields empty. Another thing, you will find that some of these fields are already filled. For example, the system uses its internal clock to fill the "Date" field for you. Also, if you were the author of the current node, the system will assume you are also the author of the new node. This means that some fields can have default values.

The program module of MicroIBIS which uses dialogue boxes, is in FIG. 9-1L. To understand what the module does, I recommend that you first read "Chapter Three" in the TOOLBOX User's Guide. This Chapter will give you a complete coverage of all screen-layout tools. Also, you will find several examples on many interesting applications.

MAJOR CONSIDERATIONS WHEN DESIGNING THE USER-INTERFACE

Mainly, your interest is in the user-interface because you want to design user-friendly systems. Paul Heckel in his book "The Elements of Friendly Software Design," writes:

"When one deals with softer problems, like communicating with people, there is no right way to solve them. We must think in different ways and look at a problem from many different angles. Each new angle might eliminate some alternative solution, suggest a new one, or give fresh insight into the problem. Each angle adds something to the image that you are building in your mind. My intention here is to focus your attention on the important elements, or angles, of friendly design so you can recognize them and think about your designs more effectively. But I have no formula to offer."

I completely agree with Mr. Heckel on this. Based on this statement, I would say that you shouldn't take our character-based textual WYSIWYG approach as a formula. Rather, you should take it as an alternative. If you like icon-based WYSIWYG programs, you might consider running your program completely in graphics mode. Of course there are tradeoffs. Your program becomes bigger, more complex, a little bit slower, and requires more development time. Another approach is the combination of both textual and graphical WYSIWYGs.

Your choice of which approach to follow depends completely on your knowledge and objectives; but then again, this statement can be misleading if you consider it without analysis. For example, which objectives are you talking about? Is it the ease-of-use of the system? Is it the spontaneous and flexible response to mistakes? Is it the design which communicates our ideas in a natural way? Also, do you need crystal-clear objectives before you start the design, or do you just need a global view and let the design evolve in the process? So as you can see, there is no start, middle, or end point in the design process. Rather, there are considerations which help you a lot if you keep it in mind.

In his above mentioned book, Paul Heckel listed 30 such considerations. All these considerations are worth discussing, but I will discuss only two of them:

- serve both the novice and the experienced user, and
- reduce the user's defensiveness, design a permissive user-interface.

Let's discuss each one of these considerations in a little bit more detail.

Designing for Both the Novice and the Experience-User

This consideration recommends that you should have tools to accommodate both the beginner and the expert. For example, our system might have a menu system as its main user-interface, with shortcut commands (hotkeys) as an alternative. If you were a beginner, you could start using the system by selecting options from a series of menus. Once you feel comfortable using the system this way, you might start demanding speed and time-saving shortcuts. This is where hotkeys come into the picture.

Take an example: In Chapter 3, I needed to go through four menus (four keystrokes) before I could view the target of a link. Let me explain: I am in the editor, I press F10 (one keystroke). This will cause the display of a hypertext menu. In this menu, there are three options: Viewing links, Adding links, and Deleting links. So I choose the "View a link" option (a second keystroke). Again, I get a menu. This menu has another three options: "view a Node-node link," "view a Point-node link," and "view a point-point link." Say I am after a node-node link, so I choose the first option (a third keystroke). Now, there might be more than one target node. So, what I get is another menu. The options in this menu are names of target nodes. I choose our target node (a fourth keystroke) and the system loads this node in the editor. On the other hand, if I use hotkeys I can reduce the number of keystrokes from four to three. How can I do this? Well, I can assign the following three hotkeys:

F10-N for viewing a node-node link,
F10-P for viewing a point-node link, and
F10-O for viewing a point-point link.

This will do it, but there is a disadvantage in using hotkeys: in a system with many menus and submenus, you might need a large number of hotkeys. A large number of hotkeys will be a burden on your memory. This is especially true when you consider that most people use more than one software package. Today, most software systems use hotkeys. This means that you have to keep track of which hotkey to use with which software. In any case, the popularity of hotkeys is an evidence of their success.

The Design of a Permissive User-Interface

To reduce the user defensiveness, Heckel recommends that we should handle the user's Fear, Uncertainty, and Doubt (FUD for short). FUD reduces our willingness to learn by browsing and exploring the system. A system which is not permissive enough to let us make a few mistakes while using it, is of little use. So, one facet of a good design is its permissiveness. To explain this, I will take a simple example. Consider the case where you want to create a new node. Here, you will take each node as a separate DOS file. So, the first thing your hypertext system does is to prompt you to enter a name for the new node. You enter a name and press ENTER. If the node doesn't already exist in the specified directory, the system will create it, but if the node does exist, the system will crash unless you design it with just such a case in mind. One way to handle this is by writing a predicate to check ahead of time if the node exists or not. Our version of this predicate is "existNODE":

```
existNODE(F2):-
  existfile(F2).

existNODE(F2):-
  cursor(R,C), Row=R+1,
  concat(F2," doesn't exist, create (y/n): ",TXT),
  lineinput(ROW,C,45,15,112,TXT,"Y",ANS),
  upper_lower(ANS1,ANS),
  frontchar(ANS1,CHAR,_),
  CHAR='Y',
  file_str(F2," "). % create the an empty node
```

This predicate is permissive in two ways. It allows you to enter a name for a node without checking if it already exists or not. It is also permissive in that it allows you to use both lower- and uppercase in entering the name of a node. Take a look at the built-in "upper_lower" predicate in the second clause. This predicate takes our answer, ANS, whether it is upper- or lowercase, and transforms it to an uppercase name, ANS1. Next, in the "frontchar" subgoal you consider the two possibilities of answering the question:

"doesn't exist, create (y/n): "

The first possibility: we enter either "y" or "n." The other possibility is to answer by entering "yes" or "no." In both cases "frontchar" will extract the first character. In the next subgoal, "CHAR='Y'," you finish the test. If "CHAR='Y' "succeeds, the last subgoal will create the file. The faulty design would be something like this:

```
existNODE(F2):-
  cursor(R,C), Row=R+1,
  concat(F2,"doesn't exist, create (y/n): ",TXT),
  lineinput(ROW,C,45,15,112,TXT,"Y",ANS),
  CHAR='Y',
  file_str(F2," ").
```

This example might be a trivial one for you, but nonetheless, it shows what I am talking about. That's how good design can result in a solid user-interface. By this, I come to the end of this chapter and the end of PART ONE. In the next Part, I will use what you have learned in PART ONE to create a complete hypertext authoring system I call "ET."

Part Two

''Extended Text''

5

Introducing ET (Extended Text):
A Hypertext Authoring and Information Retrieval System

"... the first goal of writing, like reading, is to understand; only then can one make that understanding available to others in writing. Thinking in writing is, in fact, a form of understanding—a way of shaping first thoughts—whereas communicating in writing is mostly a matter of reshaping our thoughts on paper. In brief, from first thoughts to the last word in writing, articulation precedes communication."

—From "Thinking on Paper," by V. A. Howard and J. H. Barton, page 13.

Authoring is writing. The quote above said it all. Authoring is writing because: first, it is a form of understanding and second, it is a form of communication. The order is important here. Understanding comes before communication, not the other way around. On paper, authors use style, punctuations, fonts, emphasis, and so on, to make their writings understandable. With electronic documents on the other hand, authors can use hypertext techniques to understand and express their ideas.

Examples of hypertext techniques are: 1) Representing the document as a network of nodes and links. 2) Links can have attributes. Also, you can attach procedures to the links so that when you activate a link, the system executes the attached procedure. 3) You can have different kinds of links: command links, expansion links, reference links, and replacement links. 4) You can abstract new ideas from existing text. You call these new ideas "abstractions." Examples of abstractions are: generalizations, aggregation or grouping, specializations, and filtering. 5) You can save and retrieve many revisions of the document. You call the program that manages the storage and retrieval of document revisions a "revision control system." In Chapter 7, I will discuss in more detail some of these techniques.

Books, magazines, and newspapers, are examples of paper documents. For instance, take this book as an example. How good is it in explaining hypertext depends on my writing skills. For examples of electronic documents, you can look at a few commercial hypertext systems such as IBM-PC's GUIDE and Apple-Macintosh's Hypercard. Also, you can look at the programs in PART ONE. However, leave the commercial hypertext systems aside. The programs in PART ONE explain only a few of the basics of hypertext. None of these programs is a complete system. In this chapter, I will talk about ET. ET stands for "Extended Text," not "ExtraTerrestrial." ET is a hypertext authoring system. This means that ET allows you to construct and view hypertext documents. ET shouldn't be something new to you. You already knew about the different parts of ET from your readings of PART ONE. The only difference is that I put all the parts into a single program. Without any delay, I'll introduce ET to you.

LOADING AND RUNNING ET

The main program of ET is in FIG. 5-1. As you can see, the "included" files are mostly programs from PART ONE. The rest are TOOLBOX programs. In ET, you have a complete hypertext user-interface which was developed in Chapter 4 (see "PUTTING IT ALL TOGETHER," along with FIG. 4-9 and FIG. 4-10). In PART ONE, I put the hypertext editor in the main program. In ET, the hypertext editor has its own file (see FIG. 5-3).

Fig. 5-1. The main program of ET.

```
/* ---------------------------------------------------- */
/* (ET) An Extended Text (hypertext) authoring system    */
/* ---------------------------------------------------- */

/* ************** Hypertext domain declartions ********** */

include "fig3-2.pro"   % domains and database declarations

/* ************** Turbo Prolog TOOLBOX programs ********* */

% include "fig5-2.pro"              % The title graphic screen drawing
include "c:\\toolbox\\tdoms.pro"    % TOOLBOX text domains declarations
include "c:\\toolbox\\tpreds.pro"   % TOOLBOX text predicates declaration

DATABASE
% pulldown predicates
   pdwstate(ROW,COL,SYMBOL,ROW,COL)

% line input predicates
```

(**Fig. 5-1.** continued)

```
    insmode
    lineinpstate(STRING,COL)
    lineinpflag

  % required Turbo Prolog TOOLBOX modules

  % "filename" predicate is in the TOOLBOX's "filename.pro"
  % "filename.pro" requires "lineinp.pro"
  % "lineinput" predicate is in the TOOLBOX's "lineinp.pro"

  include "c:\\toolbox\\status.pro"   % TOOLBOX status line predicate
  include "c:\\toolbox\\pulldown.pro" % TOOLBOX pulldown menu predicate
  include "c:\\toolbox\\lineinp.pro"  % TOOLBOX line input predicate
  include "c:\\toolbox\\filename.pro" % TOOLBOX file name input predicate
  include "c:\\toolbox\\menu.pro"     % TOOLBOX menu program
  include "c:\\toolbox\\boxmenu.pro"  % TOOLBOX menu program


  /* ****************************************************** */
  /* ********************** hyperMAIN ******************** */
  /* ****************************************************** */

  DATABASE - maindb
    currentFILE(STRING)
    currentPOS(INTEGER)
    currentSTR(STRING)
    currentCONFIG(STRING)

  /* ***************** hypertext modules ****************** */

  include "fig3-3.pro"      % general utility predicates
  include "fig3-9.pro"      % user-interface predicates
  include "fig2-2.pro"      % finding a hypertext point
  include "fig5-3.pro"      % hyperEDIT predicate

  /* ***************** hyperMAIN predicates *************** */

  PREDICATES
    hyperMAIN
      write_to(STRING,STRING)
      updateCURRENT(maindb)
      getCURRENT(maindb)
      ifEXIST(STRING)

  CLAUSES

  /*
            1         2         3         4         5         6         7
  01234567890123456789012345678901234567890123456789012345678901234567890123456 7
         Nodes                Edit                Configure           Quit
  */

    hyperMAIN:-
      retractall(_,hypdb),
      retractall(_,maindb),
      blankwindow,
  %   titleScreen,   % displays a graphical title screen
      textSCREEN,    % displays a text title screen
      editwindow,
      statusline,
      pulldown(112,[ curtain(7,"Nodes",["Load ",
                                        "New node",
                                        "Save",
                                        "Write to",
                                        "Directory",
                                        "Change dir.",
```

(**Fig. 5-1.** continued)

```
                                        "Operating system"
                                       ]),
                    curtain(27,"Edit",[]),
                    curtain(47,"Configure",["Load network",
                                            "Delete network",
                                            "Write to",
                                            "Save network"
                                           ]),
                    curtain(67,"Quit",[])
                  ],
                  _,_),
     removewindow,
     removewindow.

/* ****************************************************** */
/* *********************** pdwaction ******************** */
% the pulldown menu actions.
/* *************  1. NODES MENU ACTIONS ***************** */

% ****** 1.1 Load a node file (file with extension ".hyp")
 pdwaction(1,1):-
   shiftwindow(OLD),
   cursor(Row,_),
   readfilename(Row,35,15,112,hyp,"",Fname),
   ifEXIST(Fname),
   updateCURRENT(currentFILE(Fname)),
   shiftwindow(2),
   hyperEDIT(Fname,1,OUTpos),
   updateCURRENT(currentPOS(OUTpos)),
   shiftwindow(OLD).

% if first clause fails, return to menu doing nothing
 pdwaction(1,1).

% ********* 1.2 Creat a new node
  pdwaction(1,2):-
    shiftwindow(OLD),
    cursor(Row,Col), R=Row+1,
    lineinput(R,Col,40,15,112,
              "Enter new file name: ","work.ibs",NewName),
    file_str(NewName,""),
    shiftwindow(2),
    hyperEDIT(NewName,1,OUTpos),
    updateCURRENT(currentPOS(OUTpos)),
    shiftwindow(OLD).

  pdwaction(1,2).

% ********* 1.3 Save current node
pdwaction(1,3):-
  getCURRENT(currentFILE(Fname)),
  getCURRENT(currentSTR(String)),
  file_str(Fname,String).

pdwaction(1,3).

% 1.4 Write current node to another file
pdwaction(1,4):-
  shiftwindow(OLD),
  getCURRENT(currentSTR(STRING)),
  cursor(Row,Col), R=Row+1,
  readfilename(R,Col,15,112,hyp,"",Fname),
  write_to(Fname,STRING),
```

(**Fig. 5-1**. continued)

```
    shiftwindow(OLD).

  pdwaction(1,4).

  % 1.5 list current directory
  pdwaction(1,5):-
    shiftwindow(OLD),
    disk(PATH),
    dirwindow,
    dir(PATH,"*.hyp ",_,1,1,1),
    removewindow,
    shiftwindow(OLD), !.

  % if user presses ESC, then the action succeeds

  pdwaction(1,5):-
   removewindow.         % remove dirwindow

  pdwaction(1,5).

  % 1.6 Change current directory path
  pdwaction(1,6):-
    cursor(Row,Col),
    makewindow(_,_,_,_,RO,CO,_,_),
    Row1=RO+Row, Col1=CO+Col,
    changeDIR(Row1,Col1,15,112). % in "user-h.pro"

  pdwaction(1,6).

  % 1.7 A DOS shell

  pdwaction(1,7):- system("").

  /* ************** 2. EDIT CURRENTLY LOADED NODE ********* */

  pdwaction(2,0):-
    shiftwindow(OLD),
    getCURRENT(currentFILE(Fname)),
    getCURRENT(currentPOS(INpos)),
    shiftwindow(2),
    hyperEDIT(Fname,INpos,OUTpos),
    updateCURRENT(currentPOS(OUTpos)),
    shiftwindow(OLD).

  /* ********** 3. NETWORK CONFIGURATION OPTIONS ********** */

  % 3.1 Load a configuration file, a file with ".net" ext.

  pdwaction(3,1):-
    shiftwindow(OLD),
    cursor(R,_), Row=R+1,
    readfilename(Row,35,15,112,net,"",Fname),
    consult(Fname,hypdb),
    updateCURRENT(currentCONFIG(Fname)),
    shiftwindow(OLD).

  pdwaction(3,1).

  % 3.2 Delete the currently active network configuration

  pdwaction(3,2):-
    retractall(_,hypdb).

  pdwaction(3,2).
  % 3.3 Write current config. facts to a given file
```

(**Fig. 5-1**. continued)

```
pdwaction(3,3):-
  shiftwindow(OLD),
  cursor(Row,_), R=Row+1,
  readfilename(R,35,15,112,net,"",Fname),
  save(Fname,hypdb),
  shiftwindow(OLD).

pdwaction(3,3).

% 3.4 Save current config. facts to current config. file.

pdwaction(3,4):-
  getCURRENT(currentCONFIG(Fname)),
  save(Fname,hypdb).

pdwaction(3,4).

/* *************** 4. QUIT HYPERTEXT ******************** */

pdwaction(4,0):- !, fail.

pdwaction(_,_).

/* ********************** write_to ********************** */

write_to(Fname,String):-
  not(existfile(Fname)),
  file_str(Fname,String), !.
write_to(Fname,String):-
  existfile(Fname),
  file_str(Fname,Str),
  cursor(R,_), Row=R+2,
  Str <> String,
  lineinput(Row,35,30,15,112,
          "replace existing text (y/n): ","",ANS),
  upper_lower(ANS1,ANS),
  ANS1 = "Y",
  file_str(Fname,String).

/* *********************** ifEXIST ********************** */

% if the file exists return doing nothing.

ifEXIST(FileName):-
  existfile(FileName), !.

% if the file doesn't exist, ask if you want to create it.

ifEXIST(FileName):-
  makewindow(11,15,112,"",5,7,3,45),
  write("\File doesn't exist, create it (y/n): "),
  readln(Ans),
  upper_lower(Ans1,Ans),
  frontchar(Ans1,CHAR,_), CHAR = 'Y',
  file_str(FileName,""), removewindow, !.

ifEXIST(_):- removewindow, fail.      % remove window 11

/* ******************** updateCURRENT ******************* */

updateCURRENT(currentFILE(_)) :- retract(currentFILE(_)), fail.
updateCURRENT(currentPOS(_)):- retract(currentPOS(_)), fail.
updateCURRENT(currentSTR(_)):- retract(currentSTR(_)), fail.
updateCURRENT(currentCONFIG(_)):-retract(currentCONFIG(_)), fail.
```

(**Fig. 5-1.** continued)

```
updateCURRENT(FACT):- assertz(FACT,maindb).

/* *********************** getCURRENT ****************** */

getCURRENT(currentFILE(F)) :- currentFILE(F), !.
getCURRENT(currentFILE("WORK.HYP")):- file_str("WORK.HYP","").

getCURRENT(currentPOS(Pos)):- currentPOS(Pos), !.
getCURRENT(currentPOS(1)).

getCURRENT(currentSTR(Str)):- currentSTR(Str), !.
getCURRENT(currentSTR("")).

getCURRENT(currentCONFIG(F)):- currentCONFIG(F), !.
getCURRENT(currentCONFIG("CONFIG.NET")).

/* ************************* END END END **************** */

GOAL
hyperMAIN
```

Now, start your Turbo Prolog system and create three Turbo files for the programs in FIG. 5-1, FIG. 5-2, and FIG. 5-3. Before you do anything else, make sure that you have all the programs from these figures:

FIG. 5-1 (The main program of ET)
FIG. 5-2 (program displays a graphical title screen)
FIG. 5-3 (the hypertext editor module)
FIG. 3-2 (domains and database declarations)
FIG. 3-3 (utility predicates)
FIG. 3-9 (user-interface predicates)
FIG. 2-2 (predicates for finding hypertext points)

All these files can be assumed to be in the same directory. You will also need several TOOLBOX files. If you have a hard disk, you will probably have a separate directory for the TOOLBOX. For example, on my system, I use "toolbox" as the directory for all the TOOLBOX programs. Then to use a program from this directory, I simply include the program using a path name in the include string. For example, to include the TOOLBOX menu program I write:

```
include "c:\\toolbox\\menu.pro"
```

If, on the other hand, you want to install ET on a floppy diskette, then copy all the hypertext and TOOLBOX programs into the diskette and you are all set. To run ET, your first step is to load the program in FIG. 5-1. Before you run the program, make sure that you have commented the line which includes the program in FIG. 5-2, this way:

```
% include "fig5-2.pro"
```

This program displays a title screen in a graphic mode. For now, you don't need to worry about this program. I will explain it in the next chapter. Also, make sure that in the predicate "hyperMAIN," you have commented the

Fig. 5-2. Using BGI to draw a graphical title screen.

```
/* ****************************************************** */
/* Draw the title screen of the system using the BGI.     */
/* ****************************************************** */

/* To access your BGI drivers and fonts bgi_path may
need to equal "..\\BGI" */

constants
   bgi_path = ""

/* To access the GRAPDECL.PRO file you may need to
add a path: include "..\\programs\\GRAPDECL.PRO"  */

include "GRAPDECL.PRO"

PREDICATES
   titleScreen

CLAUSES

titleScreen:-
   detectgraph(GrDriver,GrMode),
   initgraph(GrDriver,GrMode,_,_,bgi_path),
   getmaxx(Xmax),
   getmaxy(Ymax),
   rectangle(0, 0, Xmax, Ymax),
   Title="Extended Text (ET 1.0)",
   settextstyle(triplex_Font,horiz_Dir,6),
   outtextxy(25,30,Title),
   settextstyle(sans_serif_Font,horiz_Dir,2),
   outtextxy(200,90,"A Hypertext System"),
   outtextxy(280,120,"By"),
   outtextxy(210,150,"Safaa H. Hashim"),
   readchar(_),
   closegraph.

/* *********************** END END END ***************** */
```

Fig. 5-3. The hypertext editor of ET.

```
/* ****************************************************** */
/* ********************* hyperEDIT ********************* */
/* ****************************************************** */

PREDICATES

  hyperEDIT(STRING,INTEGER,INTEGER)
    saveCHANGES(STRING,STRING)
    saveCHANGES1(STRING,STRING,STRING)
    saveCHANGES2(STRING,STRING,STRING)
    hyperSTATUS(STRING,STRING,INTEGER,INTEGER)
    % findHYPERtext in file "find-h.pro"
      linkOPTION(STRING,STRING,INTEGER,INTEGER)
        viewOPTION(STRING,STRING,INTEGER,INTEGER)
          searchPOINT(STRING,STRING,STRING,INTEGER)
            searchPOINT1(STRING,STRING,STRING,INTEGER)
        addOPTION(STRING,STRING,INTEGER,STRING,INTEGER)
          existNODE(STRING)
          wantTOedit(STRING)
        deleteOPTION(STRING,STRING,INTEGER,INTEGER)
```

(**Fig. 5-3.** continued)

```
          del_nnlink(STRING,STRING)
          del_pnlink(STRING,STRING)
          del_pplink(STRING,STRING)
            del_node(STRING)

CLAUSES


/* Edit the contents of a hypertext node. In this version
   of hypertext, a node is a file in the current disk
   directory. */

% flow pattern (i,i,i,o,o)

hyperEDIT(FILEname,InPos,OutPos) :-
   repeat,
     file_str(FILEname,INstr),
     MSG="End editing (ESC),  Follow hyper link (F10) ",
     edit(INstr,OUTstr,"<NODE EDITOR>",FILEname,MSG,
          InPos,"",1,1,1,1,OutPos,ReturnStatus),
     refreshstatus, % redraw the status line
     saveCHANGES1(FILEname,INstr,OUTstr),
     hyperSTATUS(FILEname,OUTstr,OutPos,ReturnStatus).


/* ************************************************** */
/* ***************** hyperSTATUS ********************* */
/* ************************************************** */
/* When ReturnStatus = 0, edit was terminated with an F10 */

hyperSTATUS(Fname,Fstr,Pos,0):-
  menu(0,35,15,112,["View a link",
                    "Add a link",
                    "Delete a link"],
       "LINK OPERATIONS",1,Choice),
  linkOPTION(Fname,Fstr,Pos,Choice), !, fail.

/* When ReturnStatus = 1, edit was terminated with an ESC */
% Ask if user want to save changes to file.
/*
hyperSTATUS(Fname,NEWstr,_,1):-
   cursor(R,_), Row=R+2,
   file_str(Fname,OLDstr),
   NEWstr <> OLDstr,
   lineinput(Row,35,30,15,112,
             "Save changes to file (y/n): ","",ANS),
   upper_lower(ANS1,ANS),
   ANS1 = "Y",
   file_str(Fname,NEWstr), !.
*/
% Exit editor without saving the changes.

hyperSTATUS(_,_,_,1).

/* *********************** linkOPTION ***************** */

% the VIEW A LINK option

linkOPTION(Fname,Fstr,Pos,1):-
  menu(0,10,15,112,["view a Node-node link",
                    "view a Point-node link",
                    "view a pOint-point link"],
       "VIEW A LINK",1,Choice),
  viewOPTION(Fname,Fstr,Pos,Choice), !.

linkOPTION(_,_,_,1). % return with no action
```

(**Fig. 5-3.** continued)

```
% the ADD A LINK option

linkOPTION(Fname,Fstr,Pos,2):-
  menu(0,35,15,112,["add a Node-node link",
                    "add a Point-node link",
                    "add a pOint-point link"],
       "ADD A LINK",1,Choice),
  cursor(R,_), Row=R+2,
  readfilename(Row,35,15,112,hyp,"",Fname2),
  addOPTION(Fname,Fstr,Pos,Fname2,Choice), !.

linkOPTION(_,_,_,2). % return with no action

% the DELETE A LINK option

linkOPTION(Fname,Fstr,Pos,3):-
  menu(0,55,15,112,["delete a Node-node link",
                    "delete a Point-node link",
                    "delete a pOint-point link"],
       "DELETE A LINK",1,Choice),
  deleteOPTION(Fname,Fstr,Pos,Choice), !.

linkOPTION(_,_,_,3). % return with no action

/* ********************** viewOPTION ******************** */

viewOPTION(S,_,_,1):-
  findall(T,nnlink(node(S),node(T)),Tlist),
  cursor(R,C), Row=R+1, Col=C+1,
  boxmenu(Row,Col,4,45,15,112,Tlist,
          "NODE-NODE LINK",1,Nchoice), Nchoice <> 0,
  nth_member(Tlist,Nchoice,TN),
  hyperEDIT(TN,1,_), !.
viewOPTION(_,_,_,1).

viewOPTION(_,FILEstr,POS,2):-
  findHyperText(FILEstr,Pos,SP),
  SP <> "",
  findall(T,pnlink(point(SP),_,node(T)),Tlist),
  cursor(R,C), Row=R+1, Col=C+1,
  boxmenu(Row,Col,4,45,15,112,Tlist,
          "POINT-NODE LINK",1,Nchoice), Nchoice <> 0,
  nth_member(Tlist,Nchoice,TN),
  hyperEDIT(TN,1,_), !.

viewOPTION(_,_,_,2).

viewOPTION(_,FILEstr,Pos,3):-
  findHyperText(FILEstr,Pos,SP),
  SP <> "",
  findall(T,pplink(point(SP),_,_,node(T)),Tlist),
  cursor(R,C), Row=R+1, Col=C+1,
  boxmenu(Row,Col,4,45,15,112,Tlist,
          "POINT-POINT LINK",1,Nchoice), Nchoice <> 0,
  nth_member(Tlist,Nchoice,TN),
  Htxt=SP,
  pplink(point(Htxt),_,point(Ttxt),node(TN)),
  file_str(TN,STR),
  searchPOINT(Ttxt,STR,"",TPos),
  hyperEDIT(TN,TPos,_), !.

viewOPTION(_,_,_,3).

/* ************************* addOPTION ***************** */
```

(**Fig. 5-3.** continued)

```
% Adding a node-node link.

addOPTION(Fname1,_,_,Fname2,1):-
  existNODE(Fname2),
  wantTOedit(Fname2),
  assert(nnlink(node(Fname1),node(Fname2))), !.
addOPTION(_,_,_,_,1).  % return with no action

% Adding a point-node link.

addOPTION(FILEname,Fstr,Pos,Fname2,2):-
  existNODE(Fname2),
  wantTOedit(Fname2),
  findHyperText(Fstr,Pos,Htxt),
  assert(pnlink(point(Htxt),node(FILEname),node(Fname2))),
  !.

addOPTION(_,_,_,_,2).  % return with no action

% Adding a point-point link.

addOPTION(Fname1,Fstr1,Pos1,Fname2,3):-
  existNODE(Fname2),
  file_str(Fname2,INstr),
  MSG="Select a hypertext point with (F10)",
  edit(INstr,Fstr2,"<EDIT TARGET>",Fname2,MSG,
       1,"",1,1,1,1,Pos2,ReturnStatus),
  ReturnStatus=0,       % editor terminated with F10
  SaveCHANGES1(Fname2,INstr,Fstr2),
  findHyperText(Fstr1,Pos1,Htxt1),
  findHyperText(Fstr2,Pos2,Htxt2),
  assert(pplink(point(Htxt1),node(Fname1),point(Htxt2),node(Fname2))),
  !.

addOPTION(_,_,_,_,3).  % return with no action

/* ******************** deleteOPTION ****************** */

% delete a nnlink

deleteOPTION(SN,_,_,1):-
  findall(T,nnlink(node(SN),node(T)),Tlist),
  cursor(R,C), Row=R+1, Col=C+1,
  boxmenu(Row,Col,4,45,15,112,Tlist,
          "NODE-NODE LINK",1,Nchoice), Nchoice <> 0,
  nth_member(Tlist,Nchoice,TN),
  X=SN, Y=TN,
  retract(nnlink(node(X),node(Y)),hypdb),
  del_nnlink(X,Y), !.

deleteOPTION(_,_,_,1).

% delete a pnlink

deleteOPTION(SN,Fstr,Pos,2):-
  findHyperText(Fstr,Pos,SP),
  SP <> "",
  findall(T,pnlink(point(SP),node(SN),node(T)),Tlist),
  cursor(R,C), Row=R+1, Col=C+1,
  boxmenu(Row,Col,4,45,15,112,Tlist,
          "NODE-NODE LINK",1,Nchoice),
  nth_member(Tlist,Nchoice,TN),
  X=SP, Y=SN, Z=TN,
  retract(pnlink(point(X),node(Y),node(Z)),hypdb),
  del_pnlink(Y,Z), !.
```

(**Fig. 5-3.** continued)

```
deleteOPTION(_,_,_,2).

% delete a pplink

deleteOPTION(SN,Fstr,Pos,3):-
  findHyperText(Fstr,Pos,SP),
  SP <> "",
  findall(T,pplink(point(SP),node(SN),point(TP),node(T)),Tlist),
  cursor(R,C), Row=R+1, Col=C+1,
  boxmenu(Row,Col,4,45,15,112,Tlist,
         "NODE-NODE LINK",1,Nchoice),
  nth_member(Tlist,Nchoice,TN),
  X=SP, Y=SN, Z=TP, W=TN,
  retract(pplink(point(X),node(Y),point(Z),node(W)),hypdb),
  del_pplink(Y,W), !.

deleteOPTION(_,_,_,3).

/* ************************** del_nnlink **************** */

% target node TN is linked only to SN
del_nnlink(SN,TN):-
  findall(SN1,nnlink(node(SN1),node(TN)),L1), L1=[SN],
  findall(TN1,nnlink(node(TN),node(TN1)),L2), L2=[],
  findall(SN1,pnlink(_,node(SN1),node(TN)),L3), L3=[],
  findall(TN1,pnlink(_,node(TN),node(TN1)),L4), L4=[],
  findall(SN1,pplink(_,node(SN1),_,node(TN)),L5), L5=[],
  findall(TN1,pplink(_,node(TN),_,node(TN1)),L6), L6=[],
  del_node(TN). % ask user before deleting target node

/* ************************ del_pnlink ***************** */

% target node TN is linked only to a point in SN

del_pnlink(SN,TN):-
  findall(SN1,pnlink(_,node(SN1),node(TN)),L1), L1=[SN],
  findall(SN1,nnlink(node(SN1),node(TN)),L2), L2=[],
  findall(TN1,nnlink(node(TN),node(TN1)),L3), L3=[],
  findall(TN1,pnlink(_,node(TN),node(TN1)),L4), L4=[],
  findall(SN1,pplink(_,node(SN1),_,node(TN)),L5), L5=[],
  findall(TN1,pplink(_,node(TN),_,node(TN1)),L6), L6=[],
  del_node(TN). % ask user before deleting target node

/* ************************ del_pplink ***************** */

% target TN only has a point linked to a point in SN

del_pplink(SN,TN):-
  findall(SN1,pplink(_,node(SN1),_,node(TN)),L1), L1=[SN],
  findall(SN1,nnlink(node(SN1),node(TN)),L2), L2=[],
  findall(TN1,nnlink(node(TN),node(TN1)),L3), L3=[],
  findall(TN1,pnlink(_,node(TN),node(TN1)),L4), L4=[],
  findall(SN1,pnlink(_,node(SN1),node(TN)),L5), L5=[],
  findall(TN1,pplink(_,node(TN),_,node(TN1)),L6), L6=[],
  del_node(TN). % ask user before deleting target node

/* *********************** del_node ******************** */

% ask the user if he wants to delete TN which is an isolated
% node in the hypertext network.

del_node(TN):-
  cursor(R,C), ROW = R+1,
  concat(TN," is not linked, delete (y/n): ",TXT),
```

(**Fig. 5-3.** continued)

```
    lineinput(ROW,C,45,15,112,TXT,"",ANS),
    upper_lower(ANS1,ANS),
    ANS1="Y",
    deletefile(TN), !.

  del_node(_).     % else return without deleting TN.

  /* ************************ searchPOINT **************** */

  searchPOINT(Hstr,Str,Nstr,Pos):-
    fronttoken(Hstr,Tok,Hstr1),
    fronttoken(Str,Tok,Str1),
    concat(Nstr,Tok,Nstr1),
    searchPOINT1(Hstr1,Str1,Nstr1,Pos), !.

  searchPOINT(Hstr,Str,Nstr,Pos):-
    fronttoken(Str,Tok,Str1),
    concat(Nstr,Tok,Nstr1),
    searchPOINT(Hstr,Str1,Nstr1,Pos).

  searchPOINT1("",_,Nstr,Pos):-
    str_len(Nstr,Pos), !.

  searchPOINT1(Hstr,Str,Nstr,Pos):-
    fronttoken(Hstr,Tok,Hstr1),
    fronttoken(Str,Tok,Str1),
    concat(Nstr,Tok,Nstr1),
    searchPOINT1(Hstr1,Str1,Nstr1,Pos).

  /* ********************* existNODE ********************* */
  /* This predicate will check when the target of the added
     link: (a) an existing node, then do nothing, else
           (b) create a new node and allow user to edit it.
  */

  existNODE(F2):-
    existfile(F2).

  existNODE(F2):-
    cursor(R,C), Row=R+1,
    concat(F2," doesn't exist, create (y/n): ",TXT),
    lineinput(ROW,C,45,15,112,TXT,"Y",ANS),
    upper_lower(ANS1,ANS),
    frontchar(ANS1,CHAR,_),
    CHAR='Y',
    file_str(F2,"").

  /* ********************* wantTOedit ******************** */
  /* Ask if user wants to inspect a target node in the editor.*/

  wantTOedit(Fname):-
    cursor(R,C), Row=R+1,
    concat("Edit target node ",Fname,TXT1),
    concat(TXT1," (y/n): ",TXT),
    lineinput(ROW,C,45,15,112,TXT,"Y",ANS),
    upper_lower(ANS1,ANS),
    frontchar(ANS1,CHAR,_),
    CHAR='Y',
    file_str(Fname,INstr),
    MSG="Terminate editing with (ESC) or (F10)",
    edit(INstr,OUTstr,"<EDIT TARGET>",Fname,MSG,
         1,"",1,1,1,1,_,_),
    file_str(Fname,OUTstr).

  wantTOedit(_). % No, user doesn't want to edit.
```

(**Fig. 5-3.** continued)

```
/* ********************** saveCHANGES ******************* */

saveCHANGES(INstr,OUTstr):-
  INstr <> OUTstr,
  msg(17,0,"To save changes use F2"), !.

saveCHANGES(_,_).

/* ********************** saveCHANGES1 ****************** */

saveCHANGES1(Fname,INstr,OUTstr):-
  INstr <> OUTstr,
  file_str(Fname,OUTstr), !.

saveCHANGES1(_,_,_).

/* ********************* saveCHANGES2 ******************* */
/* This predicate checks if the out string from the editor
   is not the same as the in string. If so it will ask if
   user wants to save changes to the file. */

saveCHANGES2(Fname,INstr,OUTstr):-
   INstr <> OUTstr,
   lineinput(4,35,30,15,112,
             "Save changes to file (y/n): ","",ANS),
   upper_lower(ANS1,ANS),
   ANS1 = "Y",
   file_str(Fname,OUTstr), !.
saveCHANGES2(_,_,_).

/* ********************* END END END END **************** */
```

"titleScreen" sub-goal this way:

```
  hyperMAIN:-
    retractall(_,hypdb),
    retractall(_,maindb),
    blankwindow,
% titleScreen, % displays a graphical title screen
    textSCREEN, % displays a text title screen
    editwindow,
    . . .
```

In this chapter, I will only use a title screen in text mode. If everything is set, run the program and sit back and wait. Turbo Prolog will clear the display and you will see the title screen of ET (see FIG. 5-4). Hit any key to continue. ET will respond by displaying its user-interface shell (see FIG. 5-5). The user-interface has a pull-down menu at the top, an editor window in the middle, and a status-line at the bottom.

In the next section, I will explain all the options for the main menu and its submenus. Also I will show you how you can use ET to create, view, and maintain a hypertext document.

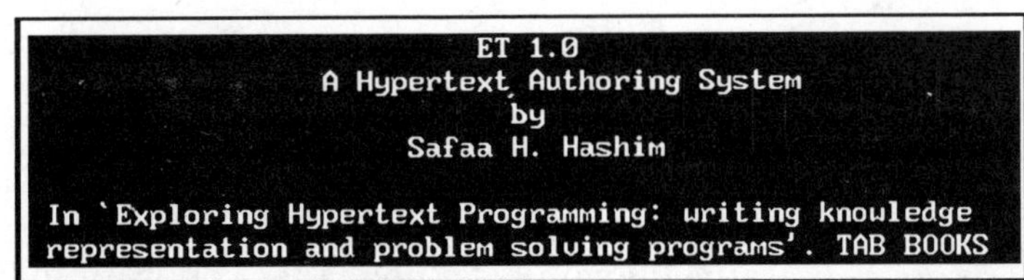

Fig. 5-4. The title screen of ET.

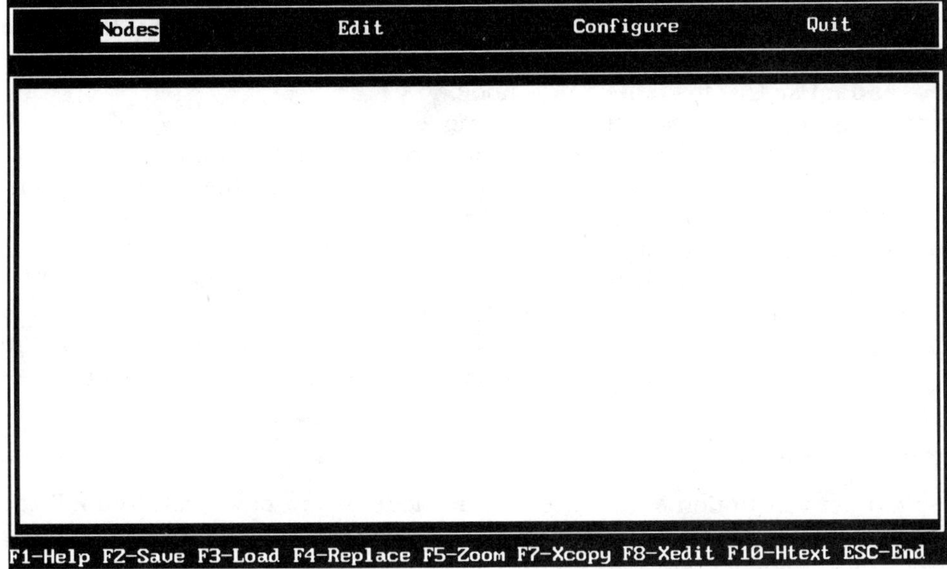

Fig. 5-5. The user-interface shell of ET.

USER GUIDE

In FIG. 5-5, you can see the main menu at the top, the editor window in the middle, and the status-line at the bottom. The main menu has four options: Nodes, Edit, Configure and Quit. You choose "Nodes" when you want to operate on nodes (load a node, create a new one, and so on). The "Edit" option puts you in the edit mode. The "Configure" option allows you to load (consult), delete, or save a network configuration file. The status-line reminds us of important commands for the hypertext editor. Now I'll talk about each item of ET in a little bit more detail.

The Nodes Submenu

When you pull down this submenu, you will get these options:

Load
New node

Save
Write to
Directory
Change dir.
Operating system

Load: Will prompt you for the filename of a node that you want to load. If you are not sure of the name, press ENTER to get a directory of hypertext files in the current directory. Hypertext files listed in the directory menu have ".hyp" as an extension. If you have entered or choosen your filename, the system will load it into the editor's window. If the file doesn't exist, ET will ask you if you want to create the file.
New node: Use this to create a new node.
Save: This option will save the current node.
Write to: You use this option to save the current node to another file.
Directory: When you want to see a list of all hypertext files in the current directory, this option will do.
Change dir.: With this option you can set the current disk drive and directory. After you do this, all future read and write operations will be from the new drive and directory.
Operating system: This option allows you to escape temporarily to DOS. To return to ET, just type "exist" at the DOS prompt.

The Edit Option

You use this option to edit the current node. If you have just fired ET, the system will have no current node. So when you choose "Edit," ET will create a "work.hyp" node for you. The editor you will be using is the Turbo Prolog editor, a WordStar compatible editor. For more details on editing commands, refer to Appendix B. The editor in Appendix B is for the hypertext-based problem solving system, MicroIBIS, which I will discuss in PART THREE. ET's editor is similar to MicroIBIS's editor, with one exception. When you press F10, while in ET's editor, you will get the hypertext menu. While in MicroIBIS, you use F10 to end editing and return to the main menu.

Another way to get help on using the editor is by pressing F1. ET will respond by displaying the Turbo Prolog's "Edit help" menu. The help menu has options such as cursor movement, insert & delete, block functions, global functions, hotkeys, WordStar functions, and so on. Also, the status-line at the bottom of the screen will remind you of these commands:

F1-Help	press F1 to get the "Editor help" menu
F2-Save	press F2 to save the current node
F3-Load	press F3 to load a new node in the editor
F4-Replace	press F4 to search and replace text
F5-Zoom	press F5 to zoom the editor-window in and out
F7-Xcopy	press F7 to copy text from external file
F8-Xedit	press F8 to edit another file

F10-Htext	press F10 to get the hypertext menu
ESC-End	press ESC to end editing and return to main menu

Here are a few comments on these commands: when you want to load a new node, I recommend that you don't use F3. Rather, use the "Load" from the "Nodes" menu. If you use F3 to load a node, the system will not be able to make the node as its current node. This will lead to many inconsistencies which might cause the system to crash. Another comment is about the F10 command. In PART ONE I used F10 as a hypertext hotkey—which means, whenever you want to view, add, or delete a link, you use F10 to get to the hypertext menu. Of course, if your hypertext operation involves point-point or point-node links, you must first position the cursor on the source point. As a reminder, a hypertext point is any text string between the "{" and "}" delimiters.

The Configure Submenu

A set of nodes is useless without a knowledge-base of the links between such nodes. In ET, as in PART ONE, I represent links by database facts. Also from PART ONE, I know that all the links in a hypertext document form a network. I call the file that contains the knowledge representation of a hypertext network a "configuration file." To distinguish network configuration files from other files, I use ".net" as their extension.

The "configure" submenu has options for loading, saving, and deleting network configuration files. Here is a summary of each option:

Load network: You use this option to load an existing configuration file.

Delete network: With this option you can delete the current network configuration. You will rarely need this option because if you want to delete a configuration file, you can do it directly from DOS. What this option does is to retract all the knowledge-base database facts so that you can start from scratch.

Write to: When you start a new hypertext document, you won't have any network configuration file to load. Go ahead and do all your work of creating nodes, points and links—but before you quit ET, use the "Write to" option to save the network to a configuration file. Remember though, when you name your network configuration file, use ".net" as the file extension.

Save network: With this option, you can save changes in network back to the configuration file.

Now, you are ready to use ET to create and view your own documents, but before you do this, take a look at the example on using ET in the next section. It will help you in getting a better understanding of the system. Remember though, ET is a prototype, not a finished product. You can expand ET by adding additional hypertext features. In Chapter 7, I will cover many of these features.

AN EXAMPLE USING ET

I will organize a list of readings into a hypertext document. The idea of this example is that I often read many books or articles on a specific topic. To help me capture the main idea in the text, I often take notes. Taking notes could take different forms such as making comments, highlighting text, and drawing connections between different chunks of text. Now, if I do this with most of my reading materials, my notebook will soon reflect a summary of what I have read. This notebook will help me integrate my comments and ideas along with the material I am reading. With ET, I can create a hypertext-based notebook.

To show you an example of this, I chose "theory of design" as my topic. The term "theory of design" is a very general term which covers many ideas on what design means. Also, in design theory I often talk about how do I design, and why do I design, and what the finished product of my design ought to look like. I will not go into more details about the "theory of design." Rather, I will concentrate on using ET to create a hypertext-based notebook on a specific "theory of design" which I call "the argumentative approach for problem-solving in design." In this approach, I consider design as a question-and-answer process. In PART TWO, I will talk in more detail about this approach when I discuss "hypertext-based problem-solving systems." For now, I will only talk about a reading-list on the "argumentative approach for design problem-solving."

A Hypertext Notebook on Design Theory

To build a hypertext document on design, first you must have a reading list on the topic. For demonstration purposes, your reading list will contain only three references. So the first node should be a text file with three references. To do this, run ET and choose the "New node" option from the "Nodes" menu. ET will then prompt to enter a name for the file. Enter `fig5-6` and ET creates the file "fig5-6.hyp" in the current disk and directory path. ET will

```
        Partial Reading List on "Design by Argumentation"


  1. Jay F. Rosenberg. The Practice of Philosophy: A Handbook
     for Beginners. Prentice-Hall, Inc. pp.13-24. 1978. Chapter
     two: {Arguments}; What They Are and How to Cope With Them.


  2. Rittel, Horst W. J. "{APIS}: a concept for an argumentative
     planning information system." Working paper # 324,
     Institute of Urban and Regional Development, CED-UCBerkeley,
     1980.

  3. Protzen, J. P. "{Reflections on the Fable of the Caliph},
     the Ten Architects and the Philosopher". JAE, V.34, summer
     1981; also Design Studies, V.3, #2, 1982.
```

Fig. 5-6. The text for a reading list of three references.

then put you in the edit mode so that you can enter the text for the node (see FIG. 5-6a). The text file ET creates is in FIG. 5-6.

Now for each item in the list you need some text to explain what it is all about. So, what you can do is to link each item, or part of an item, to an explanatory node. In other words, you can treat each item, or part of an item,

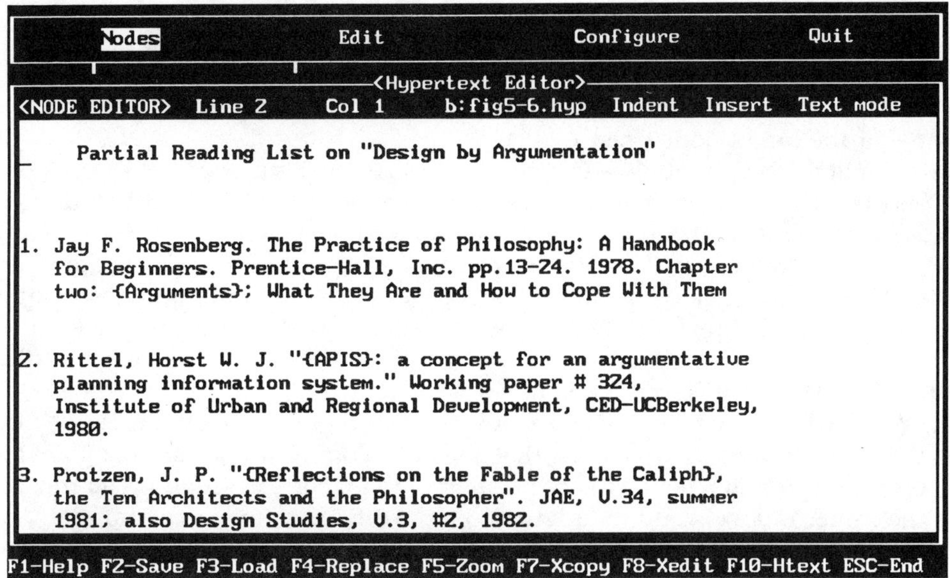

Fig. 5-6a. Entering the text for the main node.

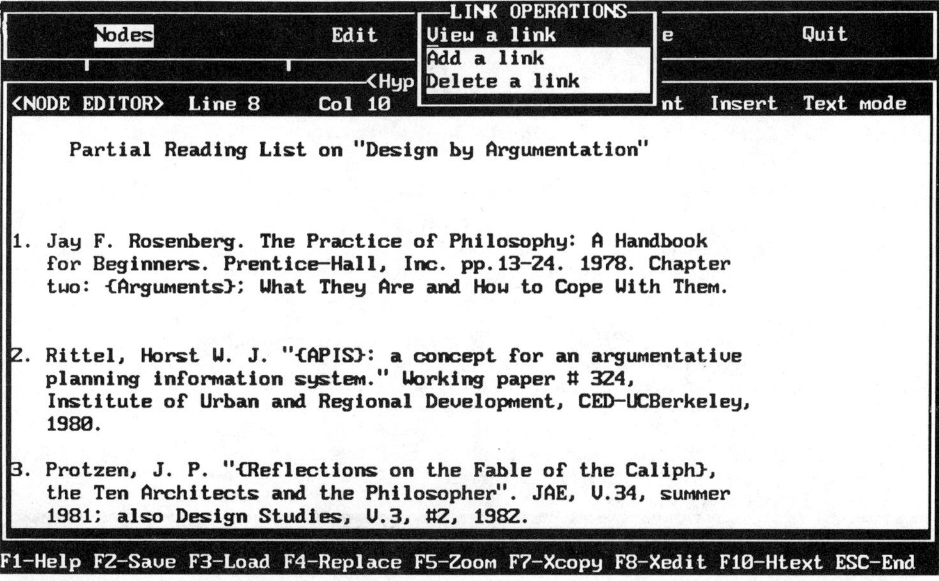

Fig. 5-6b. The "LINK OPERATIONS" menu.

as the source point in a point-node link. As you can see, there are three hypertext points in fig5-6.hyp—one point in each reference. As in PART ONE, a point is a chunk of text surrounded by "{" and "}". So far, these source points to target nodes haven't been linked. So, do some linking. To expand on the first reference, I choose the word "argument" as my point of interest. To link the point "Argument" in the first reference, I put the cursor under "Argument" and press F10. ET will display the "LINK OPERATIONS" menu (see FIG. 5-6b).

Now, I select the "Add a link" option, which I did in FIG. 5-6c; and ET will display the "ADD A LINK" menu. I need to create a point-node link, so I choose the "add a Point-node link" option. ET will respond by prompting to enter a name for the target node (see FIG. 5-6d).

Of course, the target node is a new node which ET must create first. Soon ET will find out that the node's file doesn't exist in the current directory. It will then ask if it can go ahead and create the node. Take a look at FIG. 5-6e.

When it is done, it will come back and ask if I want to edit the new node. To edit the new node, just press the ENTER key (see FIG. 5-6f)—and here I am again, in the hypertext editor. Now I enter the same excerpts from the first reference which discusses the meaning of "argument" (see FIG. 5-7a). You can see the complete text for this target node in FIG. 5-7.

When I am finished entering the text in the first target node, I press ESC to go back to the source node. Notice that the node containing the source point of a point-node link is referred to as the source node. For the second reference, I do the same. You will want to link the point "APIS" to a node explaining it. So what I have is another point-node link. All I need to do is to follow the same procedure I did before:

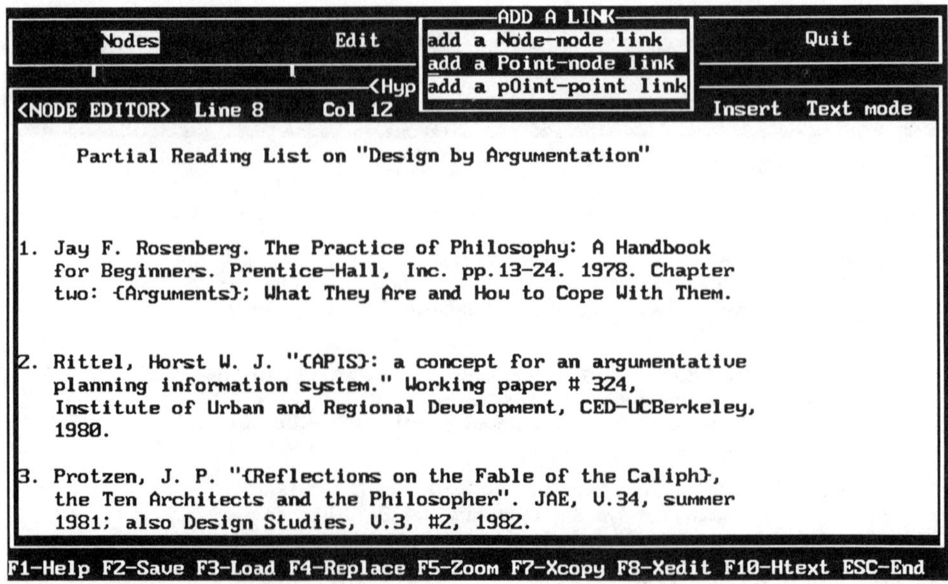

Fig. 5-6c. To link the "Argument" point to a node.

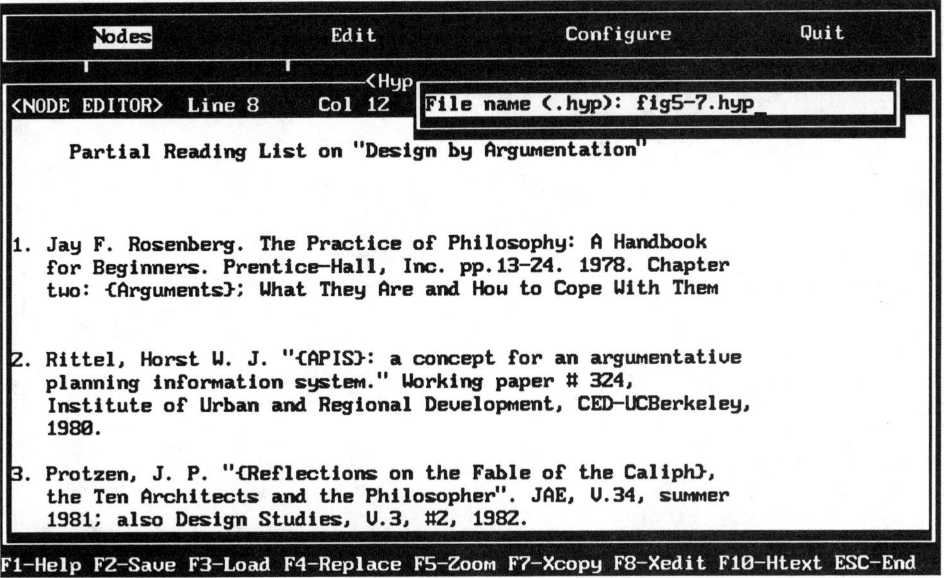

Fig. 5-6d. Entering the name for the target node.

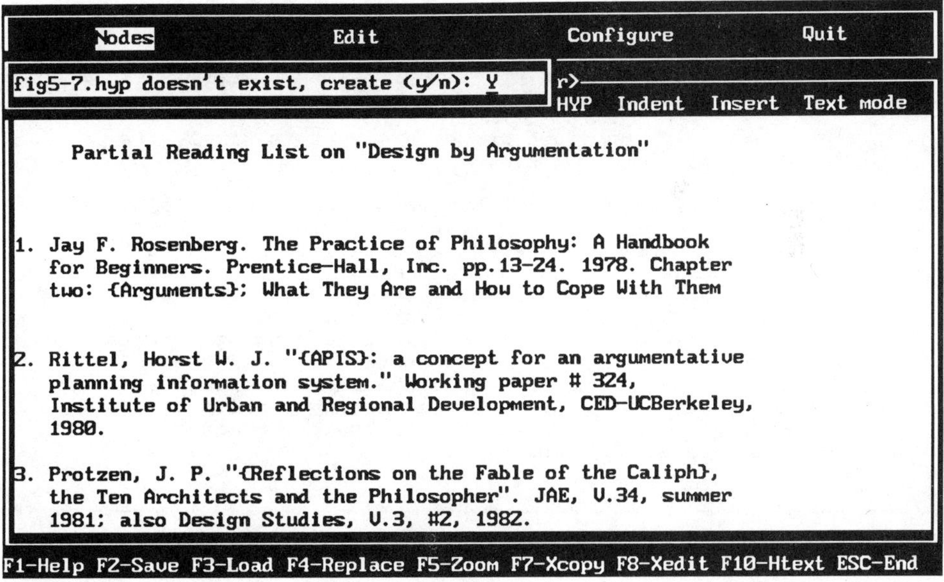

Fig. 5-6e. Creating the target node.

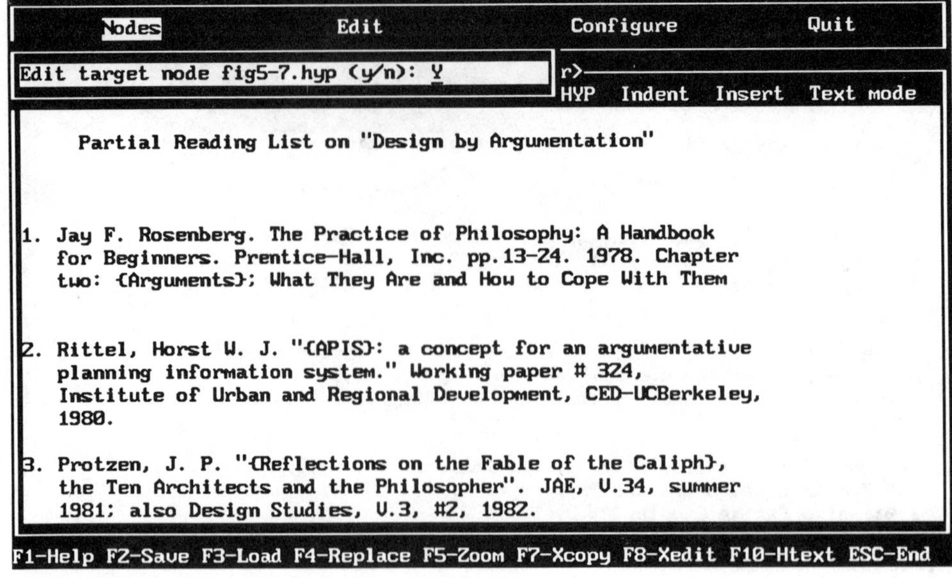

Fig. 5-6f. ET asks you if you want to edit the target node.

Excerpts From:

Jay F. Rosenberg. The Practice of Philosophy: A Handbook for Beginners. Prentice-Hall, Inc. pp.13-24. 1978. Chapter two: Arguments; What They Are and How to Cope With Them.

Definition: In its broadest sense, argument is simply the giving of reasons for beliefs.

The Structure of Arguments: An argument may be thought of as a group or bunch or series of statements. In the cleanest sort of case, one of these statements will be tagged as the intended "conclusion," expressing the target belief which requires support. Others will be marked as starting points or "premises." The conclusion is what is argued for; the premises are what is argued from. The remaining statements will attempt to illuminate the connection between the premises and the conclusion, to establish that one who grants the truth of the premises is thereby committed to granting as well the truth of the conclusion (or ought consistently to be so committed).

Fig. 5-7. Excerpts from the first reference.

- move the cursor to the "APIS" point,
- press F10,
- pick "Add a link" from the "LINK OPERATIONS" menu,
- pick "add a Point-node link" from the "ADD A LINK" menu,

- enter a name for the new target node "fig5-8.hyp"
- ET will create the node's file and asks if I want to edit the file. To edit the file, I just press ENTER.
- Once in the editor, I enter the text for the new node.

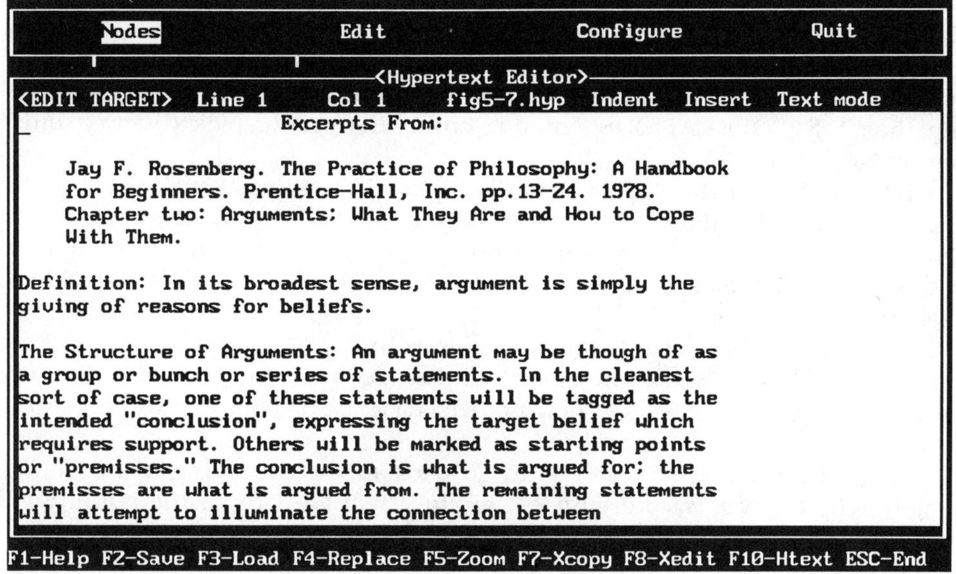

Fig. 5-7a. Entering the text for the target node.

Excerpts From:

Rittel, Horst W. J. "APIS: a concept for an argumentative planning information system." Working paper # 324, Institute of Urban and Regional Development, CED-UCBerkeley, 1980.

APIS is designed to accompany the planning process from its very beginning to the final formulation of the plan.

APIS is not supposed to have a complete record of all information needed in the planning process. It follows the opposite strategy: it tries to incorporate as little as possible into its data document collection. Its operation and use start with the "empty system." It is a "SECOND ORDER" information system.

The main purpose (there are other purposes) of APIS is to establish a discourse between those people who have the problems (giving rise to APIS's activities) and others who deal or have dealt with similar problems, or with particular aspects of the present problems. APIS role is one of scouting information and establishing communication, rather than procuring answers from its own files and collections.

Fig. 5-8. Excerpts from the second reference.

The result is the new target node in FIG. 5-8. In this node, fig5-8.hyp, were copied those portions from the second reference which describe the basic ideas behind APIS. To expand a little bit more on the purposes of APIS, I add more links. So to keep the focus of the current node on a general description of APIS, I need a new point-node link. This link will connect the point "purposes of APIS" to another node. To create this node, the node "fig5-8.hyp" must first be in the "link viewing mode." Right now I am in the "link creation mode." So if I try to press F10, ET will do nothing. To be in the "link viewing mode" I must end the "link creation mode" by pressing ESC. This will take you back to your reading list node. Now you can view the node linked to "APIS" first by choosing the "LINK OPERATIONS" menu. From this menu, pick "View a link" option (see FIG. 5-8a).

ET will display the "VIEW A LINK" menu. This time I pick the "view a Point-node link" option and enter the name "fig5-8" as my target node. If I don't know the name of the target node, I simply press the ENTER key. In response, ET will display a menu of all the target nodes, and all I need is to pick one (see FIG. 5-8b).

In this case, there is only one target node linked to the "APIS" point. Pick "fig5-8" and there it is—in the editor window (see FIG. 5-8a). Now I can link the point "purposes of APIS" to a new node (see FIG. 5-8c). This should be a direct forward task.

When I am done, I press ESC to go back to the preceding source node, which is fig5-8.hyp. By pressing ESC again, I will go back to the reading list node.

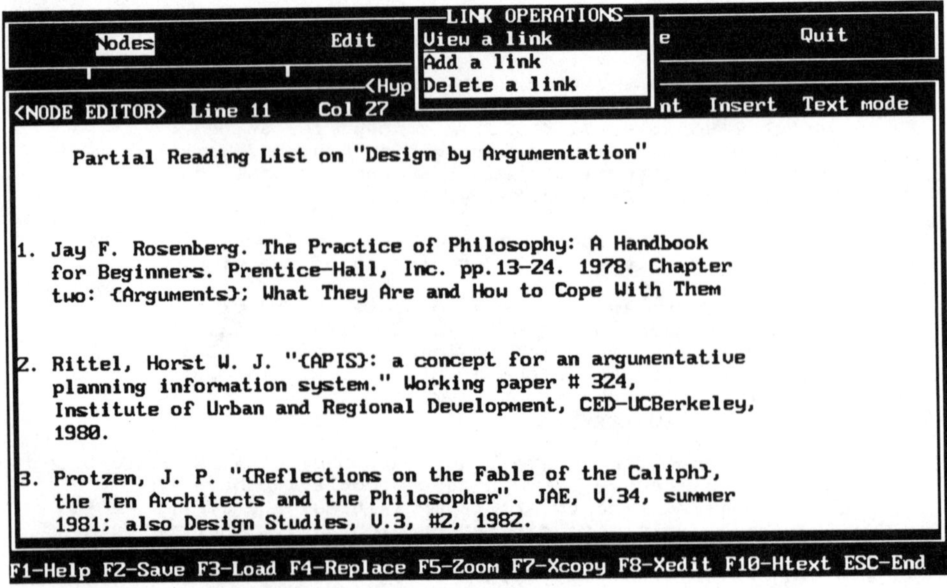

Fig. 5-8a. Viewing the point-node (APIS-fig5-8) link.

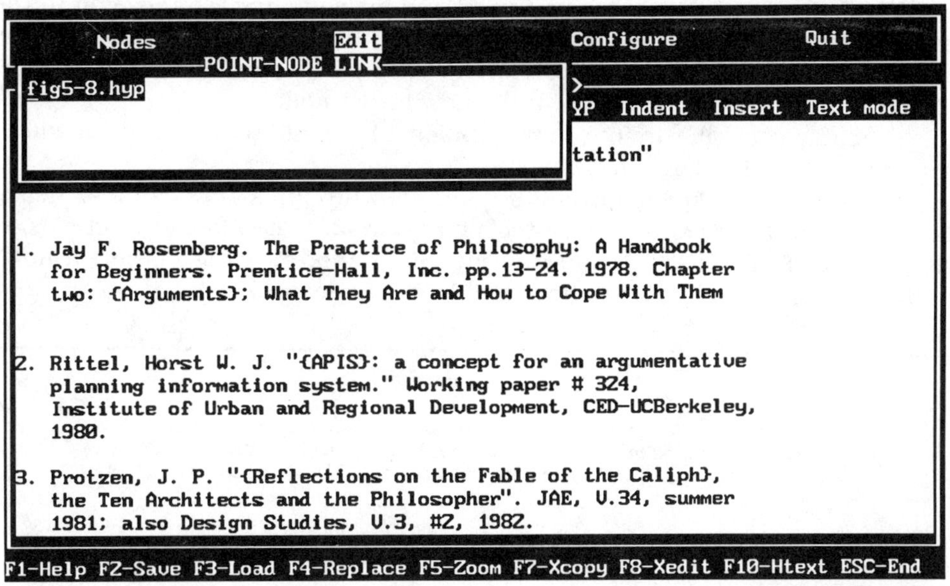

Nodes Edit Configure Quit

POINT-NODE LINK

fig5-8.hyp

YP Indent Insert Text mode

tation"

1. Jay F. Rosenberg. The Practice of Philosophy: A Handbook for Beginners. Prentice-Hall, Inc. pp.13-24. 1978. Chapter two: {Arguments}; What They Are and How to Cope With Them

2. Rittel, Horst W. J. "{APIS}: a concept for an argumentative planning information system." Working paper # 324, Institute of Urban and Regional Development, CED-UCBerkeley, 1980.

3. Protzen, J. P. "{Reflections on the Fable of the Caliph}, the Ten Architects and the Philosopher". JAE, V.34, summer 1981; also Design Studies, V.3, #2, 1982.

F1-Help F2-Save F3-Load F4-Replace F5-Zoom F7-Xcopy F8-Xedit F10-Htext ESC-End

Fig. 5-8b. ET displays a menu of all target nodes.

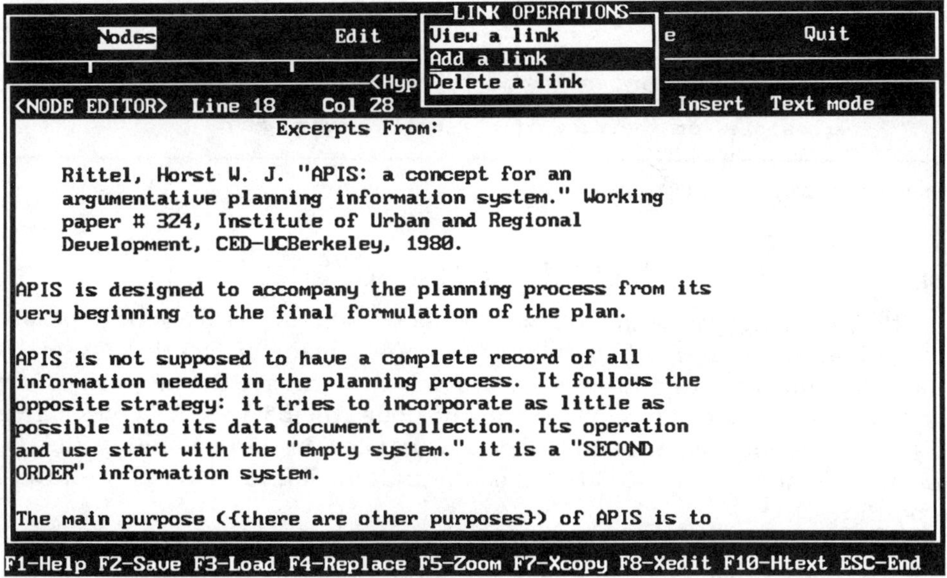

Fig. 5-8c. Adding a point-node link to a target node.

That's it. Now you know how to add a point-node link, so move on to the third reference—but try it yourself. Try to link the point "Reflections on the Fable of the Caliph" in the third reference to a new target node. You can use the text in FIG. 5-9 as the content of the new target node.

Probably you will run into some problems here and there, but with a little practice, you will feel at ease with ET.

So far I have talked about adding and viewing links. You can also delete links. To do this, first choose a source, point or node. Then by pressing F10, get the "LINK OPERATIONS" menu. From this menu, pick the "Delete a link" option. Try it yourself and see how simple it is to delete a link.

```
                    Excerpts From:

     (Protzen, J. P.) "Reflections on the Fable of the
     Caliph, the Ten Architects and the Philosopher". JAE,
     V.34, summer  1981; also Design Studies, V.3, #2, 1982.


 The author ... is "Ferdinand Gonseth, a Swiss
 philosopher. It is part of his work on the foundation of
 mathematical sciences.

 The fable addresses explicitly the problem of choice and the
 justification of choices.

 To design a plan is to CHOOSE a strategy or a set of actions
 which yields, if implemented, a desired
 side effect.

 The choices made by environmental designers and planners are
 consequential if taken together, these choices are largely
 responsible for the face of our built environment.
```

Fig. 5-9. Excerpts from the third reference.

Saving the Network Configuration to ".net" File

Before leaving you with ET, I want to show you how to save your hypertext document. As I said, my hypertext document is made of two things: several node files and one configuration file. You only need to save the network configuration in a knowledge-base file. As for the nodes themselves, ET takes care of it. Every time you create or edit a node, ET updates the corresponding files. On the other hand, to save the network configuration, you can follow one of these procedures:

- If you have already loaded a configuration file, you can choose "Save network" from the "Configure" menu. This way ET will update the existing configuration file.
- If you didn't load any configuration file, you must use the "Write to" option. First this option will prompt you to enter a name for the new configuration file. Then it will save your current configuration to that file.

- Sometimes you forget to load a configuration file, but you still use the "Save network" option. Here, ET will save the current configuration to the default "config.net" file. If this happens, no problem. You can exit temporarily to DOS and rename "config.net."

So when you save your configuration, you are saving your hypertext document. Again, this is because in ET a hypertext document is nothing but a collection of node files and one configuration file.

Documents with the Same Files, but Different Configurations

A hypertext document is nothing but a collection of regular ASCII files and a network configuration file. The configuration file is nothing but a collection of "pplink," "pnlink," and "nnlink" facts. I talked about the three kinds of links (pplink, pnlink, and nnlink) in PART ONE. These links will decide which files on the disk you can view and edit. In other words, you can create different hypertext documents using the same node-files. You do that by creating different configuration files. The nodes are the same—what matters is the way you link these node files together.

In the next chapter, I will discuss some of the programming techniques in ET. Until then, I wish you happy ETing with ET.

6

A Look Inside ET

"To explain the mind, we have to show how minds are built from mindless stuff, from parts that are much smaller and simpler than anything we'd consider smart. Unless we can explain the mind in terms of things that have no thoughts or feelings of their own, we'll only have gone around in a circle."

—*Marvin Minsky, The Society of Mind.*

Another applicable saying is the one stating that "the whole is more than the sum of its parts." In this chapter, the task is simpler than that of Minsky's. I want to explain ET, not the mind, in terms of its parts. As most of the programming behind ET is already in PART ONE.

ET FROM THE TOP: THE GENERAL STRUCTURE

The gateway to ET is the pull-down menu. In this menu, there are the four major options: Nodes, Edit, Configure, and Quit. The "Nodes" option starts a submenu of operations on nodes. The "Edit" option puts you in the hypertext-editor mode. The hypertext-editor is where all the hypertext authoring and retrieval takes place. The "Configure" option starts a submenu of hypertext network configuration file related operations. You can see a diagram for the different menu options in FIG. 6-1.

To construct this menu structure, use the TOOLBOX's pull-down menu predicate, which was discussed in Chapter 4. The call to "pulldown" is only a subgoal in the declarative definition of ET in "hyperMAIN" (see FIG. 6-2).

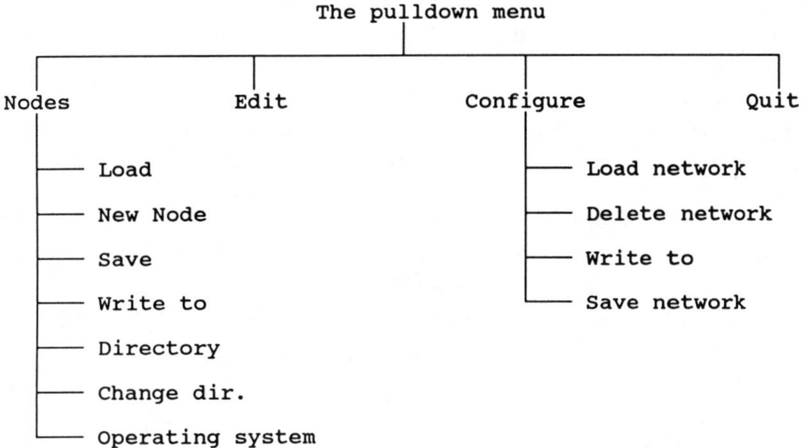

Fig. 6-1. ET's menu options.

Fig. 6-2. hyperMAIN: a declarative definition of ET.

```
/*
          1         2         3         4         5         6         7
012345678901234567890123456789012345678901234567890123456789012345678901234567
       Nodes                   Edit                    Configure            Quit
*/

  hyperMAIN:-
    retractall(_,hypdb),
    retractall(_,maindb),
    blankwindow,
%   titleScreen,   % displays a graphical title screen
    textSCREEN,    % displays a text title screen
    editwindow,
    statusline,
    pulldown(112,[ curtain(7,"Nodes",["Load ",
                                       "New node",
                                       "Save",
                                       "Write to",
                                       "Directory",
                                       "Change dir.",
                                       "Operating system"
                                      ]),
                   curtain(27,"Edit",[]),
                   curtain(47,"Configure",["Load network",
                                           "Delete network",
                                           "Write to",
                                           "Save network"
                                          ]),
                   curtain(67,"Quit",[])
                 ],
                 _,_),
    removewindow,
    removewindow.
```

Notice that in the first two subgoals of hyperMAIN, "retractall" is used to retract all database facts in the knowledge-base. This is needed to quit ET and later to go back to it. After quitting ET, the knowledge-base will still be in memory. So when starting ET the next time, you must first erase the old knowledge-base before building a new one. Because there are two kinds of database facts (hypdb and maindb) you need two calls to "retractall." Don't worry about the difference between "hyperdb" and "maindb." For now, all you need to know is that "hyperdb" is used for the hypertext knowledge-base and "maindb" for general bookkeeping purposes. I will talk more about "hyperdb" and "maindb" in "THE KNOWLEDGE-BASE" section.

After the two "retractall" subgoals, the rest of the subgoals install the user interface. Predicate "blankwindow" provides a black background for ET of 25 rows and 80 columns. Predicate "titleScreen" displays the ET logo in graphic mode. The code for "titleScreen" is in FIG. 5-2. Predicate "textSCREEN" on the other hand, uses text mode for displaying the ET logo. The "editwindow" subgoal displays the hypertext editor window. This is the window where most of our hypertext activities take place. Predicate "statusline" displays a statusline at the bottom of the screen. You can find the code for "blankwindow," "textSCREEN," "editwindow," and "statusline" in FIG. 3-10.

The main thing in "hyperMAIN" is the call to "pulldown," which was discussed in Chapter 4. With "pulldown" you can display a pull-down menu with several curtains. Each curtain can be a single option or a submenu of options. To execute pull-down menu option you need a call to "pdwaction." Each option on the pull-down menu must have one or more matching "pdwaction" clauses in the program. For example, when you pick the first option ("Load a node") from the "Nodes" submenu, Turbo tries to match the subgoal "pdwaction(1,1)" with the head of a clause in your program. For this subgoal to succeed, you must have one or more clauses with "pdwaction(1,1)" as the head. The code for all "pdwaction" clauses is in FIG. 5-1. In the next few sections, I will discuss the programming of some of these options. I'll start with "Load"—the option for loading a node.

LOADING A HYPERTEXT DOCUMENT

Say that you already have a hypertext document which was built using ET. To load this document in ET:

- first, use the "Nodes/Load" option to load a "starting node." Any node in the document can be a starting node. I talk about the programming of this option in the next section.
- second, you must load a hypertext network configuration file. The "Configure/Load network" option will do it for you.

Loading a Starting Node in the Editor: (Nodes/Load)

Now say that you already have a hypertext document which was built using ET. To load this document in ET you must use the "Nodes/Load" option.

When you pick the "Load" option from the "Nodes" menu, the pull-down menu predicate tries to match a "pdwaction(1,1)" subgoal. The matching clause should contain all the subgoals necessary to load a node from the disk. Remember that a node is nothing but a text file. FIGURE 6-3 shows the two "pdwaction(1,1)" matching clauses.

In the first clause, the first subgoal, "shiftwindow(OLD)," will retrieve the window number of the pull-down menu. You need the pull-down menu's window number so that you can shift to it after you finish loading a node in the editor's window. The "cursor(Row,_)" subgoal gives you the row number of the cursor location. Pass this number to the "readfilename" subgoal.

"Readfilename" was discussed in Chapter 4. The "readfilename" subgoal will prompt you to enter a hypertext filename. After you enter a filename, "readfilename" returns the filename as its last argument. The next subgoal, ifEXIST(Fname), will check if the file you want to load already exists in the current directory. If the file exists, ifEXIST succeeds. With the "updateCURRENT" subgoal the fact "CurrentFILE(Fname)" is asserted to the knowledge-base. "CurrentFILE" is needed to hold the name of the current node in the knowledge-base. Later when you want to save changes back to the file, all you need to do is give the goal:

```
currentFILE(Fname)
```

which will bind Fname to the name of the current file. Once updating the current filename in memory is done, ET's attention is shifted to the editor window. This is done with the subgoal "shiftwindow(2)," because 2 is the number of the editor's window. Now, the node can be edited so the subgoal "hyperEDIT" will start the hypertext editor. The subgoal "hyperEDIT(Fname,1,OUTpos)" has the flow pattern (i,i,o). This means that the filename to edit, and the cursor position in that file, need to be supplied. On its part, "hyperEDIT" will allow an edit and save of the node. Also, hyperEDIT allows an add, delete, and view of links. As for the last argument, hyperEDIT uses OUTpos to return the cursor position in the resulting node file. The next "updateCURRENT" subgoal will save the resulting cursor position as the current position in the node.

Fig. 6-3. The "pdwaction" clauses for loading a node.

```
% first, try loading the file from disk

 pdwaction(1,1):-
   shiftwindow(OLD),
   cursor(Row,_),
   readfilename(Row,35,15,112,hyp,"",Fname),
   ifEXIST(Fname),
   updateCURRENT(currentFILE(Fname)),
   shiftwindow(2),
   hyperEDIT(Fname,1,OUTpos),
   updateCURRENT(currentPOS(OUTpos)),
   shiftwindow(OLD).

% if first clause fails, return to menu doing nothing

 pdwaction(1,1).
```

It asserts a "currentPOS" fact to the knowledge-base. Thusly, all the steps necessary to load and edit a hypertext node have been done.

To return to the pull-down menu, you shift the attention of ET back to the pull-down menu window. This is the job of "shiftwindow(OLD)." Remember that the number of the pull-down menu window (OLD) through the first subgoal was retrieved.

If the first "pdwaction(1,1)" clause fails, Turbo tries to match the second one. The second clause of "pdwaction(1,1)" (see FIG. 6-3) makes sure that you return to the pull-down menu when ET fails to execute an option.

CREATING A NEW NODE: (Nodes/New node)

This is the second option in the "Nodes" submenu. To execute this option, ET must have several matching "pdwaction(1,2)" clauses. There are two "pdwaction(1,2)" clauses in ET:

```
pdwaction(1,2):-
  shiftwindow(OLD),
  cursor(Row,Col), R=Row+1,
  lineinput(R,Col,40,15,112,
    "Enter new file name: ","work.hyp",NewName),
  file_str(NewName,""),
  shiftwindow(2),
  hyperEDIT(NewName,1,OUTpos),
  updateCURRENT(currentPOS(OUTpos)),
  shiftwindow(OLD).
  pdwaction(1,2).
```

In the first clause, as in "pdwaction(1,1)," the first subgoal is "shiftwindow(OLD)." As I said, this subgoal will instantiate OLD to the window number of the pull-down menu. You need this number to go back to the pull-down menu once you are done executing an option. The "cursor(Row,Col)" subgoal retrieves the row and column of the current cursor position. The next subgoal, the TOOLBOX predicate "lineinput," will use the cursor position to prompt you to input the name of your new file. After you finish entering a filename, "lineinput" will instantiate NewName to that name, but if you just press ENTER, "NewName" will be "work.hyp." Now that ET has the name of the new file, it will create the file using the built-in predicate "file_str." "shiftwindow(2)" shifts to the editor window. The rest of the subgoals are similar to that of "pdwaction(1,1)." After you load (or create a node) and edit it, you might like to save it. Well, this is what "Nodes/Save" option is for.

SAVING A NODE: (Nodes/Save)

When you make some changes to a node using "hyperEDIT," it automatically saves the node back to the file. To explain this, take a look at the code for "hyperEDIT":

```
hyperEDIT(FILEname,InPos,OutPos) :-
    repeat,
      file_str(FILEname,INstr),
      MSG="End editing (ESC), Follow hyper link (F10) ",
      edit(INstr,OUTstr,"NODE EDITOR"FILEname,MSG,
           InPos,"",1,1,1,1,OutPos,ReturnStatus),
      refreshstatus, % redraw the status-line
      saveCHANGES1(FILEname,INstr,OUTstr),
      hyperSTATUS(FILEname,OUTstr,OutPos,ReturnStatus).
```

"HyperEDIT" will be discussed in the "Editing Hypertext" section. The main concern here is the "saveCHANGES1" subgoal. Notice that this subgoal comes after the "edit" subgoal. After you end editing, by pressing the ESC key, the built-in predicate "edit" returns the updated text of the node in "OUTstr." Then "saveCHANGES1" compares both the old text, "INstr," and the new text, "OUTstr." If "INstr" is not equal to "OUTstr," "saveCHANGES1" will save "OUTstr" to the node file "FILEname."

The "Nodes/Save" option is only applicable to the "starting node." This option has no effect on nodes linked to the starting node because of the automatic saving feature of hyperEDIT. When a hyperEDIT session is ended, it automatically saves the node. The "Nodes/Save" option is redundant.

Nonetheless, it can be used for instructional purposes. Also, you might like to take out the automatic saving capability in hyperEDIT and replace it with manual saving. Here "Nodes/Save" would be the alternative. After all, my main interest is in programming techniques, not final products. So look at the programming behind "Nodes/Save."

When you pick "Nodes/Save," the pull-down predicate executes pdwaction(1,3) which has these two clauses (also see FIG. 5-1):

```
pdwaction(1,3):-
   getCURRENT(currentFILE(Fname)),
   getCURRENT(currentSTR(String)),
   file_str(Fname,String).
pdwaction(1,3).
```

ET uses database facts, such as "currentFILE" and "currentSTR," to record the name (Fname) and text (String) of the current node. Then, all you need to do is to use "file_str" to write string "STRING" to the file "Fname."

Of course, most of the credit for the simplicity "pdwaction(1,3)" goes to "getCURRENT." "GetCURRENT" is used to retrieve the node filename, its text, and the cursor position in the text. The "getCURRENT" program is part of the main module of ET (see FIG. 5-1). To give you an idea, here is the "getCURRENT" clause for retrieving the text of the current node:

```
   getCURRENT(currentSTR(Str)):- currentSTR(Str),!.
   getCURRENT(currentSTR("")).
```

The nice thing about "getCURRENT" is that it has a default value. Also, when you retrieve the text of a node, and you don't have a current node, "getCURRENT" returns the empty string.

WRITING A NODE TO AN EXTERNAL FILE: (Nodes/Write to)

In this option, ET prompt you to enter a filename, then it copies the current node to that file. This is exactly what "pdwaction(1,4)" does:

```
pdwaction(1,4):-
  shiftwindow(OLD),
  getCURRENT(currentSTR(STRING)),
  cursor(Row,Col), R=Row+1,
  readfilename(R,Col,15,112,hyp,"",Fname),
  write_to(Fname,STRING),
  shiftwindow(OLD).
pdwaction(1,4).
```

In the first clause, "readfilename" binds Fname to a filename. Then the subgoal "write_to" writes the text (STRING) of the current node to that file (Fname):

```
write_to(Fname,String):-
  not(existfile(Fname)),
  file_str(Fname,String), !.
write_to(Fname,String):-
  existfile(Fname),
  file_str(Fname,Str),
  cursor(R,_), Row=R+2,
  Str <> String,
  lineinput(Row,35,30,15,112,
    "replace existing text (y/n): ","",ANS),
  upper_lower(ANS1,ANS),
  ANS1 = "Y",
  file_str(Fname,String).
```

If you want to write the current node to a new file, Turbo will execute the first "write_to" clause. If on the other hand, you want to write the current node to an existing file, Turbo will execute the second clause. Notice that the second clause compares the text for the current node with that of the existing file, (Str < > String). This saves us the time of writing the same text to the file.

CHANGE DIRECTORY PATH: (Nodes/Change dir.)

The core of "pdwaction(1,6)," which executes the "Change dir" option, is the "changeDIR" subgoal. Here is the code for "pdwaction(1,6)."

```
pdwaction(1,6):-
  cursor(Row,Col),
```

```
    makewindow(_,_,_,_,R0,C0,_,_),
    Row1=R0+Row, Col1=C0+Col,
    changeDIR(Row1,Col1,15,112). % see figure 3-9.
pdwaction(1,6).
```

Now take a look at "changeDIR" in FIG. 6-4. In this predicate, the first subgoal (the built-in predicate "disk") retrieves the current disk path (DISK). Then comes TOOLBOX predicate "lininput_repeat," which prompts with an input line (see FIG. 6-5). On the input line, "lineinput_repeat" first displays the current directory path (DISK). When you enter a new path, or keep the old path, it will return the new path in "NEWDISK." Next, the bound variable "NEWDISK" is passed to "changeDISK."

The first clause of "changeDISK" is "pathNAME." This predicate checks if the directory name conforms to the naming conventions. A directory name must start with a disk name (A, B, C, etc...), followed by a colon (":"), followed by a backslash ("\"), and then followed by a subdirectory name, if any. If the

Fig. 6-4. Changing the directory path.

```
/* ********************************************************** */
/* ******************** changeDIR *********************** */
/* ********************************************************** */

PREDICATES
  changeDIR(INTEGER,INTEGER,INTEGER,INTEGER)
  changeDISK(STRING)
  pathNAME(STRING)

CLAUSES

/* ************************ changeDIR ******************** */

changeDIR(ROW,COL,WATTR,FATTR):-
  disk(DISK),
  lineinput_repeat(ROW,COL,45,WATTR,FATTR,"Directory: ",DISK,NEWDISK),
  changeDISK(NEWDISK),!,
  removewindow.

changeDIR(_,_,_,_).

/* *********************** changeDISK ******************** */

changeDISK(DISK):-
  pathNAME(DISK),
  disk(DISK),!.
changeDISK(_):-
  msg(17,1,"error in directory name."), % in figure 3-9.
  fail.

/* ********************** pathNAME *********************** */

pathNAME(DISK):-
  fronttoken(DISK,_,Str),
  fronttoken(Str,":",Str1),
  fronttoken(Str1,"\\",_).

/* *********************** END END END ****************** */
```

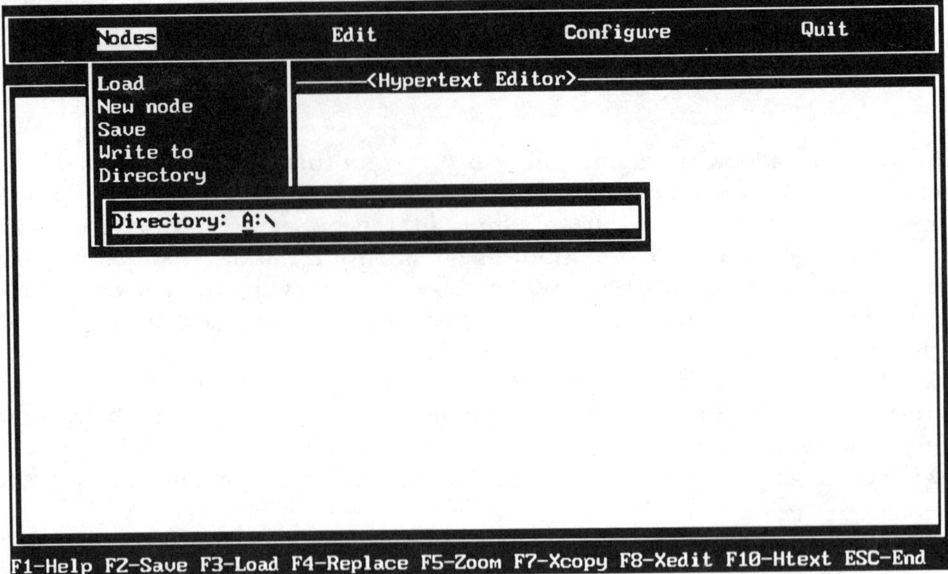

Fig. 6-5. The prompt line for changing the directory path.

directory path ("DISK") is okay, the next subgoal "disk(DISK)" makes it the current directory. The first clause of "changeDISK" will fail if you don't enter the directory path correctly. Here, Turbo will match the second clause. The second clause first issues an error message and then forces the predicate to fail. When this happens, Turbo will backtrack to "lineinput_repeat," the subgoal before "changeDISK." You will get another chance to enter the correct path name when lineinput_repeat succeeds again.

Once the directory path is set, you can list all the files in that directory by choosing the "Nodes/Directory" option.

LIST CURRENT DIRECTORY: (Nodes/Directory)

This option is an easy one to program: get the current directory path (disk(PATH)), display a window (dirwindow), then use the built-in "dir" predicate to display the directory. All these steps are subgoals of "pdwaction(1,5)":

```
pdwaction(1,5):-
  shiftwindow(OLD),
  disk(PATH),
  dirwindow,
  dir(PATH,"*.hyp",_,1,1,1),
  removewindow,
  shiftwindow(OLD),!.
% if user presses ESC, then the action succeeds
pdwaction(1,5):-
  removewindow.    % remove dirwindow
pdwaction(1,5).
```

EXIT TEMPORARILY TO DOS: (Nodes/Operating system)

This option doesn't need much explanation. All there is to it is the call to the built-in "system" predicate.

```
pdwaction(1,7):- system("").
```

EDITING HYPERTEXT: (Edit)

All the viewing, adding, and deleting of hypertext is done through the editor. The editor is the predicate "hyperEDIT." The programming of hyperEDIT was discussed in PART ONE, Chapter 2 and 3. The pull-down menu predicate "pdwaction(2,0)" starts the edit mode for us:

```
pdwaction(2,0):-
  shiftwindow(OLD),
  getCURRENT(currentFILE(Fname)),
  getCURRENT(currentPOS(INpos)),
  shiftwindow(2),     % shift to the editwindow window
  hyperEDIT(Fname,INpos,OUTpos),
  updateCURRENT(currentPOS(OUTpos)),
  shiftwindow(OLD).
```

CONFIGURING ET: (Configure)

The submenu under this option lists four operations, all having to do with network configuration files. These are operations for:

- Loading a configuration file (Configure/Load network)
- Deleting a configuration file (Configure/Delete network)
- Writing current configuration file to another file (Configure/Write to)
- Saving current configuration file (Configure/Save network)

Loading a Configuration File: (Configure/Load network)

A configuration file is not a text file; it is a knowledge-base file. So "loading" a configuration file is the consultation of the knowledge-base in that file. To consult a knowledge-base file, you must use the built-in predicate "consult." For example, to consult a configuration file called "test.net," this goal is given:

```
consult("test.net")
```

However, if the facts in the knowledge-base belong to a special database domain (a domain other than "dbasedom") you use this form:

```
consult("test.net",hypdb)
```

Here, the second argument is a symbol (hypdb) that represents the database domain. Look at "pdwaction(3,1)" which is responsible for loading the network configuration file:

```
pdwaction(3,1):-
  shiftwindow(OLD),
  cursor(R,_), Row=R+1,
  readfilename(Row,35,15,112,net,"",Fname),
  consult(Fname,hypdb),
  updateCURRENT(currentCONFIG(Fname)),
  shiftwindow(OLD).
pdwaction(3,1).
```

In the first clause, the subgoal "consult(Fname,hypdb)" loads the knowledge-base in the computer's memory.

Deleting a Configuration File: (Configure/Delete network)

When executing this option, ET will delete the whole knowledge-base from memory. To delete all database facts in a knowledge-base, use the built-in predicate "retractall." All that's needed to delete the network configuration from memory is to use "retractall" as a subgoal to "pdwaction(3,2)":

```
pdwaction(3,2):-
  retractall(_,hypdb).
pdwaction(3,2).
```

Notice that the anonymous variable "_" is used as the first argument to "retractall." This will instruct Turbo Prolog to retract from memory any hypertext database fact (a fact with "hypdb" as its database domain).

Writing the Current Configuration to a File: (Configure/Write to)

Again, this option is a very straightforward application of a built-in predicate. Here, the built-in predicate is "save." This predicate takes a filename and a database domain, and saves the current knowledge-base to that file.

```
pdwaction(3,3):-
  shiftwindow(OLD),
  cursor(Row,_), R=Row+1,
  readfilename(R,35,15,112,net,"",Fname),
  save(Fname,hypdb),
  shiftwindow(OLD).
pdwaction(3,3).
```

Saving Current Configuration to the File: (Configure/Save network)

This option is similar to "Configure/Write to." The only difference is that in "Configure/Save" ET saves the knowledge-base to the current network configuration file. While in "Configure/Write to," ET first prompts for a filename, and then saves the knowledge-base to that file. ET uses two "pdwaction(3,4)" clauses to execute the "Configure/Save" option:

```
pdwaction(3,4):-
  getCURRENT(currentCONFIG(Fname)),
  save(Fname,hypdb).
pdwaction(3,4).
```

QUITTING ET: (Quit)

When you pick the "Quit" option, Turbo executes "pdwaction(4,0)." The first clause in this predicate will cause the pull-down menu to fail. When this happens, Turbo removes the entire menu system from the screen and "pull-down" succeeds.

```
pdwaction(4,0):- !, fail.
pdwaction(_,_).
```

The cut (!) is used before "fail" to make sure that Turbo does not backtrack and tries the next pdwaction clause.

By this, I come to the end of this chapter. In the next chapter I will discuss knowledge representation for hypertext application.

7

A Database for Hypertext

"The first step in pattern recognition work begins with data taking or measurement, and the second step is the application of preprocessing and processing raw data to extract pertinent and useful features. The distinction between these two steps is merely conceptual, and in reality the two should be intimately intertwined. The purpose of feature extraction must be already present in mind when we take the 'raw' data. In other words, it is desirable that the data be already as close as possible to what may be considered as features."

—*Satosi Watanabe*, from his book *Pattern Recognition: Human and Mechanical.*

What you can learn from Watanabe's observation is that you never acquire raw data. What your senses receive and your mind recognizes is knowledge. If there is anything that you might call raw data—that is, unfiltered and unstructured data—you will not be able to recognize it as is. This is simply because without the filtering (the interpretation) which the mind does, there will be no recognition. What does this have to do with hypertext? What you want to see in hypertext is knowledge—a collection of related ideas, not a database of items. Databases and data retrieval mechanisms are tools that you can use to build efficient knowledge-based systems. The user of hypertext systems need not be aware of the database or the commands associated with it. The database (if there is any) in a hypertext system should be transparent to the user.

Up to this point, I have talked about building hypertext systems using only files. This is sufficient for most hypertext applications, especially with Turbo Prolog doing all the knowledge representation and reasoning for you. Prolog itself is a deductive relational-database system. To make things more efficient you can still use some help from databases. Turbo Prolog comes with a set of predicates for building external databases. These predicates can be used to build hypertext systems that can efficiently access a large database of nodes and links. You can have this database in memory, but if you need more room you can put it on disk or extended memory system (EMS).

In this chapter I will go over the knowledge representation scheme I have used so far in my hypertext programming in Turbo Prolog. After that, I will discuss the use of external databases in Turbo Prolog and how you can use it in writing efficient hypertext applications. The introduction of external databases will bear fruit in PART THREE when MicroIBIS, group decision support system hypertext tool, is discussed.

STRUCTURE OF KNOWLEDGE IN ET

In designing ET I used a simple database of nodes and links. Nodes are files, points are strings, and links are Prolog relations. Nodes and points are compound objects defined in the domain section of the program in this way:

```
DOMAINS
  FILENAME = STRING
  NODE = node(FILENAME)
  POINT= point(STRING)
```

On the other hand, I define the relations in the internal database section of the program in this way:

```
DATABASE - hypdb
  nnlink(NODE,NODE)
  pnlink(POINT,NODE,NODE)
  pplink(POINT,NODE,POINT,NODE)
```

These relations are needed as database predicates so you can create and delete links dynamically. This way when you need to create a new link, you assert its relation to the database. To delete an already existing link, you just need to retract its relation from the database.

Notice that the database of link relations has the label "hypdb." The "hypdb" label is used to distinguish the hypertext relations database from other databases in the program. For example, there is another database declaration section labeled "maindb." In this database bookkeeping predicates are kept on the status of the program:

```
DATABASE - maindb
  currentFILE(STRING)
  currentPOS(INTEGER)
```

```
currentSTR(STRING)
currentCONFIG(STRING)
```

Labeling internal database sections is a very handy Turbo Prolog feature. You can partition the database of facts of the program in several sections. When you consult, assert, retract, or save facts in a database you use a special form of the consult, assert, retract, and save predicates. Here are the declarations for the predicates to manipulate several internal database sections:

```
asserta(<fact>,DatabaseSectionName)
assertz(<fact>,DatabaseSectionName)
retract(<fact>,DatabaseSectionName)
retractall(<fact>,DatabaseSectionName)
save(<fact>,DatabaseSectionName)
consult(DOSFileName,DatabaseSectionName)
```

With different database sections you can add, delete, consult, or save facts from one section independent of the other. In ET you consult all the link relation predicates declared in "hypdb" section, from a file with the ".net" extension. This file is called a hypertext-network configuration file. To consult this file you would give the goal:

```
consult("config.net",hypdb).
```

On the other hand, ET creates all the facts declared in the "maindb" section at run time. This is all that you need to know to build a hypertext system using internal databases. Now on to the subject of external databases. In the next section I will show you how to create hypertext networks directly on disks, extended memory systems, or in memory using external databases.

EXTERNAL DATABASES IN TURBO PROLOG

Practical hypertext applications could have thousands of nodes and links in one network. The RAM requirements of such a network can easily exceed the capacity of the computer. With external databases you can have an efficient handling of very large hypertext networks on disk. You can put the database in memory, in a file, or in EMS-type expanded memory cards. The data stored in the database are Prolog terms (a variable, a number, a string, a compound object, or a list). In the following I will go over the basics of external databases. In this review I will give examples on building an external hypertext database. For more details on external databases please refer to the Turbo Prolog 2.0 User's Guide.

Database Selectors

For each database you create, you must give it a unique descriptor which is called a "database selector." This way you can have several external databases open simultaneously. You declare database selectors using the "db_selector'' domain this way:

```
DOMAINS
  db_selector = linkdb ; nodedb
```

You operate on a particular database by using the selector of that database.

Database Reference Numbers

When you add a new term to the database, Turbo Prolog assigns it a unique ''database reference number.'' Later you can use this reference number to retrieve, delete, or replace the term associated with it. To manipulate database terms you will need to write predicates with database terms as their arguments. To do that you need to declare the predicate arguments belonging to the standard domain ''ref.'' Here are the declarations for three predicates using the ''ref'' domain:

```
DOMAINS
  db_selector = nodedb
  refLIST = ref*
PREDICATES
  loadDBnode(ref)
  updateNODEstring(ref,STRING,STRING)
  loadDBnodes(reflist)
```

The predicate ''loadDBnode'' would load the node referenced by ''ref'' from the database. The predicate ''updateNODEstring'' retrieves the string of a node referenced by ''ref,'' updates the string, and returns it in the third argument. While ''loadDBnodes'' load all the nodes in the database ''nodedb.''

Creating, Opening, and Closing a Database File

To build an external database you must first create one. When you do that you need to tell Turbo where to place the database. You can place the database in a file, in memory, or in EMS-type extended memory. The predicate used to create and place a database, is ''db_create'' which has this declaration:

```
  db_create(DB_selector, Name, Place)
  /* Flow pattern: (i,i,i) */
```

Where DB_selector is a database selector. Place can take one of three values: in_file, in_memory, or in_ems. If you place the database in a disk file, the name of the file will be Name. If you choose to place the database in EMS or in memory, then you will need Name when you close the database.

When you create a database, it will be automatically opened for reading and writing. To read and write in a previously created database you explicitly need to open it for reading and writing. You can do that with built-in predicate ''db_open'' which has this declaration:

```
db_open(DB_selector, Name, Place)
/* flow pattern: (i,i,i) */
```

Once you are done with a database you can close it using the built-in predicate "db_close":

```
db_close(DB_selector) /* flowpattern: (i) */
```

while to delete a database you can use "db_delete":

```
db_delete(Name, Place) /* flowpattern: (i,i) */
```

There are other useful built-in predicates for manipulating external databases. You will not go into the details of describing these predicates. You will just list these predicates. For a detailed description of these predicates please refer to the User's Guide:

```
db_copy(DB-selector,Name,Place)               /* (i,i,i) */
db_openinvalid(DB_selector,Name,Place)        /* (i,i,i) */
db_flush(DB_selector)                         /* (i) */
db_garbagecollect(DB_selector)                /* (i) */
db_statistics(DB_selector,NoOfTerms,
               MemSize,FreeSize)              /* (i,o,o,o,o) */
db_chains(DB_selector, ChainName)             /* (i,o) */
db_btrees(DB_selector, BtreeName)             /* (i,o) */
```

Database Chains

Turbo Prolog's External database stores terms in chains—one chain for each set of related terms. For example, one chain might contain link relations, with another containing node relations. An external database might contain any number of chains. Using chains, you can view the database as a "table," with a chain for each relation representing the rows of the table. The columns or fields of the table are represented by the arguments of the relations. For example, you can have your hypertext nodes in one chain and the links in another. Take a look at the program in FIG. 7-1. In this program a hypertext database "hypdb" is declared with two chains "nodes" and "links."

Inserting and Retrieving Terms

To insert a term in an external database, you must insert the term into a named chain. You do this by using the built-in predicates "chain_inserta," chain_insertz," and "chain_insertafter." In FIG. 7-1 "chain_insertz" is used to add two node terms and one link term to the database "hypdb." Here are the declarations for the term insertion predicates:

```
chain_inserta(DB_Selector,Chain,Domain ,Term,Ref)
Flowpattern: (i,i,i,i,o)

chain_insertz(DB_selector,Chain,Domain,Term,Ref )
Flowpattern: (i,i,i,i,o)
```

```
chain_insertafter(DB_selector,Domain,Ref,Term,NewRef)
Flowpattern: (i,i,i,i,o)
```

Notice the flow pattern of these predicates. For every term inserted into the database, Turbo returns a unique reference number (the "o" for output in the flow pattern). Once you have this reference number, you can use it later to retrieve, replace, or delete its term in the database.

Given that you have the reference number of a term you can retrieve it from the database with "ref_term" which has this declaration:

```
ref_term(DB_selector,Domain,Ref,Term)
flowpattern: (i,i,i,o)
```

In FIG. 7-1, I used "ref_term" in "retrieveHYPnet" predicate to retrieve two node terms. Probably you have noticed that I used a different approach to retrieve "link(REF1,REF2)." This is because I wanted to use Turbo Prolog's backtracking feature to instantiate "link(REF1,REF2)" to some term in the database. The built-in predicate "chain_terms" which has the form:

```
chain_terms(DB_selector, Chain, Domain, Term, Ref)
flowpattern: (i,i,i,o,o)
```

uses backtracking to bind "Term" and "Ref" to each term and its reference number in "Chain." Other retrieval operations are possible not for terms but for reference numbers. Here is a list of built-in predicates for retrieving reference numbers:

```
chain_first(DB_selector, Chain, FirstRef)
flowpattern: (i,i,o)

chain_last(DB_selector, Chain, LastRef)
flowpattern: (i,i,o)

chain_next(DB_selector, Chain, NextRef)
flowpattern: (i,i,o)

chain_prev(DB_selector, Chain, PrevRef)
flowpattern: (i,i,o)
```

These built-in predicates return a reference number. To get the term itself, you can use "ref_term." For example, to get the next node in the database you can give the following goal:

```
chain_next(hypdb, nodes, REF),
ref_term(hypdb,nodes,REF,TERM).
```

A related term retrieval issue is searching for the term in the database. For an efficient database search you should use B+ trees (which is part of the external database system). I will not cover B+ trees here. You should review the section on B+ trees in the User's Guide.

Fig. 7-1. External database chains for nodes and links.

```
DOMAINS
  db_selector = hypdb
  nodes = node(string)
  links = link(ref,ref)

PREDICATES
  retrieveHYPnet

GOAL
% create the database hypdb.

db_create(hypdb, "hypertext.dba",in_file),

% insert node facts in nodes in hypdb

chain_insertz(hypdb,nodes,nodes,
                    node("First {hypdb} node"), REF1),
chain_insertz(hypdb,nodes,nodes,
                    node("Second hypdb node"), REF2),

% insert a link fact in links in hypdb

chain_insertz(hypdb,links,links,link(REF1,REF2),_),

% retrieve  the network

retrieveHYPnet,

% close the database

db_close(hypdb),

% delete the database file from the disk

db_delete("hypertext.dba",in_file).


CLAUSES

retrieveHYPnet :-
  chain_terms(hypdb, links, links, link(REF1,REF2), _),
  ref_term(hypdb, nodes, REF1, NODE1),
  write("The node: ",NODE1,"\n"),
  ref_term(hypdb, nodes, REF2, NODE2),
  write("\nis linked to this node: ",NODE2).

/* ******************* END END END *********************** */
```

Replacing and Deleting Terms

A term in the database is updated by replacing it with a new version of the term. The built-in predicate "term_replace" replaces an old term referenced by a reference number with a new term:

```
term_replace(DB_selector, Domain, OldTermRef, NewTerm)
flow pattern: (i,i,i,i)
```

To delete a term from the database I use "term_delete," given that I know its reference number:

```
term_delete(DB_selector, Chain, Ref)
flowpattern: (i,i,i)
```

If you need to delete a complete chain of terms, you can use "chain_delete":

```
chain_delete(DB_selector, Chain)
flowpattern: (i,i)
```

Up until now I have covered the basics of using external databases in Turbo Prolog. In the next section I will build database manipulation predicates using built-in predicates.

Building Higher Level Database Manipulation Predicates

In writing hypertext programs you will rarely use built-in predicates by themselves. The built-in external database predicates are no exception. For example, to open an external database, you need more than just using "db_-open." If the database file does not exist you must display an error message. In FIG. 7-2, the predicate "openDBfile" takes three arguments: a database selector, a database filename, and a database place for opening the database. The first subgoal of the first clause of "openDBfile" checks if the database file exists. If the database file does not exist, the first clause fails, and Turbo Prolog matches the second clause. The second clause writes a message saying that the database file doesn't exist or marked as invalid.

Also, in FIG. 7-2 is the predicate "createDBfile" which uses "db_create" to create a new database. Before creating a new database file, the first clause of "createDBfile" checks to see if the file already exists. If the file doesn't exist, the second clause uses "db_create" to create the database.

The third predicate in FIG. 7-2 is "closeDBfile." Notice the internal database fact "dbSTATUS" in the first clause of "closeDBfile." When you first create or open a database, you assert the fact "dbSTATUS(opened)." To close a database, the first clause of "closeDBfile" checks if the database is already open. Here, "dbSTATUS" succeeds and "db_close" closes the database. The last subgoal, "update," updates the database status by retracting "dbSTATUS-(opened)" and asserting "dbSTATUS(closed)."

Fig. 7-2. Creating, opening, and closing database files.

```
DOMAINS

  db_selector = hypdbdb
  file = hybtxt
  STRINGLIST = STRING*

DATABASE - currentdb
/* ********************* current database *************** */

% current system configuration used for updating

currentFILE(STRING)
```

(**Fig. 7-2.** continued)

```
dbSTATUS(SYMBOL)

/* ****************************************************** */
/*                   UTILITY PREDICATES                   */
/* ****************************************************** */

PREDICATES

update(currentdb)

CLAUSES
/* ************************ update *********************** */

update(dbSTATUS(_)):- retract(dbSTATUS(_)), fail.
update(X):- asserta(X).

/* ****************************************************** */
/*              EXTERNAL DATABASE PREDICATES              */
/* ****************************************************** */

PREDICATES

openDBfile(db_selector,STRING,place)
createDBfile(db_selector,STRING,place)
closeDBfile(db_selector)

CLAUSES

/* ********************** openDBfile ******************** */

openDBfile(DBselector,NAME,Place):-
   existfile(NAME),
   writelist(["Opening DB file ",NAME]),
   db_open(DBselector,NAME,Place),                /* @ */
   update(dbSTATUS(opened)),
   write("DB file ",NAME," is opened\n"), !.

% Database file "NAME" doesn't exist.


openDBfile(_,NAME,_):-
   write("Database file ",NAME," doesn't exist\n"), !,
   fail.


/* ***************** createDBfile ********************** */

createDBfile(_,NAME,_):-
   existfile(NAME),
   write("file already exists\n"),
   !, fail.
createDBfile(DBselector,NAME,Place):-
   closeDBfile(DBselector),
   write("creating file ",NAME,"\n"),
   db_create(DBselector,NAME,Place),              /* @ */
   update(dbSTATUS(opened)),
   write("File ",NAME," is created\n"), !.

/* ********************** closeDBfile ***************** */

closeDBfile(DBselector):-
  dbSTATUS(opened),   % we can only close an opened db file.
  db_close(DBselector),                           /* @ */
  update(dbSTATUS(closed)), !.
```

(**Fig. 7-2.** continued)

```
closeDBfile(_):- update(dbSTATUS(closed)).

/* ****************** END END END *********************** */
```

Hypertext Networks in External Databases

In this section I will show you how to build hypertext networks in external databases. Start with the domain declarations section of the program:

```
DOMAINS
  db_selector = hypdbdb
  file = hybtxt
  SOURCEref,TARGETref= ref
  ATTtype = SYMBOL
  ATTvalue = str(STRING); int(INTEGER);
             sym(SYMBOL); lst(ATTvalues)
  ATTvalues = ATTvalue*
  ATT = att(ATTtype,ATTvalue)
  ATTlist = ATT*
  REFlist=ref*
  LINKLIST   = LINK*
  STRINGLIST = STRING*
  NODE = node(ATTlist)
  LINK = link(SOURCEref,TARGETref,ATTlist)
  NET = net(REFlist)
```

In these declarations I define a node by a list of attributes. An *attribute* is a compound object with two arguments, attribute type and attribute value. For example, a node might have a label, a textual content, and a set of keywords to help identify the subject of its content:

```
node([att(label,sym(abstract)),
  att(keywords,lst([sym(database),sym(hypertext)])),
  att(contents,str("Hypertext in Ext. Database"))]).
```

As for links, a link has source and target nodes and a list of link attributes. Notice that the source and target of a link are not nodes but database reference numbers of nodes. Also, this applies to the hypertext network. A hypertext network, defined by "net(REFlist)," is just a list of reference numbers of nodes and links. As for the actual nodes and links you can save them in two database chains: "nodech" and "linkch." Take a look at the program in FIG. 7-3. In this program, fragments of a would-be hypertext system are shown.

Fig. 7-3. Hypertext system using external database.

```
DOMAINS

  db_selector = hypdbdb
  file = hybtxt
  SOURCEref,TARGETref= ref
```

(**Fig. 7-3.** continued)

```
  ATTtype = SYMBOL
  ATTvalue = str(STRING); int(INTEGER);
             sym(SYMBOL); lst(ATTvalues)
  ATTvalues = ATTvalue*
  ATT = att(ATTtype,ATTvalue)
  ATTlist = ATT*
  REFlist=ref*
  LINKLIST    = LINK*
  STRINGLIST = STRING*
  NODE = node(ATTlist)
  LINK = link(SOURCEref,TARGETref,ATTlist)
  NET = net(REFlist)

DATABASE - currentdb

/* ********************* current database *************** */
% current system configuration used for updating

currentFILE(STRING)
currentNODEatt(ATTlist)
currentLINKatt(ATTlist)
currentNODEref(ref)
currentLINKref(ref)
currentNET(REFlist)
dbSTATUS(SYMBOL)
deleteSTATUS(REFLIST)

/* ****************************************************** */
/*                1. UTILITY PREDICATES                   */
/* ****************************************************** */

PREDICATES

update(currentdb)
writelist(STRINGLIST)

CLAUSES
/* *********************** update *********************** */

update(currentFILE(_)):- retract(currentFILE(_)), fail.
update(currentNODEatt(_)):- retract(currentNODEatt(_)), fail.
update(currentLINKatt(_)):- retract(currentLINKatt(_)), fail.
update(currentNODEref(_)):- retract(currentNODEref(_)), fail.
update(currentLINKref(_)):- retract(currentLINKref(_)), fail.
update(currentNET(_)):- retract(currentNET(_)), fail.
update(dbSTATUS(_)):- retract(dbSTATUS(_)), fail.
update(X):- asserta(X).


/* ********************* listwrite ********************** */

writelist([]):- write("\n"), !.
writelist([H|T]):- write(H), writelist(T).

/* ****************************************************** */
/*       2. EXTERNAL DATABASE PREDICATES                  */
/* ****************************************************** */

PREDICATES

createDBfile(db_selector,STRING,place)
openDBfile(db_selector,STRING,place)
closeDBfile(db_selector)
```

(**Fig. 7-3.** continued)

```
makeDBfile(db_selector,STRING)
loadDBfile(db_selector,STRING)
copyDBfile(db_selector,STRING)

loadNODE(db_selector,ref)
updateNcurrent(db_selector,ref)

initCURRENTdb(db_selector,STRING)
editNODE

updateONEatt(SYMBOL,ATT)
replaceATT_in(ATT,ATTlist,ATTlist)
ATT_in(ATT,ATTlist)


CLAUSES

/* ****************** createDBfile ********************** */

createDBfile(_,NAME,_):-
   existfile(NAME),
   write("file already exists\n"),
   !, fail.
createDBfile(DBselector,NAME,Place):-
   closeDBfile(DBselector),
   write("creating file ",NAME,"\n"),
   db_create(DBselector,NAME,Place),                   /* @ */
   update(dbSTATUS(opened)),
   write("File ",NAME," is created\n"), !.

/* ********************** openDBfile ******************* */

openDBfile(DBselector,NAME,Place):-
   existfile(NAME),
   writelist(["Opening DB file ",NAME]),
   db_open(DBselector,NAME,Place),                     /* @ */

   update(dbSTATUS(opened)),
   write("DB file ",NAME," is opened\n"), !.

% Database file "NAME" doesn't exist.

openDBfile(_,NAME,_):-
   write("Database file ",NAME," doesn't exist\n"), !,
   fail.

/* *********************** closeDBfile ****************** */

closeDBfile(DBselector):-
  dbSTATUS(opened),    % we can only close an opened db file.
  db_close(DBselector),                                /* @ */
  update(dbSTATUS(closed)), !.

closeDBfile(_):- update(dbSTATUS(closed)).

/* ***************** loadDBfile ************************* */

loadDBfile(DBselector,NewFileName):-
  closeDBfile(DBselector),
  openDBfile(DBselector,NewFileName,in_file),
  initCURRENTdb(DBselector,NewFileName),
  chain_terms(DBselector,node_chain,node,_,Ref),
  loadNODE(DBselector,Ref),!.
```

(**Fig. 7-3.** continued)

```
/* ****************** makeDBfile ************************ */

makeDBfile(DBselector,NewFileName):-
  createDBfile(DBselector,NewFileName,in_file),
  update(dbSTATUS(opened)),
  initCURRENTdb(DBselector,NewFileName), !.

makeDBfile(_,_).

/* ***************** copyDBfile ************************* */

copyDBfile(DBselector,NewFileName):-
  currentFILE(NAME),
  NewFileName <> NAME,
  not(existfile(NewFileName)),
  db_copy(DBselector,NewFileName,in_file).            /* @ */

copyDBfile(_,NewFileName):-
  writelist([NewFileName," Exist, or","\n",
             "can't copy file on itself."]).


/* ******************** loadNODE *********************** */

/* this predicate checks if the REF of a node to be loaded
   is the same as the current node, if so it does nothing.
   Else it would load the new node and update the current
   db facts. */
loadNODE(_,Nref):-
  currentNODEref(Nref),
  editNODE, !.

loadNODE(DBselector,Nref):-
  currentNODEref(Cref),
  % before loading the new node, save current node
  updateNcurrent(DBselector,Cref),
  % make new node the current node
  updateNcurrent(DBselector,Nref),
  editNODE, !.

/* currently there is no current node */
loadNODE(DBselector,Nref):-
  updateNcurrent(DBselector,Nref),
  editNODE, !.

/* ****************** updateNcurrent ****************** */

/* if the node passed to updateNcurrent is an update to the
   current node (replacement) then call trem_replace.     */

updateNcurrent(DBselector,Ref):-
  currentNODEref(Ref),
  currentNODEatt(ATTlist),
  term_replace(DBselector,node,Ref,node(ATTlist)).   /* @ */

/* if the node passed to updateNcurrent is a new node ref,
   then make this node the current node.  */

updateNcurrent(DBselector,NewRef):-
  ref_term(DBselector,node,NewRef,NewNode),          /* @ */
  NewNode = node(ATTlist),
  update(currentNODEatt(ATTlist)),
  update(currentNODEref(NewRef)).

updateNcurrent(_,_).
```

(**Fig. 7-3.** continued)

```
/* ******************* initCURRENTdb ********************* */

initCURRENTdb(DBselector,NAME):-
  dbSTATUS(opened), % we only initialize when db is open
  chain_terms(DBselector,net_chain,net,NET,_),      /* @ */
  NET = net(REFlist),
  update(currentNET(REFlist)),
  update(currentFILE(NAME)), !.

/* ******************* editNODE   ************************** */

editNODE:-
  currentNODEatt(ATTlist),
  ATT_in(att(contents,str(INstr)),ATTlist),
  makewindow(1,7,7,"NODE EDITOR",0,0,24,80),
  edit(INstr,OUTstr),
  replaceATT_in(att(contents,str(OUTstr)),ATTlist,NewATTlist),
  update(currentNODEatt(NewATTlist)).

/* ******************* updateONEatt ********************* */

updateONEatt(node,ATT):-
  currentNODEatt(ATTlist),
  replaceATT_in(ATT,ATTlist,NewATTlist),
  update(currentNODEatt(NewATTlist)).

updateONEatt(link,ATT):-
  currentLINKatt(ATTlist),
  replaceATT_in(ATT,ATTlist,NewATTlist),
  update(currentLINKatt(NewATTlist)).

/* ***************** replaceATT_in ********************** */

/* replace the value of one attribute in the current node's
   list of attributes. */

replaceATT_in(_,[],_):- !, fail.
replaceATT_in(att(T,V),[att(T,_)|Rest],[att(T,V)|Rest]):-!.
replaceATT_in(ATT,[NotATT|Rest],[NotATT|Rest1]):-
  replaceATT_in(ATT,Rest,Rest1).

/* ******************* ATT_in *************************** */

/* match one attribute in a list of attributes */

ATT_in(_,[]):- !, fail.
ATT_in(att(Type,Value),[att(Type,Value)|_]):-!.
ATT_in(ATT,[_|Rest]):-
  ATT_in(ATT,Rest).

/* ****************** END END END *********************** */
```

As you can see I don't deal directly with nodes and links themselves. Rather, I mainly deal with database selectors, chain names, and reference numbers. The program shows you how to load, edit, and update the contents of nodes. Study carefully the programming techniques in FIG. 7-2. You will find many techniques which you can use in writing your own external database hypertext system. In PART THREE, I will use many of these techniques to build a hypertext-based problem solving system called "MicroIBIS."

8

Hypertext and Logic Programming

"To understand why hypertext is attracting such attention, one must understand how a hypertext "document" differs from a conventional paper document. In most conventional paper documents—such as journal articles, specifications, or novels—physical and logical structures are closely related. Physically, the document is a long linear sequence of words that has been divided into lines and pages for convenience. Logically, the document is linear too. The logic is that of sequences of building blocks. We combine words to form sentences. We group sentences to form paragraphs, and we use paragraphs to form sections and so on. If the document has a hierarchical logical structure, as do many expository documents such as journal articles, that hierarchy is presented linearly: the abstract or overview of the whole comes first, followed by the introduction, the first section, the second section, etc., until the conclusion."

—John B. Smith and Stephen F. Weiss

Of course there is more to the logical structure of documents than the division of text into words, sentences, paragraphs, sections, and so on. For example, you can talk about:

- content vs. structure of hypertext
- attributes of hypertext objects
- major and minor topics in hypertext
- categories or classes of hypertext objects
- generalizations
- installations or specializations
- aggregations
- versions of a hypertext object
- contexts in hypertext
- filters
- relations

I will refer to these characteristics of hypertext as "abstractions."

With these possible features in mind you can construct a logical model of hypertext. Then, this model can serve as the basis for building hypertext systems. What does a logical model of hypertext look like?

To start with, I will discuss abstractions in general, and then focus on a few of these abstractions.

ABSTRACTIONS

In Webster's New World Dictionary the word "abstract" is an adjective meaning "thought or thinking apart from material objects." Therefore you can say that ideas are abstract things. When you say that a piece of rock has a cubic form you are referring to the abstract idea of a cube. The idea of a cube, being an enclosed-six-square-sided object, is an invention. You can equally apply it to a piece of wood, a piece of cake, a building, and so on. It is hard to imagine a world without abstractions. Look around you, right now. Just describe what you are seeing. Congratulations—you have just used abstractions to make sense of what you see.

You might think that abstractions are only good to understand or perceive things. They are more than that. You use abstractions to invent new things (new material objects such as cars, seats, books, houses, and so on). In other words, you use abstractions to perceive and make the world around you.

Abstraction has its origin deep in philosophy. Many philosophers talked about abstractions. Aristotle (384 – 322 B.C.) was the first one to talk about it. To Aristotle, substance is composed from matter and form. Form is the word Aristotle uses for abstraction. For him, your eyes can only draw out or perceive the matter, while the mind is the one which perceives the form. By this, Aristotle gave the first account of how abstractions help you perceive the world around you. The English philosopher John Lock (1632 – 1704), gave the second account of how abstractions can help in creating new things. Listen to what Lock has to say on that:

"Man has a power to discern and distinguish; he combines simple into complex ideas; he discovers relations among ideas by holding them together in the mind; he engages in abstraction, drawing what is common from a set of ideas and in this way producing abstract or general ideas. In these procedures he is engaging in the association of ideas. It is the process of association which explains the complexity possible to thought."

Notice that I highlighted the words "abstraction" and "association." Does the word "association" look familiar to you? Vanver Bush, the father of hypertext, talked about the differences between the way data is stored and retrieved in libraries, and the way it is done in our minds (see Vanver Bush, "As we think."):

"The human mind does not work that way. It operates by association. With one item in its grasp, it snaps instantly to the next that is suggested by the association of thoughts, in accordance with some intricate web of trails carried by the cells of the brain."

As you can see, abstraction leads to association, and association is the basis of understanding and thinking. Vanver Bush suggested that we should use computer systems to support association, and hypertext is that computer system. Then for hypertext to support association it must have the ability to deal with abstractions.

WHAT ADVANTAGES THERE ARE IN USING ABSTRACTIONS

The best way to show you the advantages of using abstractions in hypertext is by demonstration. To demonstrate these advantages I must first show you how to represent them in Prolog. Once you have the representation you can use it to query the hypertext knowledge-base, and possibly deduce new knowledge as well. Here is a list of some of these advantages:

- ability to detect information relevancy,
- a logical structure of information,
- a user can impose his own structure,
- support for collaborative work,
- separation between different kinds of information in a document,
- a descriptive definition of a revision control system.

REPRESENTING ABSTRACTIONS

If the hypertext system is a procedural program—i.e., a Pascal or C program—, you can apply abstraction techniques to the program's data structure. If, on the other hand, you have a knowledge-based hypertext (e.g., ET and MicroIBIS), abstractions will be an integral part of the knowledge-base. In this book I use Prolog to write knowledge-based hypertext systems. So I will talk about abstractions being part of the knowledge-base of a hypertext system. Because I use Prolog in writing the knowledge-based systems, I will first talk about representing abstractions in Prolog.

Representing Abstractions in Prolog

To increase the expressive power of your knowledge-based system you can represent your knowledge in an explicit structure. I will use Turbo Prolog as my knowledge representation language. The program in FIG. 8-1 is a regular Turbo Prolog program expressing a knowledge-base on lectures.

Notice that most of the relationships in FIG. 8-1 are simple—i.e., binary—and the course title (e.g., Design Theory) is their common denominator. Database specialists call this common denominator the main "search-key." This search-key is used to retrieve information across different relationships. Take the "lasts" and "occupied" rules in FIG. 8-1. In the "lasts" rule I use "Course" as my search-key to retrieve "Room," "Day," "From," and "To."

Fig. 8-1. Non-structured knowledge-base.

```
DOMAINS

  SYMBOLlist = SYMBOL*


PREDICATES

teaches(SYMBOL,SYMBOL)
instructor(SYMBOL)
starts(SYMBOL,INTEGER)
ends(SYMBOL,INTEGER)
building(SYMBOL,SYMBOL)
room_number(SYMBOL,INTEGER)
day(SYMBOL,SYMBOL)
semester(SYMBOL,SYMBOL)

lasts(SYMBOL,INTEGER)
occupied(INTEGER,SYMBOL,INTEGER,INTEGER)

CLAUSES

teaches("Horst Rittel","Design Theory").
starts("Design Theory",8).
ends("Design Theory",11).
building("Design Theory","Wurster Hall").
room_number("Design Theory",492).
day("Design Theory",wednesday).
day("Design Theory",monday).
semester("Design Theory",fall).

instructor(Name):-
  teaches(Name,_).

lasts(Course,Hours):-
  starts(Course,Time1),
  ends(Course,Time2),
  Hours=Time2-Time1.

occupied(Room,Day,From,To):-
  room_number(Course,Room),
  day(Course,Day),
  starts(Course,From),
  ends(Course,To).
```

The knowledge-base of FIG. 8-1 has implicit in it the concept of "location" of a lecture. Location includes both the building and the room number for the lecture. To extract the location you can write this rule:

```
location(Course,Building,RoomNumber):-
  building(Course,Building),
  room_number(Course,RoomNumber).
```

Another implicit concept in the knowledge-base is the "time" of the lecture in terms of semester, day, starting and ending time. Again I write a "time" rule to represent this concept:

```
time(Course,Semester,Day,Starting,Ending):-
  semester(Course,Semester),
  day(Course,Day),
  starts(Course,Starting),
  ends(Course,Ending).
```

Does "location" and "time" remind you of the idea of "factorization" from your Math class. It seems that in both of these rules I "reduced" several relationships to a single one. For example, in the "time" rule the head of the rule summarizes the information in "semester," "day," "starts," and "ends." In this sense, "location" and "time" are abstractions implicit in the program. Another abstraction in the same program is the concept of "instructor." A person who teaches one or more courses is an instructor. In FIG. 8-1 you can see how to abstract the "instructor" relationship from the "teaches" relationship:

```
instructor(NAME):-
  teaches(NAME,_).
```

To make abstractions (e.g., "time," "location," and "instructor") explicit you need to add more structure to the program. One way to do this is to use compound-objects. Each abstraction is defined as a compound-object. Take a look at the program in FIG. 8-2. This program is a modified version of the one in FIG. 8-1.

The domains section in FIG. 8-2 contains definitions for four abstractions: "time," "schedule," "instructor," and "location." For example, the "schedule" abstraction:

```
schedule = schedule(semester,times)
```

is a compound object with two attributes: The "semester" of the schedule, and the list "times" for the classes of the schedule. The "times" attribute is a list of "time" abstractions:

```
time = time(day,hour,hour)
times = time*
```

Having defined abstractions as compound-objects, I can write rules in a more abstract way. For example, the "teaches" rule retrieves the whole "instructor" compound-object. In writing this rule I ignored irrelevant details about the parts of the "instructor" object. On the other hand, the "occupied" rule

Fig. 8-2. Structuring the knowledge-base.

```
DOMAINS
  semester, title, day, firstname, lastname, building = SYMBOL
  hour, room_number = INTEGER
  time = time(day,hour,hour)
  times = time*
  schedual = schedual(semester,times)
  instructor = instructor(firstname,lastname)
  location = location(building,room_number)

  SYMBOLlist = SYMBOL*

PREDICATES

course(title,instructor,schedual,location)

member(time,times)

teaches(instructor,title)
lasts(title,hour)
occupied(room_number,day,hour,hour)

CLAUSES

course("Design Theory",
       instructor(horst,rittel),
       schedual(fall,[ time(wednesday,8,11),
                       time(monday,8,11) ]),
       location(wurster_hall,492)).

teaches(Instructor,Course):-
  course(Course,Instructor,_,_).

lasts(COURSE,Hours):-
  course(COURSE,_,schedual(_,[time(_,T1,T2)|_]),_),
  Hours=T2-T1.

occupied(Room,Day,From,To):-
  course(_,_,schedual(_,Times),location(_,Room)),
  member(time(Day,From,To),Times).

member(X,[X|_]).
member(X,[_|Y]):- member(X,Y).
```

retrieves its four arguments "Room," "Day," "From," and "To" from two compound-objects ("location" and "time").

Two of the advantages for using abstractions in Prolog programs are:

- A higher descriptive and structural level than regular programs. This means the program is easier to read and understand by someone other than the programmer.
- This way, the programs are more modular. This means that changes in abstraction definitions or rules will not cause large changes in the program. For example, you can change the definition of:

```
instructor = instructor(firstname,lastname)
```

to

```
instructor = instructor(firstname,middlename, lastname)
```

without any change to the "teaches" rule.

The only disadvantage of using abstractions is that you need to write more code, which means more development time. This is not a high price to pay for the above advantages.

TYPES OF HYPERTEXT ABSTRACTIONS

In this section I will review several kinds of abstractions that are particularly useful in hypertext applications. While doing so, I will build a logical model of hypertext. I collected most of these abstractions from two pioneering articles on hypertext. The first article titled "A Survey of Hypertext" by Jeff Conklin. The second article titled "Abstraction Mechanisms in Hypertext" by Pankaj K. Garg. The logical model of hypertext is a direct forward translation of "Garg's abstraction mechanisms" into Turbo Prolog. The abstractions which I will cover are:

- content vs. structure
- hypertext objects
- attributes of hypertext objects
- major and minor ideas or topics
- bookmarks
- generalizations
- aggregates
- versions
- views or perspectives
- contexts of hypertext
- filters

These abstractions are not independent. Some of these abstractions will serve as building blocks for others. For example, the first four abstractions (content, structure, objects, and attributes) are necessary elements in representing most of the other abstractions. You can say that the first three abstractions are elementary abstractions, while the rest of the abstractions are composite. To represent both the elementary and the composite abstractions, I divide this discussion into two steps.

1) representing the elementary abstractions
2) representing some of the composite abstractions.

While doing this I will be using a logical representation of these abstractions in Prolog. This logical representation could form the basis of a logical model of hypertext.

REPRESENTING ELEMENTARY ABSTRACTIONS

Two of the elementary abstractions are "object" and "relationship" or "predicate." An object can stand for a physical or conceptual entity. A physical entity could be a database record, a file, or a text string. An example of a conceptual entity is the network structure holding hypertext nodes together.

Representing Objects

To identify objects you need object identifiers. In this case, an object identifier is either a constant Turbo Prolog atom, a compound object, or variable. For example take a look at the domains section in FIG. 8-3.

In FIG. 8-3 notice that there are simple and composite object definitions. For example, "info" (short for information) is a simple object. To define "info" I use compound objects:

```
info = str(STRING); ndx(STRING); exp(STRING);
       ref(STRING); cmd(STRING)
```

An information object could be: a text string str(STRING); an index button, ndx(STRING); an expansion button, exp(STRING); a reference button, ref-(STRING); or a command button, cmd(STRING). An example for a composite object is "item":

```
item        = item(pos,info)        /* hypertext items */
```

In "item" you define hypertext items being information objects and their positions in the hypertext node. Now you can use "item" to build more complex objects. In "obj" I do exactly that. One of "obj" definitions is "node(items)." This object, node(items), simply means that a hypertext node is a list of items. You will come to "node(items)" in the "CONTENT VS. STRUCTURE" section.

Fig. 8-3. The domains section showing object definitions.

```
DOMAINS
  pos       = INTEGER
  info      = str(STRING); ndx(STRING); exp(STRING);
              ref(STRING); cmd(STRING)
  infoLIST  = info*
  item      = item(pos,info)    /* hypertext items */
  items     = item*
  delta     = add(pos,info); rep(pos,info); del(pos,info)
  deltaseq  = delta*           /* a delta is a hypertext item */
  abs       = abs(obj,objLIST)
  obj       = sym(SYMBOL); str(STRING); chr(CHAR);
              inum(INTEGER); rnum(REAL); node(items);
              seq(deltaseq); dlt(delta); abs(obj,objLIST);
              lst(objLIST)

  objLIST   = obj*
```

Representing Relationships

Objects by themselves are meaningless. To make sense of the world of objects around you, relationships are needed. In Prolog you can represent relationships in two ways:

1) using predicates: here we can use two-place predicates, three-place predicates, and so on. . . . For example:

```
two-place predicate
  room_number_is(Course,RoomNumber)
  example: room_number_is("Introduction to AI",576)
three-place predicate
  property_of(Object,PropertyName,PropertyValue)
  example: property_of(blood,color,red)
```

You can be more explicit by using predicates to represent relationships in this way:

```
PREDICATES
  rel(SYMBOL,parm)                      % predicate or 1-place relationships
  rel(SYMBOL,parm,parm)                 % 2-place relationships
  rel(SYMBOL,parm,parm,parm)            % 3-place relationships
  rel(SYMBOL,parm,parm,parm,parm)       % 4-place relationships
```

In these predicate declarations, the first argument of the "rel" predicate is the name of the relationship. The rest of the arguments represent the related objects.

2) using compound object: in this case you treat a relationship as an object. You often use this approach in metalogical Prolog programming. For example, you can define the object "rel":

```
rel = rel(RelationName,RelatedObjects)
```

An example of this object is:

```
rel(expands_to,[peirce,"Charles Sanders Peirce,1839-1914."])
```

What I am saying here is that the predicate "expands_to" is a relation. The relation "expands_to" relates a keyword (in the example it is the first name of a person) to its full meaning. This approach gives the ability to pass relationship-objects between predicates. One of the advantages here is being able to represent the relationship between relationships. Here is an example:

```
follows(knows(X,Y),understands(X,Y)):-
  rel(understands,[X,Y,time(T1)]),
  rel(knows,[(X,Y,time(T2)]),
  T1 < T2.
```

The meta-relation "follows" represents the fact that "knowing" something is only possible after the "understanding" of that thing. I call "follows" a meta-relation because it is a relation between relations. It is a higher structural object than "knows and "understands." Now I'll stop talking about higher level structures and turn to the comparison between the content and structure of hypertext.

CONTENT vs. STRUCTURE

The word "content" usually refers to text, audio (sound), visual (graphics), or computer programming code in hypertext objects. "Structure" could mean two things: "physical structure" or "logical structure."

You can talk about the "physical" and "logical structures" for organizing hypertext objects. You usually organize regular paper documents or library reference cards in a sequential (physical) structure. The way you usually use these documents, or reference cards, is completely different. When reading a book you often jump between different sections and chapters. You rarely go from one chapter to the next or from one section to the next. I call the way I use these documents or reference cards "the logical structure" (see report by Jeff Conklin in the references section).

A few conventional paper documents—such as encyclopedias, dictionaries, and other reference works—separate "logical structure" from "physical structure." Physically, these documents are linear sequences of independent units, such as articles on specific topic or entries for individual words. Logically, they are more complex. When you read such documents you seldom read them from beginning to end. Rather, you search the document to locate a point of interest. In other words you use a random access approach to search for a certain entry. When you find what you are looking for you read that portion sequentially. However, you are likely to encounter various cross references to other entries. To get to the referenced entries you first locate the page, and volume if it is different from the current document. After you find the target entry you get to the specific point of interest of the reference.

Reference documents (e.g., encyclopedias, dictionaries, user manuals, and so on) are physically organized in a sequential way, but are used in a network-like way. When using these documents, your logical path is a network which goes forward and backward in the entire document or set of documents. Such documents are more flexible but they are also cumbersome—particularly when they appear in large, multivolume formats.

How do you differentiate between the content and structure of hypertext in your representation? In PART ONE I represented a network structure using Prolog relationships (e.g., link(nodeA,nodeB)). The content of nodes were simply text strings. In this chapter I will introduce a more elaborate representation of both structure and content.

Representing the Contents of a Node

Using Prolog terminology, a node is considered as a list of hypertext items. Each item is identified with a position. An item itself is a list of information objects. An information object could be a string of text or a hypertext button. A hypertext button could be: an index button, a command button, an expansion button, or a reference button. Items, information objects, string objects, and hypertext buttons are all abstractions. Here is a Turbo Prolog domain definition for these abstractions:

```
DOMAINS
  pos   = INTEGER
  info  = str(STRING); ndx(STRING); exp(STRING);
          ref(STRING); cmd(STRING)
  item  = item(pos,info)         /* hypertext items */
  items= item*
  node  = node(items)
```

As for the position of a hypertext item in a node, it is used to locate a certain item in a node. The position of an item depends upon the representation of a node. For example, in ET a node is a text file which has the ".hyp" extension. In these hypertext files I allow only two kinds of items: text strings and hypertext points. A hypertext point is a text string surrounded by two opposite brackets "{" and "}." Here "pos" will refer to the position of an item relative to the start of the file. For example, you have the contents of a node "N" being:

```
"From {Gibran's} masterpiece 'THE PROPHET': work is love made visible."
```

with "{Gibran's}" being a "reference point" referring to the "Gibran Kahlil Gibran," the author of "THE PROPHET." Now this node has three items:

1) From
2) {Gibran's}
3) masterpiece 'THE PROPHET': work is love made visible.

The positions of these items are: 0, 5, and 15 respectively. To use the domain definition of a node you would have this representation:

```
node([ item(0,str("From")),
  item(5,ref("Gibran's")),
  item(15,str("masterpiece 'THE PROPHET': work is
                love made visible.") ])
```

Another way to identify items within a node is by numbering them consecutively. Here "pos" will reflect the number of items in a node. Using the previous example you can have this node representation:

```
node( [ item(1,str("From")),
  item(2,ref("Gibran's')),
  item(3,str("masterpiece 'THE PROPHET': work is
                love made visible.") ])
```

Here the position of the first item is 1, the second item is 2, and the third item is 3.

Representing Properties of Objects

Object-properties help you identify and relate objects. They provide a higher level of identification than that of object-names. Properties are different from relationships. Relationships relate two or more objects to each other, while properties relate an object to its attributes. This doesn't mean you can't use relationships to represent properties. For example you can have this predicate definition of the property relationship:

```
PREDICATES
  property(OBJECTname,ATTRIBUTEname,ATTRIBUTEvalue)
```

Here the hypertext object "OBJECTname" has the property "ATTRIBUTEname" with a value of "ATTRIBUTEvalue." For example, maximum number of columns per line could be an attribute of a text node:

```
  property(introduction,number_of_lines,50)
```

Here the "number_of_lines" property of "introduction" has the value "50."

Kinds of Hypertext Objects

In Pankaj's article, "Abstraction Mechanisms in Hypertext," he talks about two kinds of hypertext objects.

1) Domain Objects, and
2) Information Objects: instances of domain objects.

A domain object contains information on the hypertext information itself. In other words, domain objects are higher level objects compared with the regular hypertext nodes. For example, you consider the guidelines on how to write a user's manual for a software system as domain information, while the user's manual itself is just an instance of the domain information. Information objects, on the other hand, are instances of predefined domain objects. So, to relate information objects to domain objects you can use an "instance_of" relationship:

```
  instance_of(InstanceObject,DomainObject)
```

and to relate all information objects belonging to the same category, you can use "instances":

```
  instances(DomainObject,ListOfInstanceObjects)
```

The set of all hypertext objects is the union of domain objects and their instance objects:

```
  union(HypertextObjects,DomainObjects,InstanceObjects)
```

Logically speaking you can define union this way:

```
DOMAINS
  SYMBOLLIST = SYMBOL*
PREDICATES
  union(SYMBOLLIST,SYMBOLLIST,SYMBOLLIST)
    in(SYMBOL,SYMBOLLIST,SYMBOLLIST)
CLAUSES
union(X,X,[]).
union([H  T],La,Lb):-
  in(H,La,La1),
  in(H,Lb,Lb1),
  union(T,La1,Lb1), !.
union([H×T],La,Lb):-
  in(H,La,La1),
  union(T,La1,Lb), !.
union([H  T],La,Lb):-
  in(H,Lb,Lb1),
  union(T,La,Lb1).
in(X,[X],[]).
in(X,[X  T],T):-!.
in(X,[H  T],[H  T1]):-
  in(X,T,T1).
```

In a strongly-defined hypertext system, every information object created must have a domain object.

COMPOSITE ABSTRACTIONS

To build composite abstractions, you use elementary abstractions. With composite abstractions you will be able to represent interesting hypertext concepts. Here are some of those composite hypertext abstractions.

Major and Minor Ideas or Topics

We can talk about the major and minor ideas of a document. For example, in an autobiography on Henry Ford, the major idea is the life of Henry Ford from childhood to his automobile manufacturing empire. One minor idea in such a biography could be the historical overview it provides on the auto industry at the turn of the century. Another minor idea could be that of politics during World War II.

Bookmarks

When reading a book or an article, and you need to stop in the middle of reading, you use tags to mark your place. If you have more than one tag in the same book you usually label these tags. For labels you often use keywords that describe the contents of the marked pages. How about having bookmarks in hypertext documents! You can do this in at least two ways:

1) By defining bookmarks as compound objects which could be part of items in the representation of a node:

```
node([item(0,str("BACK TO BASICS")),
  item(15,mark("innovation, US vs. Japan"),
  item(16,str("U.S. companies forgot that innovation
                means small but steady improvements—
                not just big breakthroughs. Now that's changing."),
  item(119,ref("BusinessWeek, 1989")]).
```

2) By defining bookmarks as attributes of hypertext objects:

```
property("BusinessWeek, 1989",
         bookmark,
         bm(15,"innovation, US vs. Japan")).
```

Here bookmark is defined as a compound-object of two arguments—the position of the mark and its label.

A very good example of using bookmarks in electronic documents is the one in the "Symbolics Document Examiner." The system allows the reader to place "bookmarks" on any page and to move swiftly between marked pages.

Generalization

Sometimes it is useful to refer to a class (category) of things rather than to a particular instance of the class. For example, in a technical paper you might use the terms natural-numbers, whole-numbers, and real-numbers. To help the non-technical reader of the paper you can provide generalization links to nodes with instances of natural, whole and real numbers. Consider this definition of a node:

```
node( [ item(1,str("In this unit we consider the set of")),
        item(2,ref("whole numbers")),
        item(3,str("and")),
        item(4,ref("natural numbers")),
        item(5,str("with the operations of ...") ]).
```

for which you need the two generalization relations:

```
rel(generalizes,"whole-numbers","the set {0,1,2,3,...}").
rel(generalizes,"natural-numbers","the set {1,2,3,...}").
```

A more familiar example of generalizations is the concept of illustration. An illustration can be a figure, a table, a photograph, an engineering drawing, an audio or a video clip. For example, in a hypertext-based tourist guide for San Francisco you might have a paragraph describing Lombard street. In that paragraph the word Lombard is a hypertext reference item:

```
node( [ item(1,ref("LOMBARD STREET,"),
        item(2,str("between Hyde and Leavenworth Str., is
                    often referred to as 'the most crooked
                    street in the world.' In a series of
                    S-curves, this one-block portion
                    descends a 40-degree slope. Stairs are
                    available. Do not try to negotiate
                    the street in a camper or trailer.") ]).
```

To give more information on the street, all you need now is to provide a relation between your reference item and an illustration abstraction. To do that you need a set of relations which should look something like this:

```
rel(illustration,X,Y):-
   rel(generalizes,illustration,List),
   member(Z,List),
   rel(Z,X,Y).
rel(generalizes,illustration,[map,picture,drawing]).
rel(picture,"LOMBARD STREET",cmd(display("LO_PIC_1"))).
rel(drawing,"LOMBARD STREET",cmd(display("LO_DRW_1"))).
rel(in_map_of, "LOMBARD STREET", "SAN FRANCISCO").
rel(map,"SAN FRANCISCO",cmd(display("SF_MAP"))).

rel(map,X,Y):-
   rel(in_map_of,X,Z),
   rel(map,Z,Y).
```

The first relation is a rule which abstracts the concept of illustration by generalizing three types of nodes: map nodes, picture nodes, and drawing nodes. When this rule is executed, its first subgoal will match the second relation, then "generalizes" fact. The third relation gives you the picture "LOMBARD STREET" as a command item. Notice that the command is expressed in the command item as a compound-object. When Turbo Prolog executes the picture relation, it will execute the command item "display("LO_PIC_1")". The fourth relation is similar in structure to the picture relation. The fifth relation specifies that the map of "LOMBARD STREET" is in the map of "SAN FRANCISCO." You need this because it is hard to find separate maps for each street or building in a city. The "in_map_of" relation is then used by the "map" rule (in the seventh relation) to locate "LOMBARD STREET."

Specialization

Specialization is the reverse of generalization. The set of numbers {0,1,2,3,...} is a specialization of the idea of whole-numbers. Figures, tables, photos are specialized forms of the idea of an illustration.

Aggregates

You could have objects which are "aggregates" of other objects. For example, you can view Turbo Prolog programs as aggregates of three kinds of sets: directives sets, declaration sets, and clauses sets. A declaration set can itself be an aggregate of domains, predicates and database declarations. This way you can talk about Turbo Prolog programs without having to bother about the details of what constitutes the program. Yet a higher level of abstraction could be the "software-project" which is a mixture of different modules written in different languages. For example, you can have a graphical-based expert-system which is an aggregate of two modules. The modules are: a graphic-interface written in C, and an inference-engine written in Turbo Prolog. With both C and the Turbo Prolog programs each being an aggregate in itself:

```
rel(aggregate,turbo_prolog,[directives,declarations, clauses]).
rel(aggregate,c,[declarations,functions]).
```

In a project like this the aggregated objects need not be dependent on each other. You might use an aggregate to capture ideas. One such idea is the plot in a novel. You can look at the plot as an aggregate of events. You can have different combinations of events forming different aggregates. Each aggregate would then stand for one possible plot. For a dramatic version of your story you can pick one plot to be the main theme. On the other hand, in a detective story you can choose to present the readers with more than one possible plot with many missing parts. This way the readers can enjoy solving the puzzle of guessing the right set of events which correctly answer all the questions.

One important thing about aggregates is to distinguish them from a simple sequence or list of objects. You should think of an aggregate in relationship to a real world abstraction (Garg, 1988). Here are some of the characteristics of aggregates:

1) An aggregate can be represented as a list of hypertext objects:

```
aggregate(ID, [ node(ID1,[item(1,"..."),...]),
  node(ID2,[item(1,"..."),...]),
  node(ID3,[item(1,"..."),...]) ]).
```

2) The constituents of an aggregate are unique. If you have two aggregates 'a' and 'b' such that:

```
  aggregate(a,List1) and
  aggregate(b,List2) and
  List1 = List2 then
  aggregates 'a' and 'b' represent one and the same aggregate.
```

3) Instances of an aggregate are formed from the instances of the objects of that aggregate. For instance, you have the aggregate 'node' such that:

```
aggregate(ID,[Characters,Plot,Location]) and
attribute(ID,type,novel) and
attribute(ID,name,X).
```

with X standing for the name of the novel, while Characters, Plot and Location, are hypertext domain objects (see our definition of hypertext domain objects earlier in this chapter). An example of the definition of such objects is the following:

```
node(ID1,[item(1,Mr. A is ...), item(2,Mrs. B is ...), ...]),
  attribute(ID1,type,characters),
  node(ID2,[item(1,"On a hot summer day, Mr. A was ..."),
            item(2,"Suddenly he felt a noise in ...")]),
  attribute(ID2,type,plot),
  node(ID3,[item(1,"It is 1983, in City C, California")]),
  attribute(ID3,type,location).
```

By instantiating the objects of the novel aggregate, you would have generated a particular novel with a certain name, characters, main plot, and location. Every different instantiation will give us a different novel.

Thus, using aggregates you can represent different versions of a novel. Of course, in writing novels you are mainly interested in picking the version you like most. In other applications, such as software projects, you might be interested in saving and retrieving all the versions of a project. For this purpose you need to address the issue of "version control" which is the next topic.

Versions

I can discuss the different "versions" of a hypertext object. For example, you can have many versions of the same node. A version of a node could serve as an alternative node or as an updated replacement of that node. To control the storage and retrieval of the different versions, you might need what many software designers call "a version control system."

In a version control system you have a hypertext object and a list of revisions for that object. To revise an object you can:

1) delete some of the information items, or
2) add new information items, or
3) change an existing information item.

One way to represent a version-control system in Prolog is to use a list of changes. If you apply this list to the current object, you would get different versions of the object. In FIG. 8-4 is shown a Turbo Prolog predicate called "revision." This predicate has the following form:

```
revision(Current,Changes,Revised)
```

where "Current" stands for the current hypertext object. The argument "Changes" stands for the list of changes that you need to apply to "Current" to get the "Revised" object.

The program in FIG. 8-4 is self-explanatory. To represent the "revision" predicate as an abstraction you can use the Metalogical predicate "rel." I intro-

Fig. 8-4. A simple revision-control predicate.

```
/* ****************************************************** */
/* **** a logical hypertext revision system ************* */
/* ****************************************************** */
/* In this system hypertext is represented as a list of
   items. An item is a compound object with two arguments:

        item(POS,hypertext-ITEM)

   POS is an INTEGER number representing the relative
   position of a hypertext-ITEM in the hypertext.
   A hypertext-ITEM could be:

           1. a chunk of text,
           2. an expansion button,
           3. a replacement button,
           4. a note button,
           5. a reference button,
           6. a command button,
           7. a keyword (index) button

    For now, we don't need to worry about the details of
    the hypertext-ITEM.  So, we will assume that a hypertext-ITEM
    is just a Turo Prolog symbol.

To try the system, load and run the program and give this goal:

Goal: revision([item(1,a),item(2,b),item(4,f)],
               REVISION,
               [item(3,c),item(4,d)]).

...and Turbo will return this answer:

REVISION = [item(1,a),item(2,b),item(3,c),item(4,d)]
1 Solution.

*/

DOMAINS
  item = item(INTEGER,SYMBOL)
  itemlist = item*

PREDICATES
  revision(itemlist,itemlist,itemlist)

CLAUSES

/* ******************** revision ************************ */
revision(X,X,[]):-!.
revision([],Y,Y).
revision([item(Pos,A)|X],Y,[item(Pos,A)|Z]):- !,
  revision(X,Y,Z).
revision([item(Pos,A)|X],[item(Pos,B)|Y],[item(Pos,B)|Z]):-
   A <> B, !,
   revision(X,Y,Z).
revision([item(Pos,A)|X],[item(Pos1,B)|Y],[item(Pos1,B)|Z]):-
  Pos > Pos1, !,
  revision([item(Pos,A)|X],Y,Z).
revision([A|X],[A|Y],Z):-
  revision(X,Y,Z).

/* ********************* END END END ******************** */
```

duced "rel" when I talked about "Representing Relationships" earlier in this chapter. In the program of FIG. 8-5 I do exactly that.

Now I'll explain how the two versions of the program, in FIG. 8-4 and FIG. 8-5 do revision control. The first clause:

```
revision(X,X,[]):-!.
```

simply states that an empty list of changes to a hypertext-object X will give the object X itself. In the second clause the opposite is done:

```
revision([],Y,Y).
```

meaning, the result of a Y list of changes to an empty hypertext object is Y itself. As for clause No. 3:

```
revision([item(Pos,A) ! X],Y,[item(Pos,A)! Z]):- !,
  revision(X,Y,Z).
```

I define the result of deleting an item A at position Pos from the hypertext-object list of items. In clause No. 4:

```
revision([item(Pos,_) ! X],
         [item(Pos,B) ! Y],
         [item(Pos,B) ! Z]) :- !,
revision(X,Y,Z).
```

I define the effect of replacing any item at position Pos with a new item B. For clause No. 5:

```
revision([item(Pos,A) !X],
         [item(Pos1,B) ! Y],
         [item(Pos1,B) ! Z]):-
  Pos > Pos1, !,
  revision([item(Pos,A) ! X],Y,Z).
```

I define the result of adding an item B at a position Pos1 which is less than the current position Pos. If none of the above clauses apply, Prolog uses clause No. 6:

```
revision([A ! X],[A ! Y],Z):-
  revision(X,Y,Z).
```

which simply ignores the list of changes and copies the current item into the resulting hypertext-object list of items. Probably by now you have realized the expressive power of Prolog as a programming language. With just a few lines of code, I have defined a complete version control system. Writing the same program in another language could easily take several pages of code.

Views or Perspectives

Most of the time, different people have a different understanding and interpretation of things. It is also possible that one person can understand some-

Fig. 8-5. A more general "revision" predicate.

```
/* ****************************************************** */
/* **** a logical hypertext revision system ************* */
/* ****************************************************** */

/* In this system hypertext is represented as a list of
   items. An item is a compound object with two arguments:

        item(POS,hypertext-ITEM)

   POS is an INTEGER number representing the relative
   position of a hypertext-ITEM in the hypertext.
   A hypertext-ITEM could be:

         1. a chunk of text,
         2. an expansion button,
         3. a replacement button,
         4. a note button,
         5. a reference button,
         6. a command button,
         7. a keyword (index) button

    For now, we don't need to worry about the details of
    the hypertext-ITEM.  So, we will assume that a hypertext-ITEM
    is just a Turo Prolog symbol.

To try the system, load and run the program and give this goal:

Goal: rel(revision,[item(1,a),item(2,b),item(4,f)],
                   REVISION,
                   [item(3,c),item(4,d)]),
 write(REVISION).
...and Turbo will return this answer:

REVISION = [item(1,a),item(2,b),item(3,c),item(4,d)] 1 Solution.

*/

DOMAINS
  item = item(INTEGER,SYMBOL)
  itemlist = item*

PREDICATES
  rel(SYMBOL,itemlist,itemlist,itemlist)

CLAUSES

/* ****************** rel ****************************** */
rel(revision,X,X,[]):-!.
rel(revision,[],Y,Y).
rel(revision,[item(Pos,A)|X],Y,[item(Pos,A)|Z]):- !,
  rel(revision,X,Y,Z).
rel(revision,[item(Pos,_)|X], [item(Pos,B)|Y],[item(Pos,B)|Z]):-
   !,
   rel(revision,X,Y,Z).
rel(revision,[item(Pos,A)|X],[item(Pos1,B)|Y],[item(Pos1,B)|Z]):-
  Pos > Pos1, !,
  rel(revision,[item(Pos,A)|X],Y,Z).
rel(revision,[A|X],[A|Y],Z):-
  rel(revision,X,Y,Z).

/* ******************** END END END ******************** */
```

thing or interpret an event in more than one way. You call these different modes of understanding, interpreting, looking, and thinking "viewpoints" or "perspectives."

Today, Researchers in Software Engineering are aware of the importance of viewpoints and perspectives in managing large software development projects. One way to deal with viewpoints in Software Engineering is mentioned in a paper by Jeff Conklin (Conklin, 1986): "In such projects the software system is presented as a hypertext network of code, specifications, documentation, and so on. Nodes in the network have multiple perspectives: Each perspective describes a different aspect of the program structure represented by the node, and provides specialized actions from that point of view." One place where this idea was in the center of the hypertext system is PIE. PIE, Personal Information Environment, is the creation of Ira Goldstein and Danny Bobrow. Several viewpoints supported in PIE are: performance views, reliability views, and management views.

Hypertext Contexts

I can talk about the "context" of hypertext objects. In the dictionary the word context refers to "the parts just before and after a word or passage that determine its meaning." In hypertext I will use "context" to refer to the different perspectives, viewpoints, or functions of hypertext objects by different users. For example, a hypertext document on a certain topic can serve as the basis for a book or an article on that topic. In this situation, I partition the objects of this document in two contexts—a book context, and an article context. An expanded version of the document objects will represent a book, and a reduced version of the same objects will represent an article.

- A single hypertext object can have multiple instances in different contexts.
- A hypertext object can serve different functions in different contexts.
- An object has a (global) identifier that identifies all the instances of that object in all the contexts, and an identifier (local) which identifies the instance of an object in a given context.
- You can use contexts to support different configurations, private workspaces, and revision history.

Filters

You can extract hypertext objects using "filters" or "search patterns." A filter allows you to extract a subset of objects from your current set of hypertext objects. For example, in a document on the "modern movement in Architecture," you can look for all nodes with information on the architect "Mies Van Der Rohe." In this case the name "Mies Van Der Rohe" will serve as a "keyword" filter. I can discuss three kinds of filters:

- strings and keywords,

- paths, and
- relations

Strings and Keywords: In searching for strings, you need an on-line algorithm for string search of predefined keywords, whole-words, leading substrings, embedded characters, and if possible the use of wildcard (regular expression) characters, such as the *, !, ?, and so on. As for keywords, you can have filters that look for:

- Keywords in Information Objects
- Keywords for Aggregations
- Keywords for Generalizations
- Keywords for Revisions

Relations: You can use relation (link) types to search for the hypertext objects (nodes). You specify the relation you are interested in, and the system would return (or highlight) all those nodes and links that match the link type in your query.

An example of a system that can filter hypertext objects using link types is Conklin's gIBIS (Conklin, 1986). gIBIS is based on Horst Rittel's "Issue Based Information Systems," IBIS. IBIS is an argumentative-based problem solving system. PART THREE of this book is devoted to a PC version of IBIS. In IBIS the nodes correspond to questions and answers. A question is an issue, and answers could be: positions from issues, arguments for and against positions, and references. Rittel suggested nine types of links as being essential to the problem solving process in IBIS. Here are a number of these link types:

- responds_to (i.e., POSITION responds_to ISSUE)
- supports (i.e., ARGUMENT supports POSITION)
- objects_to (i.e., ARGUMENT objects_to POSITION)
- suggests (i.e., POSITION suggests ISSUE)
- refers_to (i.e., POSITION refers_to REFERENCE)

Part Three

Micro Issue Based Information System

9

Introducing IBIS (Issue Based Information System): A Hypertext System for Problem Solving

"The question about the sources of our knowledge . . . has always been asked in the spirit of: 'What are the best sources of our knowledge—the most reliable ones, those which will not lead us into error, and those to which we can and must turn, in case of doubt, as the last court of appeal?' I propose to assume, instead, that no such ideal sources exist—no more than ideal rulers—and that all 'sources' are liable to lead us into error at times. And I propose to replace, therefore, the question of the sources of our knowledge by the entirely different question: 'How can we hope to detect and eliminate error?' . . .

The proper answer to my question 'How can we hope to detect and eliminate error?' is, I believe, 'By criticizing the theories or guesses.' (The latter point is highly desirable, but not indispensable; for if we fail to criticize our own theories, there may be others to do it for us.) This answer sums up a position which I propose to call 'critical rationalism'."

—Karl R. Popper, from his book "Conjectures and Refutations: The Growth of Scientific Knowledge."

In PART ONE I talked about two major hypertext applications: an information retrieval system and a problem solving system. PART TWO was mainly for building an information retrieval hypertext system. In PART THREE I will deal with a general purpose hypertext system for problem solving. My problem solving system uses a question-answering approach.

This approach allows a single user or a group of users to explore the problem space. To solve a problem this way: First you enter a statement of your goal or problem. You put this statement in the form of a question. In IBIS you call questions "issues." An issue is a controversial question. If you have a group of experts trying to solve this problem for you, they start answering your question. In IBIS there are three kinds of answers: positions, negative arguments (con arguments), and positive arguments (pro arguments). When one person answers a question, he is taking a position from an issue. If someone objects to his or her answer, I say that someone is arguing against his or her position. On the other hand, someone else might support his or her position. Here I say that someone is arguing for his or her position.

Eventually in this question-answering process, you will generate more issues which result in more positions and arguments. This process continues until you reach positions with little or no opposition. You can consider these positions as directives to solve the problem. Most often, you won't find many positions which everybody can agree on. When this happens, more questions are asked, and answered. This process could go on and on with no agreeable positions in sight. So what to do? Do you continue until you find or agree on a certain answer? Do you abandon the problem solving process, and if you do, does this mean you failed to resolve it?

There is no stopping rule for the question-answering process. You stop when you are about to run out of resources—i.e., time, money, and experts. Also you stop when you feel that you are going in circles. At any point in the process, the resulting network of questions and answers will serve as your knowledge-base. This knowledge-base represents the problem along with its proposed solutions, if any. Besides answers to problems, the network contains arguments for and against certain solutions. The arguments will help anticipate the consequences of the answers (solutions). Thus, the main advantage of this approach is its critical nature. It lets the decision maker be aware of the consequences of their decisions. Once you have a network of questions, answers, and pros and cons for the answers, you can make better decisions to deal with the problem. This approach helps you see the consequences of your actions. It uses the "critical rationalism" idea of Karl Popper's statement (the motto of this chapter).

As a decision maker, the network of questions and answers helps reach a decision. You can use the network to support or reject alternative problem solutions. This is not your typical Artificial Intelligence approach for problem solving. The inventors of this approach claim that it helps amplify our natural intelligence rather than substitute it with a piece of software. The main purpose of the computer systems here is to help the problem solver understand the problem and its alternative solutions. It helps you to bring out the pros and cons of each answer to a problem or a subproblem.

By now, you must be thinking that there is too much theory involved here with only few possible practical ideas. Before you run away, I'll show you the opposite. For the rest of this chapter, I will introduce "MicroIBIS," an "Issue Based Information System" which I wrote in Turbo Prolog. MicroIBIS will give you an idea of how to use argumentation to deal with problems such as: environmental design and planning issues, political issues, legal issues, to name just a few. These problems require thinking processes other than those used to design the structure of bridges and building. Also it is different from the systems used to control robots, fight wars, build cars, and handle dangerous materials. Argumentative thinking—i.e., critical thinking—is not intuitive thinking, it has its own logical structure. Its logical structure is the "logic of questions and answers."

RUNNING MicroIBIS

To try MicroIBIS you need to enter the complete program in FIG. 9-1. The program is a mammoth one. In Chapters 12 and 13 I will talk, in some detail, about some of the program's specific parts. For now I want you to try the system to get the feel of its operation. To do this you will need to spend a few hours entering the code in ".pro" files on your system, but once you get the code, it is worth it.

Note: If you would like to save yourself the time and effort for entering an error-free code, I suggest you order the supplementary program disks. To do this, please fill in and return the companion diskette offer at the end of the book.

If you have the companion diskettes for the book, you will find an executable version of MicroIBIS under the name "ibis.exe." To run MicroIBIS, you change the current drive to the disk drive in which you have the "ibis.exe" diskette. For example if you have the "ibis.exe" on a diskette in drive A, you make A your current drive by typing "A:," then you issue the command "ibis" and press the return key.

On the other hand, when you enter the code yourself, you get the ".exe" version by following these steps:

1) start the Turbo Prolog system,
2) load the "main-mod.pro" in the Turbo Prolog editor,
3) make sure that the current directory is the directory for the ibis source code (".pro" and ".prj" files).
4) Choose the Compile/Project option from the pull-down menu. Turbo Prolog will prompt you to enter a name for an already existing project file (a file with an ".prj" extension). Enter "ibis" for the name of the project. If you never used "projects" in Turbo Prolog, don't worry, I will talk about that in Chapter 11. After you enter the project's name, Turbo will compile and link the code for the two modules (main-mod.pro and tools-mod.pro) into an "ibis.exe" file.

Fig. 9-1a. IBIS.PRJ

```
% File name: ibis.prj


tool-mod+
main-mod
```

Fig. 9-1b. MAIN-MOD.PRO

```
% File name: main-mod.pro

project "ibis"
include "ibis-glb.pro"

PREDICATES
  runMAIN

GOAL
  runMAIN.

/* +++++++++++++++++++++++++++++++++++++++++++++++++++++++ */
% File name: "main-mod.pro"
% THIS IS THE MAIN MODULE OF THE "MicroIBIS" SYSTEM
% Version date: July 4, July 23, 1988;

/* ******************************************************* */
/*                       MicroIBIS                         */
/* "Issue Based Information System" in Turbo Prolog        */
/* ******************************************************* */

/* ******************* utility predicates *************** */
include "ibis-ut.pro"

/* ******************************************************* */
/* Additional include files needed to run MicroIBIS        */
/* ******************************************************* */

/* ***************** graphic title screen *************** */
% include "ibis-gsc.pro"


/* ********************** ibis user-interface *********** */
include "ibis-use.pro"

/* ******************** database predicates ************* */
include "ibis-db.pro"

/* ************************* ibis-map.pro **************** */
/*
a file converts external ibis-database to tree object,
which we use in a tree menu for the road-map of ibis.

also in "ibis-map.pro" we convert ibis-database to a list
of keys to be displayed in a box menu by the "nodename"
predicate.
*/

include "ibis-map.pro"

/* ********************** printing ibis ***************** */
include "ibis-prt.pro"
```

(**Fig. 9-1b.** continued)

```
/* ********************** ibis editor ****************** */
include "ibis-ed.pro"

/* ********************* ibis relations **************** */
include "ibis-rel.pro"

/* +++++++++++++++++++++++++++++++++++++++++++++++++++++ */


/* ***************************************************** */
/*              MicroIBIS - MAIN PROGRAM                 */
/* ***************************************************** */

CLAUSES

/* ********************** runMAIN ********************** */
/* ***************************************************** */

% "runMAIN" initiates the system by firing the pulldown menu.

/*
          1         2         3         4         5         6         7
012345678901234567890123456789012345678901234567890123456789012345678901234567
     Files       Nodes        Edit       Relations       Map        Setup
*/

runMAIN:-
%   graphicSCREEN,     % title graphic screen (use this of textSCREEN)
   blankwindow,
   initSETUP,  % setup the system windows attr.
   textSCREEN,     % title text screen (use this or graphiceSCREEN)
   retractall(_),
   msgwindow,
   mapwindow,
   editwindow,
   statusline,
   update(dbSTATUS(closed)),
   pulldown_attr(ATTR),
   pulldown(ATTR,[ curtain(5,"Files",["Load",
                                 "New",
                                 "Save",
                                 "sAve as",
                                 "Directory",
                                 "Change dir.",
                                 "Operating system",
                                 "Write KB to Xfile",
                                 "Print",
                                 "Quit"
                                ]),
                 curtain(17,"Nodes",["Load node",
                                  "Save node",
                                  "Delete node",
                                  "Attributes",
                                  "Nodes dir"
                                 ]),
                 curtain(29,"Edit",[]),
                 curtain(40,"Relations",[]),
                 curtain(55,"Map",[]),
                 curtain(65,"Setup",["Attr. Dialog",
                                  "Colors",
                                  "Window size",
                                  "Save new setup"])
               ],
```

(**Fig. 9-1b.** continued)

```
                  _,_).

/* ****************************************************** */
/* ********************** pdwaction ******************** */
/* ****************************************************** */
% the pulldown menu actions.

/* ********************* 1. FILES MENU ****************** */

%  ****** 1 Load an IBIS db-file

% To load a db-file we must first close the current one.

pdwaction(1,1):-
   closeDBfile(ibisdb),
   newCURSORpos(Row,Col),
   msg_attr(Wattr,Fattr),
   readfilename(Row,Col,Wattr,Fattr,ibs,"",NewName),
   openDBfile(ibisdb,NewName,in_file),  % in "ibis-db.pro"
   initCURRENTdb(NewName),
   map(REF),                  % in ibis-map.pro
   loadIBISnode(REF), !.      % in ibis-db.pro

pdwaction(1,1):- refreshSCR.

%  ****** 1.2 Creating a new IBIS db-file

pdwaction(1,2):-
   newCURSORpos(Row,Col),
   msg_attr(Wattr,Fattr),
   lineinput(Row,Col,40,Wattr,Fattr,
             "Enter new file name: ","work.ibs",NewName),
   createDBfile(ibisdb,NewName,in_file),
   update(dbSTATUS(opened)),
   initIBIS,
   initCURRENTdb(NewName), !.

pdwaction(1,2):- refreshSCR.

%  ****** 1.3 Save current IBIS db-file

pdwaction(1,3):-
  currentFILE(NAME),
  writeMSG(stay,["\n Saving ",NAME," file"]),
  db_flush(ibisdb),
  writeMSG(go,["\n",NAME," is saved"]).

pdwaction(1,3):- refreshSCR.

%  ****** 1.4 Save current IBIS db-file as another file.

pdwaction(1,4):-
  currentFILE(NAME),
  newCURSORpos(Row,Col),
  msg_attr(Wattr,Fattr),
  lineinput(Row,Col,30,Wattr,Fattr,
            "Save current IBIS as: ","",NewName),
  NewName <> NAME,
  not(existfile(NewName)),
  db_copy(ibisdb,NewName,in_file).

pdwaction(1,4):-
  writeMSG(go,["File exists, or","\n",
               "cann't copy file on itself."]).
```

(**Fig. 9-1b.** continued)

```
%  ****** 1.5 List Directory of the current path

pdwaction(1,5):-
  shiftwindow(OLD),
  disk(PATH),
  dirwindow,
  dir(PATH,"*.ibs ",_,1,1,1),
  removewindow,
  shiftwindow(OLD), !.

% if user presses ESC, then the action succeeds

pdwaction(1,5):-
 shiftwindow(DIRnum),            % check if directory window is
 windowNUM(dirwindow,DIRnum),    % still on screen, if so then
 removewindow.                   % remove dirwindow

%  ****** 1.6 Change current directory path

pdwaction(1,6):-
  cursor(Row,Col),
  makewindow(_,_,_,_,RO,CO,_,_),
  Row1=RO+Row, Col1=CO+Col,
  msg_attr(Wattr,Fattr),
  changeDIR(Row1,Col1,Wattr,Fattr).

%  ****** 1.7 Exit temporarly to DOS

pdwaction(1,7):- system("").

%  ****** 1.8 Write IBIS knowledge-base to external file

pdwaction(1,8):- dumpIBIS.   % in IBIS-prt

%  ****** 1.9 Print current IBIS to  PRINTER or to DOS FILE

pdwaction(1,9):- printIBIS.  % in IBIS-prt

%  ****** 1.10 QUIT IBIS
pdwaction(1,10):-
   msg_attr(Wattr,Fattr),
   lineinput(5,40,30,Wattr,Fattr,
            "Are you sure (y/n) ? ","",ANS),
   upper_lower(ANS1,ANS),
   ANS1 = "Y",
   removewindow,
   removewindow,
   removewindow,
   writeMSG(stay,["\n Closing the IBIS database file"]),
   closeDBfile(ibisdb),
   !,
   removewindow,
   removewindow,
   retractall(_),
   exit.

pdwaction(1,9):- refreshSCR.

/* ********************** 2. NODES MENU ****************** */

%  ****** 2.1 Load an IBIS node
pdwaction(2,1):-
  dbSTATUS(opened),
  newCURSORpos(ROW,COL),
  chain_terms(ibisdb,ibisch,ibis,IBIS,_),
```

(**Fig. 9-1b.** continued)

```
   msg_attr(Wattr,Fattr),
   nodename(ROW,COL,Wattr,Fattr,IBIS,"",NodeName,NODEref),!,
   getNODE(NODEref,NODE),
   NODE = node(_,_,_,_,STR),
   update(currentREF(NODEref)),
   update(currentNstr(STR)),
   update(currentCpos(1)),
   writeMSG(stay,["\nLoading ",NodeName," node."]),
   refreshNODE,
   writeMSG(go,["\n",NodeName," is loaded"]), !.

pdwaction(2,1):-
   dbSTATUS(closed),
   writeMSG(go,["\nIBIS database file is not open"]).

pdwaction(2,1):- refreshSCR.

%  ****** 2.2 Save the node currently in the editor

pdwaction(2,2):-
   dbSTATUS(opened),
   currentNstr(STR),
   currentREF(REF),
   getNODE(REF,NODE),
   NODE=node(N,K,A,D,_),
   term_replace(ibisdb,node,REF,node(N,K,A,D,STR)), !.

pdwaction(2,2):-
   dbSTATUS(closed),
   writeMSG(go,["\n IBIS database file is not open"]).

pdwaction(2,2):- refreshSCR.

%  ****** 2.3 Erase a node and remove its links

pdwaction(2,3):-
   currentREF(REF),
   cursor(R,C), RR=R+1, CC=C+1,
   msg_attr(Wattr,Fattr),
   lineinput(RR,CC,30,Wattr,Fattr,"Are you sure (y/n)? ","",ANS),
   upper_lower(ANS1,ANS),
   ANS1="Y",
   chain_terms(ibisdb,ibisch,ibis,IBIS,IBISref),
   deleteIBIS(REF,IBIS,NEWibis,DELibis),
   term_replace(ibisdb,ibis,IBISref,NEWibis),
   nodesINibis(DELibis,[],REFlist),
   deleteNODES(REFlist),
   clearCURRENT.

pdwaction(2,3).

%  ****** 2.4 Display and accept changes in node information.

pdwaction(2,4):-
   currentREF(REF),
   getNODE(REF,NODE),
   NODE = node(Ntype,Ktype,A,D,STR),
   displayINFO(Ntype,Ktype,A,D,Ktype1,A1,D1),
   updateNattr(REF,STR,Ntype,Ktype,A,D,Ktype1,A1,D1).


pdwaction(2,4).

%  ****** 2.5 Directory of nodes in current file.
```

(**Fig. 9-1b.** continued)

```
pdwaction(2,5):- writeMSG(go,["option is inactive"]).

/* ************** 3. EDIT CURRENTLY LOADED NODE ********* */

pdwaction(3,0):-
  dbSTATUS(opened),
  currentREF(REF),
  currentNstr(INstr),
  currentCpos(INpos),
  getNODEname(REF,NODEname),
  getNODE(REF,NODE),
  NODE=node(Ntype,_,_,_,_),
  shiftwindow(OLD),
  changestatus(
"F1-Help F2-Xsave F3-Load F4-Replace F5-Zoom F7-Xcopy F8-Xedit (F10 or ES
End"),
  windowNUM(editwindow,Enum),
  shiftwindow(Enum),
  ibisEDITOR(NODEname,Ntype,REF,INstr,INpos,OUTstr,OUTpos),
  changestatus(
" >>>>>>>>>>>>>>>>>>>>>>>>> Select from pulldown menu
<<<<<<<<<<<<<<<<<<<<<<<<<"),
  shiftwindow(OLD),
  update(currentCpos(OUTpos)),
  update(currentNstr(OUTstr)), !.

pdwaction(3,0):-
  dbSTATUS(closed),
  writeMSG(go,["\n IBIS database file is not open"]).

pdwaction(3,0):- refreshSCR.

/* ********************** 4. RELATIONS MENU ************* */

% 4 Relations between current node and other nodes

pdwaction(4,0):-
  dbSTATUS(opened),
  currentREF(REF),
  currentNstr(Str),
  getNODE(REF,Tnode),  % in ibis-db.pro
  Tnode=node(N,K,A,D,Str1),
  saveCURRENT(REF,Str,N,K,A,D,Str1),
  relates_to(REF,_,_,_,Tnode), !.

pdwaction(4,0):-
  dbSTATUS(closed),
  writeMSG(go,["IBIS file is not open"]).

pdwaction(4,0):-
  refreshNODE.

/* ********************** 5. MAP MENU ******************* */

% 5 a Road-Map of the IBIS tree; the map is a tree menu.

/* I tried using "repeat" so if a subtree is deleted,
   ifNODEdeleted will fail causing backtracking to map
   so we get a new drawing of IBIS after the deletion.
   But unfortunately this repeat causes redrawing of IBIS
   even when I am just pressing ESC in treemenu, because ESC
   causes treemenu to fail, and thus "map" to fail, which
   backtrack repeats and this causes redrawing of map
   without any possible exit except loading a new node.
```

(**Fig. 9-1b.** continued)

```
In the first clause, when user presses F10, the f10action
predicate is activated otherwise if return is pressed
control is passed to loadIBISnode else if ESC is pressed,
this clause fails and control is passed to next clause.

*/

pdwaction(5,0):-
    dbSTATUS(opened),
    map(REF),               % in ibis-map.pro
    ifNODEdeleted(REF),     % in ibis-db.pro
    loadIBISnode(REF), !.   % in ibis-db.pro

pdwaction(5,0):-
  dbSTATUS(closed),
  writeMSG(go,["IBIS file is not open"]).

pdwaction(5,0):-
  changestatus(
" >>>>>>>>>>>>>>>>>>>>>>> Select from pulldown menu <<<<<<<<<<<<<<<<<<<<<<<").


/* ************************* 6. Setup ****************** */

% change attribute status, show or hide.

pdwaction(6,1):-
  pulldown_attr(Attr),
  menu(3,67,Attr,Attr,["Show",
                      "Hide"],"",1,Choice),
  attrCHOICE(Choice).  % in ibis-db.pro

pdwaction(6,1).

% Change the window attributes

pdwaction(6,2):-
  pulldown_attr(Attr),
  menu(4,67,Attr,Attr, ["Editor",
                        "Message",
                        "Road-map",
                        "Pulldown",
                        "Status line",
                        "Dialog box"],"",1,Choice),
  window_color(Choice).  % in ibis-use.pro

pdwaction(6,2).

% Change window sizes

pdwaction(6,3):-
  pulldown_attr(Attr),
  menu(5,67,Attr,Attr, ["Editor",
                        "Message",
                        "Road-map"],"",1,Choice),
  window_size(Choice),   % in ibis-use.pro
  refreshstatus.

pdwaction(6,3):- refreshstatus.

% Save current setup
pdwaction(6,4):-
  save("ibis.sys",setupdb), !.
```

(**Fig. 9-1b.** continued)

```
pdwaction(6,4):-
  writeMSG(go,["Can't save to ibis.sys"]).

/* ****************************************************** */
/* ***** USING THE HYPERTEXT HOTKEY F10 ***************** */
/* ****************************************************** */

PREDICATES
  mapCHOICE(ref,INTEGER)

CLAUSES

/* *********************** f10action ******************* */
/*
   f10action is a predicate added to the tree menu to
   accomodate special functions, in MicroIBIS I use f10 for
   a hypertext hotkey. When a user presses f10 while the
   cursor is on a selection (an IBIS node) a menu of
   possible operations will appear. The user can select the
   operation to perform on that node, add to it, delete it
   and its subtrees, contract its subtrees to one node,
   expand an already contracted subtree, and show, author,
   date and knowledge type in a node.
*/

f10action(NODEref):-
  cursor(R,C),
  pulldown_attr(Attr),
  menu(R,C,Attr,Attr,
       ["Relations","Delete","Attr","Contract","Expand"],
       map,1,Choice),
  mapCHOICE(NODEref,Choice).

/* ************************** mapCHOICE **************** */

%  ********* Relations menu, same as in pulldowm menu
%  This is basically an ADD LINK menu

mapCHOICE(REF,1):-
  getNODE(REF,Tnode),
  Tnode=node(N,K,A,D,STR1),
  currentNstr(STR),
  saveCURRENT(REF,STR,N,K,A,D,STR1),  % in ibis-db.pro
  relates_to(REF,_,_,_,Tnode).        % in ibis-rel.pro

%  ********* Delete an IBIS node and its subtree

mapCHOICE(REF,2):-
  cursor(R,C), RR=R+1, CC=C+1,
  dialog_attr(Wattr,Fattr),
  lineinput(RR,CC,30,Wattr,Fattr,"Are you sure (y/n)? ","",ANS),
  upper_lower(ANS1,ANS),
  ANS1="Y",
  chain_terms(ibisdb,ibisch,ibis,IBIS,IBISref), !,
  deleteIBIS(REF,IBIS,NEWibis,DELibis),
  term_replace(ibisdb,ibis,IBISref,NEWibis),
  nodesINibis(DELibis,[],REFlist), % get all refs of deleted subtree
  deleteNODES(REFlist), % and delete all the nodes in that subtree
  update(deleteSTATUS(REFlist)), % in ibis-ut.pro
  clearwindow,                   % clear mapwindow
  ifCURRENTdeleted(REFlist), !.  % in ibis-db.pro

/* Notice that after we delete a node, its REF number will still
   be passed back by treemenu, and thus by map(IBIS,REF), then
   loadIBISnode(REF) will try to load it and this will cause
   a problem because the third clause of loadIBISnode will try to
```

(**Fig. 9-1b.** continued)

```
    load that node, and REF is not valid. This is why we need
    ifNODEdeleted in the road-map option in the pulldown menu.

    ifCURRENTdeleted is used to clear the current node if it was
    one of the deleted nodes in the process. */

  mapCHOICE(_,2).

%  ********* Information on the selected node

mapCHOICE(REF,3):-
  getNODE(REF,NODE),
  NODE = node(Ntype,Ktype,A,D,STR),
  displayINFO(Ntype,Ktype,A,D,Ktype1,A1,D1),
  updateNattr(REF,STR,Ntype,Ktype,A,D,Ktype1,A1,D1).

mapCHOICE(_,3).

/*
%  ********* Contract the IBIS subtree starting at the
%  currently selected node to a single node in the tree

mapCHOICE(REF,4):-

%  ********* Expand an already contracted subtree to its
%  original shape

mapCHOICE(REF,5):-
*/

/* +++++++++++++++++++++++++++++++++++++++++++++++++++++++ */

/* ****************** END END END ********************** */
```

Fig. 9-1c. TOOL-MOD.PRO

```
% File name: tool-mod.pro

project "ibis"
include "ibis-glb.pro"

/* ****************************************************** */
/* A TURBO PROLOG TOOLBOX MODULE                          */
/* ****************************************************** */
/* ****************************************************** */
/* TURBO PROLOG TOOLBOX                                   */
/* ****************************************************** */

% THE TOOLBOX's domains and predicate declarations

include "tpreds.pro"

/* ************** TOOLBOX lineinput tool **************** */

include "lineinp.pro"

/* *************** TOOLBOX readfilename tool ************ */

include "filename.pro"

/* *************** TOOLBOX status line tool ************* */
```

(**Fig. 9-1c.** continued)

```
include "status.pro"

/* *********** TOOLBOX screen-layout tools ************** */

include "scrhnd.pro"

/* **************** TOOLBOX menu tools ****************** */

include "menu.pro"        /* Regular menu predicate */
include "pulldown.pro"    /* Pulldown menu predicates */
include "boxmenu.pro"     /* Box menu predicates */

/* ************** a relationship-tree menu ************** */
% This is a modified version of the TOOLBOX tree.pro

include "tree2.pro"        /* Tree menu predicate */

/* ***************************************************** */
/*       a dialog-box utility predicates file            */
/* UTILITIES WHICH USE THE TOOLBOX SCREEN-LAYOUT TOOLS    */
/* ***************************************************** */
include "ibis-dia.pro"      /* Dialog-boxes for IBIS nodes */

/* ******************* END END END ********************** */
```

Fig. 9-1d. IBIS-GLB.PRO

```
% File name: ibis-glb.pro


/* ***************************************************** */
/* Global declarations for the IBIS system               */
/* ***************************************************** */

/* ***************************************************** */
GLOBAL DOMAINS
/* ***************************************************** */

/* ****************** TOOLBOX tdoms.pro file ************ */

ROW, COL, LEN, ATTR   = INTEGER
SYMBOLLIST = SYMBOL*
STRINGLIST = STRING*
INTEGERLIST = INTEGER*
KEY     = cr; esc; break; tab; btab; del; bdel; ctrlbdel; ins;
          end ; home ; fkey(INTEGER) ; up ; down ; left ; right ;
          ctrlleft; ctrlright; ctrlend; ctrlhome; pgup; pgdn;
          ctrlpgup; ctrlpgdn; char(CHAR) ; otherspec

% modified treemenu domains
  SELECTOR = ref
  TREE = tree(string,string,selector,treelist)
  TREELIST = tree*

% pulldown menu domains

 MENUELEM=  curtain(COL,STRING,STRINGLIST)
 MENULIST=  MENUELEM*

% screen handeling
  FNAME=SYMBOL
  TYPE = int(); str(); real()

/* ******************** IBIS domains ******************* */
```

(**Fig. 9-1d.** continued)

```
  db_selector = ibisdb
  file = ibistxt

  SOURCE,TARGET,RELATION = STRING
  AUTHOR,DATE,TEXT = STRING
  Ntype,Ktype = STRING
  REL = rel(SOURCE,RELATION,TARGET)
  RELLIST=REL*
  REFLIST=ref*

% A node has a knowledge type, an author, a date, and text

  NODE = node(Ntype,Ktype,AUTHOR,DATE,TEXT)

% keys are numbers used to generate symbolic names for ibis nodes

% an ID is a pair of two things: A node symbolic name, and its REF

  KEYS = keys(INTEGER,INTEGER,INTEGER,INTEGER)
  ID   = id(STRING,REF)
  IDLIST = ID*

% The ibis tree of nodes

   IBIS = ibis(RELATION,NTYPE,REF,ibislist)
   IBISLIST = ibis*

/* ******************************************************* */
GLOBAL PREDICATES
/* ******************************************************* */

/* from tpreds.pro */
nondeterm repeat

/* box menu */

  boxmenu(ROW,COL,ROW,COL,ATTR,ATTR,STRINGLIST,STRING,INTEGER,
          INTEGER) - (i,i,i,i,i,i,i,i,i,o)

/* readfilename */

  readfilename(ROW,COL,ATTR,ATTR,STRING,STRING,STRING)
  - (i,i,i,i,i,i,o)

/* menu */

  menu(ROW,COL,ATTR,ATTR,STRINGLIST,STRING,INTEGER,INTEGER)
  - (i,i,i,i,i,i,i,o)
/* pulldown menu */

  pulldown(ATTR,MENULIST,INTEGER,INTEGER) - (i,i,o,o)
nondeterm  pdwaction(INTEGER,INTEGER) - (i,i)

/* lineinput */

  lineinput(ROW,COL,LEN,ATTR,ATTR,STRING,STRING,STRING)
  - (i,i,i,i,i,i,i,o)
  nondeterm lineinput_repeat(ROW,COL,LEN,ATTR,ATTR,STRING,STRING,STRING)
  - (i,i,i,i,i,i,i,o)

/* STATUS */
  makestatus(ATTR,STRING) - (i,i)
  nondeterm tempstatus(ATTR,STRING) - (i,i)
  removestatus
```

(**Fig. 9-1d.** continued)

```
     refreshstatus
     changestatus(STRING) - (i)

   /* tree menu */

     treemenu(SYMBOL,TREE,SELECTOR) - (i,i,o)
   nondeterm  f10action(SELECTOR) - (i)
  /* ibis-dialog box predicates */
    getNattr(STRING,STRING,STRING) - (o,o,o)
    nodeDIALOG(STRING,STRING,STRING) - (o,o,o)
    displayINFO(STRING,STRING,STRING,
                STRING,STRING,STRING,STRING) - (i,i,i,i,o,o,o)

  /* ibis utility predicates */
    update(dbasedom) - (i)

  /* IBIS system windows */

              blankwindow
  nondeterm   editwindow
  nondeterm   msgwindow
  nondeterm   mapwindow
  nondeterm   dirwindow
  nondeterm   dialogwindow(STRING) - (i)
  nondeterm   statusLINE

    windowNUM(SYMBOL,INTEGER) - (i,i) (i,o) (o,i)

  /* ****************************************************** */
  GLOBAL DATABASE
  /* ****************************************************** */

  % predicates used in tree menu
    treewindow(ROW,COL)
    treechoice(SELECTOR)

  % predicates used in PULLDOWN
    pdwstate(ROW,COL,SYMBOL,ROW,COL)

  % predicates used in LINEINP
    insmode
    lineinpstate(STRING,COL)
    lineinpflag

  % predicates used in SCRHND
    actfield(FNAME)                /* Actual field */
    screen(SYMBOL,DBASEDOM)        /* Saving different screens */
    value(FNAME,STRING)            /* value of a field */
    field(FNAME,TYPE,ROW,COL,LEN)  /* Screen definition */
    txtfield(ROW,COL,LEN,STRING)
    windowsize(ROW,COL).
    notopline

    /* DATABASE PREDICATES USED BY VSCRHND */
    windowstart(ROW,COL)
    mycursord(ROW,COL)

    deleteON

  /* ******************** current database *************** */
  % current system configuration used for updating

    currentFILE(STRING)
    currentNtype(STRING)
    currentKtype(STRING)
    currentAUTHOR(STRING)
```

(**Fig. 9-1d.** continued)

```
    currentDATE(STRING)
    currentNstr(STRING)
    currentREF(ref)
    currentNdialog(STRING)
    currentCpos(INTEGER)
    currentNODE(NODE)
    currentIBIS(IBIS)
    dbSTATUS(SYMBOL)
    deleteSTATUS(REFLIST)

  %  relationLIST(STRING,STRINGLIST,STRINGLIST)

  GLOBAL DATABASE - setupdb

  pulldown_attr(ATTR)
  edit_attr(ATTR,ATTR)
  msg_attr(ATTR,ATTR)
  map_attr(ATTR,ATTR,ATTR)
  status_attr(ATTR)
  aux_edit_attr(ATTR,ATTR)
  dialog_attr(ATTR,ATTR)
  edit_size(INTEGER,INTEGER,INTEGER,INTEGER)
  msg_size(INTEGER,INTEGER,INTEGER,INTEGER)
  map_size(INTEGER,INTEGER,INTEGER,INTEGER)

  /* ************************* END END END ***************** */
```

Fig. 9-1e. IBIS-USE.PRO

```
% File name: ibis-use.pro

/* ******************************************************* */
/* USER INTERFACE UTILITIES                                 */
/* ******************************************************* */
/*
DATABASE - setupdb

pulldown_attr(ATTR)
edit_attr(ATTR,ATTR)
msg_attr(ATTR,ATTR)
map_attr(ATTR,ATTR,ATTR) % the last attr is for highlighting choice
status_attr(ATTR)
aux_edit_attr(ATTR,ATTR)
dialog_attr(ATTR,ATTR)
*/

PREDICATES
/* @ these predicate are in ibis-glb.pro
blankwindow
editwindow
msgwindow
mapwindow
dirwindow
dialogwindow(STRING)

windowNUM(SYMBOL,INTEGER)
statusLINE
*/

refreshNODE
clearCURRENT
refreshSCR
```

(**Fig. 9-1e.** continued)

```
textSCREEN

initSETUP  % intialize system windows attribute
window_color(INTEGER)
  window1_color(SYMBOL,INTEGER)
  window2_color(INTEGER,SYMBOL,INTEGER)
update_attr(SYMBOL,ATTR,ATTR)
window_size(INTEGER)
newCURSORpos(INTEGER,INTEGER)
% msg(ROW,COL,STRING)
writeMSG(SYMBOL,STRINGLIST)
listwrite(STRINGLIST)

CLAUSES

/* ******************** SYSTEM WINDOWS ****************** */

% blank window
blankwindow :- makewindow(1,7,0,"",0,0,25,80).

% edit window
editwindow :-
  edit_attr(Wattr,Fattr),
  edit_size(R,C,Rsize,Csize),
  makewindow(2,Wattr,Fattr,
           "IBIS-EDITOR",
           R,C,Rsize,Csize).

% directory window
dirwindow :-
  msg_attr(Wattr,Fattr),
  cursor(R,C), Row=R+1,
  makewindow(3,Wattr,Fattr,"Directory",Row,C,8,45).

% message window
msgwindow :-
  msg_attr(Wattr,Fattr),
  msg_size(R,C,Rsize,Csize),
  makewindow(4,Wattr,Fattr,"Messages",R,C,Rsize,Csize).

% treemenu window
mapwindow :-
  map_attr(Wattr,Fattr,_),
  map_size(R,C,Rsize,Csize),
  makewindow(5,Wattr,Fattr,"IBIS-MAP",R,C,Rsize,Csize).

% a dialog window
dialogwindow(NodeType):-
  dialog_attr(Wattr,Fattr),
  makewindow(6,Wattr,Fattr,NodeType,5,15,15,50).

% main status line
statusLINE:-
  status_attr(Attr),
  makestatus(Attr,
" >>>>>>>>>>>>>>>>>>>>>>> Select from pulldown menu <<<<<<<<<<<<<<<<<<<<<<<").


/* **************** windowNUM ************************** */

windowNUM(blankwindow,1).
windowNUM(editwindow,2).
windowNUM(dirwindow,3).
windowNUM(msgwindow,4).
```

(**Fig. 9-1e.** continued)

```
windowNUM(mapwindow,5).
windowNUM(dialogwindow,6).
windowNUM(pdwmenu,81).
windowNUM(status,83).

/* ******************** refreshNODE ********************* */
refreshNODE:-
   shiftwindow(OLD),
   currentNstr(STR),
   windowNUM(editwindow,Enum),
   shiftwindow(Enum),
   window_str(STR),
   shiftwindow(OLD).

refreshNODE.

/* ********************** clearCURRENT ****************** */
% clear the contents of current node from editor window.

clearCURRENT:-
  shiftwindow(OLD),
  windowNUM(editwindow,Enum),
  shiftwindow(Enum),
  clearwindow,
  retract(currentREF(_)),
  update(currentNstr("")),
  update(currentCpos(1)),
  shiftwindow(OLD).

/* ***************** refreshSCR ************************* */
refreshSCR:-
   windowNUM(pdwmenu,Pnum),
   windowNUM(mapwindow,Mnum),
   windowNUM(editwindow,Enum),
   shiftwindow(Mnum),
   shiftwindow(Enum),
   shiftwindow(Pnum).

refreshSCR.

/* *********************** textSCREEN ****************** */
% display the system version information.

textSCREEN:-
  map_attr(Wattr,Fattr,_),
  makewindow(11,Wattr,Fattr,"",7,10,9,60),
  write("\t\t       MicroIBIS 1.0"),
  write("\n\t An Issue Based Information System Shell"),
  write("\n\t\t\t    by "),
  write("\n\t\t      Safaa H. Hashim"),
  write("\n\n(c) TAB Books Inc., Exploring Hypertext Programming, 1988")
  write("\n\t\t Press any key to continue."),
  repeat,
    inkey(_),  % repeat waiting for a key to be pressed.
  !,
  removewindow.

/* *********************** initSETUP ******************* */

initSETUP:-
  existfile("ibis.sys"),
  consult("ibis.sys",setupdb), !.

% otherwise use default setup.
```

(**Fig. 9-1e.** continued)

```
initSETUP:-
  update1(pulldown_attr(112)),
  update1(edit_attr(15,112)),
  update1(msg_attr(15,112)),
  update1(map_attr(15,112,79)),
  update1(status_attr(112)),
  update1(aux_edit_attr(15,79)),
  update1(dialog_attr(15,31)),
  update1(map_size(3,0,17,36)),
  update1(msg_size(20,0,4,36)),
  update1(edit_size(3,36,21,44)).
/* *********************** window_color ***************** */
window_color(1):-
  windowNUM(editwindow,NUM),
  window1_color(editwindow,NUM).

window_color(2):-
  windowNUM(msgwindow,NUM),
  window1_color(msgwindow,NUM).

window_color(3):-
  windowNUM(mapwindow,NUM),
  window1_color(mapwindow,NUM).

window_color(4):-
  windowNUM(pdwmenu,NUM),
  window2_color(2,pdwmenu,NUM).

window_color(5):-
  windowNUM(status,NUM),
  window2_color(2,status,NUM).

window_color(6):-
  dialogwindow("dialog box"),
  windowNUM(dialogwindow,NUM),
  window1_color(dialogwindow,NUM),
  removewindow.
window_color(_).
/* *********************** window1_color **************** */
window1_color(Wname,Wnum):-
  pulldown_attr(Attr),
  menu(5,70,Attr,Attr,["Frame","Screen"],"",1,Choice),
  window2_color(Choice,Wname,Wnum).
/* *********************** window2_color **************** */
% setting the frame color

window2_color(1,Wname,NUM):-
  shiftwindow(OLD),
  shiftwindow(NUM),
  colorsetup(1),
  makewindow(_,Wattr,Fattr,_,_,_,_,_),
  update_attr(Wname,Wattr,Fattr),
  shiftwindow(OLD).

% setting the screen color

window2_color(2,Wname,NUM):-
  shiftwindow(OLD),
  shiftwindow(NUM),
  colorsetup(0),
  makewindow(_,Wattr,Fattr,_,_,_,_,_),
  update_attr(Wname,Wattr,Fattr),
```

(**Fig. 9-1e.** continued)

```
    shiftwindow(OLD).

  /* ********************** update_attr ****************** */
  update_attr(editwindow,Wattr,Fattr):-
    update1(edit_attr(Wattr,Fattr)).

  update_attr(msgwindow,Wattr,Fattr):-
    update1(msg_attr(Wattr,Fattr)).

  update_attr(mapwindow,Wattr,Fattr):-
    update1(map_attr(Wattr,Fattr,79)).

  update_attr(pdwmenu,Wattr,_):-
    update1(pulldown_attr(Wattr)).

  update_attr(status,Wattr,_):-
    update1(status_attr(Wattr)).

  update_attr(dialogwindow,Wattr,Fattr):-
    update1(dialog_attr(Wattr,Fattr)).

  /* ********************** window_size ****************** */

  % resizing the edit window
  window_size(1):-
    shiftwindow(OLD),
    windowNUM(editwindow,NUM),
    shiftwindow(NUM),
    resizewindow,
    makewindow(_,_,_,_,R,C,Rnum,Cnum),
    update1(edit_size(R,C,Rnum,Cnum)),
    shiftwindow(OLD).

  % resizing the message window
  window_size(2):-
    shiftwindow(OLD),
    windowNUM(msgwindow,NUM),
    windowNUM(mapwindow,Mnum),
    windowNUM(editwindow,Enum),
    shiftwindow(NUM),
    resizewindow,
    makewindow(_,_,_,_,R,C,Rnum,Cnum),
    update1(msg_size(R,C,Rnum,Cnum)),
    shiftwindow(Mnum),
    shiftwindow(Enum),
    shiftwindow(OLD).

  % resizing thye map window
  window_size(3):-
    shiftwindow(OLD),
    windowNUM(mapwindow,NUM),
    shiftwindow(NUM),
    resizewindow,
    makewindow(_,_,_,_,R,C,Rnum,Cnum),
    update1(map_size(R,C,Rnum,Cnum)),
    shiftwindow(OLD).

  /* ********************** writeMSG ******************** */
  writeMSG(stay,Msgs):-
     windowNUM(msgwindow,MSGnum),
     shiftwindow(MSGnum),
     listwrite(Msgs),
     write("\n").
  writeMSG(go,Msgs):-
```

(**Fig. 9-1e.** continued)

```
    windowNUM(msgwindow,MSGnum),
    shiftwindow(MSGnum),
    listwrite(Msgs),
    repeat,
      inkey(_), !,
    refreshSCR.
/* ********************* listwrite ********************** */
% inkey is used instead of keypressed, which was found to cause
% some problems in the dialog box program.

listwrite([]):- write("\n"), !.
listwrite([H|T]):- write(H), listwrite(T).
/* ****************** newCURSORpos ********************** */
newCURSORpos(ROW,COL):-
   cursor(R,C),
   makewindow(_,_,_,_,RO,CO,_,_),
   ROW=R+RO, COL=C+CO.
/* ************************************************** */
/* A TOOL FOR CHANGING THE DIRECTORY PATH            */
/* ************************************************** */
PREDICATES
  changeDIR(INTEGER,INTEGER,INTEGER,INTEGER)
  changeDISK(STRING)
  pathNAME(STRING)

CLAUSES

changeDIR(ROW,COL,WATTR,FATTR):-
  disk(DISK),
  lineinput_repeat(ROW,COL,45,WATTR,FATTR,"Directory: ",
                   DISK,NEWDISK),
  changeDISK(NEWDISK),!,
  removewindow.
changeDIR(_,_,_,_).

changeDISK(DISK):-
  pathNAME(DISK),
  disk(DISK),!.
changeDISK(_):-
  writeMSG(go,["\nerror in directory name."]), % in "user-h.pro"
  fail.

pathNAME(DISK):-
  fronttoken(DISK,_,Str),
  fronttoken(Str,":",Str1),
  fronttoken(Str1,"\\",_).

/* ********************** END END END **************** */
```

Fig. 9-1f. IBIS-DB.PRO

```
% File name: ibis-db.pro

/* ************************************************** */
/* IBIS DATABASE MANIPULATION PREDICATES              */
/* ************************************************** */
```

(**Fig. 9-1f.** continued)

```
PREDICATES

openDBfile(db_selector,STRING,place)
createDBfile(db_selector,STRING,place)
closeDBfile(db_selector)

loadIBISnode(ref)
nodesINibis(IBIS,REFLIST,REFLIST)
  nodesINibisL(IBISLIST,REFLIST,REFLIST)
deleteNODES(REFLIST)
ifNODEdeleted(REF)
ifCURRENTdeleted(REFLIST)

updateNstr(ref,STRING)
updateNcurrent(ref)
updateNattr(ref,STRING,STRING,STRING,STRING,STRING,
                      STRING,STRING,STRING)
getIBIS(IBIS)
getNODE(ref,NODE)
initCURRENTdb(STRING)
knowledgeTYPE(STRING)
saveCURRENT(ref,STRING,STRING,STRING,STRING,STRING,STRING)
initIBIS                    % defining an initial ibis tree
attrCHOICE(INTEGER)

CLAUSES

/* *********************** openDBfile ******************** */
openDBfile(DBselector,NAME,Place):-
   existfile(NAME),
   writeMSG(stay,["Opening DB file ",NAME]),
   db_open(DBselector,NAME,Place),
   update(dbSTATUS(opened)),
   writeMSG(go,["DB file ",NAME," is opened"]), !.

% Database file "NAME" doesn't exist.

openDBfile(_,NAME,_):-
   writeMSG(go,["Database file ",NAME," doesn't exist"]), !,
   fail.

/* ******************** createDBfile ******************* */

createDBfile(_,NAME,_):-
   existfile(NAME),
   writeMSG(go,["file already exists"]),
   !, fail.
createDBfile(DBselector,NAME,Place):-
   closeDBfile(DBselector),
   writeMSG(stay,["creating file ",NAME]),
   db_create(DBselector,NAME,Place),
   update(dbSTATUS(opened)),
   writeMSG(go,["File ",NAME," is created"]), !.

/* *********************** closeDBfile ****************** */

closeDBfile(DBselector):-
  dbSTATUS(opened),   % we can only close an opened db file.
  db_close(DBselector),
  update(dbSTATUS(closed)), !.

closeDBfile(_):- update(dbSTATUS(closed)).

/* ******************** loadIBISnode ******************** */
```

(**Fig. 9-1f.** continued)

```
/* This predicate checks if the REF of a node to be loaded
   is the same as the current node, if so it does nothing.
   Else it would load the new node and update the current
   db facts. */

loadIBISnode(Nref):-
  currentREF(Nref),
  refreshNODE, !.

loadIBISnode(Nref):-
  currentREF(Cref),
  % So before loading the new node, save current node
  currentNstr(Cstr),
  updateNstr(Cref,Cstr),
  % Make new node the current node
  updateNcurrent(Nref),
  refreshNODE, !.

loadIBISnode(Nref):-
  updateNcurrent(Nref),
  refreshNODE.

/* ******************* updateNcurrent ******************* */

updateNcurrent(REF):-
  ref_term(ibisdb,node,REF,NODE),
  NODE = node(Ntype,Ktype,A,D,STR),
  update(currentREF(REF)),
  update(currentNstr(STR)),
  update(currentNtype(Ntype)),
  update(currentKtype(Ktype)),
  update(currentAUTHOR(A)),
  update(currentDATE(D)),
  update(currentCpos(1)),
  fail.

updateNcurrent(_).
/* ********************** updateNattr ******************* */

updateNattr(_,_,_,K,A,D,K,A,D):- !.
updateNattr(REF,STR,N,_,_,_,K1,A1,D1):-
  term_replace(ibisdb,node,REF,node(N,K1,A1,D1,STR)).

/* ********************** updateNstr ******************** */

updateNstr(REF,STR):-
  ref_term(ibisdb,node,REF,OLDnode),
  OLDnode = node(N,K,A,D,_),
  term_replace(ibisdb,node,REF,node(N,K,A,D,STR)),
  fail.
updateNstr(_,_).


/* ******************** nodesINibis ********************* */

nodesINibis(ibis(_,_,REF,[]),L,[REF|L]):-!.
nodesINibis(ibis(_,_,REF,[H|T]),OLD,NEW):-
  nodesINibis(H,[REF|OLD],TEMP),
  nodesINibisL(T,TEMP,NEW).

nodesINibisL([],L,L):-!.
nodesINibisL([H|T],OLD,NEW):-
  nodesINibis(H,OLD,TEMP),
  nodesINibisL(T,TEMP,NEW).
```

(**Fig. 9-1f.** continued)

```
/* ******************** deleteNODES ******************** */

deleteNODES([]):-!.
deleteNODES([REF|T]):-
  term_delete(ibisdb,nodech,REF),
  deleteNODES(T).

/* ******************* ifNODEdeleted ******************* */

ifNODEdeleted(_):- deleteSTATUS([]), !.

ifNODEdeleted(REF):-
  deleteSTATUS(REFlist),
  member(REF,REFlist),
  update(deleteSTATUS([])), !, fail.

ifNODEdeleted(_):- update(deleteSTATUS([])).

/* ******************* ifCURRENTdeleted ***************** */

ifCURRENTdeleted(REFlist):-
  currentREF(REF),
  member(REF,REFlist),
  clearCURRENT.

ifCURRENTdeleted(_).

/* ******************** initCURRENTdb ******************* */

initCURRENTdb(NAME) :-
  dbSTATUS(opened), % we only initialize when db is open
  getIBIS(IBIS),
  IBIS=ibis("root","issue",REF,_),
  updateNcurrent(REF),
  update(currentFILE(NAME)), !.

/* ************************* getIBIS ******************** */
/* for efficient use of the global stack a call to ref_term
   must be followed by "fail" to release the allocated space
   (see TURBO PROLOG user guide page 339 ) */

getIBIS(IBIS):-
  chain_terms(ibisdb,ibisch,ibis,IBIS,_),
  update(currentIBIS(IBIS)),
  fail.

getIBIS(IBIS):- currentIBIS(IBIS).

/* ************************ getNODE ********************* */

getNODE(REF,NODE):-
  ref_term(ibisdb,node,REF,NODE),
  update(currentNODE(NODE)),
  fail.

getNODE(_,NODE):- currentNODE(NODE).

/* ********************** initIBIS ********************* */

initIBIS:-
  shiftwindow(OLD),
  nodeDIALOG(Kstr,Author,Date),
  knowledgeTYPE(Kstr),
  INstr="", INpos=1,
```

(**Fig. 9-1f.** continued)

```
   MSG="Enter your issue",
   changestatus(
"F1-Help F2-Xsave F3-Load F4-Replace F5-Zoom F7-Xcopy F8-Xedit (F10 or ESC)-
End"),
   windowNUM(editwindow,Enum),
   shiftwindow(Enum),
   edit(INstr,OUTstr,"<NODE EDITOR>","I1",MSG,
           INpos,"",1,1,1,1,_,_),
   changestatus(
" >>>>>>>>>>>>>>>>>>>>>>>>> Select from pulldown menu
<<<<<<<<<<<<<<<<<<<<<<<<"),
   chain_inserta(ibisdb,nodech,node,
                 node("issue",Kstr,Author,Date,OUTstr),REF),
   chain_inserta(ibisdb,ibisch,ibis,ibis("root","issue",REF,[]),_),
   shiftwindow(OLD).

/* ************************ Ktype ************************ */

knowledgeTYPE("conceptual").
knowledgeTYPE("factual").
knowledgeTYPE("deontic").
knowledgeTYPE("instrumental").
knowledgeTYPE("explanatory").

/* ********************** saveCURRENT ******************** */

saveCURRENT(_,STR,_,_,_,_,STR):-!.
saveCURRENT(REF,STR,N,K,A,D,_):-
   term_replace(ibisdb,node,REF,node(N,K,A,D,STR)).

/* ********************* attrCHOICE ********************** */
attrCHOICE(1):- update(currentNdialog("on")).
attrCHOICE(2):- update(currentNdialog("off")).

/* ********************* END END END END **************** */
```

Fig. 9-1g. IBIS-PRT.PRO

```
% File name: ibis-prt.pro

/* ******************************************************** */
/* PRINTING IBIS TREE TO A PRINTER OR FILE                  */
/* DUMPING IBIS KNOWLEDGE BASE TO EXTERNAL FILE             */
/* ******************************************************** */

/* The predicates in this file write the contents of nodes
   to the current output device. The output is directed by
   the openwrite, and writedevice (built-in) predicates.
   The redirection is done via the print option in the file
   menu--see the file ibis-run.pro  this file must be
   included after:
      all toolbox files ,
      ibis-use, and
      ibis-map */
/* ******************************************************** */
/* Types of printing, depth first or breadth first.         */
/* ******************************************************** */

PREDICATES
  printDF(TREE)
    printDF1(STRING,STRING,TREE)
    printDFlist(STRING,STRING,TREELIST)
```

(**Fig. 9-1g.** continued)

```
CLAUSES

/* ************************ printDF ********************* */

printDF(tree("root",Name,REF,TREElist)):-
  ref_term(ibisdb,node,REF,NODE),
  NODE = node(Ntype,_,_,_,STR),
  write("\nThe main issue"," (",Name,") is:"),
  write("\n\n",STR),
  printDFlist(Ntype,Name,TREElist).

printDF1(Ntype,Name,tree(Rel,Name1,REF,[])):-
  ref_term(ibisdb,node,REF,NODE),
  NODE = node(Ntype1,_,_,_,STR),
  write("\n\n\n",Ntype1," (",Name1,") ",Rel," ",
               Ntype," (",Name,"):"),
  write("\n\n",STR), !.

printDF1(Ntype,Name,tree(Rel,Name1,REF,TREElist)):-
  ref_term(ibisdb,node,REF,NODE),
  NODE = node(Ntype1,_,_,_,STR),
  write("\n\n\n",Ntype1," (",Name1,") ",Rel," ",
               Ntype," (",Name,"):"),
  write("\n\n",STR),
  printDFlist(Ntype1,Name1,TREElist), !.

/* ********************** printDFlist ****************** */
printDFlist(Ntype,Name,[Htree]):-
  printDF1(Ntype,Name,Htree), !.

printDFlist(Ntype,Name,[Htree|TREElist]):-
  printDF1(Ntype,Name,Htree),
  printDFlist(Ntype,Name,TREElist).

/* ***************************************************** */
/* ********************* printIBIS ********************** */
/* ***************************************************** */

PREDICATES
  printIBIS
    printCHOICE(INTEGER)

CLAUSES

printIBIS:-
  dbSTATUS(opened),
  newCURSORpos(Row,Col),  % in ibis-use.pro
  pulldown_attr(ATTR),
  menu(Row,Col,ATTR,ATTR,["Printer","File"],"print",1,CHOICE),
  printCHOICE(CHOICE), !.

printIBIS:-
  writeMSG(go,["IBIS DB file is not open"]).

printCHOICE(1):-
  writeMSG(stay,["printing IBIS"]),
  writedevice(printer),
  chain_terms(ibisdb,ibisch,ibis,IBIS,_), !,
  getTREE(keys(0,0,0,0),_,IBIS,TREE),   % in ibis-map.pro
  printDF(TREE),
  writedevice(screen),
  refreshSCR.
```

(**Fig. 9-1g.** continued)

```
printCHOICE(2):-
  newCURSORpos(Row,Col),
  readfilename(Row,Col,15,112,txt,"",FileName),
  writeMSG(stay,["Writing IBIS to ",FileName]),
  openwrite(ibistxt,FileName),
  writedevice(ibistxt),
  chain_terms(ibisdb,ibisch,ibis,IBIS,_), !,
  getTREE(keys(0,0,0,0),_,IBIS,TREE),
  printDF(TREE),
  writedevice(screen),
  closefile(ibistxt),
  refreshSCR.
printCHOICE(_):- writedevice(screen).

/* ****************************************************** */
/* DUMPING AN IBIS EXTERNAL DATABASE FILE TO A TEXT FILE   */
/* ****************************************************** */

PREDICATES
   dumpIBIS
     dumpDba
       wrIBIS(IBIS)
       wrNODE

CLAUSES
/* *********************** dumpIBIS ******************** */
dumpIBIS:-
  dbSTATUS(opened),
  newCURSORpos(Row,Col),
  readfilename(Row,Col,15,112,txt,"",FileName),
  writeMSG(stay,["Writing IBIS KB to ",FileName]),
  openwrite(ibistxt,FileName),
  writedevice(ibistxt),
  dumpDba,
  writedevice(screen),
  closefile(ibistxt),
  refreshSCR, !.

dumpIBIS:- writeMSG(go,["IBIS DB file is not open"]).

/* ************************ dumpDba ******************** */
dumpDba:-
  chain_terms(ibisdb, ibisch, ibis, IBIS, _),
  write("\n\n\n ******** THE IBIS TREE ********\n\n"),
  wrIBIS(IBIS),
  write("\n\n\n ******** THE NODES ********\n\n"),
  wrNODE,
  write("\n\n\n ******** END OF KB ********\n\n").

/* ************************ wrIBIS ********************** */
wrIBIS(X) :- write(X), nl.

/* ************************ wrNODE ********************** */
wrNODE:-
  chain_terms(ibisdb, nodech, node, Term, _),
  write(Term), nl, fail.
wrNODE.

/* ****************************************************** */
```

Fig. 9-1h. IBIS-UT.PRO

```
% File name: ibis-ut.pro

/* ****************************************************** */
/* UTILITY PREDICATES                                     */
/* ****************************************************** */

PREDICATES

%@ in ibis-glb.pro
%@ update(dbasedom)
update1(setupdb)

concat_list(STRINGLIST,STRING)
  concat_list1(STRINGLIST,STRING,STRING)

member(REF,REFLIST)
member(STRING,STRINGLIST)

CLAUSES
/* *********************** update ********************** */

update(currentNtype(_)):- retract(currentNtype(_)), fail.
update(currentKtype(_)):- retract(currentKtype(_)), fail.
update(currentAUTHOR(_)):- retract(currentAUTHOR(_)), fail.
update(currentDATE(_)):- retract(currentDATE(_)), fail.
update(currentNdialog(_)):- retract(currentNdialog(_)), fail.
update(deleteSTATUS(_)):- retract(deleteSTATUS(_)), fail.
update(currentREF(_)):- retract(currentREF(_)), fail.
update(dbSTATUS(_)):- retract(dbSTATUS(_)), fail.
update(currentIBIS(_)):- retract(currentIBIS(_)), fail.
update(currentNstr(_)):- retract(currentNstr(_)), fail.
update(currentCpos(_)):- retract(currentCpos(_)), fail.
update(currentFILE(_)):- retract(currentFILE(_)), fail.
update(currentNODE(_)):- retract(currentNODE(_)), fail.

update(X):- asserta(X).

/* *********************** update1 ********************* */

update1(edit_attr(_,_)):- retract(edit_attr(_,_),setupdb), fail.
update1(msg_attr(_,_)):- retract(msg_attr(_,_),setupdb), fail.
update1(map_attr(_,_,_)):- retract(map_attr(_,_,_),setupdb), fail.
update1(dialog_attr(_,_)):- retract(dialog_attr(_,_),setupdb), fail.
update1(status_attr(_)):- retract(status_attr(_),setupdb), fail.
update1(aux_edit_attr(_,_)):- retract(aux_edit_attr(_,_),setupdb), fail.
update1(edit_size(_,_,_,_)):- retract(edit_size(_,_,_,_),setupdb), fail.
update1(msg_size(_,_,_,_)):- retract(msg_size(_,_,_,_),setupdb), fail.
update1(map_size(_,_,_,_)):- retract(map_size(_,_,_,_),setupdb), fail.

update1(X):- asserta(X,setupdb).

/* *********************** concat_list ***************** */

concat_list(LIST,STR):-
  concat_list1(LIST,"",STR).

concat_list1([],STR,STR):-!.
concat_list1([H|T],OLDstr,NEWstr):-
  concat(OLDstr,H,MIDstr),
  concat_list1(T,MIDstr,NEWstr).

/* ************************* member ******************** */
```

(**Fig. 9-1h.** continued)

```
member(H,[H|_]):-!.
member(H,[_|T]):- member(H,T).
/* ********************* END END END ******************** */
```

Fig. 9-1i. IBIS-MAP.PRO

```
% File name: ibis-map.pro

/* ***************************************************** */
/* GENERATING BOX AND TREE MENUS OF IBIS NODES           */
/* ***************************************************** */

/*

To try the program by itself uncomment these declarations
NOTE: For testing the program change any REF domain to INTEGER.
      Also, comment out the getNODEname predicate because it needs
      external database domain input.

include "tdoms.pro"

DOMAINS
  KEYS = keys(INTEGER,INTEGER,INTEGER,INTEGER)
  ID   = id(STRING,INTEGER) % integer is ref
  IDLIST = ID*

  RELATION,NTYPE=STRING
  IBIS = ibis(RELATION,NTYPE,INTEGER,ibislist) % INTEGER is ref
  IBISLIST = ibis*

  % treemenu domains
  SELECTOR = INTEGER  % selector has a ref domain
  TREE = tree(string,string,selector,treelist)
  TREELIST = tree*

DATABASE

% predicates used in lineinp
insmode
lineinpstate(STRING,COL)
lineinpflag

% predicates used in tree menu
treewindow(ROW,COL)
treechoice(SELECTOR)

include "tpreds.pro"
include "lineinp.pro"
include "boxmenu.pro"
include "status.pro"
include "tree2.pro"  % A modified version of tree.pro
*/

/* +++++++++++++++++++++++++++++++++++++++++++++++++++++ */

PREDICATES

map(REF)

% map uses getTREE

nodename(ROW,COL,ATTR,ATTR,IBIS,STRING,STRING,REF)
```

(**Fig. 9-1i.** continued)

```
% nodename uses getTREE & getIDlist

nodename1(ROW,COL,ATTR,ATTR,IDLIST,STRING,STRING,REF)
    % uses strTOref
    nodename2(ROW,COL,ATTR,ATTR,IDLIST,STRING,REF)
      getSTRlist(IDLIST,STRINGLIST)
      pickREF(INTEGER,IDLIST,STRING,REF)

strTOref(STRING,IDLIST,REF)
refTOstr(REF,IDLIST,STRING)

getNODEname(REF,STRING)

getTREE(keys,keys,IBIS,TREE)
  getNODEtype(keys,keys,NTYPE,STRING)
  getTREElist(keys,keys,IBISLIST,TREELIST)

getIDlist(TREE,IDLIST)
  getIDlist1(STRING,TREELIST,IDLIST,IDLIST)

reverse(IDLIST,IDLIST,IDLIST)


CLAUSES


/* ****************************************************** */
/* *********************** MAP ************************** */
/* ****************************************************** */
% notice that we use a modified version of treemenu in "tree2.pro"

map(REF):-
  chain_terms(ibisdb,ibisch,ibis,IBIS,_),
  getTREE(keys(0,0,0,0),_,IBIS,TREE),
  changestatus(
"F1:Help F5:Zoom F10:HypTxtMenu Cr:Select Arrow:move-around Ctrl-arrow:move-
fast"),
  treemenu(right,TREE,REF),
  changestatus(
" >>>>>>>>>>>>>>>>>>>>>> Select from pulldown menu <<<<<<<<<<<<<<<<<<<<<<"),
 !.

/* *********************** getNODEname ***************** */

getNODEname(REF,NAME):-
  chain_terms(ibisdb,ibisch,ibis,IBIS,_), !,
  getTREE(keys(0,0,0,0),_,IBIS,TREE),
  getIDlist(TREE,IDlist),
  refTOstr(REF,IDlist,NAME).

/* ***************** getTREE & getTREElist ************* */
/* getTREE takes an ibis tree and converts it to a tree

   suitable for the treemenu predicate.
   Flow pattern:   (i,o,i,o)
*/

getTREE(Keys,Keys1,ibis(Rel,Node,Sel,[]),
                  tree(Rel,STR,Sel,[])):-
  getNODEtype(Keys,Keys1,Node,Str), !.
getTREE(Keys,Keys3,ibis(Rel,N,Sel,[H|T]),
                  tree(Rel,Str,Sel,[Htree|Ttree])):-
  getNODEtype(Keys,Keys1,N,Str),
  getTREE(Keys1,Keys2,H,Htree),
  getTREElist(Keys2,Keys3,T,Ttree), !.
```

(**Fig. 9-1i.** continued)

```
getTREElist(Keys,Keys,[],[]):-!.
getTREElist(Keys,Keys2,[Hnode|Tnodes],[Htree|Ttrees]):-
  getTREE(Keys,Keys1,Hnode,Htree),
  getTREElist(Keys1,Keys2,Tnodes,Ttrees), !.

/* *********************** getNODEtype ******************* */
/* This predicate converts a node type to a string:
   for a node of issue type which is "issue(REF)" it will
   give STR=I# The # is a number generated by the system to
   reflect the number of the nodes, for example it could
   be I5, P3, A13, or R7. */

getNODEtype(keys(I,P,A,R),keys(I1,P,A,R),"issue",Str):-
  I1=I+1,
  str_int(Istr,I1),
  concat("I",Istr,Str), !.

getNODEtype(keys(I,P,A,R),keys(I,P1,A,R),"position",Str):-
  P1= P+1,
  str_int(Pstr,P1),
  concat("P",Pstr,Str), !.

getNODEtype(keys(I,P,A,R),keys(I,P,A1,R),"argument",Str):-
  A1=A+1,
  str_int(Astr,A1),
  concat("A",Astr,Str), !.

getNODEtype(keys(I,P,A,R),keys(I,P,A,R1),"reference",Str):-
  R1=R+1,
  str_int(Rstr,R1),
  concat("R",Rstr,Str), !.
/* *********************** getIDlist ******************** */

getIDlist(tree(_,Str,REF,TreeList),[id(Str,REF)|IDlist]):-
  getIDlist1(Str,TreeList,[],IDlist1),
  reverse(IDlist1,[],IDlist).

getIDlist1(_,[],L,L):-!.
getIDlist1(ID1,[tree(_,ID2,REF,L2)|L1],OldL,NewL):-
  concat(ID1,ID2,ID),
  getIDlist1(ID2,L2,[id(ID,REF)|OldL],TempL),
  getIDlist1(ID1,L1,TempL,NewL).

/* *********************** reverse *********************** */
reverse([X|Y],M,N):-
  reverse(Y,[X|M],N).
reverse([],N,N):-!.

/* ***************************************************** */
/* ********************** NODENAME ********************** */
/* ***************************************************** */

nodename(ROW,COL,WATTR,FATTR,IBIS,OLD,NODEname,REF):-
  getTREE(keys(0,0,0,0),_,IBIS,TREE),
  getIDlist(TREE,IDLIST),
  TXT = "Node name:",
  lineinput_repeat(ROW,COL,40,WATTR,FATTR,TXT,OLD,NAME),
  nodename1(ROW,COL,WATTR,FATTR,IDLIST,NAME,NODEname,REF),!,
  write(NODEname), readln(_),
  removewindow, !.

/* ******************** nodename1 ********************** */

nodename1(ROW,COL,WATTR,FATTR,IDLIST,"",NODEname,REF):- !,
```

(**Fig. 9-1i.** continued)

```
    ROW2=ROW+3,
    nodename2(ROW2,COL,WATTR,FATTR,IDLIST,NODEname,REF).
  nodename1(_,_,_,_,IDLIST,NAME,NAME,REF):-
    strTOref(NAME,IDLIST,REF).

  /* ********************** nodename2 ********************* */

  nodename2(ROW,COL,WATTR,FATTR,IDlist,NODEname,REF):-
    getSTRlist(IDlist,STRlist),
    boxmenu(ROW,COL,6,40,WATTR,FATTR,STRlist,
            "Nodes directory",1,Choice),
    pickREF(Choice,IDlist,NODEname,REF), !.

  nodename2(_,_,_,_,_,_,_):-fail.

  /* *********************** strTOref ******************** */

  strTOref(STR,[id(STR,REF)|_],REF):-!.
  strTOref(STR,[_|L],REF):- strTOref(STR,L,REF).

  /* *********************** refTOstr ******************** */

  refTOstr(REF,[id(STR,REF)|_],STR):-!.
  refTOstr(REF,[_|L],STR):- refTOstr(REF,L,STR).


  /* ********************* getSTRlist ******************** */

  % translate a list of ID pairs into a list of ID strings

  getSTRlist([],[]):-!.
  getSTRlist([id(STR,_)|IDlist],[STR|STRlist]):-
    getSTRlist(IDlist,STRlist).

  /* ********************* pickREF ********************** */

  pickREF(1,[id(STR,REF)|_],STR,REF):-!.
  pickREF(NUM,[_|T],STR,REF):-
    NUM1=NUM-1,
    pickREF(NUM1,T,STR,REF).

  /* +++++++++++++++++++++++++++++++++++++++++++++++++++++ */

  /* ***************************************************** */
  /* **************** TESTING PREDICATES ***************** */
  /* ***************************************************** */

  /* To use the testing predicates, you must change every REF
     domain into an INTEGER domain above.

  PREDICATES
    testmap
    testnodename

    mapwindow

  CLAUSES

  mapwindow :- makewindow(5,15,112,"IBIS road-map",3,0,21,80).

  testmap:-
    mapwindow,  % in "ibis-use.pro"
    map(ibis("root","issue",1,
          [ibis("responds-to","position",2,
               [ibis("objects-to","argument",3,[]),
```

(**Fig. 9-1i.** continued)

```
                 ibis("supports","argument",4,[])
                ]),
            ibis("responds-to","position",5,
                [ibis("supports","argument",6,[]),
                 ibis("refered-to-by","reference",7,[])
                ]),
            ibis("generalizes","issue",8,
                [ibis("responds-to","position",9,
                     [ibis("objects-to","argument",10,[]),
                      ibis("supports","argument",11,[])
                     ])
                ])
           ]),
            "",NodeName,REF),
    write("Node name= ",NodeName,"\nREF= ",REF),
    readln(_).
*/
/* +++++++++++++++++++++++++++++++++++++++++++++++++++ */

/* ************************* END END END ***************** */
                 ibis("supports","argument",4,[])
                ]),
            ibis("responds-to","position",5,
                [ibis("supports","argument",6,[]),
                 ibis("refered-to-by","reference",7,[])
                ]),
            ibis("generalizes","issue",8,
                [ibis("responds-to","position",9,
                     [ibis("objects-to","argument",10,[]),
                      ibis("supports","argument",11,[])
                     ])
                ])
           ]),
       REF),
   write("REF = ",REF),
   readln(_).

testnodename:-
   nodename(1,1,2,4,
       ibis("root","issue",1,
           [ibis("responds-to","position",2,
                [ibis("objects-to","argument",3,[]),
```

Fig. 9-1j. TREE2.PRO

```
% File name: tree2.pro

/* ******************************************************** */
/*
                             Treemenu (V.2)

(treemenu is copyright of Borland International)
(modified version of the TURBO PROLOG TOOLBOX TREE MENU)
(Copyright 1986, Borland International.)

modifications are in:

1. predicate "listsum" is now tail recursive (more efficient).
2. Arrows pointing to parent nodes are added.
3. the arcs between nodes are labeled with relation names.
   to facilitate this tree definition.
```

(**Fig. 9-1j.** continued)

```
   4. predicate draw_right is now tail recursive, the
      draw_rightlist appears at the end of draw_right, not in
      the middle.
   5. a new predicate "writetext1" was added for writing labels.

*/
/* ****************************************************** */
/*
include "tdoms.pro"

DOMAINS
  SELECTOR=INTEGER
  TREE = tree(STRING,STRING,SELECTOR,TREELIST)
  TREELIST = TREE*

DATABASE
  treewindow(ROW,COL)
  treechoice(SELECTOR)
*/

DOMAINS
  ROWLIST=ROW*
  COLLIST=COL*

PREDICATES
% @ treemenu(SYMBOL,TREE,SELECTOR)  /* in ibis-glb.pro  */
  treeaction(SELECTOR)
% @  f10action(SELECTOR)    /* in ibis-glb.pro */
  draw(symbol,TREE)
  writetext(ROW,COL,INTEGER,STRING,SELECTOR)
  writetext1(ROW,COL,STRING,COL)
  treeline_ver(ROW,ROW,COL)
  treeline_ver1(ROW,ROW,COL)
  treeline_hor(COL,COL,ROW)
  treeline_hor1(COL,COL,ROW)
  scr_ch(ROW,COL,CHAR)
  lastinlist(ROW,ROWLIST)
  lastinlist(COL,COLLIST)
  listsum(ROWLIST,ROW,ROW)
  listsum(COLLIST,COL,COL)
  treekeyact(KEY)
  just(ROW,COL)
  just1(ROW,COL,ROW,COL)
  just2(ROW,COL)
  nodelistlen(ROWLIST,INTEGER)
  nodelistlen(COLLIST,INTEGER)
  remove_treechoice
  newupdate(DBASEDOM)
  treedrop(INTEGER,STRING,STRING)


CLAUSES

/* ********************* treeline_ver ******************* */

/* draw vertical lines connecting elements in the tree */
  treeline_ver(R1,R2,C):-
    treewindow(STROW,STCOL),          /* find the starting position */
    makewindow(_,_,_,_,_,_,ROWS,COLS), /* returns the tree windows size */
    C>=STCOL, C<STCOL+COLS-2, R1<STROW+ROWS-2,
    R2>=STROW, SLROW=STROW+ROWS-2,
    max(STROW,R1,STROW1), min(R2,SLROW,SLROW1),
    CC=C-STCOL, RR1=STROW1-STROW, RR2=SLROW1-STROW,
    treeline_ver1(RR1,RR2,CC),fail.
```

(**Fig. 9-1j.** continued)

```
   treeline_ver(_,_,_).

/* ******************** treeline_ver1 ******************* */

  treeline_ver1(R1,R2,C):-
    R2>R1, R=R1+1,
    scr_char(R1,C,'°'),
    treeline_ver1(R,R2,C).

/* ********************** treeline_hor **************** */

/* draw horizontal lines connecting elements in the tree */
  treeline_hor(C1,C2,R):-
    treewindow(STROW,STCOL),
    makewindow(_,_,_,_,_,_,ROWS,COLS),
    SLCOL=STCOL+COLS-2,
    R>=STROW, R<STROW+ROWS-2, C1<SLCOL, C2>STCOL,
    max(STCOL,C1,STCOL1), min(C2,SLCOL,SLCOL1),
    RR=R-STROW, CC1=STCOL1-STCOL, CC2=SLCOL1-STCOL,
    treeline_hor1(CC1,CC2,RR),fail.
  treeline_hor(_,_,_).

/* ********************** treeline_hor1 **************** */

  treeline_hor1(C1,C2,R):-
    C2>C1, C=C1+1,
    scr_char(R,C1,'á'),
    treeline_hor1(C,C2,R).

/* ************************* scr_ch ******************** */

/* write a character in a tree window  */
  scr_ch(R,C,CH):-
    treewindow(STROW,STCOL), makewindow(_,_,_,_,_,_,ROWS,COLS),
    R>=STROW, R<STROW+ROWS-2, C>=STCOL, C<STCOL+COLS-2, !,
    RR=R-STROW, CC=C-STCOL,
    scr_char(RR,CC,CH).
  scr_ch(_,_,_).

/* ************************* treedrop ****************** */

  treedrop(0,TEXT,TEXT):-!.
  treedrop(N,TEXT,TEXT1):-frontstr(N,TEXT,_,TEXT1).

/* ************************* writetext ****************** */

  writetext(ROW,COL,ATTR,TEXT,SELECT):-
    str_len(TEXT,LEN),
    treewindow(STROW,STCOL), makewindow(_,_,_,_,_,_,ROWS,COLS),
    ROW>=STROW, ROW<STROW+ROWS-2, COL<STCOL+COLS-2, COL+LEN>STCOL,
    REALROW=ROW-STROW,
    RSTART=COL-STCOL,
    REND=RSTART+LEN,
    VST=STCOL-STCOL, VEND=VST+COLS-2,
    max(RSTART,VST,RSTART1), min(REND,VEND,REND1),
    REALLEN=REND1-RSTART1,
    DROP=RSTART1-RSTART,
    treedrop(DROP,TEXT,TEXT1),
    field_str(REALROW,RSTART1,REALLEN,TEXT1),
    field_attr(REALROW,RSTART1,REALLEN,ATTR),
    cursor(R,C),
    R=REALROW,
    C>=RSTART1, C<RSTART1+REALLEN,    !,
    field_attr(R,RSTART1,REALLEN,79),
    assert(treechoice(SELECT)).
  writetext(_,_,_,_,_).
```

(**Fig. 9-1j.** continued)

```
/* *************************** writetext1 **************** */

writetext1(ROW,COL,TEXT,COLAFTERTEXT):-
  str_len(TEXT,LEN),
  COLAFTERTEXT=COL+LEN,
  treewindow(STROW,STCOL), makewindow(_,_,_,_,_,_,ROWS,COLS),
  ROW>=STROW, ROW<STROW+ROWS-2, COL<STCOL+COLS-2, COL+LEN>STCOL,
  REALROW=ROW-STROW,
  RSTART=COL-STCOL,
  REND=RSTART+LEN,
  VEND=COLS-2,
  max(RSTART,0,RSTART1), min(REND,VEND,REND1),
  REALLEN=REND1-RSTART1,
  DROP=RSTART1-RSTART,
  treedrop(DROP,TEXT,TEXT1),
  field_str(REALROW,RSTART1,REALLEN,TEXT1), !.

writetext1(_,C,_,C).

/* **************************** listsum ****************** */

  listsum([],S,S):-!.
  listsum([H|T],OS,NS):-TS=OS+H,listsum(T,TS,NS).

/* ********************** lastinlist ******************* */

  lastinlist(RMAX,[RMAX]) :- !.
  lastinlist(RMAX,[_|T]) :- lastinlist(RMAX,T).

/* ********************* nodelistlen ******************* */

  nodelistlen([],0):-!.
  nodelistlen([_|T],N):-
    nodelistlen(T,X),
    N=X+1.

/* ********************** newupdate ******************** */

  newupdate(_):-retract(treewindow(_,_)),fail.
  newupdate(X):-assert(X).

/* ************************** just *********************** */

/* Cursor window control */
  just(R,C):-
    cursor(ROW,COL),        /* current cursor pos */
    RR=ROW+R, CC=COL+C,
    makewindow(_,_,_,_,_,_,ROWS,COLS),
    ROWSS=ROWS-3, COLSS=COLS-3,
    just1(RR,CC,ROWSS,COLSS).

/* ************************ just1 *********************** */

/* move cursor and control windows */
  just1(R,C,_,_):-R<0,!,cursor(0,C),just2(R,0).
  just1(R,C,_,_):-C<0,!,cursor(R,0),just2(0,C).
  just1(R,C,ROWS,_):-R>ROWS,!,cursor(ROWS,C),DR=R-ROWS,just2(DR,0).
  just1(R,C,_,COLS):-C>COLS,!,cursor(R,COLS),DC=C-COLS,just2(0,DC).
  just1(R,C,_,_):-cursor(R,C),fail.

/* ************************* just2 ********************** */

/* scroll tree in window with cursor and update tree position */
  just2(DR,DC):-
```

(**Fig. 9-1j.** continued)

```
    scroll(DR,DC),  /* scroll is a Turbo Prolog standard predicate */
    treewindow(R,C),!,
    CC=C+DC, RR=R+DR,
    newupdate(treewindow(RR,CC)),
    fail.

/* *********************** treekeyact ****************** */

/* Tree input key action */
  treekeyact(right):-just(0,1).
  treekeyact(ctrlright):-just(0,5).
  treekeyact(left):-just(0,-1).
  treekeyact(ctrlleft):-just(0,-5).
  treekeyact(up):-just(-1,0).
  treekeyact(pgup):-just(-5,0).
  treekeyact(down):-just(1,0).
  treekeyact(pgdn):-just(5,0).
  treekeyact(ctrlhome):-treewindow(R,C),!,RR=-R,CC=-C,just2(RR,CC).
  treekeyact(end):-cursor(_,C),makewindow(_,_,_,_,_,_,_,COLS),
    DC=COLS-3-C,just(0,DC).
  treekeyact(home):-cursor(_,C),DC=-C,just(0,DC).
  treekeyact(cr):-treechoice(CHOICE), !, treeaction(CHOICE).
  treekeyact(esc).

/* *******************************************************
@@@ F10 is a hypertext hotkey that displays hypertext
   operations menu
******************************************************* */
  treekeyact(fkey(10))   :-
    treechoice(CHOICE), !,
    f10action(CHOICE). % f10action is a hotkey action


/*treekeyact(fkey(1)):-help.  If helpsystem is used */

  treekeyact(fkey(5)):-
     makewindow(_,_,_,_,R,C,RN,CN),
     R=0, C=0, RN=24, CN=80,
     clearwindow,
     map_size(MR,MC,MRN,MCN),
     resizewindow(MR,MC,MRN,MCN), !, fail.

  treekeyact(fkey(5)):-
     clearwindow,
     resizewindow(0,0,24,80), !, fail.

/* ******************** remove_treechoice *************** */

  remove_treechoice:- retract(treechoice(_)), fail.
  remove_treechoice.

/* ****************************************************** */
/* ***********************draw_right ******************* */
/* ****************************************************** */
/* @@@ This is a modified version of draw_right */

PREDICATES
  draw_right(TREE,ROW,ROW,COL,COL,COL,COL,ROW)
  draw_rightlist(STRING,STRING,SELECTOR,TREELIST,
                 STRINGLIST,STRINGLIST,
                 ROWLIST,ROWLIST,
                 ROW,ROW,
                 COL,COL,COL,COL,ROW)
  connect_nodesright(STRINGLIST,ROW,COL,INTEGER,COL,COL,ROWLIST)
  con_nodesright(STRINGLIST,ROW,COL,ROW,ROW,COL,COL,ROWLIST)
  cornerright(ROW,ROW,ROW,ROW,CHAR)
```

(**Fig. 9-1j.** continued)

```
    check_lastright(ROW,COL,ROWLIST)

  CLAUSES

  draw_right(_,_,_,_,_,_,_):-
    keypressed, !,
    readkey(KEY),
    treekeyact(KEY),
    fail.

  draw_right(tree("root",NAME,SELECT,[]),
             CURROW,NEWCURROW,
             _,CURCOL,CURCOL,_,RESROW):- !,
    NEWCURROW=CURROW+2,
    RESROW=NEWCURROW,
    writetext(RESROW,CURCOL,112,NAME,SELECT).

  draw_right(tree(RELATION,NAME,SELECT,[]),
             CURROW,NEWCURROW,
             _,CURCOL,CURCOL,COLSTEP,RESROW):- !,
    NEWCURROW=CURROW+2,
    str_len(RELATION,LEN),
    CURCOL1=CURCOL+LEN+COLSTEP,
    RESROW=NEWCURROW,
    writetext(RESROW,CURCOL1,112,NAME,SELECT).

  draw_right(tree("root",NAME,SELECT,TREELIST),
             CURROW,NEWCURROW,
             LASTNAMECOL,NEXTNAMECOL,CURCOL,COLSTEP,RESROW):- !,
    draw_rightlist("",NAME,SELECT,TREELIST,
                   [],_,
                   [],_,
                   CURROW,NEWCURROW,
                   LASTNAMECOL,NEXTNAMECOL,CURCOL,COLSTEP,RESROW).

  draw_right(tree(RELATION,NAME,SELECT,TREELIST),
             CURROW,NEWCURROW,
             LASTNAMECOL,NEXTNAMECOL,CURCOL,COLSTEP,RESROW):-
    draw_rightlist(RELATION,NAME,SELECT,TREELIST,
                   [],_,
                   [],_,
                   CURROW,NEWCURROW,
                   LASTNAMECOL,NEXTNAMECOL,CURCOL,COLSTEP,RESROW).

  /* ************************ draw_rightlist ************** */

  draw_rightlist(RELATION,NAME,SELECT,[],
                 RELlist,RELlist,
                 NodeRowList,NodeRowList,
                 CurRow,CurRow,
                 NEXTNAMECOL,NEXTNAMECOL,CURCOL,COLSTEP,RESROW):-
    str_len(NAME,NAMELEN),
    str_len(RELATION,RELLEN),
    CURCOL1=CURCOL+1+NAMELEN+COLSTEP+COLSTEP+RELLEN,
    CURCOL2=CURCOL+COLSTEP+RELLEN,
    nodelistlen(NODEROWLIST,LEN),
    listsum(NODEROWLIST,0,SUM),
    RESROW=SUM div LEN,
    COLAFTERarrow=1+CURCOL2+NAMELEN,
    COLAFTERdash=2+CURCOL2+NAMELEN,
    COLAFTERname=CURCOL2+NAMELEN,
    connect_nodesright(RELlist,RESROW,COLAFTERdash,
                       LEN,CURCOL1,COLSTEP,NODEROWLIST),
    writetext(RESROW,CURCOL2,112,NAME,SELECT),
```

(**Fig. 9-1j.** continued)

```
  scr_ch(RESROW,COLAFTERname,'<'),
  scr_ch(RESROW,COLAFTERarrow,'á'),
  check_lastright(RESROW,COLAFTERdash,NODEROWLIST), !.

draw_rightlist(RELATION,NAME,SELECT,[H|T],
               RELlist,ResRELlist,
               NodeRowList,ResNodeRowList,
               CurRow,CurRow2,
               LNCOL,LNCOL2,CURCOL,COLSTEP,RESROW):-
  H=tree(Rel,_,_,_),
  str_len(NAME,NAMELEN),
  str_len(RELATION,RELLEN),
  CURCOL1=CURCOL+1+NAMELEN+COLSTEP+COLSTEP+RELLEN,
  draw_right(H,CurRow,CurRow1,LNCOL,LNCOL1,CURCOL1,COLSTEP,Noderow),
  draw_rightlist(RELATION,NAME,SELECT,T,
                 [Rel|RELlist],ResRELlist,
                 [Noderow|NodeRowList],ResNodeRowList,
                 CurRow1,CurRow2,
                 LNCOL1,LNCOL2,CURCOL,COLSTEP,RESROW).
/* ********************** check_lastright **************** */

check_lastright(ROW,_,[ROW|_]):-!.

check_lastright(ROW,COL,[_|LIST]):-!,
  check_lastright(ROW,COL,LIST).

check_lastright(ROW,COL,_):-
  scr_ch(ROW,COL,'Ç').
/* ****************** connect_nodesright **************** */

connect_nodesright([REL],ROW,COL,1,COL1,COLSTEP,_) :-!,
  treeline_hor(COL,COL1,ROW),
  writetext1(ROW,COL1,REL,COL2),
  COL3=COL2+COLSTEP,
  treeline_hor(COL2,COL3,ROW).

connect_nodesright(Rlist,ROW,COL,_,COL1,COLSTEP,[RMAX|L]):-
  lastinlist(RMIN,[RMAX|L]),
  con_nodesright(Rlist,ROW,COL,RMIN,RMAX,COL1,COLSTEP,[RMAX|L]).

con_nodesright(_,_,_,_,_,_,_,[]).

con_nodesright(_,_,COL,_,_,_,_,[R1,R2|_]):-
  R22=R2+1,
  treeline_ver(R22,R1,COL), fail.

con_nodesright([Hrel|Trel],ROW,COL,RMIN,RMAX,COL1,COLSTEP,[ROW1|T]):-
  CC=COL+1,
  treeline_hor(CC,COL1,ROW1),
  writetext1(ROW1,COL1,Hrel,COL2),
  COL3=COL2+COLSTEP,
  treeline_hor(COL2,COL3,ROW1),
  cornerright(ROW,RMIN,RMAX,ROW1,CORNCHAR),
  scr_ch(ROW1,COL,CORNCHAR),
  con_nodesright(Trel,ROW,COL,RMIN,RMAX,COL1,COLSTEP,T).
/* ********************** cornerright ****************** */

cornerright(RMIN,RMIN,_,RMIN,'ô') :- !.

cornerright(RMAX,_,RMAX,RMAX,'ê') :- !.

cornerright(_,RMIN,_,RMIN,'Ö') :- !.

cornerright(_,_,RMAX,RMAX,'â') :- !.
```

(**Fig. 9-1j.** continued)

```
cornerright(RMIDT,_,_,RMIDT,'é') :- !.

cornerright(_,_,_,_,'û').


/* ************************** draw ********************** */

/* draw a tree in the selected direction */

  draw(right,TREE):-
    draw_right(TREE,0,_,0,_,0,3,_).

/* ************************* treemenu ******************* */

/* @@@@@ modified version @@@@@ */
/* treemenu constructs and displays a box diagram of a tree structure */

  treemenu(DIRECTION,TREE,CHOICE) :-
        shiftwindow(OLD),
        windowNUM(mapwindow,NUM),
        shiftwindow(NUM),
        clearwindow,
        newupdate(treewindow(0,0)),
        repeat,
          remove_treechoice,
          draw(DIRECTION,TREE),
          readkey(KEY),
          treekeyact(KEY), !,
        shiftwindow(OLD),
  not(KEY=esc),
  treechoice(CHOICE),!.

treeaction(_).

/* ****************** END END END *********************** */
```

Fig. 9-1k. IBIS-REL.PRO

```
% File name: ibis-rel.pro

/* ****************************************************** */
/*                     IBIS RELATIONS                     */
/* ****************************************************** */
/* To test the relations section uncomment these declarations
DOMAINS
  SOURCE,TARGET,RELATION,NTYPE=STRING
  STRINGLIST=STRING*
  IBIS= ibis(RELATION,NTYPE,ref,IBISLIST)
  IBISLIST = IBIS*
  RELLIST = rel(SOURCE,ELATION,TARGET)

DATABASE
  relationLIST(STRING,STRINGLIST,STRINGLIST)
*/

PREDICATES

insertIBIS(ref,ref,STRING,NTYPE,IBIS,IBIS)
  insertIBISlist(ref,ref,STRING,NTYPE,IBISLIST,IBISLIST)

deleteIBIS(ref,IBIS,IBIS,IBIS)
  deleteIBISlist(ref,IBISLIST,IBISLIST,IBIS)
```

(**Fig. 9-1k.** continued)

```
CLAUSES

/* ************************** insertIBIS ***************** */

/* insertIBIS inserts an ibis node "Sref" that has a relation
   Srel to a source node Tref. If the target node is found to
   be the current node of the ibis subtree, then we insert
   the new (source) node as one of its children. */

insertIBIS(Tref,Sref,Srel,Stype,
           ibis(Trel,Ttype,Tref,LIST),
           ibis(Trel,Ttype,Tref,[ibis(Srel,Stype,Sref,[])|LIST]) ).

/* Else continue searching the ibis tree for a node that has
   the same "Tref" */

insertIBIS(Tref,Sref,Srel,Stype,
           ibis(REL,TYPE,REF,[H|T]),
           ibis(REL,TYPE,REF,[NewH|T])):-
  insertIBIS(Tref,Sref,Srel,Stype,H,NewH), !.

insertIBIS(Tref,Sref,Srel,Stype,
           ibis(REL,TYPE,REF,[H|T]),
           ibis(REL,TYPE,REF,[H|NewT])):-
  insertIBISlist(Tref,Sref,Srel,Stype,T,NewT).

/* ******************** insertIBISlist ****************** */

insertIBISlist(_,_,_,_,[],[]):- fail.

insertIBISlist(Tref,Sref,Srel,Stype,[H|T],[NewH|T]):-
  insertIBIS(Tref,Sref,Srel,Stype,H,NewH), !.

insertIBISlist(Tref,Sref,Srel,Stype,[H|T],[H|NewT]):-
  insertIBISlist(Tref,Sref,Srel,Stype,T,NewT).
/* *********************** deleteIBIS ******************** */
/* Delete a subIBIS and its subtrees and return
   the resulting IBIS without the deleted subIBIS, and
   the subIBIS */

deleteIBIS(REF,ibis("root",_,REF,_),_,_):-!,fail.

deleteIBIS(REF1,ibis(REL,TYP,REF,[ibis(REL1,TYP1,REF1,L)|T]),
                ibis(REL,TYP,REF,T),
                ibis(REL1,TYP1,REF1,L)):-!.

deleteIBIS(REF1,ibis(_,_,REF2,[]),_,_):-
  A=REF1, B=REF2, not(A=B),!,fail.

deleteIBIS(REF1,ibis(REL,TYP,REF,[H|T]),
                ibis(REL,TYP,REF,[NewH|T]),
                DeletedIBIS):-
  deleteIBIS(REF1,H,NewH,DeletedIBIS), !.

deleteIBIS(REF1,ibis(REL,TYP,REF,[H|T]),
                ibis(REL,TYP,REF,[H|NewT]),
                DeletedIBIS):-
  deleteIBISlist(REF1,T,NewT,DeletedIBIS), !.

/* ********************** deleteIBISlist **************** */

deleteIBISlist(_,[],_,_):-!, fail.
deleteIBISlist(REF,[ibis(REL,TYP,REF,L)|T],
                   T,
                   ibis(REL,TYP,REF,L)):-!.
```

(**Fig. 9-1k.** continued)

```
deleteIBISlist(REF,[H|T],[NewH|T],DeletedIBIS):-
  deleteIBIS(REF,H,NewH,DeletedIBIS), !.

deleteIBISlist(REF,[H|T],[H|NewT],DeletedIBIS):-
  deleteIBISlist(REF,T,NewT,DeletedIBIS).

/* ****************************************************** */

PREDICATES

/*
readRELATIONS(STRING)
getRELATIONS(STRING,RELLIST)
  getONE(STRING,STRING,STRING,STRING)


assertRlist(RELLIST)
  assertRlist1(STRING,RELLIST,STRINGLIST,STRINGLIST,RELLIST)
*/

relationLIST(STRING,STRINGLIST,STRINGLIST)

relates_to(ref,ref,STRING,NODE,NODE)
  matchRELATION(INTEGER,INTEGER,STRINGLIST,STRINGLIST,
                STRING,NTYPE)

CLAUSES

/* ********************** relates_to ******************** */

relates_to(Tref,Sref,Rel,node(Stype,Ktype,A,D,OUTstr),
                         node(Ttype,_,_,_,_)):-
  relationLIST(Ttype,RELlist,NtypeLIST),!,
  pulldown_attr(Attr),
  menu(2,43,Attr,Attr,RELlist,Ttype,1,Choice),
  matchRELATION(Choice,1,RELlist,NtypeLIST,Rel,Stype),
  getNattr(Ktype,A,D),
  concat_list1(["Edit this node as an <",Stype," ",Rel," ",
               Ttype,">."],"",MSG),
  shiftwindow(OLD),
  windowNUM("editwindow",NUM),
  shiftwindow(NUM), clearwindow,
  edit("",OUTstr,"<NODE EDITOR>",Stype,MSG,
        1,"",1,1,1,1,_,_), !,
  chain_inserta(ibisdb,nodech,node,
                node(Stype,Ktype,A,D,OUTstr),Sref),
  chain_terms(ibisdb,ibisch,ibis,IBIS,REF),!,
  insertIBIS(Tref,Sref,Rel,Stype,IBIS,NewIBIS),
  term_replace(ibisdb,ibis,REF,NewIBIS),
  update(currentIBIS(NewIBIS)),
  update(currentREF(Sref)),
  update(currentCpos(1)),
  update(currentNstr(OUTstr)),
  shiftwindow(OLD).
/*
/* ********************* readRELATIONS ****************** */

readRELATIONS(FILENAME):-
  existfile(FILENAME),
  file_str(FILENAME,STR),
  getRELATIONS(STR,RELlist),
  assertRlist(RELlist), !.
  % this will assert relationLIST facts to the database.
```

(**Fig. 9-1k.** continued)

```
readRELATIONS(FILENAME):-
  writeMSG(go,["\n",FILENAME," doesn't exist."]).

/* ********************* getRELATIONS ******************* */

getRELATIONS("",[]):-!.
getRELATIONS(STR,LIST):-
  frontchar(STR,'\n',STR1),
  getRELATIONS(STR1,LIST), !.
getRELATIONS(STR,[rel(S,R,T)|L]):-
  getONE(STR,"",S,STR1),  !,
  getONE(STR1,"",R,STR2), !,
  getONE(STR2,"",T,STR3), !,
  getRELATIONS(STR3,L).

getONE("",N,N,""):-!.
getONE(STR,N,N,STR1):-
  frontchar(STR,'\n',STR1), !.
getONE(STR,N,N,STR1):-
  frontchar(STR,' ',STR1), !.
getONE(STR,O,N,STR2):-
  fronttoken(STR,"-",STR1),
  concat(O,"-",O1),
  getONE(STR1,O1,N,STR2), !.
getONE(STR,O,N,STR2):-
  fronttoken(STR,TOK,STR1),
  concat(O,TOK,O1),
  getONE(STR1,O1,N,STR2).

/* ********************* assertRlist ******************** */

assertRlist([]):-!.
assertRlist([rel(S,R,T)|L]):-
  assertRlist1(T,[rel(S,R,T)|L],Rlist,Slist,L1),
  asserta(relationLIST(T,Rlist,Slist)),
  assertRlist(L1).

/* ********************** assertRlist1 ****************** */

assertRlist1(_,[],[],[],[]):-!.
assertRlist1(T,[rel(S,R,T)|L],[R|RL],[S|SL],L1):-
  assertRlist1(T,L,RL,SL,L1), !.
assertRlist1(T,[rel(S,R,T1)|L],RL,SL,[rel(S,R,T1)|L1]):-
  assertRlist1(T,L,RL,SL,L1).
*/

/* ***************************************************** */
/* ******************* default relationLIST ************* */

relationLIST("issue",
            ["responds-to","replaces","suggested-by",
             "questions","generalizes","specializes",
             "referenced-by"],
            ["position","issue","issue","issue","issue",
             "issue","reference"]).

relationLIST("position",
            ["supports","objects-to","suggested_by",
             "questions","referenced-by"],
            ["argument","argument","issue","issue",
             "reference"]).

relationLIST("argument",
            ["supports","objects-to","suggested_by",
             "questions","referenced-by"],
```

(**Fig. 9-1k.** continued)

```
             ["argument","argument","issue","issue",
              "reference"]).

relationLIST("reference",
             ["referenced-by"],["reference"]).

/* ********************** matchRELATION **************** */

matchRELATION(NUM,NUM,[H1|_],[H2|_],H1,H2):-!.
matchRELATION(NUM,Count,[_|T],[_|T1],H1,H2):-
  Count1=Count+1,
  matchRELATION(NUM,Count1,T,T1,H1,H2).

/* ************************************************** */
/*
GOAL

% Testing deleteIBIS

deleteIBIS(6,
           ibis("root","issue",1,[
                  ibis("responds-to","position",2,
                      [
                      ibis("supports","argument",3,[]),
                      ibis("objects_to","argument",4,[])
                      ]),
                  ibis("generalizes","issue",5,
                      [
                      ibis("responds-to","position",6,
                          [
                          ibis("supports","argument",9,[])
                          ]),
                      ibis("responds-to","position",7,[])
                      ])          ]),
           ResultIBIS,DeletedIBIS),

write(ResultIBIS,"\n\n",DeletedIBIS),
readln(_).

% Testing insertIBIS

insertIBIS(6,8,"objects-to","argument",
           ibis("root","issue",1,[
                  ibis("responds-to","position",2,
                      [
                      ibis("supports","argument",3,[]),
                      ibis("objects_to","argument",4,[])
                      ]),
                  ibis("generalizes","issue",5,
                      [
                      ibis("responds-to","position",6,[]),
                      ibis("responds-to","position",7,[])
                      ])          ]),

           IBIS),
write(IBIS), readln(_).
*/
/* **************** END OF IBIS-REL.PRO ************** */
```

Fig. 9-1I. IBIS-DIA.PRO

```
% File name: ibis-dia.pro

/* ********************************************************* */
/* A program that uses the TOOLBOX screen-layout tools.    */
/* ********************************************************* */

/* @@@@@@@@@@@@@@@@@@@@@@@@@@@@@@@@@@@@@@@@@@@@@@@@@@@@@@@@@@
To run "dialog.pro" by itself, uncomment these declarations

include "tdoms.pro"

DOMAINS
  FNAME=SYMBOL
  TYPE = int(); str(); real()

DATABASE
  /* Database declarations used in scrhnd */
  insmode                         /* Global insertmode */
  actfield(FNAME)                 /* Actual field */
  screen(SYMBOL,DBASEDOM)         /* Saving different screens */
  value(FNAME,STRING)             /* value of a field */
  field(FNAME,TYPE,ROW,COL,LEN) /* Screen definition */
  txtfield(ROW,COL,LEN,STRING)
  windowsize(ROW,COL).
  notopline

  /* DATABASE PREDICATES USED BY VSCRHND */
  windowstart(ROW,COL)
  mycursord(ROW,COL)

  /* Database declarations used in lineinp */
  lineinpstate(STRING,COL)
  lineinpflag

/********************************************************** */
/*                      Include tools                        */
/********************************************************** */
include "tpreds.pro"
include "menu.pro"
include "status.pro"
include "lineinp.pro"
include "scrhnd.pro"                        /* Or vscrhnd.pro */
@@@@@@@@@@@@@@@@@@@@@@@@@@@@@@@@@@@@@@@@@@@@@@@@@@@@@@@@@@@@ */

CLAUSES
/**********************************************************
  Field action
*********************************************************** */
  field_action(_):-fail.

/**********************************************************
  Field_value
********************************************************** */
field_value(FNAME,VAL):-value(FNAME,VAL),!.

field_value("date",V):-
  date(Y,M,D),
  str_int(Year,Y), str_int(Month,M), str_int(Day,D),
  concat(Day,"-",S1), concat(S1,Month,S2),
  concat(S2,"-",S3), concat(S3,Year,V).

field_value("author",V):-
  currentAUTHOR(V).
```

(**Fig. 9-1l.** continued)

```
field_value("ktype",V):-
  currentKtype(V).

/*********************************************************
  noinput
********************************************************* */
% noinput("outntype").
% noinput("outktype").
% noinput("outauthor").
% noinput("outdate").

noinput(_):-fail.

/* ******************************************************* */
%@  in ibis-glb.pro
%@ PREDICATES
%@ getNattr(STRING,STRING,STRING)
%@ nodeDIALOG(STRING,STRING,STRING)
%@ displayINFO(STRING,STRING,STRING,STRING,STRING,STRING,STRING)
/* ******************************************************* */

/* *********************** getNattr ********************* */
getNattr(Ktype,A,D):-
  currentNdialog("on"),
  nodeDIALOG(Ktype,A,D),
  update(currentAUTHOR(A)),
  update(currentKtype(Ktype)), !.

getNattr("","","").

/* ************************* nodeDIALOG ***************** */

% A dialog-box for extracting node information

nodeDIALOG(Ktype,Author,Date):-
  consult("ndialog.scr"),
  createwindow(off),
  scrhnd(off,_),
  field_value("author",Author),
  field_value("date",Date),
  field_value("ktype",Ktype),
  retractall(value(_,_)),
  retractall(field(_,_,_,_,_)),
  retractall(txtfield(_,_,_,_)),
  retractall(windowsize(_,_)),
  removewindow, !.

nodeDIALOG("","",""):- removewindow.

/* *********************** displayINFO ****************** */

% display the node info in a screen-layout
% flow pattern: (i,i,i,i,o,o,o)

displayINFO(Ntype,Ktype,Author,Date,Ktype1,Author1,Date1):-
  consult("nodeinfo.scr"),
  asserta(value("outntype",Ntype)),
  asserta(value("outktype",Ktype)),
  asserta(value("outauthor",Author)),
  asserta(value("outdate",Date)),
  createwindow(off),
  scrhnd(off,_),
  field_value("outktype",Ktype1),
  field_value("outauthor",Author1),
```

(**Fig. 9-1l.** continued)

```
    field_value("outdate",Date1),
    retractall(value(_,_)),
    retractall(field(_,_,_,_,_)),
    retractall(txtfield(_,_,_,_)),
    retractall(windowsize(_,_)),
    removewindow, !.
/* ************************* END END END **************** */
```

Fig. 9-1m. IBIS-ED.PRO

```
% File name: ibis-ed.pro

/* ******************************************************* */
/*                       IBIS EDITOR                       */
/* ******************************************************* */
/*

ibisEDITOR(NodeName,NodeType,REF,INstr,INpos,OUTstr,OUTpos)

   flow pattern: (i,i,i,i,i,o,o)
*/


PREDICATES

ibisEDITOR(STRING,ntype,ref,STRING,INTEGER,STRING,INTEGER)


CLAUSES

ibisEDITOR(Nname,Ntype,_,INstr,INpos,OUTstr,OUTpos):-
  MSG = "End editing with ESC or F10",
  edit(INstr,OUTstr,Ntype,Nname,MSG,INpos,"",1,1,1,1,OUTpos,_).

/* ************************* END END END ***************** */
```

Fig. 9-1n. IBIS-GSC.PRO

```
% File name: ibis-gsc.pro

/* ******************************************************* */
/* Draw the title screen of the system using the BGI.      */
/* ******************************************************* */
/* To access your BGI drivers and fonts bgi_path might
need to equal "..\\BGI" */

constants
   bgi_path = ""

/* To access the GRAPDECL.PRO file you might need to
add a path: include "..\\programs\\GRAPDECL.PRO"  */

include "GRAPDECL.PRO"

PREDICATES
  graphicScreen

CLAUSES
```

(**Fig. 9-1n.** continued)

```
graphicScreen:-
   detectgraph(GrDriver,GrMode),
   initgraph(GrDriver,GrMode,_,_,bgi_path),
   setbkcolor(blue), setcolor(white),
   getmaxx(Xmax), getmaxy(Ymax),
   rectangle(0, 0, Xmax, Ymax),
   Title="Turbo IBIS ",
   settextstyle(triplex_Font,horiz_Dir,9),
   outtextxy(50,0,Title),
   textheight(Title,H), H1=H+2,
   setlinestyle(solid_line,$FFFF,thick_WIDTH),
   setcolor(red),line(50,H1,530,H1), setcolor(white),
   settextstyle(sans_serif_Font,horiz_Dir,2),
   outtextxy(225,120,"(Version 1.0)"),
   outtextxy(100,180,"An Issue Based Information System Shell"),
   outtextxy(280,200,"By"), outtextxy(210,220,"Safaa H. Hashim"),
   setlinestyle(solid_line,$FFFF,thick_WIDTH),
   setcolor(red), rectangle(50,170,530,245), setcolor(white),
   settextstyle(default_Font,horiz_Dir,1),
   outtextxy(80,290,
             "(c) TAB Books Inc., Exploring Hypertext Programming, 1990."),
   outtextxy(170,330,"---- PRESS ANY KEY TO START ----"),
   readchar(_), closegraph.

/* *********************** End of ibis-gsc ************** */
```

Fig. 9-1o. IBIS-GSC.PRO

```
% File name: ibis-gsc.pro

/* **************************************************** */
/* Draw the title screen of the system using the BGI.    */
/* **************************************************** */

/* To access your BGI drivers and fonts bgi_path might
need to equal "..\\BGI" */

constants
   bgi_path = ""

/* To access the GRAPDECL.PRO file you might need to
add a path: include "..\\programs\\GRAPDECL.PRO"  */

include "GRAPDECL.PRO"

PREDICATES
  graphicScreen

CLAUSES

graphicScreen:-
   detectgraph(GrDriver,GrMode),
   initgraph(GrDriver,GrMode,_,_,bgi_path),
   setbkcolor(blue),
   setcolor(white),
   getmaxx(Xmax),
   getmaxy(Ymax),
   rectangle(0, 0, Xmax, Ymax),
   Title="Turbo IBIS ",
   settextstyle(triplex_Font,horiz_Dir,9),
```

(**Fig. 9-10.** continued)

```
    outtextxy(50,0,Title),

    textheight(Title,H), H1=H+2,
    setlinestyle(solid_line,$FFFF,thick_WIDTH),
    setcolor(red),
    line(50,H1,530,H1),
    setcolor(white),

    settextstyle(sans_serif_Font,horiz_Dir,2),
    outtextxy(225,120,"(Version 1.0)"),
    outtextxy(100,180,"An Issue Based Information System Shell"),
    outtextxy(280,200,"By"),
    outtextxy(210,220,"Safaa H. Hashim"),

    setlinestyle(solid_line,$FFFF,thick_WIDTH),
    setcolor(red),
    rectangle(50,170,530,245),
    setcolor(white),
    settextstyle(default_Font,horiz_Dir,1),
    outtextxy(80,290,"(c) TAB Books Inc., Exploring Hypertext Programming,
            1990."),
    outtextxy(170,330,"---- PRESS ANY KEY TO START ----"),
    readchar(_),
    closegraph.
/* *********************** End of ibis-gsc ************** */
```

Now you can exit Turbo Prolog, and run MicroIBIS from DOS. All you need to do is enter "ibis" at the DOS prompt. The first thing you see will be the system's title screen. FIGURE 9-2 shows the title screen. Notice that I use graphics in my screen design. I used the "Borland Graphic Interface" (BGI) for this. The Prolog code for drawing the title screen is in FIG. 9-10. When you are done with the title screen, hit any key and voilà, you are in the MicroIBIS environment.

(Version 1.0)

An Issue Based Information System Shell
By
Safaa H. Hashim

(c) TAB Books Inc., Exploring Hypertext Programming, 1988.

---- PRESS ANY KEY TO START ----

Fig. 9-2. The introduction screen to MicroIBIS.

THE MicroIBIS ENVIRONMENT

Once in MicroIBIS, you will notice its user-interface, which is very similar to the Turbo Prolog interface. The main items in this interface are:

- a pull-down menu
- an editor window
- the IBIS Road-Map window
- a message window, and
- a status line

Take a look at FIG. 9-3. You will see these items. When you use IBIS, you might find it better if some windows are smaller in size while others are larger. Also, when you first fire MicroIBIS, your screen will be in Black and White but how about colors? MicroIBIS allows you to change the colors for some items in the user-interface.

FIGURE 9-3 shows the default configuration for the user-interface. To change window sizes and colors, you need to change the default configuration. You do this by choosing the "setup" option from the pull-down menu. See FIG. 9-4.

For changing the size of a window choose the "Setup/Window size" option. For changing the color of a user-interface item choose the "Setup/ Colors" option. When you are done customizing your IBIS, you can save the new setup by choosing the "Setup/Save new setup" option. To know more about the operation of MicroIBIS please refer to the MicroIBIS user guide in Appendix B.

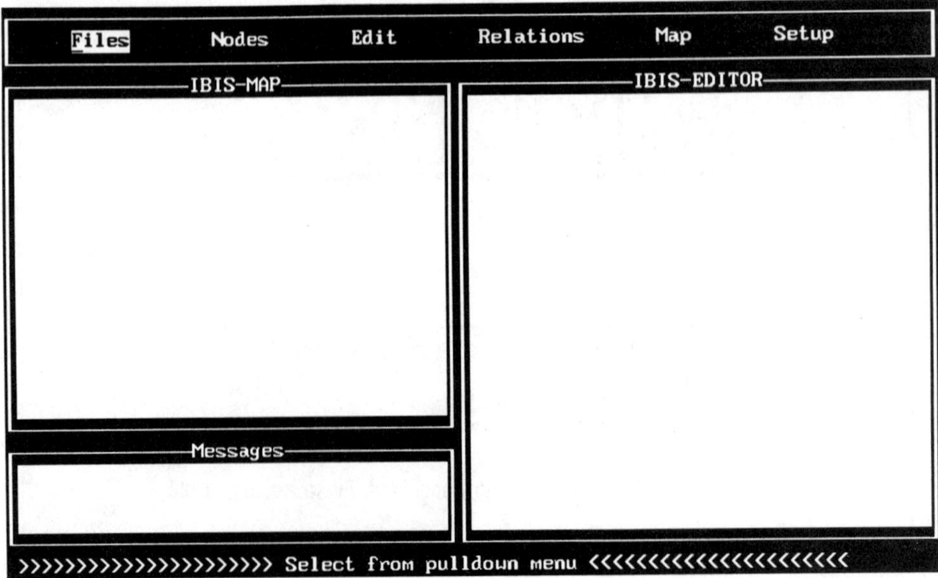

Fig. 9-3. The default user-interface configuration.

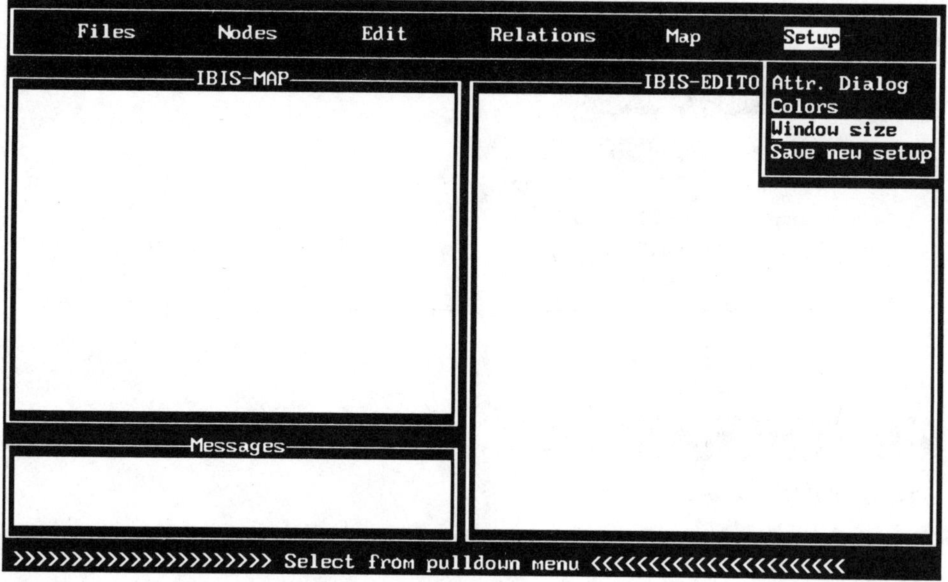

Fig. 9-4. Using "Setup" to customize the user-interface.

Now you are ready to see MicroIBIS in action. To do this you need a sample problem. I will choose a simple problem which has to do with issues of public policy. It is about wildfires in national parks. The issue came to my mind while reading an article about the wildfires in the Yellowstone National Park. This is an 85-year-old park that was on fire in June 1988.

However, this chapter is already a long one, and the problem of fighting wildfires will have to wait one more chapter. In Chapter 10 I will discuss the theory of IBIS and in Chapter 11 I will be ready to deal with the wildfires problem. In the rest of this chapter, I will help you get acquainted with MicroIBIS.

Creating a New Problem File

To start the problem solving process in MicroIBIS, you need a new database file. When you create a new IBIS file, you choose the File/New option. When you hit the ENTER key, the program prompts you to enter a filename; or hit ENTER to use the default "work.ibs" file. IBIS will create a new database file and open it for writing. The next thing it does is to create the root node. The root node is the statement of the main problem.

After it creates the new file, IBIS prompts you with a dialogue box with slots for:

- name of person asking the question, enter your name.
- date of node, the system fills the slot for you.
- type of knowledge in the node (you enter a knowledge type here). I will talk about types of knowledge when I discuss the theory of IBIS. For now, leave this slot empty.

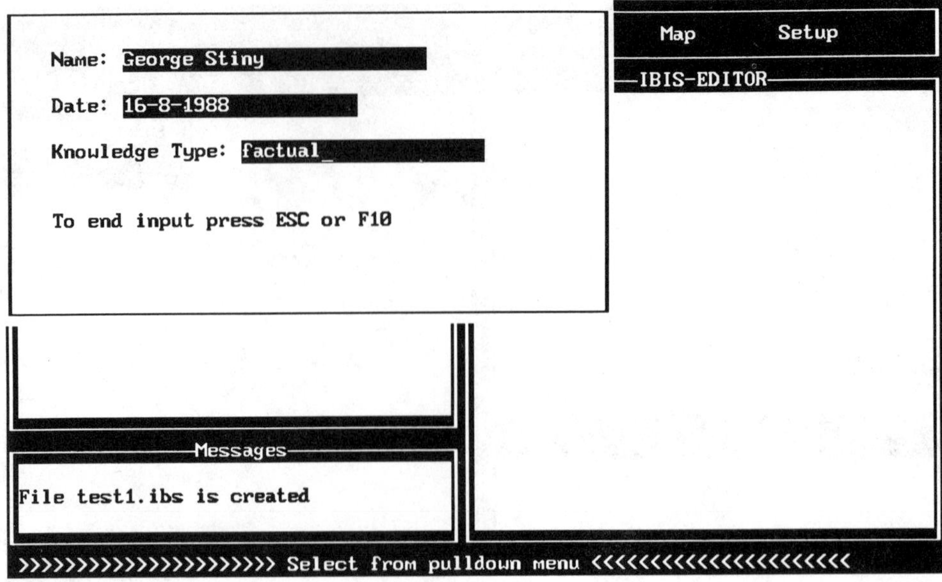

Fig. 9-5. Entering the attributes for the root issue.

You use the arrow keys or the return key to move between slots. Take a look at FIG. 9-5.

When you finish entering the information, press the ESC or F10 key to exit the dialogue box. IBIS will put you in the editor with a message at the bottom reading "Enter your issue." FIGURE 9-6 shows a screen of the system at that moment.

While you are in the editor, enter some questions representing a problem you want to solve. To exit the editor, press ESC or F10. To answer your question, use the "Relations" menu.

Establishing Relationships in IBIS (extending the network)

You use the "Relations" menu to link the current node to a target node. The options in this menu are relationship names. Each name represents a link type. The link types in this menu are dependent on the type of your current node. So for each node type (i.e., issue node, position node, argument node, and reference node), there is a different "Relations" menu. In your case, the current node is an issue node. When you pull down the "Relations" menu, you will notice that it has the word "issue" as a title.

In the issue "Relations" menu, there are seven possible types of links. Pick the first one, "responds-to." When you do so, IBIS will put you in the editor with a message at the bottom reading:

```
Edit this node as a <position responds-to issue>.
```

to remind you that you are establishing a relation between an issue node and a

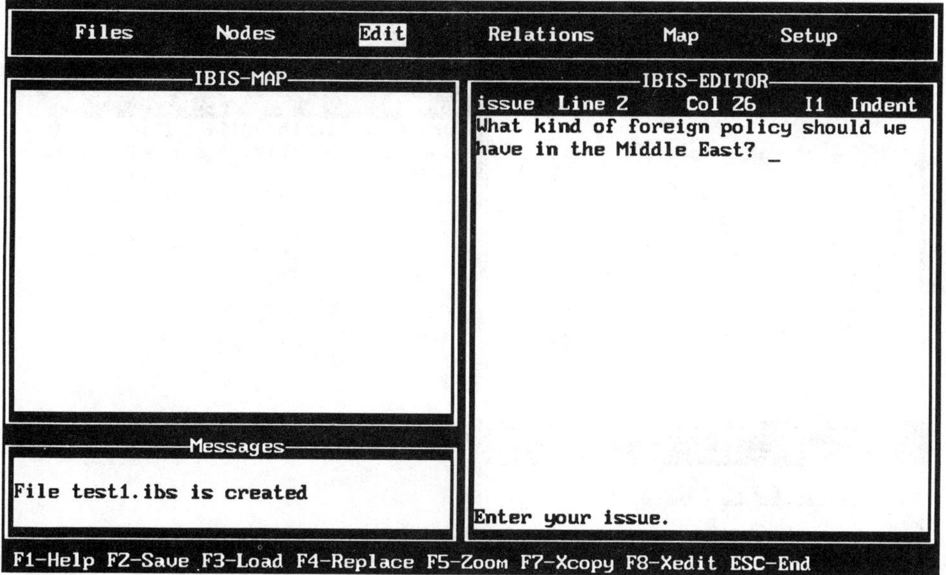

Fig. 9-6. Editing the root issue.

position node. Enter the text for your position, and end editing with ESC or F10. In hypertext terms, what you have just done is the linking of two nodes. You created a link called "responds-to" between a source node (a position node) and a target node (an issue node). As you can see, you are back talking hypertext. Even more, IBIS can show you a graphical representation of what you just did. This is what I have the "Map" for.

Viewing the IBIS Knowledge Structure

Choose the Map option from the pull-down menu. IBIS will show you a graph with an arc labeled "responds-to" between two nodes, "I1" and "P1." The I and P stand for issue and position respectively. I call this graphic representation of the IBIS knowledge-base a "Road-Map." See FIG. 9-7 for an idea of the IBIS-MAP.

While in the "IBIS-MAP" window, you can do these operations:

1) use the road map to view the knowledge-base,
2) load a node in the editor,
3) link to a new node,
4) delete a part of the knowledge-base, and
5) view or change the node attributes.

For instance, to load the main issue in the editor, you move the cursor using the arrow keys until it is under I1. Press ENTER and the root issue is instantly loaded in the editor window. For operations 2 to 5, you use a hyper-

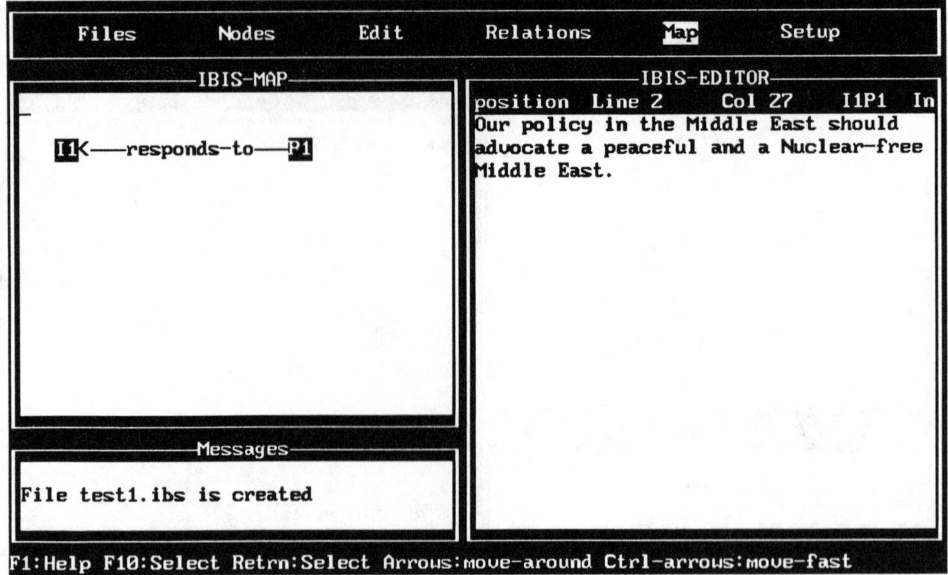

Fig. 9-7. The IBIS-MAP, a graphic representation of the knowledge-base.

text hotkey. As before, we use F10 for the hotkey. Place the cursor on a node and press the hotkey to get the "map" menu. By the way, notice the status line in the lower part of the screen. It tells you about the keys you can use while in the IBIS-MAP mode.

This is enough for now. To quit MicroIBIS, you choose the "File/Quit" option, and respond "yes" to the input line. In the next chapter I will go over the theory of the Issue Based Information System. In Chapter 11, I will use a complete example of problem solving using MicroIBIS.

10

The Theory of Problem Solving by Argumentation

"The search for scientific bases for confronting problems of social policy is bound to fail, because of the nature of these problems. They are 'wicked' problems, whereas science has developed to deal with 'tame' problems. Policy problems cannot be definitively described. Moreover, in a pluralistic society there is nothing like the indisputable public good: there is no objective definition of equity; policies that respond to social problems cannot be meaningfully correct or false; and it makes no sense to talk about 'optimal solutions' to social problems unless severe qualifications are imposed first. Even worse, there are no 'solutions' in the sense of definitive and objective answers."

—Horst Rittel and Melvin Webber, from "Dilemmas in the General Theory of Planning."

This quotation summarizes the properties of a wide range of problems. Planning, design, politics, and law are just a few areas where you can find many "wicked" problems, but very few "tame" ones. Horst Rittel, a professor of planning and design at the University of California at Berkeley, wrote extensively on design and planning problems. He was the first to recognize the difference between scientific and planning problems. In this chapter I will summarize Rittel's IBIS theory on which I based MicroIBIS. By scientific problems I mean something like solving mathematical equations, finding new theories, designing bridges, and playing chess. By planning problems I mean something like fighting crime, designing transit systems, marketing new products, developing a housing project, issuing a tax law, negotiating international treaties, and so on.

In this chapter I will discuss a theory for dealing with "wicked" problems. As a practical programming book, you expect more than just theories. So I will discuss and compare methods dealing with both "tame" and "wicked" problems. Next, I will concentrate on an "Issue Based Information System" as our method to handle "wicked" problems. MicroIBIS is our Turbo Prolog implementation of issue based information theory. First, you need a clear idea about "wicked" and "tame" problems, and this is what I will do in the next section.

TAME vs. WICKED PROBLEMS

The search for problem-solving techniques first started in the industrial age. The pressing problem at that time was that of "efficiency" in the industrial process. To solve a problem, you need some kind of a theory to help you define the problem. Once you have a theory of what your problem is, you start looking for a way to deal with it. In other words, you look for a theory to define the problem and a method to solve the problem. This is exactly what the industrial age problem solvers did. They looked for and found an existing economical definition of efficiency based on classical physics. In this definition, efficiency is a state by which you can perform a task with minimum input and maximum output. After all, this definition of efficiency was behind many useful inventions: the steam engine, the mill, the automobile, the production line, and so on. It was also behind most of the impressive engineering projects such as steel bridges, concrete dams, and high-rise buildings.

Impressed by these industrial accomplishments, policy makers, planners, and designers were anxious to try new ideas to their problems. They wanted to solve the housing problem created by mass migration from the countryside to the city. They wanted to solve health problems, transportation, crime and many other problems caused by industrialization. This way they came to define planning and policy making in terms of minimum input and maximum output.

In short, they thought they can use science to solve social problems. When things didn't work out—i.e., when crime started to increase, when housing projects deteriorated into slums, when transportation became an issue—they put the blame on anything other than their borrowed principles—but no one can blame them. Science did provide desperately needed solutions for many problems. For example, they were able to cure many diseases, pave roads, build sewage systems, and connect cities with trains to move goods and people in masses. Why can't they then use science and its method to solve management and social problems?

It turns out that there are basic differences between scientific or technological-type problems and social or planning-type problems. Rittel calls scientific or technological-type problems as "tame problems." On the other hand, he calls social or planning-type problems as "wicked problems." He suggests that there are 10 distinguishing differences between tame and wicked problems.

(1) There is no definitive formulation of a wicked problem. To solve a tame problem, first collect all the information you need to understand the problem. Next, use the information to formulate the problem. The last step is to solve the problem.

In wicked problems, you can't define the problem independent from your attempt to solve it. In other words, to understand and describe a wicked problem, you must generate a number of possible solutions in advance. Why? To answer your question, I'll use an example.

Consider the problem of how to solve the parking situation in the downtown area. To understand this problem, you must have some idea of what constitutes not having any parking problems. For instance, it would be nice to park your car within walking distance of your office; or leave your car in the train station's parking lot. Then, you can take a train to your downtown office. Yet another solution is to live within walking distance of your office. This way you don't need to worry about driving and parking at all.

Now, having these three alternatives, you can have an idea about the kind of information you need. For the first solution, you can ask, are there enough parking spaces for people working or visiting in the downtown area? If not, you have the first reason for the parking problems. For the second solution, we can ask, is there adequate public transportation (trains, buses, and so on) that connects the downtown with other parts of the city? If not, you have another reason for the parking problems. This will lead you to ask why there is inadequate public transportation, and you take it from there. For the third solution, to live within walking distance of downtown, you can have few questions. First of all, are there enough housing projects downtown? If so, the next question is: are they expensive? Can you afford them?

As you can see, the proposed solutions helped you to understand better the parking problem. Also, the deeper analysis you make of a solution and its consequences, the better ideas you have about the problem. Still, you will not be able to have an exhaustive formulation of the problem. There will always be solutions and consequences of solutions that you didn't think of.

(2) Wicked problems have no stopping rule. When an engineer designs a robot, he knows when it is finished and when people can start using it. When a mathematician solves an equation, he knows when he has a solution. Also, when a chess player makes his move, he knows if he will win, lose, or continue the game.

With wicked problems, the situation is different. When dealing with wicked problems there are no stopping rules. This is because, from (1) in the above, the process for solving a wicked problem is identical to the process of understanding it. Also you know that you can't have an exact formulation of a wicked problem. This means that you are not sure if you have a sufficient understanding of the problem. In turn, you won't be sure whether the solution at hand is a sufficient one. With more effort, you can always find better solutions.

However, if you can't find a satisfactory solution, when can you stop? You stop because of external—i.e., problem independent—considerations. You stop either because you ran out of money, time, or patience. When you stop, you take your latest solution as a "good enough" solution.

(3) Solutions to wicked problems are not true-or-false, but good-or-bad. When someone says they have a solution for a tame problem, you can judge their solution to be either right or wrong. A mathematician's solution to an equation can be either correct or false. A robot designed by an engineer can either work or not work. A chess player's move can lead him to a win, lose, or tie game. In these tame problems, an independent party can check if the solution is true or false.

In wicked problems, you can't say that there are true or false solutions. Also if you are working in a group to solve a problem, no one can claim or judge the correctness of a solution. In a group, it is quite possible that you find as many judgments as there are members in the group. The judgment of one member is always related to something else—e.g., personal interest, ideology, religion. Then, you are better off if you express your solutions as "better-than," "worse-than," "good," "bad," "good enough," or "satisfactory."

(4) There is no immediate and no ultimate test of a solution to a wicked problem. You can always test the solution for a tame problem and see how good it has been. For example, as a robot engineer you can try the robot in different situations and measure its performance. As a chess player, you can always try a move and see your opponent's reaction to it. If your opponent was unable to make a good move, you will know right away that your move was an effective one. Also, in future games he will always consider using the same move when he faces the same conditions.

On the other hand, in wicked problems, a solution will generate a chain of consequences. The solution will generate these consequences over an extended period of time. The direct consequences of a solution might be satisfactory, but in the next cycle of consequences you might find unsatisfactory side-effects. In other words, you can't tell ahead of time the full consequences of your current decisions. As for the downtown parking problem, you might come up with a solution by making a new building regulation. Say that one of the new regulations will require all new buildings to have enough parking spaces or floors as part of the design. After passing the regulation, and many buildings were built, some side-effect might happen that you didn't anticipate. For example, all people working in downtown who have their own parking spaces, will drive to work on a daily basis. As a result there will be heavy traffic in and out of the downtown.

(5) Every solution to a wicked problem is a "one-shot operation"; because there is no opportunity to learn by trial-and-error, every attempt counts significantly. In solving tame problems you can always try—and if you failed, you can try again. If your chess move didn't work out, try something else next time. In wicked problems you can't do that. The consequences of your actions already took place and you can't do anything about it. The traffic problem you created by solving the downtown parking problem is an example. Many accidents already took place and people died or were injured in these accidents. Your solution already left traces that you can't undo. Also if you want to reverse your actions, it would be too difficult to do so. For example, you can't tear down multi-story parking lots. Also, if you reduce the parking space, you will be back where you started. You have to resolve the parking problem once more. This in turn is not an easy, or inexpensive thing to do as with the redesign of a robot or the mechanic failure in a factory.

(6) Wicked problems do not have an enumerable (or an exhaustively describable) set of potential solutions, nor is there a well-described set of permissible operations that might be incorporated into the plan. Tame problems, on the other hand, have a definite set of solutions. Chess has a finite set of rules. Mathematics, chemistry, and physics all have a finite set of formulas that you use to find answers to the questions.

However, in dealing with wicked problems, you can never be sure that your solutions are all that's there. There is always the possibility that there are other solutions that you couldn't think of. In your solution to the parking problem, you suggested three answers:

- provide more parking space,
- use more public transportation to substitute for personal use of cars, and
- provide more living units within a walking distance from the downtown area.

First I thought that these were all the possible solutions. Right now, I find another solution:

- encourage the use of bicycles and motorcycles. After all, bicycles and motorcycles take less parking space than cars.

Now, what do you think? Are these all the possible solutions for our parking problem? I don't think so. To prove this here is another solution:

- introduce strict parking rules, and increase fines on parking tickets.

How about that. Now it is your turn to try looking for a solution. Remember that a solution is an attempt to understand the problem. Your solution might come from an understanding that the parking problem is a symptom of another problem. For example, in the last alternative, you believe that there are enough parking spaces, but people don't respect parking rules. This is because some people don't respect parking zones, and others park longer than they are supposed to. So enforcing parking rules will help solve the parking problem.

(7) Every wicked problem is "essentially unique." In a tame problem such as chess, you group moves in classes. You have opening games, closing games, and so on. In mathematics you can find rules for classifying families of problems given certain conditions. For wicked problems, there are no classes of problems. This means that you can't have a set of actions or procedures which are applicable to a group of wicked problems. What "essentially unique" means, Rittel himself explains:

"By 'essentially unique' we mean that, despite long lists of similarities between a current problem and a previous one, there always might be an additional distinguishing property that is of overriding importance."

Here, Rittel warns you not to be fooled by the extensive similarities between problems. Taking these similarities as basis to transfer solutions could prove disastrous. Take, for example, the housing problems in the emerging cities in third world countries. The first thing the housing authorities of these countries do is to build apartment buildings. The apartment building is a well-known and successful western approach to solve the housing problem. Most of the time this approach doesn't work well in third world countries. The third world city may share many similarities with the developed city, but third world farmers moving to the city are not American farmers moving to the city.

(8) You can consider every wicked problem to be a symptom of another problem. You came across this situation in (6) when you considered parking problems as a symptom for the problem of not respecting parking rules. Another example: you can consider war as a symptom of economic competition. Still you consider economic competition as a symptom of limited markets and limited resources.

At which level you should attack the problem is totally dependent on your own knowledge. This usually causes the problem of narrowing the solution space. An architect will always recommend building new projects to help the sagging economy of a city. A businessman, on the other hand, will recommend converting small businesses to franchise stores to help reduce the cost of operations. There is no logical or natural level to start with, but if a problem is a symptom of another problem, then you should first attend to the cause and not to the symptom.

(9) Sometimes there is a discrepancy in representing wicked problems. To explain this, I can go in different directions. Also, your choice of explanation determines the nature of the problem's resolution. In science, when you want to explain a hypothesis—i.e., an unproved theory that is tentatively accepted to explain certain facts—you use this rule:

"Assuming that H is a valid hypothesis—i.e., a hypothesis whose conclusions follow necessarily from its conditions—of the form 'E if C,' and given condition C, effect E must occur."

If effect E does occur, my confidence in the hypothesis H increases, but if the effect E does not occur, then I reject H as a hypothesis.

In wicked problems, you might explain the nonoccurrence of effect E by saying that something prevented it from occurring. Also you can say that the effect E did occur but you didn't see or record its occurrence. So you can always explain the nonoccurrence of E and continue to hold the hypothesis H. Take the "parking problem in the downtown area" as an example.

Assume that you want to increase the parking space in downtown areas. You built multi-story parking lots. You introduced laws that require new buildings to have enough parking space for their tenants. After a few years, however, you still have parking problems. Someone will say that increasing parking space didn't work. One possible response is to admit that you still have parking problems, but you can say that if you didn't increase the parking space a few years ago, the situation would be worse. This way you can keep your hypothesis that increasing parking space solves the problem. In addition you should increase parking space on a periodic basis to keep the problem under control. As you can see, you were able to rescue your hypothesis, "adding parking space solves parking problems," even though the effect didn't take place. Another answer as to why you still have parking problems is to claim that the measure was effective. You did solve the problem, and by doing so you encouraged more businesses and tourism. This increase in business and tourism caused an additional demand on parking space. To show that you solved the original problem you say that all workers in the downtown have their own parking space.

In dealing with wicked problems, you don't have a specific rule to determine the "right" explanation. Some reasons for this are:

- wicked problems are unique (see 7 above), so you can't compare explanations across solutions to two similar wicked problems.
- you can't experiment with a solution to a wicked problem (see 4 above) because every solution is a one-shot operation (see 5 above). This means you can't verify if one explanation is right and the other is wrong.

What all this means is that: your choice of explanation has no logical basis. So, explanations are always dependent on the "world-view" of the problem solver.

(10) The planner, designer, or policy maker has no right to be wrong. In solving tame problems, someone can be wrong with little or no blame at all. A physicist advancing a new theory of atomic reaction can be wrong and no one would blame him, but an architect, designing a house for the elderly, is liable if something goes wrong with his design. If a person falls on a staircase, the architect is responsible for this. The architect should have anticipated the dangers of falling on the steps. In dealing with wicked problems, there is no second time to everything. Thus, no immunity is tolerated.

DEALING WITH TAME PROBLEMS:
Problem Solving Approach of the First Generation

A well-known method in dealing with scientific problems is the "hypothetico-deductive" method. You normally associate this method with the procedures of mathematics and physics. It uses the logical concept of "deduction." Deduction is a reasoning mode in which you consider the conclusion to be true if the conditions (premises) are all true. The hypothetico-deductive method consists of making explicit through deduction all that is implicit in a set of premises.

In science, this method is used to confirm a hypothesis about the world. To do this you join the hypothesis to a set of confirmed premises to deduce "observations sentences," which you can test. An observation sentence is a statement about something you can observe. The value of the hypothesis depends upon the significance of its role in helping to deduce observation sentences which turn out to be both true and interesting. Even if you finally find that an interesting hypotheses is untrue, still, this hypothesis can have value in leading the way to other hypotheses which can be confirmed.

Scientists showed that the "hypothetico-deductive" method is a powerful tool in science. Most of our scientific discoveries are related, one-way or another, to this method. Even more, some scientists and philosophers went a little bit further, to suggest using the "hypothetico-deductive" method in solving social issues. Carl Hempel, a leading twentieth century Philosopher of science, holds that the "hypothetico-deductive" method is also valid for the social sciences. For more discussion on the "hypothetico-deductive" method, you can read Hempel's book "Philosophy of Natural Science."

During World War II, the military asked scientists to help in the war effort. Scientists found a very good opportunity to apply their method to practical problems. For example, the British asked a team of their scientists to help solve the German submarine problem. The British sent large amounts of depth charges to knock out enemy submarines but without much luck. The scientists started collecting facts. They noted that the depth charges were dropped from aircraft. These charges were set so that the charge did not go off until at least 35 feet below the surface, but German submarines were intact. Using their method, British scientists formed a hypothesis. To test their hypothesis, they asked this question: Why not try to set the charges so they go off at a shallower depth and see what happens? The military thought this was a stupid question. After all, you expect submarines to be submerged to take advantage of the water as a cover, but that was exactly what the scientist's hypothesis is all about. Their hypothesis is that the Germans perhaps knew that the depth charges are set for 35 feet. As a countermeasure, German submarines tried to stay closer to the surface during a raid. Sure enough, after a few experiments by the British, their submarine kill went up significantly as a result of setting the charges at a shallower depth.

Operations Research

The success of scientific method in the military in World War II was outstanding, but at that time they were looking for a new name for the scientific method. Probably because of its use in helping military operations, they called it "operations research (OR)." After the war, and as a consequence of its success during the war, there was a large interest in using "operations research" to solve nonmilitary problems. Scientists tried to solve problems like marketing, finance, transportation, and many other policy problems. With the computer on the scene, scientists saw the opportunity to use it in automating some parts of their approach. It also opened the door for further developments.

The scientist, armed with the computer and his widened perspective, began to think of his approach as the "systems approach." This was as a result of his interest in making his method the basis for a new science, the science of "decision making." He wanted to make decision-making a logical and coherent process where no personal idiosyncrasies would occur. A good reference on this approach is the book by C. West Churchman, which has the title (you guessed it) "The Systems Approach."

The Systems Approach

The systems approach is a label for a number of problem-solving methods employing "system analysis." System analysis means attacking problems of planning in a rational, straightforward, systematic way. The person doing "systems analysis" is the "system analyst," the designer, or the expert.

If you ask many proponents of the systems approach, they will agree on certain characteristics of a system analyst. Take a look at four of these characteristics as Rittel puts them:

1) The system analysts attitude should be somewhat detached from the problem at hand. He always tries to be rational, objective and scientific in attacking his problems.
2) A system analyst tries to maximize the effectiveness of his solution. He tries to get an optimal solution. An optimal solution is the best solution you can get given a set of constraints you must satisfy.
3) He doesn't seek piecemeal improvements. Rather, he always attempts to grasp the whole of the system.
4) You know that: a system analyst tries to grasp the whole of the system. You know that any system, as a whole, has many facets. You also know that problems of planning are not the responsibility of any single discipline. Such a context calls for a system analyst to have an "interdisciplinary" background. This is perhaps why some system designers like to call themselves generalists in contrast to the specialist of a single field.

To get his job done, the system analyst usually uses a set of predefined procedures. An interesting part of the theory of the systems approach is this: the procedures, used in systems analysis and their order, are independent from the person applying them. This means, if two people use the same set of procedures in the same order, they would get the same or similar results. Of course you are not surprised by this revelation. After all, if you were all objective, shouldn't you get similar results, if not the same one. As for the procedures and their order, I will discuss this in the next section.

The Procedure of the Systems Approach

Basically, the systems approach is characterized by a certain sequence of steps. Different text books have a different number of these steps, but the content and the order of these steps are the same. I use an eight-step version (See "On the Planning Crisis. . . ," by Horst Rittel).

1) understand the problem,
2) gather information to help you further understand the problem in its particular context,
3) analyze the information from step 2,
4) generate alternative solutions,
5) evaluate the alternative solutions and pick the best,
6) test the solution at hand,
7) modify the solution, learn from your mistakes, and save your knowledge for the next similar problem.

It turns out that you can use the same number and order of these steps to solve a wide range of problems. In the late fifties and early sixties, universities started many programs using this approach for basic research. An example is the research in Artificial Intelligence (AI). Even though the research in AI had its problems at that time, some practical applications started to show up in the middle and late seventies. Many consider the emerging field of expert systems as one of the most promising AI applications to solve real problems. So take a look at expert systems and see its similarities and differences with the systems approach.

Expert Systems

To fix automobiles, you need automobile experts who can tell you what went wrong with them. You need computer design experts to build faster and cheaper computers. You need quality assurance experts to analyze a certain design before you send it to the production line. You need financial market experts to advise you where to invest your money. Those experts developed their experience over time. In the early stages of their career, they used manuals and user-guides to solve problems, but over time they accumulated knowledge of their own. So, to capture such valuable experiences in computer programs, "knowledge engineers" are trained to build expert systems.

Expert Systems are computer programs that mimic the human problem solver. You can consider the knowledge engineer as the equivalent of the system analyst in the systems approach, but in expert systems you find a major shift from the basic ideas behind the systems approach. The best way to see this shift is to look at the differences between them:

- unlike the system analyst, the knowledge engineer doesn't have the skills to solve the problem by himself. Rather, he uses his analytic skills to capture the problem solving skills of others in a computer program.

- in expert systems, you can use rules of thumb to solve the problem. These rules of thumb are blueprints of personal experience. In the systems approach, the system analyst would not allow this. The system analyst is more interested in basic rules.
- In the systems approach, the system analyst is the generalist who must be interdisciplinary. In expert systems, the knowledge engineer is the specialist who helps others record their experience.
- Many decision makers consider the systems approach equally applicable both to engineering and policy problems. For example, in the 1960s, Governor Brown of California asked the aerospace industry to submit four systems science designs for crime, sanitation, information, and transportation. In expert systems, the picture is different. So far most of our expert systems deal with tame problems.

Examples of these expert systems are MOLGEN, ACRONYM, AM, MYCIN, PROSPECTOR, XCON, to name just a few. MOLGEN, a program developed by M. Stefik at Stanford University, helps the molecular geneticist in planning scientific experiments. ACRONYM, developed by R. Brooks and T. Binford at Stanford University, can locate objects in an image given that it has a database of these objects. AM, developed by D. Lenate, at Stanford University also, is an experimental program for automatic theory formation in mathematics. MYCIN, also developed at Stanford University, can prescribe treatment for infectious diseases. PROSPECTOR can analyze geological information obtained from a field of observations. It uses this analysis to make predictions about the possible existence of minerals in a certain site. XCON, developed by Digital Equipment Corporation, can automatically determine optimal configurations of VAX computers according to customer's needs and the available options.

DEALING WITH WICKED PROBLEMS: Problem Solving Approach of the Second Generation

So far, all the problem solving systems discussed deal with tame problems. Right at this moment I can imagine you saying something like this: Oh, I see, but how about systems for wicked problems? My answer is yes. I think you can build systems to deal with wicked problems, but these systems should have a different structure from those you use for tame problems. Professor Horst Rittel, in his research at UC Berkeley, wrote several papers discussing the differences. He outlined the logical structure of a new approach for dealing with wicked problems. He calls his approach, a "systems approach of the second generation." While all other systems—i.e., operations research, expert systems, and so on—are variations of the "systems approach of the first generation."

In the systems approach of the second generation, Rittel talks about an argumentative process for problem solving. In this process, a single person or a group of people deals with a problem using a question-and-answer technique. The meat of this approach is this: by asking and answering crucial questions, you can understand the problem in a better way. Also, you can know better the consequences of any solutions you suggest. This way, you avoid many unexpected and undesired after-effects. Rittel developed a logical structure for writing systems using this question-and-answer process. The term he uses for these systems is "Issue Based Information Systems," or simply "Issue Systems." The word "Issue" means a controversial question. Rittel introduced Issue systems in the early and middle 1970s. For the rest of this chapter, I will give you a brief description of issue systems and their logical structure.

ISSUE BASED INFORMATION SYSTEMS

In general, you come to know that you have a problem when the "desired state" is not the "current state." In other words, the "ought-to-be" state is inconsistent with the current state. For example, if the current state of the problem is:

"drunk drivers are the cause of eighty percent of car accidents."

then the ought-to-be state could be:

"eliminate or at least minimize the accidents caused by drunk drivers."

When you have such a situation, the first thing to do is to ask the main question. The main question is the statement of the problem. For the "car accidents" problem, the main question could be something like this:

"How do you eliminate, or at least minimize, accidents caused by drunk drivers?"

Any answer to resolve the inconsistency between the "ought-to-be" state and the current state will then be a controversial answer. Here is an *issue* (a question with potentially controversial answers). This is why I call questions, including the main question, issues. The main question becomes the main issue. If you visualize the product of the problem solving process as a tree—i.e., tree structure—of questions and answers, the main issue will be the "root issue." Here I must confess that the actual structure of this question-and-answer process forms a network rather than a tree. I will talk about this later when I talk about the structure of issue systems. For now, let's move along and talk about how a problem and its solutions will look like in an issue system.

KNOWLEDGE REPRESENTATION IN ISSUE SYSTEMS

An important part of any problem solving process is the issue of knowledge representation. In AI, you use knowledge representation techniques to represent a problem and its solutions in the computer. Here is a list of some AI knowledge representation techniques:

- Predicate Calculus
- Production Systems

- Nonmonotonic Reasoning systems—e.g., Truth Maintenance System (TMS)
- Semantic Networks
- Frames
- Scripts

For example, in most expert systems rules and facts are used for knowledge representation. This is done by using Predicate Calculus or Production Systems. Turbo Prolog is a good programming language in which to write expert systems by using rules and facts. Prolog is a Logic Programming Language based on a form of First Order Predicate Calculus which is called "Horn Clauses." In this book I use Turbo Prolog, a powerful version of Prolog for personal computers.

In issue systems, the question-and-answer format is our knowledge representation, but there is more to it than just simple questions and answers. There are two levels of knowledge representation in issue systems:

- representing the kind of knowledge in each question and in each answer. I call this the typology of knowledge in issue systems.
- representing the categories of questions and answers in relation to each other. I call this the typology of relations in issue systems.

TYPOLOGY OF KNOWLEDGE IN ISSUE SYSTEMS

OK, an issue system is a questions-and-answers system, but what kind of questions and answers are they? Rittel would tell you that you can "know" five types of questions-and-answers. As for questions (issues) you can have:

1) a "factual" issue—"What is the case?"
2) a "deontic" issue—"What ought to be the case?"
3) an "instrumental" issue—"How do we do it?"
4) an "explanatory" issue—"Why is the case so?"
5) a "conceptual" issue—"What do you mean?"

So much for knowing, but if you know something, you don't know many other things. So there are also five types of ignorance. Five kinds of ignorance will cause five kinds of questions—those who don't know and want to know will ask questions. Also, five kinds of knowing will give us five kinds of answers—those who know will answer the questions of those who don't.

Knowing the Author and Date of Questions and Answers

Another aspect of an issue system from the knowledge point of view, is that knowledge is always someone's knowledge. So an issue is someone's issue. This means that you need to keep a record of who asked what. Also, the problem solving process might extend over a period of time. So to keep an accurate record you save the date and time of each entry. The author's name and date of an entry are important for information retrieval and reasoning in issue systems.

TYPOLOGY OF RELATIONS IN ISSUE SYSTEMS

In an issue system, most questions are issues. You can have an issue replacing an issue. For example, you can replace the issue:

I1 = How can you increase the income of corporation X?

with the issue:

I2 = How can you increase productivity in corporation X?

You can represent this relation between issue I1 and I2 using Prolog relations. In Turbo Prolog, you can do it this way:

```
replaces(issue(I2),issue(I1)).
```

Here "issue(I1)" and "issue(I2)" are compound-objects—terms. The whole thing is a Turbo Prolog fact. Another relation between two issues is the "suggests" relation. You can say "issue I1 suggests issue I3":

I3 = How can you reduce spending in corporation X?

```
suggests(issue(I1),issue(I3)).
```

Other relations between two issues are "generalizes" and "specializes." In Turbo Prolog you can write these relations this way:

I4 = How can we expand corporation X?
I5 = How can we increase income and reduce spending in corporation X?

```
generalizes(issue(I4),issue(I1)).
specializes(issue(I5),issue(I1)).
```

OK, now that you know something about issues, how about answers? Answers are different. There are at least three kinds of answers:

(1) Positions from an Issue. Assume that someone asks the question:

I = "How can you increase productivity?

You might answer this question by saying:

P1 = To increase productivity you must increase the number of workers on each production line.

and my answer could be:

P2 = To increase productivity you must add more production lines.

Here you say that you responded to issue I with position P1, while I responded-to the same issue with P2. If you represent issues and positions as Turbo Prolog compound terms, then you can represent the relation "responds-to" as a Turbo Prolog clause. For example, you can represent the questions and answers for our productivity problem with two Turbo Prolog facts:

```
responds_to(position(P1),issue(I)).
responds_to(position(P2),issue(I)).
```

To make things more clear, you can include the name of a person responding to an issue in the clause. This way you know who is responding. Also, you know if someone responded with more than one position. For example, you can write:

```
responds_to(Name1,position(P1),issue(I)).
responds_to(Name1,position(P2),issue(I)).
responds_to(Name2,position(P3),issue(I)).
```

(2) Arguing for and against other's Positions and Arguments. When you disagree with someone's response to an issue, your objection goes on record—but it won't do simply to disagree, to claim, or even to point out, that you don't like someone's answer. You must say what's wrong, what your interpretation is of the answer, and why you think the answer is wrong. Such answers are called "arguments."

On one hand, you can "argue for" or support a given position. On the other hand, you can "argue against" or "object to" a given position. Take an example: We take a position P by a person NAME1 from issue I. Another person NAME2 wants to argue against NAME1's position—but you would like to argue for his position. Here is how this is represented in Turbo:

```
responds_to(NAME1,position(P),issue(I)).
objects_to(NAME2,argument(A1),position(P)).
supports(safaa,argument(A2),position(P)).
```

Arguments are not only for and against positions. You can also argue for and against someone else's argument. For example NAME1—to defend his position P from issue I, he can argue against NAME2's argument. Furthermore, to strengthen his position, he can support the argument for his position. Here are his two arguments:

```
objects_to(NAME1,argument(A3),argument(A1)).
supports(NAME1,argument(A4),argument(A2)).
```

(3) References for the Issues, Positions and Arguments. Of course, you look better if you have a list of those who agree with you as references for your issues, arguments, and positions. You can make a reference to a person, a book, an article, results from a survey, and so on. Using the previous example you can have:

```
refers_to(NAME1,issue(I),reference(F)).
refers_to(NAME1,position(P),reference(F1)).
refers_to(safaa,argument(A2),reference(F1)).
```

Notice that NAME1 and safaa both used the same reference, F1. To sum up this discussion on the typology of relations in issue systems, refer to FIG. 10-1.

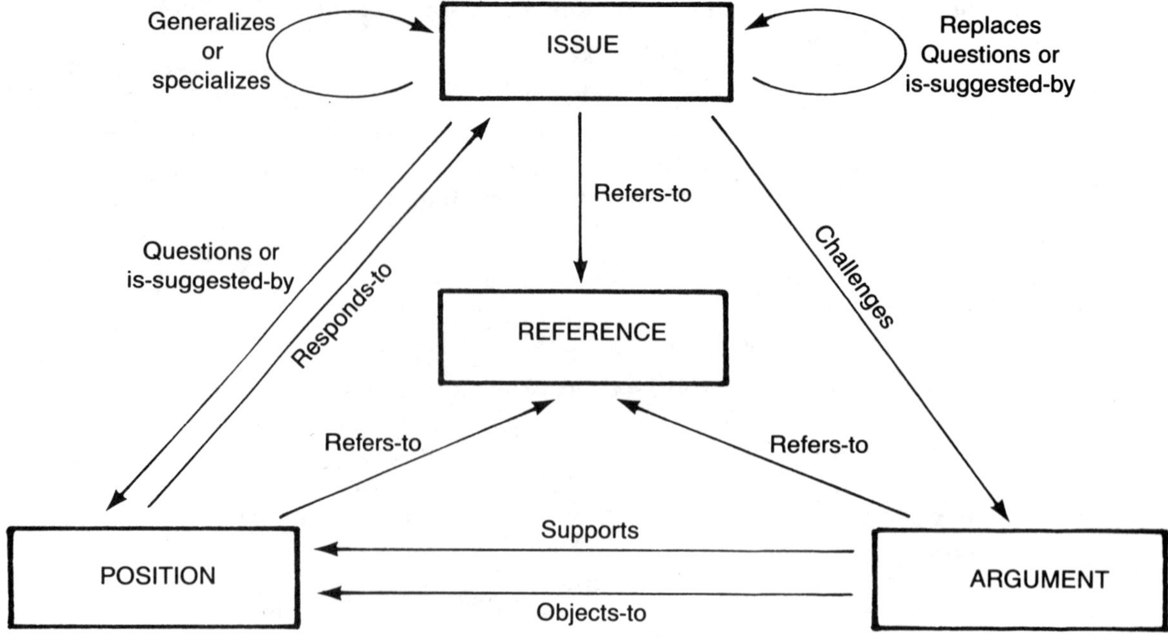

Fig. 10-1. These are all the relations forming a network of nodes.

In FIG. 10-1 you will see all the relations talked about in this section. Notice that they form a network of nodes linked together. I labeled these links with relations such as "responds_to," "suggests," "replaces," and so on. In the next section, I discuss in some detail how to use this network in problem solving.

STRUCTURE OF ISSUE SYSTEMS

In an issue system, problem solving is inherently an evolutionary process done by an individual or a group. A main characteristic of this approach is that the understanding of the problem evolves as you attempt to solve the problem. Also, each problem is a unique problem. When you start a new problem, you start with an empty system. The system's information evolves with the process. How does this happen? When someone asks a question in a group, you or someone else in the group will supply an answer. So the more questions asked, the more answers you need, and thus the more information you might get.

While asking and answering questions, you are also building a network of nodes. A node in an issue system is either an issue, position, argument, or a reference. The links between these nodes are relations—responds-to, objects-to, support, and so on (see FIG. 10-1). These links can have many characteristics. For example, they can be one-way or two-way links. Also, links can have procedural and declarative attachments. A "procedural attachment" is a procedure that can take its input from one node and direct its output to another node. The topic of procedural attachments is an advanced one—I will not cover it in this book, but to make it up to you I will discuss link directions. In the next section, I will show you how you can move in one or two directions in the IBIS network.

Active and Passive Links

Links can represent either a one-way relation or a two-way relation. A one-way relation is a relation with either a passive or active form. A two-way relation is a relation with both its passive and active forms. Here are some examples of passive and active relations:

supports(argument(A),position(P)). ——— active
supported-by(position(P),argument(A)). ——— passive
refers_to(issue(I),reference(R)). ——— active
referenced_by(reference(R),issue(I)). ——— passive

Of course you don't need both directions as facts in your system. You can always write a Turbo Prolog rule to transform one to another. Here are two rules to transform the passive into active and vice versa of the "supports" relation:

```
supports(X,Y):- supported_by(Y,X).
supported_by(X,Y):- supports(Y,X).
```

Remember that you should always append these rules at the end of all other "supports," or "supported_by" facts. Now go back to the network structure of issue systems.

Arguments and Positions That Raise Issues

To extend the issue system network you add more links. In IBIS, adding links could mean raising new issues, taking positions from issues, arguing for or against a position, and so on. The best way to extend an IBIS network is by raising new issues. You can raise new issues using different relations. Here are some examples:

suggests(issue(OLD),issue(NEW)).
replaces(issue(NEW),issue(OLD)).
questions(issue(NEW),issue(OLD)).
suggests(argument(OLD),issue(NEW)).
questions(issue(NEW),argument(OLD)).
generalizes(issue(NEW),issue(OLD)).
specializes(issue(NEW),issue(OLD)).

and so on. So far so good, but when do you stop? If you are lucky, all or most of your terminal nodes turn out as action positions—e.g., the case is like this, you should do this and that, you should do it this way, and so on. An action node is a position with very few or no negative arguments. In issue systems, most of the time you stop because of some external considerations—you run out of time, money, patience. In any case, an issue system helps to solve a problem after taking into consideration the field of issues, positions, and arguments produced by this procedure.

You must keep in mind that you don't build an issue system to generate a clean cut solution. Rather, an issue system is meant to keep problem solvers from disregarding aspects that would show themselves as important after the fact. An issue system "invites controversy; it asks for more deliberated reasoning that leads to a plan" (Rittel 1980, "APIS: A Concept. . ."). Also, you should know that issues, positions, and arguments are all dependent on the interest and world view of the participants.

The IBIS method breaks the problem solving process down into sub-processes consisting of the resolving of various issues—issues being questions arising while trying to solve a problem, and resolving being the process of deriving appropriate answers to these issues. In dealing with issues, the first step in the IBIS procedure is to generate that issue. Once you have the issue, you can try resolving it using these three steps:

- proposing candidate answers, i.e., possible answers to the issue under consideration.
- arguing the pros and cons of the candidate answers.
- selecting candidate answers for inclusion in the resolution of the issue.

ISSUE SYSTEMS AND HYPERTEXT

In hypertext, information is stored in a network of nodes connected by links. IBIS is an argumentative problem solving system that uses a network of nodes. The nodes in IBIS are connected by links representing relations between these nodes. From what I have just said about hypertext and IBIS, it seems that they use similar structures. IBIS is "isomorphic" to hypertext. Two entities are isomorphic when they have the same structure.

In hypertext, you can view the nodes; and in some systems you can view the network itself, through an interactive browser. To add, delete, or change links in the network, you can use a menu fired by a hotkey. These functions are considered the minimum in any hypertext system. With these functions you can extend, contract, view, and change the network. You can use the isomorphism between IBIS and hypertext to build a working IBIS system. In other words, you can consider IBIS as a hypertext system for problem solving using the argumentative approach. I should mention that Rittel introduced IBIS in the early 1970's. Also he wrote the first IBIS system on an APPLE-II computer.

The idea of marrying IBIS to hypertext is not my invention. Rittel's system on the APPLE-II existed before the 1980's reincarnation of hypertext. Another IBIS-based hypertext system is the MCC's "Design Journal." The Microelectronic and Computer Technology Corp (MCC) is the software development think tank in Austin Texas. The "Design Journal" helps designers to save their ideas and communications with clients in an IBIS format. The most interesting part of the "Design Journal" is its graphical browser. You can use this browser to edit the network. To know more about the "Design Journal," take a look at Begeman and Conklin's article (see references in Appendix A).

MicroIBIS: AN IBIS SHELL PROGRAMMED IN TURBO PROLOG

In PART ONE, I talked about writing Turbo Prolog programs to add, delete, and change links. In PART TWO, I developed "ET" a hypertext system for information retrieval. This chapter develops all the theory you need to build a problem-solving system. So all you need is to use the programming skill learned in PART ONE and TWO to write a Turbo Prolog IBIS system. I wrote a sample IBIS program which I call "MicroIBIS." You can use MicroIBIS as is without any modifications or additions, but before you start using it on your own you will need a tutorial. Chapter 11 serves this purpose very well. In Chapter 11, I take a problem, analyze it, and propose a few solutions using MicroIBIS. For additional help, try MicroIBIS's user's guide in Appendix B. On the other hand, if you prefer to enhance or develop your own IBIS, I suggest reading Chapters 12 and 13 first.

In MicroIBIS, I don't use a network of nodes—I use a tree structure. This way I can give you a simple view of the IBIS method. Extending the tree structure to a network shouldn't be a difficult task. I already talked about programming the network structure in PART ONE and TWO. The tree structure has another advantage—writing a graphical browser for a tree structure is easier than writing a graphical browser for a network. Writing a graphical browser for a network requires extensive graphics programming in Turbo Prolog. Graphical programming in Turbo Prolog is an advanced topic which deserves a book of its own. You can use text graphics to build a tree browser for IBIS. This is exactly what I did in MicroIBIS. I modified the Turbo Prolog TOOLBOX "treemenu" predicate to work as a browser. I call the MicroIBIS browser "IBIS-ROAD-MAP."

11
Deciding on a Firefighting Policy in National Parks:
A Problem-Solving Example Using MicroIBIS

> "There are two modes of acquiring knowledge, namely by reasoning and experience. Reasoning draws a conclusion and makes us grant the conclusion, but does not make the conclusion certain, nor does it remove doubt so that the mind may rest on the intuition of truth, unless the mind discovers it by the path of experience."
>
> —*Roger Bacon (c. 1220 – 1292) philosopher and scientist*

As Bacon suggests, it is one thing to know new facts by reasoning from already known facts and rules, but it is another thing to be certain about the product of our reasoning. What is the connection between Bacon's statement and our IBIS approach? In Chapter 10 I explained the rationale, the reasoning, behind it. To anchor this rationale to the depth of your understanding, you need practice. With practice you will gain experience in solving problems using IBIS. This experience is the only judge for the success or failure of the IBIS approach.

In Chapter 9 I introduced you to MicroIBIS in a speedy way, and in Chapter 10 I discussed the theory behind it. In this chapter you will use MicroIBIS to build a knowledge-base on firefighting policies for national parks. MicroIBIS is ideal for problem-solving by a group of people. For firefighting in national parks you need an acceptable policy for all interest groups. It has to be acceptable to those who live and do business in and around the parks. It also must be acceptable to nature lovers, and ecologists. In short, for a policy to be a successful one, all those who have an interest must participate in the debate.

SELECTING A GROUP OF PARTICIPANTS TO SOLVE THE PROBLEM

The first step in conducting the argumentative process is to select the participants. One way to do this is by asking the representatives of each interest group to step forward. Take a representative from the parks rangers. Also, you need a prominent ecologist with good credentials. A government representative is very welcome in the group. Also, you need representatives from the park neighbors—those who live and do business in and around the park. Did I forget something? Yes, I forgot to include you in the group. So you are a member of the debate and I expect you to actively participate in it. You can raise issues, take positions, advance negative as well as positive arguments, and show your references.

OK, how am I going to get such a group together? You and I are here but how about the others? Well, one way to do this is by collecting the viewpoints of the different interest groups from newspapers and magazines. Also, with today's advancement in telecommunications you can use teleconferencing. Teleconferencing is an open telephone line between a group of people. You can ask one member of the group to use MicroIBIS to record the debate. I choose the first approach—not because it is better, but because it is simpler and still very effective. What I did was to collect articles from different newspapers and magazines on a particular incident. The incident was the disastrous fire in the Yellowstone national park in 1988. I used MicroIBIS to reconstruct the debate out of these articles.

From the newspaper articles, I got a few viewpoints from those in different interest groups. In short, I got all the ingredients for the debate: the people interested in debating the issue, the tool which is MicroIBIS—but is that all? How about the decision maker! Who will decide what to do after you have built your argumentative knowledge base? How about you? You can be a member as well as the decision maker.

Now, the stage is set for MicroIBIS to do its thing. Now take a look at some background for the problem.

FIRE IN THE PARK

"Nature is the Art of God."—Dante (1265 – 1321) Italian poet.

In 1972, the United States park services adopted a new fire fighting policy for the nation's national parks. The policy is known as the "free-burn" policy, also called the "let-it-burn" policy. The policy advocates that natural fires, occurring because of lightning, should be allowed to go out on their own—but in June 1988 a naturally occurring wildfire in the Yellowstone national park caused a controversy. The fire started in June and was still going strong at the time of the writing of this book—September of the same year. In three months the fire burned one half of the 2.2 million-acre park. Many reports in local and national newspapers started to debate the issue of what went wrong. The debate focuses on these two issues:

1) What kind of policy is needed to deal with natural and artificial wildfires in national parks? Also, should the "let-it-burn" policy be kept, or abandoned?
2) Who is to blame for the huge loss in such national landmarks (one half of Yellowstone's 2.2 million acres)? Also, who is to blame for the loss in tourism, considering that it took 100 to 200 years for nature to bring Yellowstone to its state before the fire.

Now assume that you are a decision maker who must cast his vote on fire fighting policies. You will use MicroIBIS to form an information network to help you shape a decision. To do that, MicroIBIS allows you to analyze the problem in a network of nodes. A node in the network can be a *question node* (issue node: Here I'll save the text for a controversial question), which I will call "Issue"—or an *answer node*. An answer to a question can take several forms:

1) A "Position": your *position* from an issue is your explanation or solution for a problem. Every answer has its pros and cons. These pros and cons are also answers which are called arguments.
2) An "Argument": an *argument* is an answer for an issue, a position, or to another argument. Arguments are of two kinds:

   Negative arguments: a *negative argument* is an argument against an issue, against a position, or against another argument.

   Positive arguments: a *positive argument* is an argument supporting an issue, supporting a position, or supporting another argument.

3) Sometimes it is better to have references for issues, positions, and arguments. A "Reference" gives authority. It shows that other people have already studied the issue, position, or argument under consideration. It makes the questions and answers more legitimate.

MicroIBIS TO THE RESCUE

To make up your minds about these two issues, build a network of questions and answers using MicroIBIS. So fire up the system and create a new file called "Yellow.ibs." FIGURE 11-1 gives an idea of this step. Use the ".ibs" extension to differentiate the IBIS database files from other files.

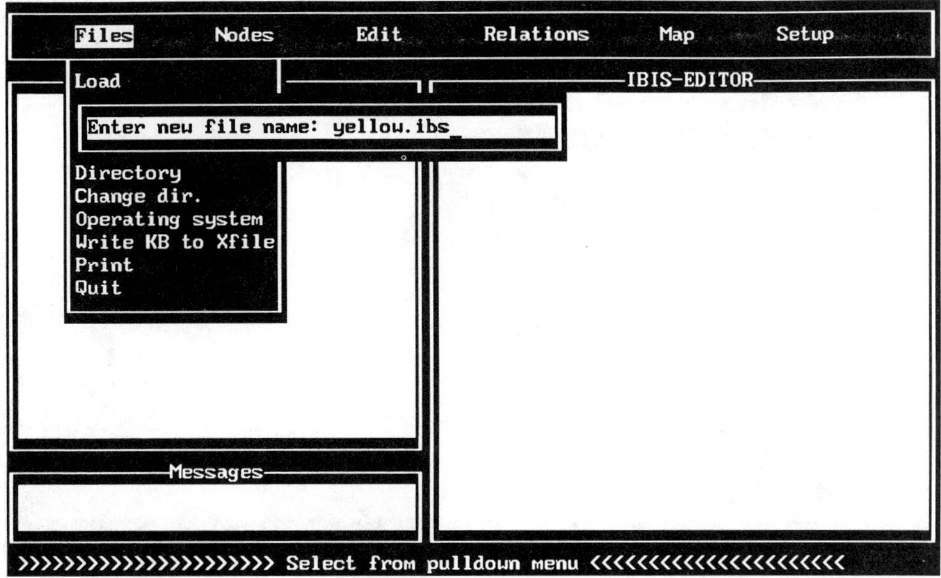

Fig. 11-1. Creating a new IBIS database file.

MicroIBIS creates the file and throws you into a dialogue box. The system assumes that each new IBIS must start with a main issue, so it creates a new database file with the first entry being an issue node.

The Attributes Dialogue Box

The dialogue box is MicroIBIS's way of asking you to specify the attributes of a new node. The dialogue box has fields for:

- the name of the person raising the issue, which you should supply.
- the date of entering the issue, so you can know when the issue was first raised. The system will supply the date for you. MicroIBIS allows you to change the date if you want to do so.
- the kind of issue you are about to enter. There are five kinds of issues corresponding to five kinds of knowledge. These are: factual issues, conceptual issues, explanatory issues, instrumental issues, and deontic issues. MicroIBIS expects you to supply that.

This is exactly what I did in FIG. 9-5, but for the fire fighting problem I entered different values. See FIG. 11-2 for the attributes of the root issue.

Once you are done with the dialogue box, you can press ESC or F10 to exit and save the attributes of the root node. The next thing you know, you are in the node editor with a message, at the bottom of the window, telling you to enter the issue. FIGURE 11-3 gives you an idea about this stage.

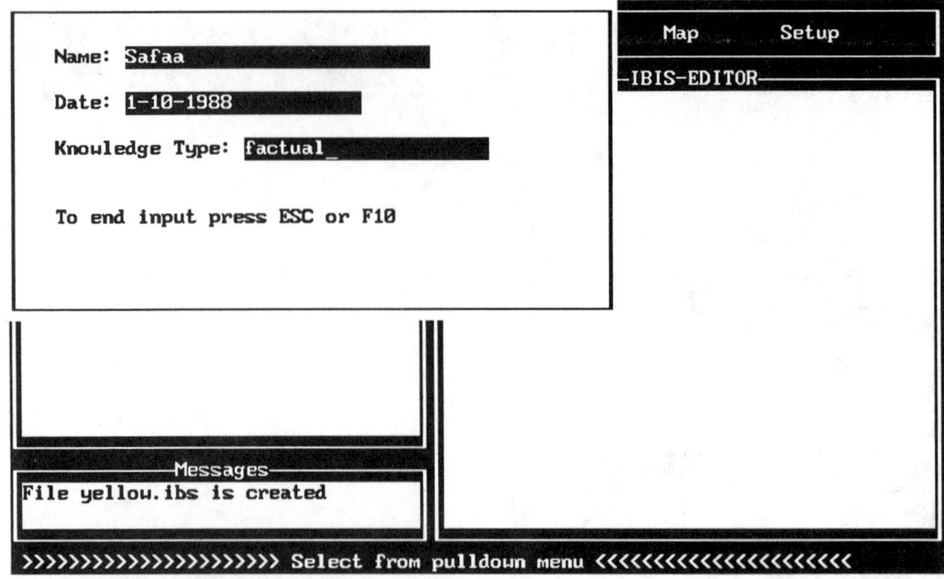

Fig. 11-2. Entering the attributes of the root issue.

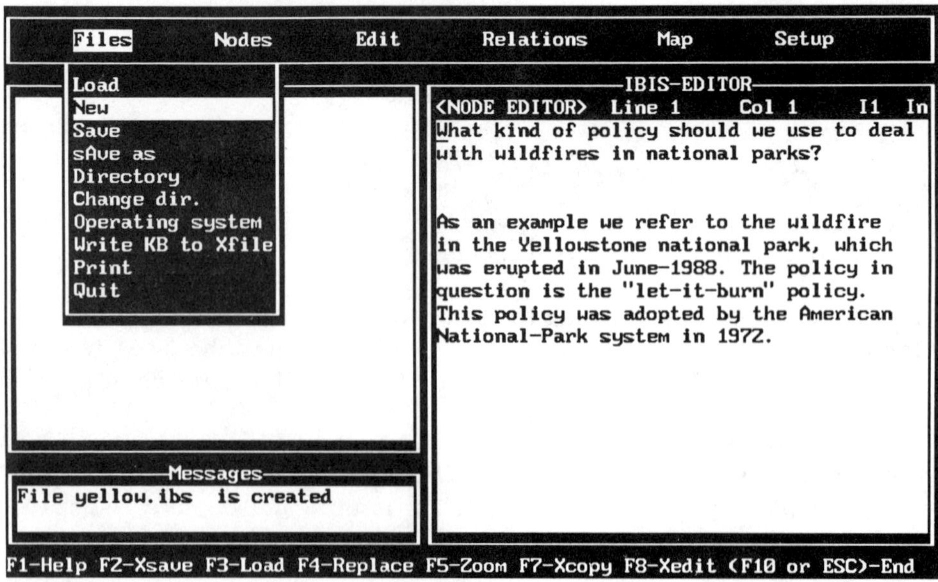

Fig. 11-3. Entering the root issue using the IBIS-EDITOR.

The Main Issue

To solve any problem, the first thing you need to do is to state your problem. In the IBIS approach you put the problem statement in a question form. The first question in an IBIS is what is called the "main issue," (see FIG. 11-3).

When entering the main issue, you should be concise and to the point. In other words, your question must be a focused one. Some times it is quite hard to put the whole problem into one statement. In such a situation you might like to start the issue with a major question that captures the whole issue. Then, you can add separate paragraphs for a more detailed breakdown of the major issue. Even better, you can add the additional information as a separate node or nodes. For example, you could add some background information about the Yellowstone national park. You can do that by using a separate "reference" node.

Adding a Reference Node

To add a reference you use the "Relations/referenced-by" option from the pull-down menu. In this case, after you entered the text for the main issue, you exit the editor by pressing ESC. Now you are back in the pull-down menu. You choose the "Relations/referenced-by" option to create a new node for the background information (see FIG. 11-4). MicroIBIS will put you in the node editor again, so you can start entering your reference. In FIG. 11-5, you entered some general background information about the Yellowstone national park, to help understand the main issue.

You finish entering the text in the reference node by pressing the ESC key. MicroIBIS will automatically save the text in the new reference node. To continue the argumentation process, you must go back to the issue. How do you do that? You can go to an already existing node in two ways. One way is to use the "Nodes/Load node" option. The other way is to use the IBIS-MAP to locate and view the contents of nodes. Now use the IBIS-MAP to get back to the main

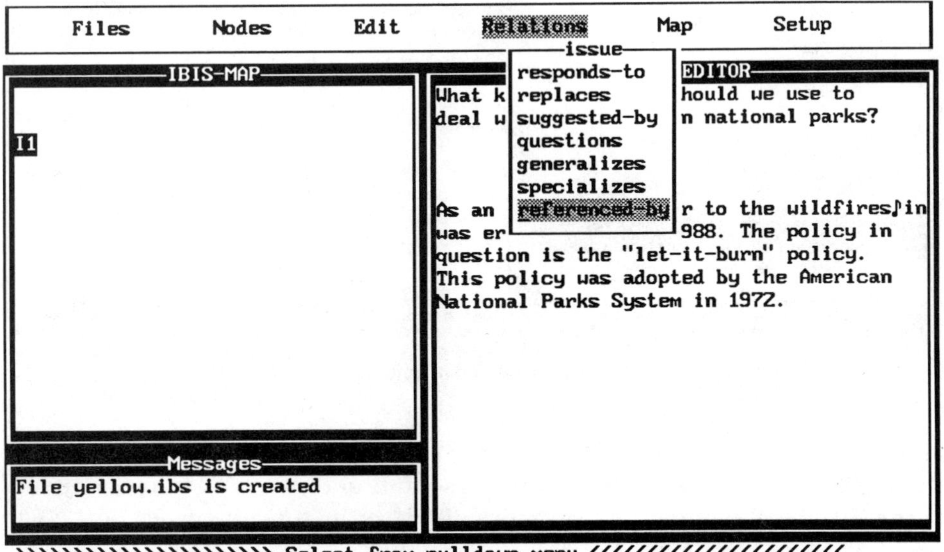

Fig. 11-4. More information is put on the issue in a reference.

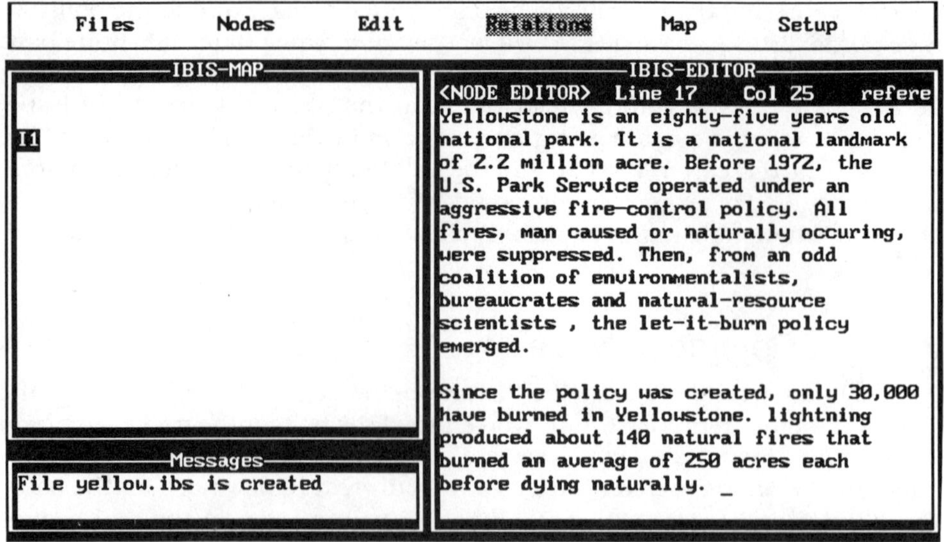

Fig. 11-5. Entering the text for the reference material.

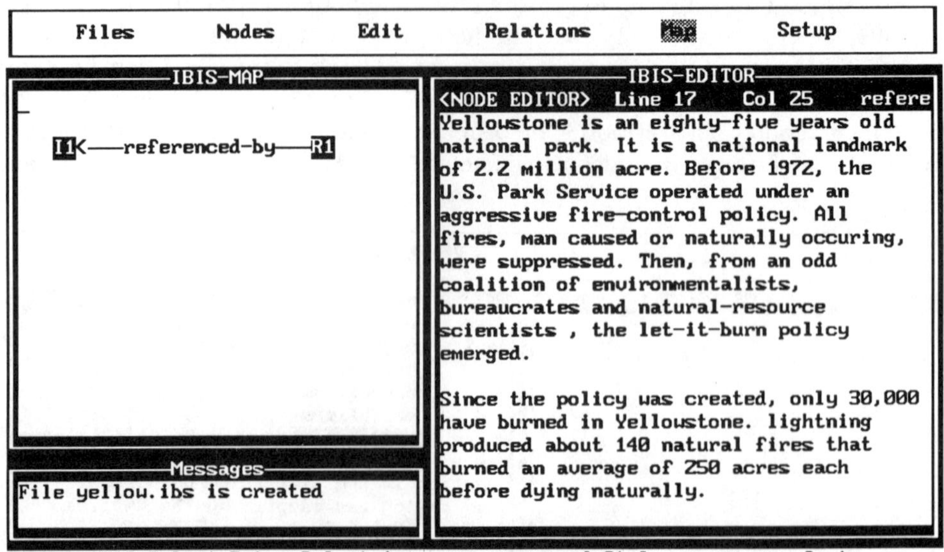

Fig. 11-6. Viewing the IBIS-MAP of a root issue and its reference.

issue. To do that, you choose the "Map" option from the pull-down menu. MicroIBIS will display a graphical representation of the IBIS knowledge-base in the IBIS-MAP window. The cursor will be in the top-left-corner of the window. Take a look at FIG. 11-6.

Viewing Nodes and Links in MicroIBIS

The IBIS-MAP is a graphical representation of the IBIS knowledge-base. In IBIS-MAP you can see the nodes and the links between these nodes. Each link will have a label. The label of a link is the name of the relationship between the two nodes.

At present, MicroIBIS uses a tree structure instead of a network. You know, from Chapter 10, that a network is better than a tree in representing the problem-solving process in IBIS. In PART ONE and PART TWO I discussed the use of networks in hypertext. For this book, a tree-based IBIS is sufficient for exploring the use of hypertext in problem-solving. In Chapter 13 I will show you how I wrote the IBIS-MAP code. You can modify it to reflect a network structure instead of a tree structure.

How do you use the IBIS-MAP? Using IBIS-MAP involves its three main advantages:

- First, to move around in the IBIS-MAP window, use the arrow keys. To move faster you can use CTRL-arrow for fast horizontal movement. Also, you can use PGUP and PGDN for fast vertical movement. Try using these keys to move around in the map. You will notice that you can scroll left, right, up, or down in the window. Your IBIS-MAP can be as large as you want. You are not limited to the size of your monitor's screen. IBIS-MAP is a virtual map.
- Second, to pick a node, place the cursor on the node and press the ENTER key. Notice the change in the background color of the node, when you move the cursor on the node. After you press the ENTER key, MicroIBIS loads the node in the IBIS-EDITOR window. Now, you can choose the Edit option from the pull-down menu to edit the node.
- Third, when you put the cursor on a node and press F10, you get a hypertext menu. F10 is the hypertext hotkey. You use this menu to operate on the node you have just selected. You create new links by choosing the relationships option. You delete a whole IBIS sub-tree by selecting the Delete option. Also, you can view the node attributes by selecting the "Attr" option. FIGURE 11-7 gives you an idea about the hypertext menu.

An important aspect of the IBIS-MAP is the status-line at the bottom of the screen. The status-line lists most of the commands you need while in the IBIS-MAP window. Now it is time to go back to the main issue of the wildfires problem.

Modifying the Main Issue

As a member of the argumentation group, I want to modify the main issue by suggesting a new version of it. To do that I must: first have the main issue (I1) as the current issue, FIG. 11-3. Second, I choose the Relations/Specializes option, FIG. 11-8. Third, I enter the text for the new issue (I2) in the IBIS-EDITOR, FIG. 11-9. Done with entering the text, I exit the editor. Fourth, I can view the updated IBIS map by choosing the Map option, FIG. 11-10.

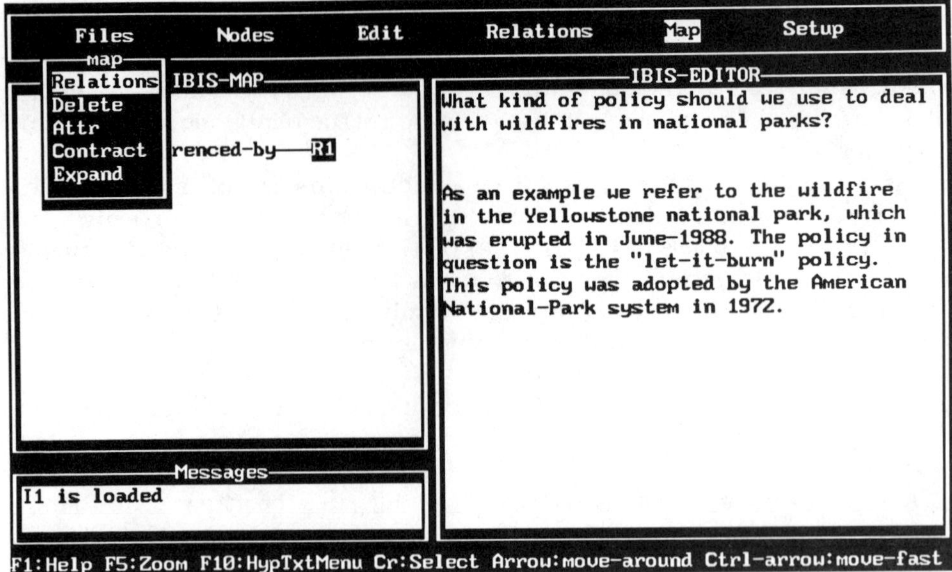

Fig. 11-7. Operating on a node using the hypertext menu.

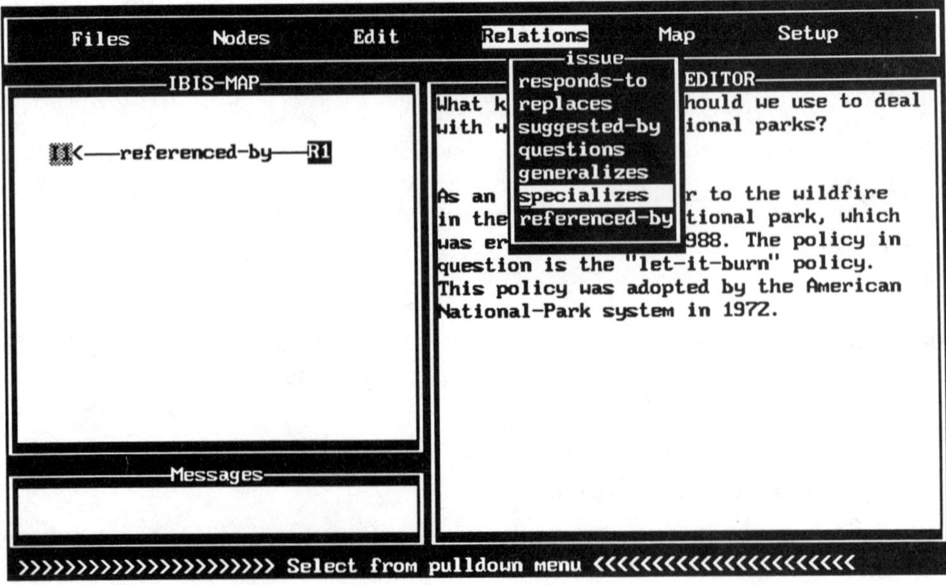

Fig. 11-8. Specializing the main issue in a new issue.

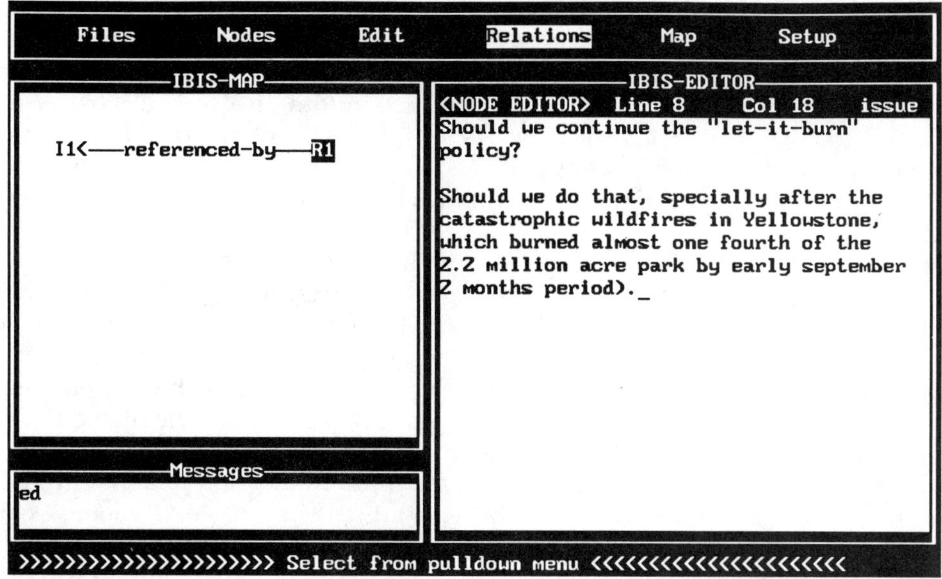

Fig. 11-9. Entering the text for the new issue.

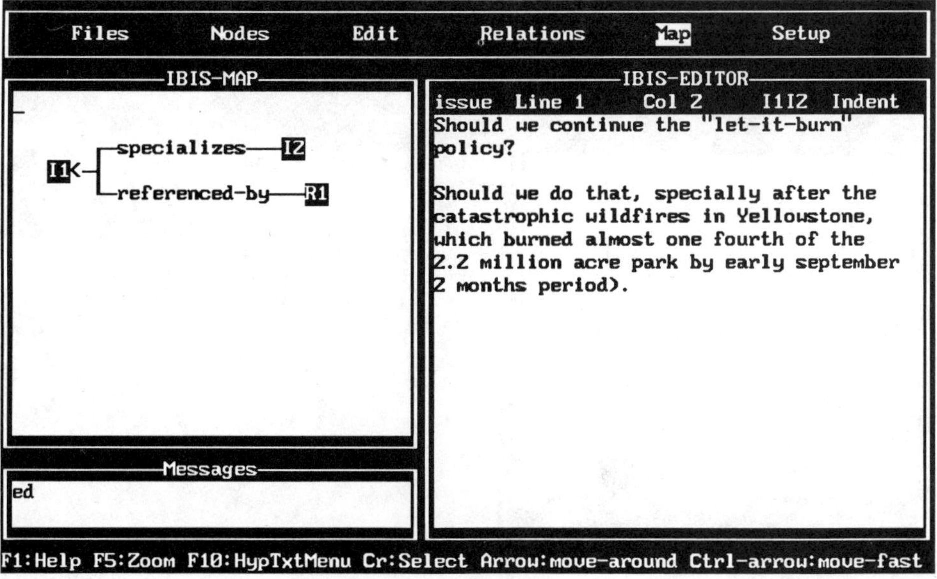

Fig. 11-10. MicroIBIS shows the new issue (I2) in its MAP.

I entered the new issue, but how about the attributes of this issue. Each MicroIBIS's node must have four attributes: node type, author name, knowledge type, and date. So, where is the dialogue box? When I entered the main issue, MicroIBIS displayed the dialogue box automatically (FIG. 11-2). Why didn't it do the same for the new issue? Well, except for the main issue, MicroIBIS doesn't automatically ask you to enter the attributes of a new node. There are three ways to enter the attributes of a node:

1) By selecting the "Setup/Attr.Dialog/Show" option. This way, every time I create a new node—i.e., establishing a new relationship—MicroIBIS will automatically display the dialogue box. FIGURE 11-11 shows you how to do that.
2) For an already existing node, I can select the "Nodes/Attributes" option. I can use this for the new issue (I2). In FIG. 11-12 you can see the dialogue box for the attribute values of the I2 issue.
3) Another way to enter or change the attribute-values of a node is through the hypertext menu in the IBIS-MAP. While in the IBIS-MAP mode, I can place the cursor on the node whose attributes I want to change. Then, by using the hypertext hotkey (F10) I get the hypertext (map) menu. Now, I can choose the "Attr" option to get the dialogue box. Once I am in the dialogue box, I can edit its attribute-fields (see FIG. 11-12).

It is time to come up with some answers. Ask the group to take some positions from the new issue (I2).

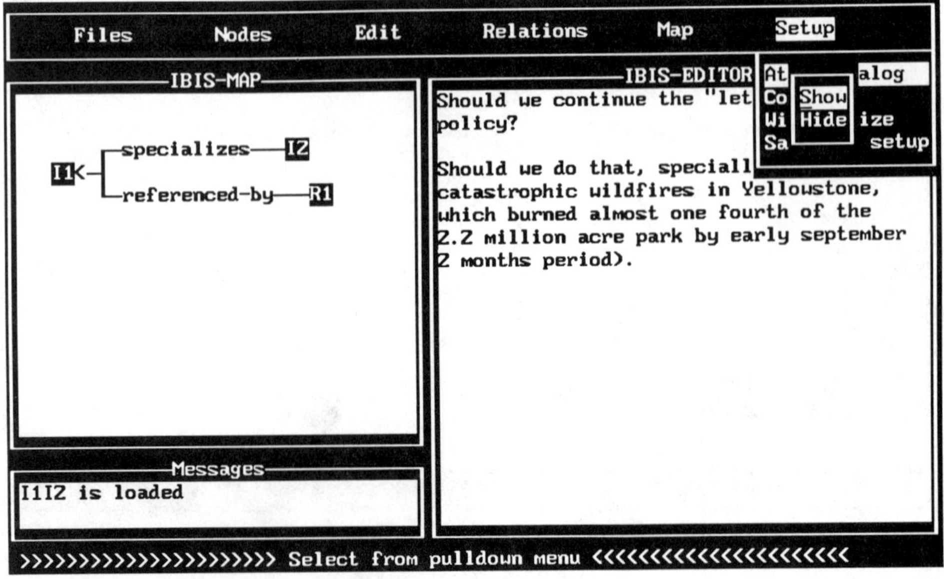

Fig. 11-11. Changing the attributes-dialogue-box status.

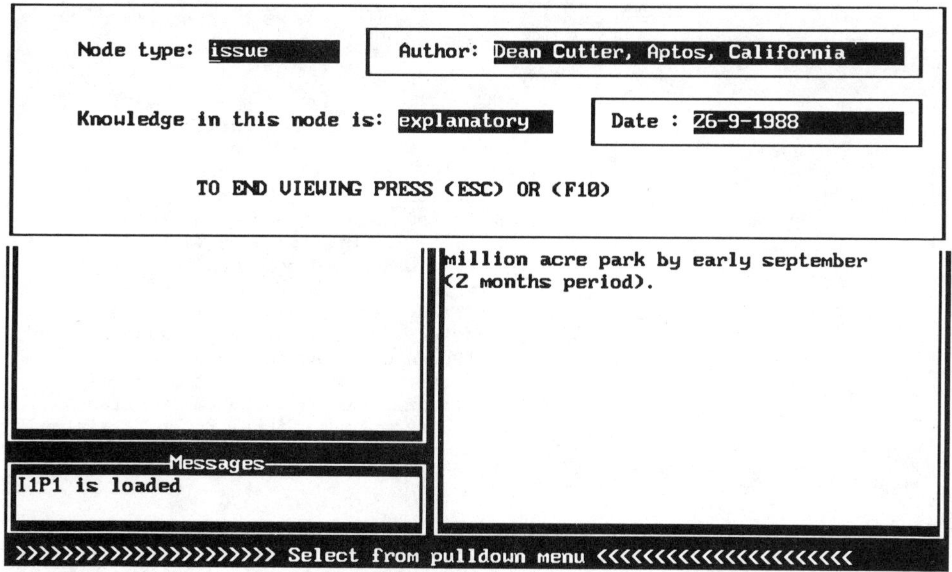

Fig. 11-12. Viewing and changing the attributes of a node.

Taking Positions from an Issue

With I2 as the current issue, choose the Relations/Responds-to option from the pull-down menu. If you had set MicroIBIS to "Setup/Attr-Dialog-/Show" you will first see the attribute dialogue box. You will assume that the person answering I2 is a neighbor of the Yellowstone Park, and not in favor of the let-it-burn policy. He will explain why the let-it-burn policy is a harmful one to parks like Yellowstone. So, his position will contain an explanatory knowledge. After entering the attributes values in the dialogue box, MicroIBIS puts you in the IBIS-EDITOR. FIGURE 11-13 shows the position in the IBIS-EDITOR window.

Arguing Against a Position

As in any group discussion, you agree with some answers and disagree with others. When you disagree you advance an argument against the answer you don't like. This is exactly what the Yellowstone ecologist, a member of our IBIS group, does. He wants to argue against the position that the let-it-burn policy is harmful. As an ecologist, he explains why the let-it-burn policy should be kept. In this sense, his argument is an explanatory one. In FIG. 11-14 you can see the text for this argument.

So far you have been a silent member of our IBIS group. Probably you would like to participate in the process. Try to argue for or against the position that the let-it-burn policy is harmful. For me, I would like to support the position that the let-it-burn policy is a harmful one.

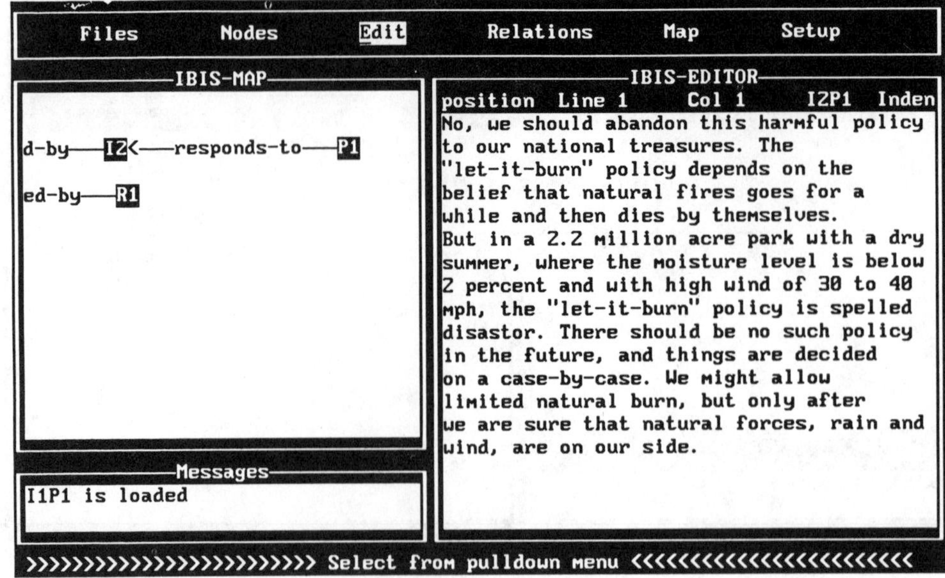

Fig. 11-13. Responding to the current issue (I2).

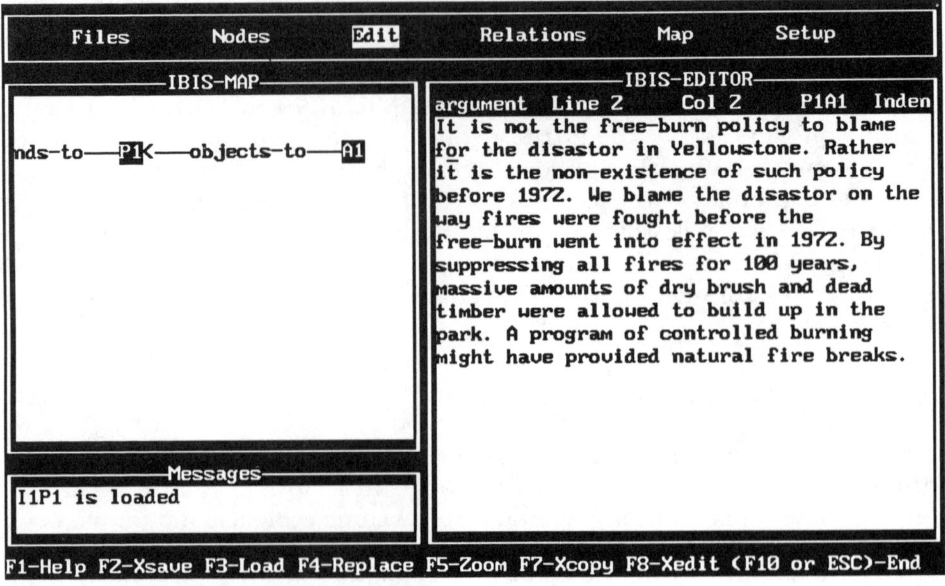

Fig. 11-14. Arguing against the current position.

An Argument Supporting a Position

Because of my position against the continuation of the free-burn policy, I will support the position taken by the Yellowstone residents. With that position as the current node, I choose the "Relations/Supports" option and enter the text for my argument. Take a look at my supporting argument in FIG. 11-15.

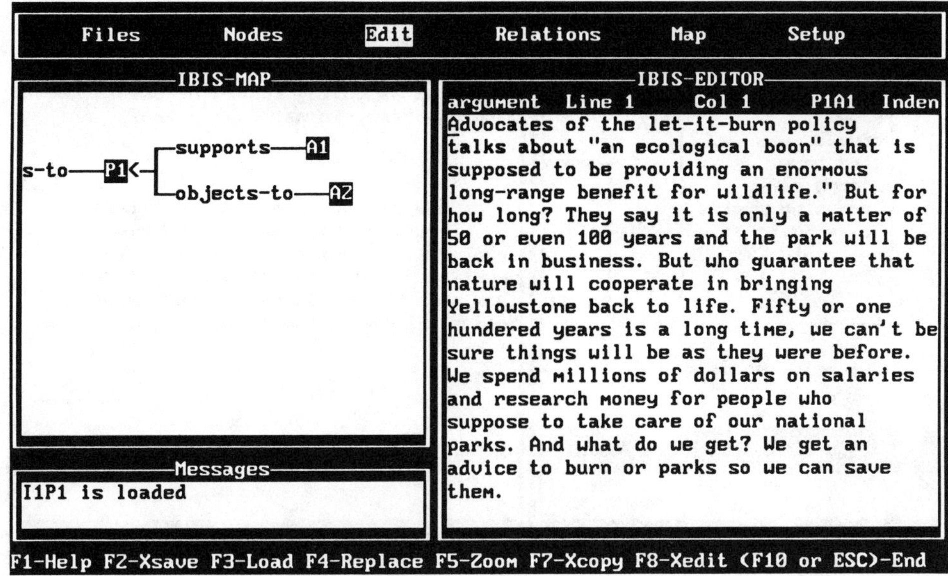

Fig. 11-15. Supporting the current position.

Arguing For and Against an Argument

Now you have two arguments related to one position. One argument is against the position, and the other supports it. It seems, with the two arguments balancing against each other, that the position by the Yellowstone residents is not encouraging. Another member wanted to submit his position from I2 for argument. The process continues—some will take supporting positions, others will take opposing positions. Also, you might have members opposing the arguments of others. I call an argument opposing another argument a "counter-argument." Still, some members might support the arguments of others. You can see some examples of arguments opposing or supporting other arguments in the listing of the whole Yellowstone IBIS in FIG. 11-17.

PRINTING THE WHOLE IBIS

Suppose you are solving a problem with MicroIBIS and you want to see the whole IBIS in one piece. How can you do that? To do that you can use the File/Print option from the pull-down menu. With this option you can print the whole IBIS either to the printer, or to an external text file. The real advantage of this option is when you want to print IBIS to an external text file. The text file will be in ASCII format. You can use your favorite word processor to edit and print the file as a final report. This report will represent the group analysis and solution of the problem. In FIG. 11-16 I show you how to choose the File-/Print/File option. FIGURE 11-17, on the other hand, shows the resulting text file for the Yellowstone IBIS.

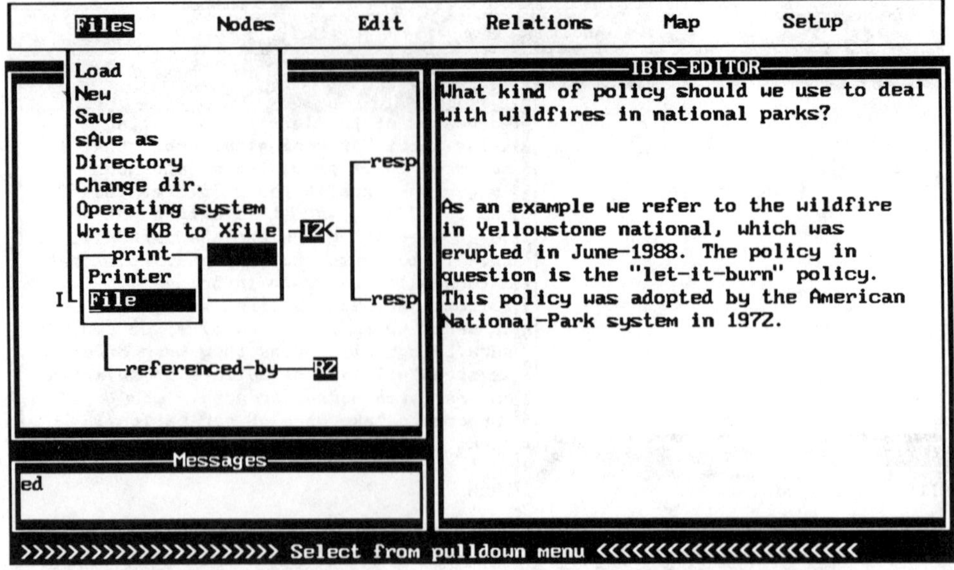

Fig. 11-16. Printing the whole IBIS to an external text file.

Fig. 11-17. The Yellowstone IBIS text file.

```
The main issue (I1) is:

    What kind of policy should we use to deal with wildfires
    in national parks?

    As an example we refer to the wildfire in Yellowstone
    national, which erupted in June 1988. The policy in
    question is the "let-it-burn" policy. This policy was
    adopted by the American National Park system in 1972.


issue (I2) suggested-by issue (I1):

    Should we continue the "let-it-burn" policy?

    Should we do that, especially after the catastrophic
    wildfires in Yellowstone burned almost one-fourth
    of the 2.2 million acre park by early September  (2
    month period).


position (P1) responds-to issue (I2):

    Yes, I think we should continue the let burn policy.

    As firefighters well know, a let burn
    policy under the right conditions is necessary to
    prevent disastrous wildfires in the future.

    Nearly all major wildfires, including Yellowstone,
    happened because fire suppression allows brush and trees
    to accumulate to critical levels.
```

(**Fig. 11-17.** continued)

Wildlife and plants actually flourish after a fire's passing. Open areas allow growth of sun-loving plants which sustain a chain of insects, birds, mammals and other organisms.

Wisely administered, controlled burns reduce the risk of devastating uncontrollable fires and promote healthy ecosystems. Naturally.

argument (A1) objects-to position (P1):

On the eve of Labor day, plumes of Yellowstone smoke are drifting over the Midwest and beyond, and businesses in neighboring Montana, Wyoming and Idaho towns that rely exclusively on Park visitors are suffering.

I've heard the story that Yellowstone will be a better place, and I can't believe my ears. I lived along the Yellowstone river for 23 years and I manage the Chico Hot Springs Resort in Pray, where business is off 50 percent. It was an insane thing to do, and I'm as mad as the grizzly. And he's mad when there are no berries and he's hungry.

argument (A2) objects-to argument (A1):

I think the argument that the fire in Yellowstone will hurt tourism business in the area is not acceptable.

I predict that curiosity will bring more visitors to Yellowstone next year than ever before: "Nobody ever heard of Mount St. Helens until it errupted. Now it's a major tourist attraction."

argument (A3) supports position (P1):

Really, the fire is almost superficial in an ecological sense. There are few real changes.

One of the problems, he says, is the human view of the forest and an impatience with the cycles of life and death on the land.

It is part of the outlook we inherited from Europe that says we have to tame or conquer nature. We need to live with the ecosystem, not conquer it.

I believe that wildfires in the park should be allowed to burn, to go wherever it wants to go, as long as it does not endanger life or burn down buildings.

This is one of the very few areas in the world where natural processes are allowed to go on. There is no place left that is 100 percent pure, but Yellowstone is as close as they come.

I am not worried about the Yellowstone that was lost in the fire. The new forest that emerges from the fires will be a fantastic lab for science to study.

argument (A4) objects-to argument (A3):

(**Fig. 11-17.** continued)

<Harold R. Walt, professor of management at the University of San Francisco, is chairman of California Board of Forestry.>

It is astonishing to find that some people still describe the fires in Yellowstone National Park in positive, if not lyrical terms. Thus we read about "an ecological boon" that is supposed to be providing an enormous "long-range benefit for wildlife." It is sheer rationalization of an ill-concevied management policy being defended by the beleaguered National Park Service. I would suggest a description more apt for this national tragedy: madness.

There are three basic elements to the fire suppression equation: Fuel, weather, and topography. In their deadly way they combined to create a tragic scene in which four major convection columns of smoke rose 40,000 feet--nearly eight miles into the heavens. Of these elements, only the first (fuel) can be controlled by man. And that is the heart of the problem. The dominant forest species of the park, lodgepole pine, grows like cornstalks, and about as close togther.

As the weaker trees die, they fall in place to form a perfect bonfire setting --crisscrossed logs and piles of dried fuel waiting for ignition. The "hands-off" policy of the park set the stage for the present inferno.

In the congressional oversight hearings being planned, it is appropriate to raise several questions. Answers must be sought, not in an antagonistic "whodunit" approach, but rather in the spirit that America can't tolerate a repeat of this episode.

issue (I3) suggested_by argument (A4):

Can we develop a more effective early fire warning system?

position (P2) responds-to issue (I3):

Yes. Yellowstone fires should not have been allowed to get out of hand. They could have been predicted. Computer models are available to warn of discernible fire-hazard trends, and steps should have been taken early in the summer for contingency plans.

Of course, predictions like these are not 100 precent accurate, but they would enable fire control officials to make their best decision with the best possible information in hand. Thus an early agreement should have been reached to assume an aggressive fire suppression attitude and initiate a prompt and well-organized attack effort on all lightning strikes.

reference (R1) referenced-by argument (A3):

Just off one of the main highways in Yellowstone Park, across a marsh where wild elk sometimes graze, there is

(**Fig. 11-17.** continued)

a ghostly forest of gray-colored lodgepole pines, killed in a wildfire 12 years ago.

"This is what people will see when they look out the car windows in Yellowstone in the year 2000," said Don Despain, the park's chief research biologist. It was a preview in miniature of the huge blazes that have roared over the Yellowstone country this summer.

Despain walked through the grove the other morning, pointing out what the fire had done and how the forest had renewed itself. The burned Yellowstone forests will still be full of standing trees in the summer of the year 2000. When the trees fall, they will stay on the forest floor for a century, because it takes that long for lodgepoles to rot in the dry Yellowstone climate.

But by that summer, new trees, some of them seven or eight feet tall, will have sprung up. The ground will be covered with green plants, some of them different from the plants that were there when the fire came. Before the fire, the forest was thick and there was not much sunlight, but there will be patches of wild strawberry and liverwort, a primitive plant that once was thought of as a folk medicine.

In June or July there will be wildflowers, clover and violets. There will also be a green slime of algae, which grows when there is plenty of sunlight.

The forest that summer will be alive--but a somewhat different life from what was there before. The fires usually mean a big decline in small animals, and this decline lasts for as many as a dozen years. "But eventually, most of the species that were there, plants, animals and insects, come back. Five years after a fire, 90 percent of the species that were there are back."

position (P3) responds-to issue (I2):

No, we should abandon this policy that is harmful to our national treasures.

The "let-it-burn" policy depends on the belief that natural fires go for a while and then die by themselves. But in a 2.2 million park with a dry summer, where the moisture level is below 2 percent and with high winds of 30 to 40 mph, the "let-it-burn" policy spells disaster. There should be no such policy in the future, with things decided on a case-by-case basis. We might allow limited natural burn, but only after we are sure that natural forces, rain and wind, are on our side.

argument (A5) objects-to position (P3):

It is not the free-burn policy that is to blame for the disaster in Yellowstone. Rather it is the non-existence of such policy before 1972.

We blame the disaster on the way fires were fought before the free-burn went into effect in 1972. By suppressing all fires for 100 years, massive amounts of

(**Fig. 11-17.** continued)

```
     dry brush and dead timber were allowed to build up in
     the park. A program of controlled burning might have
     provided natural fire breaks.


 argument (A6) supports position (P3):

     Advocates of the let-it-burn policy talk about "an
     ecological boon" that is supposed to be providing an
     enormous long-range benefit for wildlife.  But for how
     long? They say it is only a matter of 100 or even 50
     years and the park will be back in business. But who
     guarantees that nature will cooperate in bringing
     Yellowstone back to life. Fifty or one hundred years
     is a long time, no one can be sure things will be as they
     were before. We spend millions of dollars on salaries
     and research money for people who are supposed to take care
     of our national parks. And what do we get? We get
     advice to burn our parks so we can save them.


 reference (R2) referenced-by issue (I1):

     Yellowstone is an eighty-five year old national park.
     It is a national landmark of 2.2 million acres. Before
     1972, the U.S. Park Service operated under an aggressive
     fire-control policy. All fires, man caused or naturally
     occuring, were suppressed. Then, from an odd coalition
     of environmentalists, bureaucrats and natural-resource
     scientists, the let-it-burn policy emerged.

     Since the policy was created, only 30,000 trees have burned in
     Yellowstone.  Lightning produced about 140 natural fires
     that burned an average of 250 acres each before dying
     naturally.

    <From the SanFrancisco Examiner, Sunday, September 4,
    1988, page A-15.>
```

To help decision makers solve a problem, it is better to have both textual and graphical representations of an IBIS. In MicroIBIS you can do both. By printing IBIS to an external file, you get the textual part, FIG. 11-17. For the graphical part, use the map option to view the IBIS-MAP. To print the IBIS-MAP, use SHIFT-PrtSC to directly print the map on the printer. Another way is to use memory-resident copy tools, such as the one in SideKick. For example, in SideKick, you can use F4 to copy the IBIS-MAP to a file. Once the map is in SideKick, you can edit the map before you print it. Remember, in MicroIBIS version 1.0 the graphics are just text-graphics. MicroIBIS version 1.0 operates only in text mode. FIGURE 11-18 gives you an idea of the complete IBIS-MAP for the Yellowstone IBIS.

WRITING THE IBIS KNOWLEDGE-BASE TO AN EXTERNAL FILE

When solving a problem in MicroIBIS, you enter the attributes of each node using a dialogue box. As for the text of a node, you use the IBIS-EDITOR.

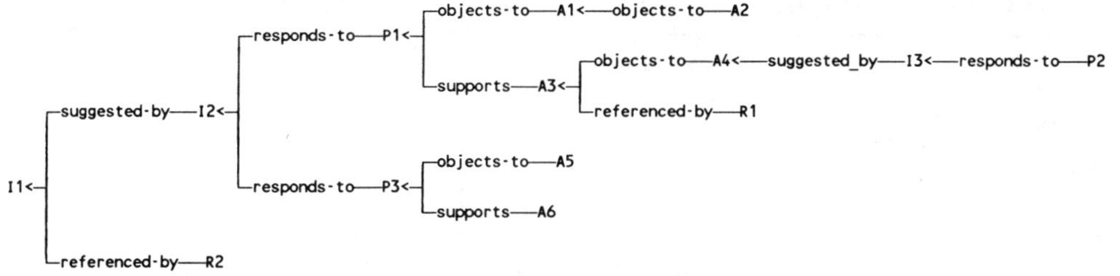

Fig. 11-18. The IBIS-MAP for the Yellowstone problem.

MicroIBIS, on its part, processes the input and builds the graphical structure in an IBIS-MAP. In MicroIBIS the knowledge-base is written as a set of Prolog relationships. These relationships constitute the knowledge-base of MicroIBIS. In other words, the knowledge-base is what MicroIBIS knows about the problem. It is his internal representation of the problem—and attributes in a dialogue box, text in the IBIS-EDITOR, and the IBIS-MAP are MicroIBIS's external representations of the problem.

In other words, MicroIBIS saves its knowledge on a problem in two parts: A single "ibis" fact, and several "node" facts. The "ibis" fact represents the nested tree structure of IBIS (see FIG. 11-19a), and the "node" facts represent the attributes and contents of each node in IBIS (see FIG. 11-19b). You can get the "ibis" fact and the "node" facts of an IBIS by using the "File/Write KB to Xfile" option. When you choose this option, MicroIBIS will ask you to enter a filename. MicroIBIS will use this file to save the "ibis" fact and the "node" facts.

I added the "Write KB to Xfile" to help you understand the internal representation of a problem. It is true that when solving a problem in MicroIBIS you don't need this internal representation, but if you are planning to add some AI features to MicroIBIS, you should know how the program saves and processes its data. With Turbo Prolog you can operate on the knowledge-base to analyze and draw conclusions about issues, positions, and arguments. One application could be the automatic generation of issues. Another application is to check if a position does address the issue at hand or tries to avoid answering it. I can think of many other applications—each deserves a chapter of its own.

To conclude this chapter, I recommend that you use MicroIBIS to solve a problem of your own. Once you have done that, you will have a better understanding of the argumentative process of problem-solving. You can extend your MicroIBIS to allow the user to add his own argumentation rules—but first, you must understand the philosophy behind it. I often like to think of MicroIBIS as a book, which in order to understand it, you have to read and live its contents. Writers often recommend this to their readers, as in this quotation from Ezra Pound:

"No man understands a deep book until he has seen and lived at least part of its contents."

To learn more about the internals of MicroIBIS, I included a detailed analysis of the program in the next two chapters.

Fig. 11-19a. Representing the IBIS-MAP as a Prolog relation.

```
******** THE IBIS TREE ********

ibis("root","issue",1,
     [ibis("suggested-by","issue",4,
           [ibis("responds-to","position",8,
                 [ibis("objects-to","argument",B,
                       [ibis("objects-to","argument",C,[])
                       ]),
                  ibis("supports","argument",9,
                       [ibis("objects-to","argument",D,
                             [ibis("suggested_by","issue",E,
                                   [ibis("responds-to","position",F,[])
                                   ])
                             ]),
                        ibis("referenced-by","reference",A,[])
                       ])
                 ]),
            ibis("responds-to","position",5,
                 [ibis("objects-to","argument",6,[]),
                  ibis("supports","argument",7,[])
                 ])
           ]),
      ibis("referenced-by","reference",3,[])
     ]).
```

Fig. 11-19b. The node relations of the Yellowstone IBIS.

```
******** THE NODES ********

node("position","explanatory","Harold R. Walt","14-9-1988.",
     "Yes. \n\nYellowstone fires should not have been\nallowed
      to get out of hand. They could\nhave been predicted.
      Computer models\nare available to warn of discernible\nfire-hazard
      trends, and steps should\nhave been taken early
      in the summer for\ncontingency plans.\n\nOf course,
      predictions like these are\nnot 100 precent accurate,
      but they would\nenable fire control officials to
      make\ntheir best decision with the best\npossible
      information in hand. Thus an\nearly agreement should
      have been reached\nto assume an aggressive fire
      suppression\nattitude and initiate a prompt and
      well\norganized attack effort on all
      lightning\nstrikes.")

node("issue","factual","Harold R. Walt","14-9-1988",
     "Can we develop a more effective early \nfire warning
     system?") node("argument","explanatory","Prof. Harold
     Walt. UCSF","12-9-1988","<Harold R. Walt, professor of
     management\nat the University of San Francisco,
     is\nchairman of California Board of \nForestry.>\n\nIt
     is astonishing to find that some \npeople still
     describe the fires in \nYellowstone National Park in
     positive, \nif not lyrical terms. Thus we read \nabout
     \"an ecological boon\" that is \nsupposed to be
     providing an enormous \n\"long-range benefit for
     wildlife.\" \nIt is sheer rationalization of an \nill-
     conceived management policy being\ndefended by the
     beleaguered National \nPark Service. I would  suggest a
     \ndescription more apt for this national \ntragedy:
     madness.\n\nThere are three basic elements to the
     \nfire suppression equation: Fuel,\nweather, and
```

(**Fig. 11-19b.** continued)

```
      topography. In their\ndeadly way they combined to
      create a\ntragic scene in which four major\nconvection
      columns of smoke rose\n40,000 feet--nearly eight miles
      into\nthe heavens. Of these elements, only \nthe first
      (fuel) can be controlled by\nman. And that is the heart
      of the \nproblem. The dominant forest species\nof the
      park, lodgepole pine, grows like\ncornstalks, and about
      as close togther.\n\nAs the weaker trees die, they fall
      in\nplace to form a perfect bonfire setting\n--
      crisscrossed logs and piles of dried \nfuel waiting for
      ignition. The \n\"hands-off\" policy of the park set
      the\nstage for the present inferno.\n\nIn the
      congressional oversight\nhearings being planned, it is
      \nappropriate to raise several questions. \nAnswers
      must be sought, not in an \nantagonistic \"whodunit\"
      approach, but\nrather in the spirit that America
      can't\ntolerate a repeat of this episode.\n\n")

node("argument","explanatory","Yellowstone chief ranger","15-9-1988",
      "I think the argument that the fire in\nYellowstone
      will hurt tourism business\nin the area is not
      acceptable. \n\nI predict that curiosity will bring
      more\nvisitors to Yellowstone next year than\never
      before \"Nobody ever heard of Mount\nSt. Helens until
      it errupted.\ Now its a\nmajor tourist
      attraction.\"\n\n")

node("argument","factual","Yellowstone resident","15-9-1988",
      "On the eve of Labor day, plumes of\nYellowstone smoke
      are drifting over the\nMidwest and beyond, and
      businesses in\nneighboring Montana, Wyoming and
      Idaho\ntowns that rely exclusively on Park\nvisitors
      are suffering.\n\nI've heard the story that
      Yellowstone\nwill be a better place, and I
      can't\nbelieve my ears. I lived along the\nYellowstone
      river for 23 years and I \nmanage the Chico Hot Springs
      Resort in\nPray, where business is off 50 percent.\nIt
      was an insane thing to do, and I'm\nas mad as the
      grizzly. And he's mad\nwhen there are no berries and
      he's\nhungry.\n")

node("reference","factual","Park's research biologist","12-9-1988",
      "Just off one of the main highways in\nYellowstone
      Park, across a marsh where\nwild elk sometimes graze,
      there is a\nghostly forest of gray-colored
      lodgepole\npines, killed in a wildfire 12 years
      ago.\n\n\"This is what people will see when they\nlook
      out the car windows in Yellowstone\nin the year 2000,\"
      said Don Despain, the\npark's chief research biologist.
      It was\na preview in miniature of the huge blazes\nthat
      have roared over the Yellowstone\ncountry this
      summer.\n\nDespain walked through the grove the \nother
      morning, pointing out what the fire\nhad done and how
      the forest had renewed\nitself. The burned Yellowstone
      forests \nwill still be full of standing trees in\nthe
      summer of the year 2000. When the\ntrees fall, they
      will stay on the forest\nfloor for a century, because
      it takes\nthat long for lodgepoles to rot in the\ndry
      Yellowstone climate.\n\nBut by that summer, new trees,
      some of\nthem seven or eight feet tall, will
      have\nsprung up. The ground will be covered\nwith green
      plants, some of them different\nfrom the plants that
      were there when the\nfire came. Before the fire, the
      forest\nwas thick and there was not much sunlight\n,
      but there will be patches of wild\nstrawberry and
```

(**Fig. 11-19b.** continued)

```
      liverwort, a primitive \nplant that once was thought of
      as a folk\nmedicine.\n\nIn June or July there will
      be\nwildflowers, clover and violets. There \nwill also
      be a green slime of algae,\nwhich grows when there is
      plenty of\nsunlight. \n\nThe forest that summer will be
      alive--but\na somewhat different life from what
      was\nthere before. The fires usually mean\na big
      decline in small animals, and this\ndecline lasts for
      as many as a dozen \nyears. \"But eventually, most of
      the\nspecies that were there, plants, animals\nand
      insects, come back. Five years after\na fire, 90
      percent of the species that\nwere there are back.\n")

node("argument","explanatory","Park's research biologist","10-9-1988",
      "Really, the fire is almost superficial.  In\nan
      ecological sense, there are few real\nchanges.\n\nOne of
      the problems, he says, is the\nhuman view of the forest
      and an\nimpatience with the cycles of life and\ndeath
      on the land.\n\nIt is part of the outlook we
      inherited\nfrom Europe that says we have to tame
      or\nconquer nature. We need to live with
      the\necosystem, not conquer it.\n\nI believe that
      wildfires in the park\nshould be allowed to burn, to go
      wherever\nit wants to go, as long as it does
      not\nendanger life or burn down buildings.\n\nThis is
      one of the very few areas in the\nworld where natural
      processes are allowed\nto go on. There is no place left
      that is\n100 percent pure, but Yellowstone is as\nclose
      as they come.\n\nI am not worried about the
      Yellowstone\nthat was lost in the fire. The new
      forest\nthat emerges from the fires will be a
      \nfantastic lab for science to study.\n\n")

node("position","deontic","Dean Cutter, Aptos,California","9-10-1988",
      "Yes, I think, we should continue the\nlet burn policy.
      \n\nAs firefighters well know,\na let
      burn policy under the right\nconditions is necessary to
      prevent\ndisastrous wildfires in the future.\n\nNearly
      all major wildfires, including\nYellowstone, happened
      because fire\nsuppression allows brush and trees
      to\naccumulate to critical levels. \n\nWildlife and
      plants actually flourish\nafter a fire's passing. Open
      areas allow\ngrowth of sun-loving plants which
      sustain\na chain of insects, birds, mammals and\nother
      organisms.\n\nWisely administered, controlled
      burns\nreduce the risk of devastating uncontrollable\nfires
      and promote healthy ecosystems.\nNaturally.")

node("argument","explanatory","A Yellowstone ecologist","4-9-1988",
      "It is not the free-burn policy to blame\nfor the
      disaster in Yellowstone. Rather\nit is the non-
      existence of such policy\nbefore 1972. \n\nWe blame the
      disaster on the way fires\nwere fought before the free-
      burn went\ninto effect in 1972. By suppressing
      all\nfires for 100 years, massive amounts of\ndry brush
      and dead timber were allowed to\nbuild up in the park.
      A program of\ncontrolled burning might have
      provided\nnatural fire breaks.\n\n")

node("argument","explanatory","Safaa","13-9-1988",
      "Advocates of the let-it-burn policy\ntalk about \"an
      ecological boon\" that is\nsupposed to be providing an
      enormous\nlong-range benefit for wildlife.\" But
      for\nhow long? They say it is only a matter of\n50 or
```

(**Fig. 11-19b.** continued)

```
        even 100 years and the park will be\nback in business.
        But who guarantee that\nnature will cooperate in
        bringing \nYellowstone back to life. Fifty or one
        \nhundred years is a long time, no can be\nsure things
        will be as they were before.\nWe spend millions of
        dollars on salaries\nand research money for people who are
        \nsupposed to take care of our national\nparks. And what
        do we get? We get \nadvice to burn or parks so we can
        save\nthem. \n")

    node("position","explanatory","A neighbour of Yellowstone","4-9-1988",
        "No, we should abandon this policy that is harmful \nto our
        national treasures. \n\nThe \"let-it-burn\" policy
        depends on the \nbelief that natural fires go for
        a\nwhile and then die by themselves.\nBut in a 2.2
        million park with a dry \nsummer, where the moisture
        level is below\n2 percent and with high winds of 30 to
        40\nmph, the \"let-it-burn\" policy spells
        \ndisaster. There should be no such policy\nin
        the future, with things decided\non a case-by-case basis.
        We might allow\nlimited natural burn, but only
        after\nwe are sure that natural forces, rain and\nwind,
        are on our side.\n")

    node("issue","explanatory","Dean Cutter, Aptos,California","26-9-1988",
        "Should we continue the \"let-it-
        burn\"\npolicy?\n\n\nShould we do that, especially
        after the\ncatastrophic wildfires in
        Yellowstone,\nwhich almost one-fourth of the
        2.2\nmillion acre park by early September \n(2 month
        period).\n") node("reference","factual","San Francisco
        Examiner","4-9-1988","Yellowstone is an eighty-five
        year old\nnational park. It is a national landmark\nof
        2.2 million acre. Before 1972, the\nU.S. Park Service
        operated under an\naggressive fire-control policy.
        All\nfires, man caused or naturally occuring,\nwere
        suppressed. Then, from an odd\ncoalition of
        environmentalists,\nbureaucrats and natural-
        resource\nscientists, the let-it-burn
        policy\nemerged.\n\nSince the policy was created, only
        30,000\n trees have burned in Yellowstone.  Lightning\nproduced
        about 140 natural fires that\nburned an average of 250
        acres each\nbefore dying naturally.\n\n- From the
        San Francisco Examiner, Sunday,\nSeptember 4, 1988, page
        A-15.\n")

    node("issue","factual","Safaa","1-9-1988",
        "What kind of policy should we use to deal\nwith
        wildfires in national parks? \n\n\n\nAs an example we
        refer to the wildfire \nin Yellowstone national, which
        was \nerupted in June-1988. The policy in\nquestion is
        the \"let-it-burn\" policy.\nThis policy was adopted by
        the American\nNational-Park system in 1972.\n\n")
```

12

Knowledge Representation for Hypertext-Based Problem Solving in MicroIBIS

"We all start from 'naive realism,' i.e., the doctrine that things are what they seem. We think that grass is green, that stones are hard, and that snow is cold. But physics assures us that the greenness of grass, the hardness of stones, and the coldness of snow are not the greenness, hardness, and coldness that we know in our own experience, but something very different. The observer, when he seems to himself to be observing a stone, is really, if physics is to be believed, observing the effects of the stone upon himself. Thus science seems to be at war with itself: when it most means to be objective, it finds itself plunged into subjectivity against its will. Naive realism leads to physics, and physics, if true, shows that naive realism is false. Therefore naive realism, if true, is false; therefore it is false."

—Bertrand Russell (1872–1970)—An English philosopher—From his "An Inquiry Into Meaning and Truth," 1940, pp. 14–15.

You might wonder what this quotation is doing here. This book is not a book on epistemology. I have two reasons for recalling these lines from Bertrand Russell's work on the theory of knowledge.

The first reason is an intellectual one—to show the effect of argumentation on shaping thought. Russell, a winner of the 1952 Nobel prize in Literature, is a very convincing writer. You and I might have a hard time arguing against Russell's ideas, but there are those who can argue against Bertrand Russell. For instance, Albert Einstein has this argument against Russell's statement:

"No matter how much one may admire the acute analysis which Russell has given us in his latest book on Meaning and Truth, it still seems to me that even there the specter of metaphysical—i.e., beyond physics—fear has caused some damage. For this fear seems to me, for example, to be the cause for conceiving of the "thing" as a bundle of "qualities," such that the "qualities" are to be taken from the sensory raw material. Now the fact that two things are said to be one and the same thing, if they coincide in all qualities, forces one to consider the geometrical relations between things as belonging to their qualities. (Otherwise one is forced to look upon the Eiffel Tower in Paris and a New York skyscraper as 'the same thing.') However, we see no 'metaphysical' danger in taking the thing (the object in the sense of physics) as an independent concept into the system together with the proper spatio-temporal structure." —Albert Einstein (1879 – 1955), From "Ideas and Opinions," pp. 34 – 35, Dell Publishing Co., Inc.

The second reason, and the most important one, is my need as a programmer to bridge between the effect of the program and its underlying theory. In MicroIBIS, it is true that "what-you-see-is-what-you-get" (WYSIWYG), but you still can't see the relation between the IBIS idea and the Turbo Prolog program underlying it. Also, you can't see the relation between the hypertext of MicroIBIS and its Turbo Prolog code.

The MicroIBIS you knew from Chapters 9, 10 and 11, is a knowledge-based system I wrote in Turbo Prolog. The purpose of this chapter is to help you understand the knowledge engineering behind MicroIBIS. Bertrand Russell's concern mainly has to do with the general theory of knowledge. Still, I think his concern has an impact on building intelligent systems. In knowledge-based systems, you must easily relate between what the program does and its knowledge representation. In MicroIBIS I tried to do that through an option in the File menu. This option (the "File/Write KB to Xfile" option) writes the knowledge representation of an IBIS to an external text file. MicroIBIS uses this knowledge representation to manage a specific IBIS problem-solving session.

REPRESENTING THE LOGICAL STRUCTURE OF ISSUE SYSTEMS

Issue systems are problem exploration systems. The theory behind issue systems is the theory of argumentation. To talk about representing logical structure of issue systems, I must first talk about representing the logical structure of argumentation.

In Chapter 10, I talked about capturing the logic of argumentation using the predicate calculus syntax of Prolog—but how do you capture such representation in a practical computer system? You might answer by saying that: a Prolog program is a practical computer system! Also, you might add: "the structure of argumentation will be the knowledge-base of such a program." This is an answer, but it is not a complete answer. A Prolog program isn't necessarily a practical computer system. Besides, argumentation is only the logical basis of our system. We still need a user-interface to the argumentation process. At the end of Chapter 10, I talked about such a user-interface: it is hypertext. Hypertext is the most appropriate user-interface for the computer-based argumentation. In Chapter 10 I showed how the network-formed nodes, points, and links in hypertext can capture the argumentation process in issue systems.

What is needed now is a general knowledge representation which captures both the argumentation process as well as the hypertext interface to that process. The hypertext interface will help you to add, change, delete, and view the network of argumentation in an issue system. So, how do you do that? Well, you already have the ingredients for this representation. You have the Turbo Prolog representation of hypertext from PART ONE. You also have the relational structure of argumentation from Chapter 10. All you need to do is to put these two ideas together. In the next section you will work on building the knowledge representation model of MicroIBIS. This will give a clear idea of writing knowledge-based systems which use hypertext as one of its features.

USING TURBO PROLOG TO REPRESENT THE LOGIC OF ISSUE SYSTEMS

I said that hypertext forms an appropriate user-interface for issue systems. Here is an example: consider the position "P" from an issue "I" which you usually put in this relational form:

responds_to(position(P),issue(I)).

In hypertext you would consider the issue "I" as one node and the position "P" as another node. Whereas the relation "responds_to" will be the link between these two nodes. Here is a sketch of this hypertext representation:

node(I) <——— responds_to ——— node(P)

As for the "issue" and "position" predicates, I will consider them as attributes of a hypertext node. That is to say, node(I) has the attribute of being an issue, and the node(P) has the attribute of being a position. To design a Prolog representation of this approach, first you will look at representing nodes.

Representing an IBIS Node in Turbo Prolog

You already know that you save the text for issues, positions, arguments and references in hypertext nodes. To represent this in Turbo Prolog I use these domain declarations:

```
DOMAINS
  TEXT = string
  NODE = node(TEXT)
```

Here a node is a "compound-object" with one argument. The single argument of a node object is a string of the text of an issue, position, argument, or reference. As I said in the previous section, you identify the text in a node being an issue by having the word "issue" as an attribute of that node. I call this kind of attribute a "Node-type" attribute. In other words, all nodes in an issue system will have a node-type attribute. In terms of Turbo Prolog you will have this declaration:

```
DOMAINS
  TEXT, Ntype = string
  NODE = node(Ntype,TEXT)
```

So for example you can argue about the deregulation of the Airlines industry. The federal government started deregulating the Airlines in 1978. Deregulation means that Airline companies can set their own ticket prices. The main purpose of the deregulation, or the argument supporting it, is to ensure that American citizens have the opportunity of having a low-priced air transportation. Now, after more than a decade, the deregulation is an issue again. The deregulation example is based on an article from the *San Francisco Chronicle* (see references in Appendix A). When reading the article I thought of reconstructing it in an argumentative style. The main issue which I wanted to have an answer for was:

"The deregulation of the Airlines industry, is it good or bad?"

Now, using compound-object domain declaration of a node, I can write:

node("issue", "The deregulation of the Airlines industry, is it good or bad?").

You might respond to this issue with the position:

"Deregulation is good."

then you can capture this position in a node such as this one:

node("position", "Deregulation is good").

To add more substance, assume that you have a supporting argument such as this one:

"Travelers have saved more than $100 billion in air fares in the past decade."

This argument would go into a node by itself:

node("argument", "Travelers have saved more than $100 billion in air fares in the past decade.").

As for the logical form of this representation, notice that in:

issue(I)

the word "issue" is the predicate symbol—i.e., relation name. While in:

node("issue",I)

"issue" is just a string value for the node-type parameter of "node." Notice that I treat "issue" as a regular object. Here I treated "issue" on the same level of the object it describes—i.e., the predicate "issue" and its object "I" have the same level of abstraction in the "node" representation. This is not a new approach. Logicians have a name for it—they call it "reification." Reification means the treatment of abstract ideas as if they were observable objects. So I will leave it here and continue working on the representation of nodes in Prolog. If you need or want to know more about "reification," a good reference would be the book "Prolog and Natural-Language Analysis," by Fernando Pereira (see Appendix A for references).

Besides the "node-type" attribute, there can be other node attributes. For instance, the "type of knowledge" represented in a node is another attribute. The "Knowledge type" of a node can be factual, conceptual, instrumental, explanatory, or deontic. Two more important attributes of a node could be: name of the person who created the node, and the date when the node was first created. In general, you have to represent, at least, these four attributes:

- Node-type: the text in a node could represent an issue, a position, an argument, or a reference.
- Knowledge Type: the text in a node could represent factual, conceptual, instrumental, explanatory, or deontic knowledge.
- Author Name: name of person raising an issue, responding to an issue, or arguing for or against a position.
- Date of Node: this is the date when the node was first created.

There can be other attributes, but these four are the basic ones. So, how do you represent a node with these four attributes? You already have a representation with one attribute—i.e., the "node-type" attribute. All you need is to extend it to include four attributes. Here is the Turbo Prolog declaration for the new representation:

```
DOMAINS
    TEXT, Ntype, Ktype, AUTHOR, DATE = STRING
    NODE = node(Ntype,Ktype, AUTHOR, DATE, TEXT)
```

This representation is a very compact one. If you use regular Prolog syntax you will need more than one compound object. Take a look at an alternative representation:

```
DOMAINS
  TEXT    = text(STRING)
  Ntype   = issue(); position(); argument(); reference()
  Ktype   = factual(); conceptual(); instrumental();
            explanatory(); deontic()
  AUTHOR  = author(STRING)
  DATE    = date(STRING)
  NODE    = node(Ntype, Ktype, AUTHOR, DATE, TEXT)
```

Got it! Now, to move on and start the representation of relations between nodes.

Representing Relationships between Nodes in Turbo Prolog

In Prolog, relations are represented as predicates. You can have a relation between two things—a binary relation. For example, the "objects-to" relation is binary. You can write "objects-to," using the node representation from the previous section:

```
objects_to(
  node("argument",
       "explanatory",
       author("Taha"),
       date("10-31-1988"),
       "Airlines traveling safety is not that good as
       airlines are neglecting proper maintenance because of
       economic pressures, less-experienced flight crews
       and understaffed air-traffic control towers."),
  node("position",
       "factual",
       author("Philip"),
       date("10-13-1988"),
       "the deregulation of airline industry didn't effect
       the safety of travel by air.")
         ).
```

So, it seems that all you need is to declare the set of all relations, in an issue system, as predicates. For example, you might have the following predicates representing a set of relations:

```
DOMAINS
  TEXT, Ntype, Ktype, AUTHOR, DATE = STRING
  NODE = node(Ntype, Ktype, AUTHOR, DATE, TEXT)
PREDICATES
  responds_to(NODE,NODE)
  responded_to_by(NODE,NODE)
  replaces(NODE,NODE)
```

```
  generalizes(NODE,NODE)
  specializes(NODE,NODE)
```

Of course, you have to have a clauses section where you enter one or more facts for each relation in the predicates section—but every time you need to add a new relation-fact or delete an old one, you have to modify the clauses section. This is not a practical thing to do, especially when you need to add and delete relation-facts at run time. This means that you must have the ability to assert or retract relations to the knowledge-base. In Turbo Prolog, to allow assertion and retraction of predicates, you must first declare them as database facts, such as here:

```
DOMAINS
  TEXT, Ntype, Ktype, AUTHOR, DATE = STRING
  NODE = node(Ntype, Ktype, AUTHOR, DATE, TEXT)
DATABASE - ibisdb
  responds_to(NODE,NODE)
  responded_to_by(NODE,NODE)
  replaces(NODE,NODE)
  generalizes(NODE,NODE)
  specializes(NODE,NODE)
```

In Turbo Prolog V.2, you can have multiple database declaration sections. This is why you need to label the database section as "ibisdb" database. This way you can assert and retract from a specific database section using the built-in predicates, assert/2, asserta/2, assertz/2, retract/2, retracta/2, and retractz/2. The "2" after the predicate name means that the predicate has two arguments. Take a look at assert/2 and retract/2 here:

```
assert ( <fact> , DatabaseName)
retract( <fact> , DatabaseName)
```

So it seems that you are in better shape now! Are you? It turns out that this representation doesn't have enough flexibility either. For example, if you like to do some reasoning with relations, you will need to pass a relation as an argument to predicates. In this case you need to treat a relation as an object rather than as a predicate. In reasoning about relations—i.e., links—I am trying to establish relations between relations. I call this kind of programming "Metalogical programming."

An example of reasoning about relations is the ability to collect a list of all possible relations from an issue node. In MicroIBIS I did exactly that. When you choose the Relations option from the pull-down menu, you will get a list of relations. The names of relations in this list is dependent on the "node-type" of the current node. If the current node is an "issue," you have one list of relations. Also, if the current node is a "position," you have a different list of relations (see FIG. 12-1). So how did I do that in MicroIBIS?

In MicroIBIS you represent relations as compound-objects. This way you can pass individual relation and lists of relations as arguments to other predi-

```
issue           position        argument        reference
responds-to     supports        supports        referenced-by
replaces        objects-to      objects-to
suggested-by    suggested_by    suggested_by
questions       questions       questions
generalizes     referenced-by   referenced-by
specializes
referenced-by
```

Fig. 12-1. The four "relations" menus of MicroIBIS.

cates. Here is our updated representation of nodes and relations in Turbo Prolog:

```
DOMAINS
  TEXT, Ntype, Ktype, AUTHOR, DATE, RELATION = STRING
  SOURCE, TARGET = Ntype
  NODE   = node(Ntype, Ktype, AUTHOR, DATE, TEXT)
  REL    = rel(SOURCE, RELATION, TARGET)
  RELlist = REL*
```

Notice that I defined "rel" to be an infix binary relation. In an infix binary relation, you place the relation name between two related things. The relation "John likes Mary" is an infix one because the relation name, "likes," is between the two related names. Another thing about "rel" is that it isn't a relation between two nodes, as you might have expected, such as this one:

```
REL = rel(NODE,RELATION,NODE)
```

Rather, "rel" is a relation between two "node-type" attribute values (issue, position, argument, or reference). This is because in this current version of MicroIBIS you only need a simple bookkeeping process of relations. The idea is this: given a current node (an issue, a position, an argument, or a reference), what are the possible relations that you can have with it? To answer this request, put all the relations possible with the current node in a list. Here is an example: if the current node is a position, you want the "Relations" menu to have all the possible relations with a "position." The result is the list of relations in the menu titled "position" in FIG. 12-1.

So the reasoning with relations in MicroIBIS is limited to the collection of their names. You can extend this representation to allow additional features. One possible extension could be the addition of "procedural attachments" to hypertext links. Here is an example:

```
REL = rel(SOURCE,RELATION,TARGET,CONDITIONS,CLAUSEid)
```

The "CLAUSEid" argument stands for an ID number of a fact or a rule that you execute when Turbo satisfies the "CONDITIONS." This is a very powerful extension to the notion of links in hypertext. It gives links an active status in the network. For now I will leave "rel" in its simplest form and move on to the general structure of these relations in MicroIBIS.

Representing the IBIS Structure in Turbo Prolog

The general structure of an IBIS can be a tree-based structure or a network-based structure. A network structure is more suitable for IBIS and hypertext. In PART TWO I used a network-based structure for writing the "ET" hypertext system. In MicroIBIS I use a tree structure. I do this for instructional reasons, not for practical ones. I have a couple reasons for this: first, tree structures are simpler than network structures. Second, with tree structures I can easily use text-graphics to display the tree in text mode. The IBIS-MAP in MicroIBIS is built using ASCII graphic characters. A graphic-mode version of MicroIBIS is in preparation. For this book, our text-mode version will do. So I'll talk about representing a tree structure of issue systems.

In a tree based representation of IBIS, the main "issue" is the root node of the tree. Except for the root node, every node must link to at least one parent node. The root node has no parent nodes. Also, every node can have one, many, or no child nodes linked to it. Our tree structure is a strictly hierarchical one. For instance, IBIS-MAP, the tree of MicroIBIS, allows nodes to have only one parent node. Another restriction, in IBIS-MAP, is that cross-level links are not allowed. A cross-level link is a link between two nodes that are more than

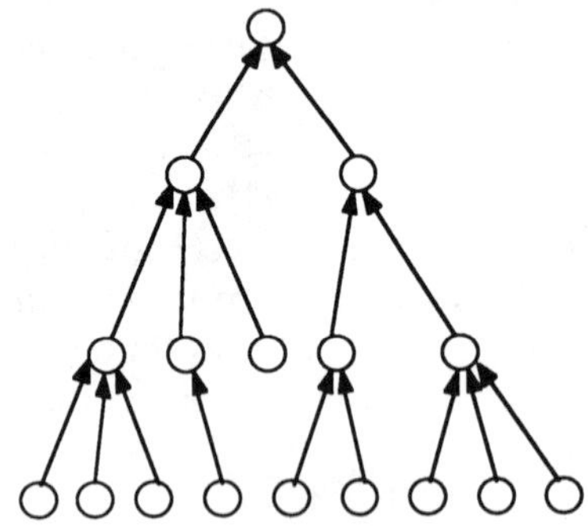

The IBIS-MAP tree

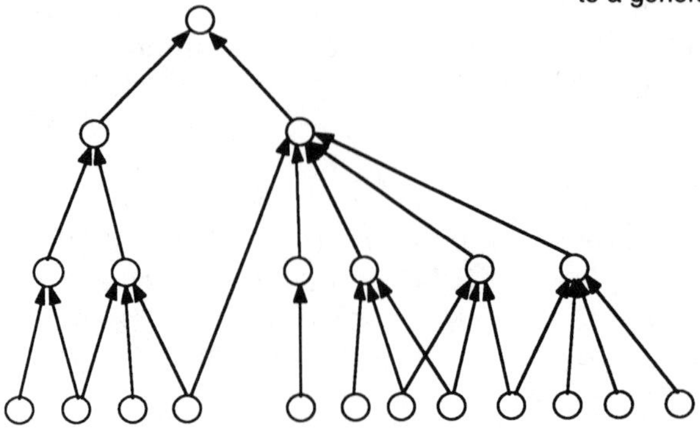

A general tree (a cascade)

Fig. 12-2. Comparing the IBIS-MAP tree to a general (cascade) tree.

one level apart. In FIG. 12-2 you can see the difference between an IBIS-MAP like tree and a more general type of a tree.

As you can see, with a general tree-based structure you are closer to a network-based structure. Another name of this general tree-based structure is what is called a "cascade." Most researchers on issue systems recommend that you represent your IBISs as cascades, not networks. Their argument is that in an issue system you always start from the root node—the main issue. Then, you expand from this node in a general, non-hierarchical, tree-based structure. In a network there is no such thing as a root node, or levels of expansion. This theoretical discussion of structure is very interesting, but you need to see some representations to have a better idea on using these structures in an IBIS program. In the next section I will talk about representing the tree structure of IBIS-MAP in MicroIBIS.

The Tree-Based Representation of MicroIBIS

The structure of argumentation in MicroIBIS is a simple one. I use a "recursive" representation which I call (guess what) "ibis." A recursive representation is a one which refers to itself. The structure "ibis" is a Turbo Prolog compound-object. Take a look at its declaration along with the other two objects, "node" and "rel":

```
DOMAINS
  TEXT, Ntype, Ktype, AUTHOR, DATE, RELATION = STRING
  SOURCE, TARGET = Ntype
  NODE  = node(Ntype, Ktype, AUTHOR, DATE, TEXT)
  REL   = rel(SOURCE, RELATION, TARGET)
  RELlist = REL*
  IBIS = ibis(RELATION,NTYPE,REF,IBISlist)
  IBISlist = IBIS*
```

As you can see, the two main elements of the issue system, "node" and "rel," and their general structure, "ibis," are compound-objects. I said that "ibis" has a recursive representation. What makes it recursive? Notice that the last argument, "IBISlist," is itself defined in terms of "ibis." This way I have each ibis containing other ibis's. Another element of this representation is the "REF" argument. This argument is an "external database" reference number of an ibis node. Now, I'll talk a little bit about saving the issue structure using Turbo Prolog's external database.

Why do you use reference numbers rather than the nodes themselves? If you had a node instead of the "REF" argument, you would get this "ibis" declaration:

```
IBIS = ibis(RELATION, NTYPE, NODE, IBISlist)
IBISlist = IBIS*
```

A major disadvantage of this representation is its complexity. The complexity arises from mixing knowledge in nodes with the structure of the inter-node relations. It makes more sense to have an ID for each node—and the ID, not the node, is the one that goes into the structure, but how do we get these IDs? With a short review of Turbo Prolog V.2 features I found the answer. The answer is Turbo Prolog's "External databases." In Chapter 8 you reviewed the basic elements of "external databases" in Turbo Prolog. With external databases, you can save our IBIS knowledge-base in chains. Then, you can create one chain for saving nodes, and a second chain for saving the "ibis" structure. To do that you use the built-in predicate "chain_inserta" or "chain_insertz." Both of these predicates have the same declaration and flow pattern. For instance, the declaration and flow pattern of "chain_inserta" are:

```
Declaration: chain_inserta(Dbase,Chain,Domain,Term,Ref)
FlowPattern: (i,i,i,i,o)
```

What is important for you here is the last argument of "chain_inserta" or "chain_inserta." The "Ref" argument, meaning reference, is the ID you are after. Notice the flow pattern, "Ref" is an Output argument. Turbo Prolog generates a special "Ref" whenever you insert a new term in the knowledge-base. You can use this "Ref" to extract its respective term from the knowledge-base. What this tells you is: you can have the IBIS structure independent from the node representations. The only connection is the node "ref" numbers. As you can see it turns out that the structure:

```
IBIS = ibis(RELATION,NTYPE,REF,IBISlist)
```

is an appropriate one. Another thing in this representation, is the "RELATION" argument. This argument records the relation between the current node and its parent node. For example, if you have an IBIS of three nodes (a root issue, with one position responding to it and an issue replacing it), how do you represent this IBIS using the "ibis" object? First, make a map of this IBIS (a map is a graph representation of the IBIS tree). In FIG. 12-3a you can see such a graph. From this graph you can build a comparable "ibis" object (see FIG. 12-3b).

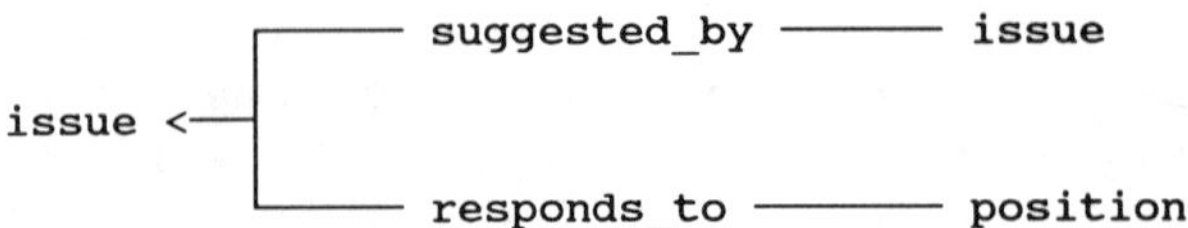

Fig. 12-3a. The map of a sample IBIS.

Fig. 12-3b. The "ibis" object of Fig. 12-3a IBIS.

```
IBIS = ibis("root","issue",REF1,
           [
            ibis("responds_to",position,REF2,[]),
            ibis("suggested_by","issue",REF3,[])
           ]).
```

Notice that you don't need to use the "rel" object to represent relations between nodes. Relations are already represented in the "ibis" object. In other words, the knowledge in:

```
rel(issue,replaces,issue), and
rel(position,responds_to,issue)
```

is already represented in the "ibis" object. So, it seems that all you need to represent an IBIS are two things: an "ibis" object and several "node" objects.

Now that I am done with representing the structure in MicroIBIS, I should move on to a new topic. I already started the new topic. It is about assembling the IBIS knowledge-base in an external database. Before you do that, I suggest that you take a look at the complete domains declarations of MicroIBIS in the global domains section in FIG. 9-1d.

ASSEMBLING IBIS KNOWLEDGE-BASE IN EXTERNAL DATABASE

In the last three sections, I talked about representing knowledge of IBIS using Turbo Prolog. The knowledge representation was in three parts: nodes, relations, and their general structure. To represent nodes I used the "node" object:

```
NODE = node(Ntype, Ktype, AUTHOR, DATE, TEXT)
```

Also, to represent relations I used the "rel" object:

```
REL = rel(SOURCE, RELATION, TARGET)
```

and, to represent the general structure I used the "ibis" object:

```
IBIS = ibis(RELATION,NTYPE,REF,IBISlist)
```

but, later, I found that relations are part of the "ibis" object. Thus, I don't need to assert or retract "rel" objects. Rather, I only need to update the "ibis" object. In MicroIBIS, I give "rel" a very minor role in the representation.

The knowledge-base of an IBIS can be a very large one. If you were to use internal knowledge-bases, you would be using up valuable memory space. In External databases you can assemble the whole database in memory, in a separate file, or in extended memory. In MicroIBIS I assemble the knowledge-base in an external file. Turbo Prolog provides more efficient ways (chains, and B+ trees) to save and retrieve knowledge in external databases, than that of an internal knowledge-base. (For more on chains and B+ trees in external databases, see Chapter 8.)

So, in the case of MicroIBIS, you need to save "node" and "ibis" in an external database. For each IBIS problem, I use a single database file. As a convention, I use the ".ibs" extension to distinguish IBIS database files from other files.

How to Create and Open IBIS Files

In MicroIBIS, you create a new IBIS file by choosing the "Files/New file" option from the main menu. This will cause the execution of the pull-down menu predicate's "pdwaction(2,1)" clauses. These clauses are part of "main-mod.pro" in FIG. 9-1b. Here is the code for the two clauses:

```
pdwaction(1,2):-
  newCURSORpos(Row,Col),
  msg_attr(Wattr,Fattr),
  lineinput(Row,Col,40,Wattr,Fattr,
            "Enter new file name: ","work.ibs",NewName),
  createDBfile(ibisdb,NewName,in_file),
  update(dbSTATUS(opened)),
  initIBIS,
  initCURRENTdb(NewName),!.
pdwaction(1,2):- refreshSCR.
```

My main concern here is the "createDBfile" predicate. This predicate creates a new IBIS file. This predicate is part of "ibis-db.pro" in FIG. 9-1f. Take a look at the two clauses of "createDBfile":

```
createDBfile(_,NAME,_):-
  existfile(NAME),    % check if file NAME already exists
  writeMSG(go,["file already exists"]),
  !, fail.
createDBfile(DBselector,NAME,Place):-
  closeDBfile(DBselector),
  writeMSG(stay,["creating file ",NAME]),
  db_create(DBselector,NAME,Place),
  update(dbSTATUS(opened)),
  writeMSG(go,["File ",NAME," is created"]),!.
```

If the file you want to create already exists, your "createDBfile" subgoal will match the first clause. Otherwise, Turbo matches the second clause. The first subgoal of this clause will close the currently open IBIS database file, if any. The next subgoal will display a message saying that Turbo will start creating the new file.

To create a database file, use the built-in predicate "db_create," which has this declaration form:

```
db_create(DBselector,File_name,Place)
```

DBselector is a database selector domain, File_name is the name of the IBIS database file, and Place is storage media where the file is saved. Place can either be: in_memory, in_file, or in_ems. In MicroIBIS's case, the database selector domain is "ibisdb," see "ibis-glb.pro" in FIG. 9-1d. Here is the domain declaration of our database selector:

```
db_selector = ibisdb
```

As for the "Place" for IBIS database files, it is "in_file." This means that Turbo will create IBIS databases in external files on floppy or hard disks. Once you create an IBIS database file it will automatically be open for reading and writing.

How to Open (load) Existing IBIS Files

To load an existing IBIS file, you choose the Files/Load option—but "loading an IBIS file" is not the proper phrase. I should write "opening an IBIS file." This is because MicroIBIS uses files on disk—it doesn't load them in the system's memory. The system uses "pdwaction(1,1)" to execute the "Files/Load" option:

```
pdwaction(1,1):-
  closeDBfile(ibisdb),
  newCURSORpos(Row,Col),
  msg_attr(Wattr,Fattr),
  readfilename(Row,Col,Wattr,Fattr,ibs,"",NewName),
  openDBfile(ibisdb,NewName,in_file),   % in"ibis-db.pro"
  initCURRENTdb(NewName),
  map(REF),                  % in ibis-map.pro
  loadIBISnode(REF),!.  % in ibis-db.pro
pdwaction(1,1):- refreshSCR.
```

The "openDBfile" subgoal in the first clause takes care of opening the IBIS file. The code for "openDBfile" is part of "ibis-db.pro" in FIG. 9-1f. It has two clauses. The first clause succeeds if the file you want to open exists and is a valid database file:

```
openDBfile(DBselector,NAME,Place):-
  existfile(NAME),
  writeMSG(stay,["Opening DB file ",NAME]),
  db_open(DBselector,NAME,Place),
  update(dbSTATUS(opened)),
  writeMSG(go,["DB file ",NAME," is opened"]),!.
```

This clause uses the built-in predicate "db_open" to open the file for reading and writing. The arguments for "db_open" are: DBselector, this is the ibis database files selector, which is "ibisdb;" the second argument is "NAME," which is the name of the file we want to open; the third argument "Place," as you know by now, is "in_file." Now you know how to open an IBIS file. How do you close it? The answer to this question is the subject of the next section.

How to Close (save) IBIS Files

You need to close a database file when you want to create a new file, load an existing file, or when you want to quit MicroIBIS. This is why you have "closeDBfile" as a subgoal for predicates which create and load IBIS files. For instance "createDBfile" has "closeDBfile" as a subgoal. Also, in "pdwaction(1,1)" "closeDBfile" is a subgoal. So take a look at the code for "closeDBfile":

```
closeDBfile(DBselector):-
  dbSTATUS(opened),      % we can only close an opened db file.
  db_close(DBselector),
  update(dbSTATUS(closed)), !.
closeDBfile(_):- update(dbSTATUS(closed)).
```

In the first clause of "closeDBfile," the first subgoal "dbSTATUS" checks to see if you already have an opened IBIS file. If "dbSTATUS" succeed you need to close the current file before you open another one. To close a file, you use the built-in predicate "db_close." The only argument of "db_close" is a database selector—in this case it is "ibisdb." After Turbo closes the current file, you must update the database status. This is why you need a second "closeDBfile" clause. The second clause uses the "update" predicate to change the database status from "opened" to "closed." The code for "update" is in the "ibisut.pro" file in FIG. 9-1h. Now you know how to create, open, and close IBIS files. How do we insert, change, and delete objects from the database? As you might have guessed, the answer is in the next section.

How to Add and Retrieve Objects in an IBIS File

Once a database file is open, you can start inserting terms in it. In this case, the terms will be "node" objects and the "ibis" object. Our IBIS database file will have two chains: one chain to save "node" objects, and another chain to save the "ibis" object. To insert objects in a chain you use the built-in predicates "chain_inserta," and "chain_insertz." Both predicates have the same declaration and flow pattern. Here is the declaration and flow pattern of "chain_inserta":

```
Declaration: chain_inserta(DBselector,Chain,Domain,Term,Ref)
FlowPattern: (i,i,i,i,o)
```

For IBIS database files, "DBselector" is "ibisdb." The "Chain" argument should be a name for the chain in question. In this case, there should be two chain names. In MicroIBIS, I use "nodech" as a name for the chain containing "node" objects. As for the chain containing the "ibis" object, I use "ibisch." I'll give two examples to show you how to insert nodes and their ibis structure. To insert a node in a database chain, write:

```
chain_inserta(ibisdb,nodech,node,
              node(Ntype,Ktype,Author,Date,Ntxt),REF)
```

To insert an "ibis" structure, write:

```
chain_inserta(ibisdb,ibisch,ibis,
              ibis("root","issue",REF,[]),_)
```

When inserting a node, Turbo returns a REF-number. Later you can use this number to retrieve and update these nodes. On the other hand, when you insert the "ibis" object, you don't need Turbo to return a REF-number. This is because you only have one ibis structure per database file. So to show that you don't need the REF-number I use the anonymous variable.

Once you have inserted nodes and their ibis structure, you can retrieve them using these built-in predicates:

```
chain_terms,
chain_first,
chain_last,
chain_next,
chain_prev, and
ref_term
```

You can build very sophisticated term retrieval techniques using these built-in predicates. In MicroIBIS, I find "ref_term" to be sufficient for most of my node-retrieval needs. To retrieve a node (term) with "ref_term" I must give this goal:

```
ref_term(ibisdb,node,REF,TERM)
```

because "ibisdb" is the database selector, and node is the domain of all "node" objects. To get the node (TERM), you must supply the REF-number of that node.

There is an important thing to know about "ref_term": every time you retrieve a term from an external database with "ref_term," Turbo Prolog places that term on the global stack. The system won't release the space occupied by that term until the program fails and backtracks to a point before the call to "ref_term." This is why I use the predicate "getNODE" in MicroIBIS. The predicate "getNODE" takes a REF_number of a node and returns its compound object:

```
getNODE(REF,NODE):-
  ref_term(ibisdb,node,REF,NODE),
  update(currentNODE(NODE)),
  fail.
getNODE(_,NODE):- currentNODE(NODE).
```

Notice that in the first clause, I first retrieve a "node" object with "ref_term" then I update the currentNODE fact. Then, "fail" will cause Turbo to backtrack and try the second clause. The second clause will simply succeed. The predicate "getNODE" is in "ibis-db.pro" in FIG. 9-1f.

Now I am done with retrieving nodes, how do I retrieve the "ibis" structure. This should be a straightforward task! I know that there is only one "ibis" object for each IBIS file. All I need to do is to use the built-in predicate "chain_terms." This way I don't need to give any REF_number to get my "ibis" structure. Again, as with "ref_term," I need to backtrack after every call to chain_terms. So, I need to write a predicate similar to "getNODE." I call it, guess what, "getIBIS":

```
getIBIS(IBIS):-
  chain_terms(ibisdb,ibisch,ibis,IBIS,_),
  update(currentIBIS(IBIS)),
  fail.
getIBIS(IBIS):- currentIBIS(IBIS).
```

In fact, I don't need a subgoal for the second clause. I can just write:

```
getIBIS(_).
```

Now that you can add and retrieve nodes and their structure, you need to know how to update them. So I'll talk about that.

How to Update Objects of an IBIS File

When you change the author, date, or text of a node, you need to update its object in the IBIS file. In MicroIBIS, to update attributes or text of a node you use the built-in "term_replace" predicate. For example, the main menu option "Nodes/Save" uses "term_replace" to save your changes to the current node. When you choose this option, Turbo executes pdwaction(2,2). The "term_replace" subgoal in the first clause of pdwaction(2,2) takes care of saving the changes. Here is the code for this clause:

```
pdwaction(2,2):-
  dbSTATUS(opened),
  currentNstr(STR),
  currentREF(REF),
  getNODE(REF,NODE),
  NODE=node(N,K,A,D,_),
  term_replace(ibisdb,node,REF,node(N,K,A,D,STR)), !.
```

but sometimes, you only need to replace the attributes of a node without changing its text string. On other occasions, you want to do the reverse: change the text string and leave the attributes unchanged. To do these two operations, I use two of my own predicates, "updateNattr" and "updateNstr":

```
/* *********************** updateNattr ******************** */
updateNattr(_,_,_,K,A,D,K,A,D):- !.
updateNattr(REF,STR,N,_,_,_,K1,A1,D1):-
  term_replace(ibisdb,node,REF,node(N,K1,A1,D1,STR)).
  /* *********************** updateNstr ******************** */
updateNstr(REF,STR):-
  ref_term(ibisdb,node,REF,OLDnode),
  OLDnode = node(N,K,A,D,_),
  term_replace(ibisdb,node,REF,node(N,K,A,D,STR)),
  fail.
updateNstr(_,_).
```

Both of these predicates are in "ibis-db.pro" in FIG. 9-1f. Their flow patterns are:

updateNattr: (i,i,i,i,i,i,i,i)
updateNstr: (i,i)

In "updateNattr," the first clause checks if the new attributes are the same as the old ones. If this is the case, "updateNattr" does nothing—it just succeeds and exits without trying the second clause. If there is an attribute that is different from its comparable old one, the first clause will fail. When this happens, Turbo will match the second clause. In this clause, the "term_replace" subgoal, substitutes the new attributes for the old one of the given node.

To replace the text string of a node, I use "updateNstr." This predicate, unlike "updateNattr" substitutes the new string, STR, for the old one without checking if the two strings are equal. Notice the use of "fail" in the first clause. Why did I do that? Does this remind you of something from the previous section? Yes, it is "ref_term." I need to "fail" my "ref_term" call to release the space occupied by the "node" term. Turbo won't release the stack space until the program fails and backtracks to a point before the call to "ref_term."

OK, I talked about replacing "node" objects. How about their "ibis" structure? To replace the "ibis" object you can give these subgoals:

```
chain_terms(ibisdb,ibisch,ibis,IBIS,IBISref),
term_replace(ibisdb,ibis,IBISref,NEWibis).
```

The first subgoal will retrieve the REF-number of our "ibis" structure. Then, "term_replace" will substitute "NEWibis" for the old one. You can see this sequence of subgoals in MicroIBIS, when you erase a node and want to update your "ibis" structure to reflect these changes. Take a look at the first clause of "pdwaction(2,3)" in FIG. 9-1b. I will talk about this clause in the next section when I discuss the deletion of nodes from the IBIS.

How to Delete Objects from an IBIS File

Sometimes you need to delete a node, without replacing it. What do you do? To delete a node is not as simple as it seems. Beside deleting the node itself, you need to delete all its links to other nodes. In MicroIBIS, links, as you know, are relations. You record relations to and from a node in the "ibis" structure. So, after you delete a node you need to delete its links in the "ibis" structure. The best thing to do is to see a predicate that does just that. When you choose "Nodes/Delete" from the main menu, Turbo executes "pdwaction(2,3)":

```
pdwaction(2,3):-
  currentREF(REF),
  cursor(R,C), RR=R+1, CC=C+1,
  msg_attr(Wattr,Fattr),
  lineinput(RR,CC,30,Wattr,Fattr,"Are you sure
            (y/n)?","",ANS),
  upper_lower(ANS1,ANS),
```

```
ANS1="Y" ,
chain_terms(ibisdb,ibisch,ibis,IBIS,IBISref),        /* 1 */
deleteIBIS(REF,IBIS,NEWibis,DELibis),                /* 2 */
term_replace(ibisdb,ibis,IBISref,NEWibis),           /* 3 */
nodesINibis(DELibis,[ ],REFlist),                    /* 4 */
deleteNODES(REFlist),                                /* 5 */
clearCURRENT.
```

In this clause, the first few subgoals make sure that you really want to delete the node in question. After this comes the part where you start deleting the node and its links—the subgoals labeled 1 to 5. Here is what each one of these does:

1) "Chain_terms" retrieves the "ibis" structure and its REF-number.
2) "DeleteIBIS" takes the REF-number of the node you want to delete and the "ibis" structure. In return, "deleteIBIS" generates two IBIS substructures, NEWibis and DELibis. DELibis, is an IBIS substructure with the REF-number of the node you want to delete as its root. All other nodes in DELibis, are either direct or indirect children of the node you want to delete. Newibis, on the other hand, is your original IBIS structure after taking out the DELibis substructure. I will not go into the details of how "deleteIBIS" does that. I leave this to you (see FIG. 12-4.).
3) "Term_replace" will replace our original IBIS structure with the new ibis structure, NEWibis. I talked about this in the previous section, so I will skip talking about it here.
4) "NodesINibis" takes an IBIS substructure and returns a list of all the REF-numbers in that structure. I use this predicate to get a list of all REF-numbers in the deleted IBIS substructure, DELibis.
5) "DeleteNODES" takes a list of REF-numbers of "node" objects, REFlist, and deletes these objects from the IBIS database. This predicate uses the built-in predicate "term_delete" to recursively delete "node" objects:

```
deleteNODES([ ]):-!.
deleteNODES([REF ! T]):-
    term_delete(ibisdb,nodech,REF),
    deleteNODES(T).
```

To delete a "node" object using "term_delete" you only need three things:

1) an IBIS database selector—in this case it is ibisdb.
2) the name of the chain from which you want to delete objects. For nodes, the chain name is "nodech."
3) the REF-number of the node you want to delete.

By this we have covered all the important operations on nodes and their IBIS structure in MircoIBIS, but to make MicroIBIS easy to use, these operations are not visible to the user. You interface to these operations through a user-interface, but you can study these operations by monitoring their effect

Fig. 12-4. Deleting an IBIS substructure with "deleteIBIS"

```
/* ********************** deleteIBIS ******************** */
/* Delete a subIBIS and its subtrees and return both:
   The resulting IBIS without the deleted subIBIS, and
   also return the subIBIS */

deleteIBIS(REF,ibis("root",_,REF,_),_,_):-!,fail.

deleteIBIS(REF1,ibis(REL,TYP,REF,[ibis(REL1,TYP1,REF1,L)|T]),
                ibis(REL,TYP,REF,T),
                ibis(REL1,TYP1,REF1,L)):-!.

deleteIBIS(REF1,ibis(_,_,REF2,[]),_,_):-
  A=REF1, B=REF2, not(A=B),!,fail.

deleteIBIS(REF1,ibis(REL,TYP,REF,[H|T]),
                ibis(REL,TYP,REF,[NewH|T]),
                DeletedIBIS):-
  deleteIBIS(REF1,H,NewH,DeletedIBIS), !.

deleteIBIS(REF1,ibis(REL,TYP,REF,[H|T]),
                ibis(REL,TYP,REF,[H|NewT]),
                DeletedIBIS):-
  deleteIBISlist(REF1,T,NewT,DeletedIBIS), !.

/* ********************** deleteIBISlist **************** */

deleteIBISlist(_,[],_,_):-!, fail.
deleteIBISlist(REF,[ibis(REL,TYP,REF,L)|T],
                   T,
                   ibis(REL,TYP,REF,L)):-!.
deleteIBISlist(REF,[H|T],[NewH|T],DeletedIBIS):-
  deleteIBIS(REF,H,NewH,DeletedIBIS), !.

deleteIBISlist(REF,[H|T],[H|NewT],DeletedIBIS):-
  deleteIBISlist(REF,T,NewT,DeletedIBIS).
```

on the knowledge-base. All you need is an option to copy the knowledge-base to an external file, which you can view at any time. Viewing the knowledge-base is the topic of the next section. So get on with it.

VIEWING THE KNOWLEDGE-BASE OF AN IBIS

Imagine yourself being a user of MicroIBIS. Do you need to worry about how it stores and uses its knowledge-base? I am not talking about someone who might want to modify the system. I am talking about someone who only wants to use MicroIBIS—as is—to deal with problems. I think, if you are such a user, you will need to concentrate on the argumentation process. You needn't worry about how MicroIBIS creates IBIS database files. Also you needn't worry about how it represents nodes and their IBIS structure. The user-interface should take care of receiving and answering your queries and action. This is what MicroIBIS does: It takes care of translating your input to representations of nodes, relations, and structures.

On the other hand, as a programmer, you might like to view the knowledge-base in MicroIBIS. Here, you would like to see the set of "node" objects and their "ibis" object. MicroIBIS allows you to copy the knowledge-base of the current IBIS to an external text file. To do this, you use the "Files/Write KB to Xfile." When you choose this option, the system will retrieve the "ibis" structure and "node" objects and write them to the external text file. The predicate which does this is "dumpDBa," in "ibis-prt" in FIG. 9-1i. This predicate will first extract the "ibisch" chain and directly write it to the file, using the "wrIBIS" predicate. Next, it will extract all "node" objects from the "nodech" chain and directly write them to the text file, using the "wrNODE" predicate. In Chapter 13 I will go into the details of programming the "Files/Write KB to Xfile" option. See the section titled "COPYING THE IBIS KNOWLEDGE-BASE TO AN EXTERNAL FILE." That's it for now folks, and see you next chapter.

13

Analyzing the Program Structure of MicroIBIS

"Four chief causes of error among men are: authority; custom; the opinion of the unskilled majority; concealment of ignorance under pretense of wisdom."

—Roger Bacon (c. 1220 – 1292) philosopher and scientist

This quotation both agrees and disagrees with the argumentative approach in IBIS. Bacon and IBIS agree on the negative role of authority in decision making. IBIS encourages group problem-solving. Group problem-solving helps reduce the authority of experts. In a group, problem analysis and decision making is a collective effort. Also, Bacon and IBIS agree on custom and concealment of ignorance as sources for error in decision making. Here, I will leave it for you to make the connection. On the other hand, Bacon and IBIS disagree on the opinion of the the unskilled majority. In IBIS the opinion of unskilled majority is still of importance. For Bacon, the unskilled majority is a source of error in decision making. In IBIS, this unskilled majority will be the one most affected by the outcome of argumentation.

After this brief encounter with the theory of problem solving, I go back to discussing the programming of issue systems. In this chapter I talk about some of the major programming techniques in MicroIBIS. These techniques include:

- the general design of the program structure and the use of some hypertext features.

- the modular programming approach of Turbo Prolog.
- copying the issue system to printers and external files.
- copying the knowledge-base to printers and external files.

So I'll start with the first technique: The general structure of the program.

THE GENERAL STRUCTURE OF MicroIBIS

The issue of the general structure of a system is a design issue. So what kind of a strategy do you need to design MicroIBIS. There can be many strategies one can follow. I can think of three possible strategies. The first is what I call the *organic* or *functional* strategy. This is the strategy which calls for a design closer to the natural way of doing things. In terms of IBIS, this means that our design should reflect the natural way of doing argumentation. The second strategy is to concentrate on the practicality and efficiency of a design. This strategy favors having a practical and efficient system over that which models our natural way of thinking. This doesn't mean you can't have designs with the best of both strategies. On the contrary, you would define a third strategy as one which tries to have a natural design without compromising its efficiency and practicality. In MicroIBIS I tried to follow the third strategy.

Let's turn to what it means to have a natural, efficient, and practical design of an issue system. You start with the natural or organic feature of an issue system.

The regular way of group problem-solving involves what I call the "meeting sessions" approach. In this approach, when you have a certain problem you organize a meeting to discuss a certain topic. In this case the topic is the main issue. Only those who are interested in understanding and resolving the main issue will attend the meeting. If you couldn't resolve the issues you raised in the meeting, and you ran out of time, you adjourn the meeting. To continue the process you arrange a second session, a third session, and so on. You do that until you either reach some conclusion, or you can't have more time, money, or people to support future sessions.

So, to design a natural system, you should have some kind of a "meeting sessions" interface. This interface of course will use several computer resources to give you the feeling that you are in a meeting environment. Computer resources could include a windowing system, an iconic interface (Macintosh-like interface), colors, database, and artificial intelligence capability.

On the meaning of efficiency of an issue system, I could cite the system's speed in responding to your requests. Response speed covers the time the system requires to create, load, update, or delete nodes. The less time it takes to do these operations, the more efficient it is.

As for practicality, the elements of effectiveness, cost, and performance of the system are the major issues which you should consider. Is the system more effective than actual meeting sessions in understanding and resolving problems? For example, if the system makes it difficult to see the general picture of the argumentation, participants will walk away from it, and never use it again. Cost could be another factor in our decision to use a computer-based IBIS. For example, a group might need to solve a problem using a network-based system which supports a multimedia interface, but if the cost of using such a system is prohibitive, regular meetings would still be the right way to go.

Putting the General Design Aspects to Work

Having the aspects of a natural, efficient, and practical system in mind, now look at the design of MicroIBIS. I'll start with the user-interface. In MicroIBIS, the user-interface uses a hierarchical menu based approach. On the top level you have the pull-down menu. From this pull-down menu you can get to other resources. In the lower level of the user-interface, you have predicates for menus, dialogue boxes, line-input prompts, and status lines. In terms of resources you have:

- a powerful editor, the IBIS-EDITOR.
- a graphic interface of the IBIS tree, the IBIS-MAP.
- a message system to report activities and problems.
- a status line to help you in using the system.
- system setup tools to change the color and size of windows.

Each one of these resources has its own screen window. Users can only access the IBIS-EDITOR, the IBIS-MAP, and the setup tools. They can't send messages to the message window or to the status line.

It's time to talk programming, but because of the size of the MicroIBIS program I can only focus on parts of it. In the following few sections I will talk about the hierarchical menu structure. Also, when you come to the Map option, I will talk about hypertext programming, but for now I will start with the pull-down menu.

THE PULL-DOWN MENU: The Gateway to MicroIBIS

The firing point of MicroIBIS is the predicate "runMAIN" in "main-mod-.pro" of FIG. 9-1b. This predicate should give you a clear idea of the general structure of MicroIBIS. Take a look at it in FIG. 13-1.

In this predicate, I start by covering the whole screen with a blank background window. To initialize the system attributes I use "initSETUP," which asserts facts about the size and position of resource windows:

```
initSETUP:-        /* 1 */
    existfile("ibis.sys"),
    consult("ibis.sys",setupdb), !.
initSETUP:-        /* 2 */
    updatel(pulldown_attr(112)),
    updatel(edit_attr(15,112)),
    updatel(msg_attr(15,112)),
```

Fig. 13-1. Predicate runMAIN: firing the MicroIBIS system.

```
/* ************************ runMAIN ********************** */
/* ****************************************************** */

% "runMAIN" initiate the system by firing the pulldown menu.

/*
          1         2         3         4         5         6         7
01234567890123456789012345678901234567890123456789012345678901234567890123456 7
     Files       Nodes       Edit        Relations      Map        Setup
*/

runMAIN:-
   blankwindow,
   initSETUP,       % setup the system windows attr.
   textSCREEN,      % title text screen (use this or graphiceSCREEN)
   retractall(_),
   msgwindow,
   mapwindow,
   editwindow,
   statusline,
   update(dbSTATUS(closed)),
   pulldown_attr(ATTR),
   pulldown(ATTR,[ curtain(5,"Files",["Load",
                                  "New",
                                  "Save",
                                  "sAve as",
                                  "Directory",
                                  "Change dir.",
                                  "Operating system",
                                  "Write KB to Xfile",
                                  "Print",
                                  "Quit"
                                 ]),
                   curtain(17,"Nodes",["Load node",
                                   "Save node",
                                   "Delete node",
                                   "Attributes",
                                   "Nodes dir"
                                  ]),
                   curtain(29,"Edit",[]),
                   curtain(40,"Relations",[]),
                   curtain(55,"Map",[]),
                   curtain(65,"Setup",["Attr. Dialog",
                                     "Colors",
                                     "Window size",
                                     "Save new setup"])
               ],
               _,_).

/* ****************************************************** */
```

```
updatel(map_attr(15,112,79)),
updatel(status_attr(112)),
updatel(aux_edit_attr(15,79)),
updatel(dialog_attr(15,31)),
updatel(map_size(3,0,17,36)),
updatel(msg_size(20,0,4,36)),
updatel(edit_size(3,36,21,44)).
```

The first clause of "initSETUP" looks for a knowledge-base file "ibis.sys." If "ibis.sys" exists, "initSETUP" consults its knowledge-base. When you change colors and sizes of windows and save them, MicroIBIS appends these changes to "ibis.sys." If "ibis.sys" doesn't exist in the current directory, "initSETUP" will assert a default set of setup facts using the "update1" predicate. You can try this technique yourself by entering and running the program in FIG. 13-2.

There are two sets of goals in the commented GOAL section. Try these goals in this order:

Goal: initSETUP, putwindow.
Goal: update1(win_attr(4,6,5,0,10,80)), putwindow.

Fig. 13-2. Using a knowledge-base of window attributes.

```
/* ********************************************************* */

DOMAINS
  Sattr, Fattr, Rstart, Cstart, Rsize, Csize = INTEGER

DATABASE - setupdb
  win_attr(Sattr,Fattr,Rstart,Cstart,Rsize,Csize)

PREDICATES
  initSETUP
  update1(setupdb)
  putwindow

% GOAL
% /* 1. */ initSETUP, putwindow.
% /* 2. */ update1(win_attr(4,6,5,0,10,80)), putwindow.

CLAUSES

/* ************************* update1 ********************* */

  update1(win_attr(_,_,_,_,_,_)) :-
    retract(win_attr(_,_,_,_,_,_),setupdb), fail.

  update1(X) :- asserta(X,setupdb).

/* *************************** initSETUP ***************** */

  initSETUP :-
    existfile("test.sys"),
    consult("test.sys",setupdb), !.

  initSETUP :-
    update1(win_attr(112,15,5,0,10,80)).

/* ************************* putwindow ****************** */

  putwindow :-
    win_attr(Sattr,Fattr,Rstart,Cstart,Rsize,Csize),
    makewindow(1,Sattr,Fattr,"TEST",Rstart,Cstart,Rsize,Csize),
    Write("\n Press any key"), readln(_),
    removewindow.

/* *********************** END END END ****************** */
```

See how "putwindow" uses the default setting in the first goal, while in the second goal "putwindow" uses the attributes I assert using "update1." Got it!

Back to FIG. 13-1 and "runMAIN." After setting up the system, I display the system title screen and the copyright notice. Next, the "retractall(_)" subgoal makes sure that the system's knowledge-base is empty. The next four subgoals (msgwindow, mapwindow, editwindow, and status line) will display the system resource windows. A window predicate first reads the asserted attribute and size of the window before it creates the window.

Window making predicates are in FIG. 9-1e. As for the "Pulldown" predicate, I already discussed it in Chapter 4, so you already know how it works.

Now to start reviewing the different submenus of the pull-down menu.

The Files Menu

The Files menu collects basic operations on the IBIS file. In FIG. 13-3 you can see the file menu and its "print" submenu.

The print submenu allows you to print the IBIS tree to either the printer or an external file—but I'll start from the top. After you choose the Files option from the pull-down menu, the system displays its Files "curtain." In each curtain there are a set of options. In the files menu the options are the ones in FIG. 13-3. I suggest that you take a look at the predicates pdwaction(1,1) to pdwaction(1,9) in FIG. 9-1b. Notice that the second clause of most "pdwaction" predicates is there to refresh the system windows. For example, to save the current IBIS file to the disk I use these two clauses of "pdwaction(1,3)":

```
pdwaction(1,3):-
    currentFILE(NAME),
    writeMSG(stay,["\n Saving ",NAME," file"]),
    db_flush(ibisdb),
    writeMSG(go,["\n",NAME," is saved"]).
pdwaction(1,3):- refreshSCR.
```

The first clause will save the current file and, after it finishes, Turbo will execute the second clause. What the second clause does is return control to the pull-down menu. It does that by using "refreshSCR" to make the pull-down

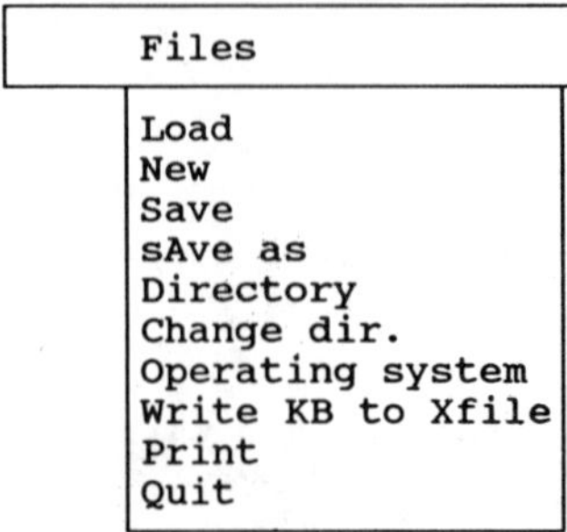

Fig. 13-3. The Files menu and its Print submenu.

window the current window. Take a look here:

```
refreshSCR:-
  windowNUM(pdwmenu,Pnum),
  windowNUM(mapwindow,Mnum),
  windowNUM(editwindow,Enum),
  shiftwindow(Mnum),
  shiftwindow(Enum),
  shiftwindow(Pnum).
refreshSCR.
```

If, for any reason, the first clause of "refreshSCR" fails, the second clause will succeed. The second clause is the insurance policy against any unexpected failures in shifting between different windows. In other words, it allows you to continue developing the system even if you can't get the user-interface right the first time. Eventually, you will not need the second clause of "refreshSCR" once you are done with the final design of the system. I find this technique a very useful one, and a time saving one. I would suggest using it as a "Computer Aided Software Engineering" (CASE) tool. It helped me develop a workable system to express my design ideas without worrying about many programming details. Let's move on and talk about another part of the menu system. This time it is a submenu: the print submenu.

The Print Submenu. There are two options in this submenu (see FIG. 13-3). You can use the first option (the "Printer" option) to get a hard copy of the current IBIS file. On the other hand if you want an ASCII file version of the current IBIS file, you should choose the second option (the "File" option).

The main reason to print an IBIS, or copy it to an external text file, is to be able to put it in a linear text form. A linear text, as you know, is something like a report or a book. Notice that the Printer's output is just a list of issues, positions, arguments and references. To make this output more appealing as the final report on analyzing the problem, I use the second option. With the "File" option, you can copy the current IBIS database file to an ASCII file. Later, you can use your favorite word processor and edit and print the final report. For example, in Chapter 11, I printed the Yellowstone IBIS to an external file (see FIG. 11-16 and FIG. 11-17). You can take the Yellowstone text file and use any word processor to prepare a comprehensive report on the problem. Of course, when editing the text file you should not change the content of the IBIS, only check the form.

Someone might ask the question: Why do I need draft or final hardcopies of an IBIS if I can use computers instead? It is true that you can use the IBIS-MAP to review and edit the different nodes and links, but there will always be the need to use paper and pencil to contemplate plans and actions. Two major advantages of a printout of an IBIS are: its portability and ease of use compared to that of computers.

Now turn to the programming side of the Print submenu. The pull-down predicate for displaying the Print submenu is "pdwaction(1,9)":

```
pdwaction(1,9) :- printIBIS.        % in ibis-prt.pro
```

Fig. 13-4. Predicate "printIBIS" printing IBIS to printer or to external file.

```
/* ********************************************************** */
/* ********************* printIBIS ********************** */
/* ********************************************************** */

PREDICATES
  printIBIS
    printCHOICE(INTEGER)

CLAUSES

printIBIS:-
  dbSTATUS(opened),
  newCURSORpos(Row,Col),  % in ibis-use.pro
  pulldown_attr(ATTR),
  menu(Row,Col,ATTR,ATTR,["Printer","File"],"print",1,CHOICE)
  printCHOICE(CHOICE), !.

printIBIS:-
  writeMSG(go,["IBIS DB file is not open"]).

printCHOICE(1):-
  writeMSG(stay,["printing IBIS"]),
  writedevice(printer),
  chain_terms(ibisdb,ibisch,ibis,IBIS,_), !,
  getTREE(keys(0,0,0,0),_,IBIS,TREE),    % in ibis-map.pro
  printDF(TREE),
  writedevice(screen),
  refreshSCR.

printCHOICE(2):-
  newCURSORpos(Row,Col),
  readfilename(Row,Col,15,112,txt,"",FileName),
  writeMSG(stay,["Writing IBIS to ",FileName]),
  openwrite(ibistxt,FileName),
  writedevice(ibistxt),
  chain_terms(ibisdb,ibisch,ibis,IBIS,_), !,
  getTREE(keys(0,0,0,0),_,IBIS,TREE),
  printDF(TREE),
  writedevice(screen),
  closefile(ibistxt),
  refreshSCR.

printCHOICE(_):- writedevice(screen).

/* ********************************************************** */
```

The printing predicates, including "printIBIS," are all in the file "ibis-prt.pro" in FIG. 9-1g. I extracted "printIBIS" in FIG. 13-4.

In "printIBIS" I use the Turbo Prolog TOOLBOX "menu" predicate to display the "print submenu." If I haven't loaded or created an IBIS file, the first clause will fail. The second clause will take care of sending a message to remind me of that. For each option in the "print submenu" there is a "printCHOICE" clause. The first "printCHOICE" is for sending IBIS to the printer. The second "printCHOICE" is for copying IBIS to an external file. There is also a third clause for "printCHOICE." After it finishes printing an IBIS, Turbo matches the third clause to make sure that you interact with MicroIBIS through the screen. In both cases, writing to a printer or to an external file, you use "printDF" to do the job. Take a look at it in FIG. 9-1g to see how it does that. After all, I took you half the way through the code. You shouldn't have any difficulty finding your way in it. In the next section I will review the Nodes menu.

The Nodes Menu

In this menu, all the operations possible on nodes are listed. If you don't have MicroIBIS up and running, you can see the Nodes menu in FIG. 13-5. To execute this menu, the system uses clauses "pdwaction(2,1)" to "pdwaction(2,4)." These clauses are part of "main-mod.pro" in FIG. 9-1b, but to save you from flipping the pages backward and forward, I list these clauses in FIG. 13-6.

```
Nodes
-------------
Load node
Save node
Delete node
Attributes
Nodes dir
```

Fig. 13-5. The Nodes menu.

Fig. 13-6. Executing the Node menu options.

```
/* ******************************************************** */
/* ********************** 2. NODES MENU **************** */
/* ******************************************************** */

%  ****** 2.1 Load an IBIS node
pdwaction(2,1):-
  dbSTATUS(opened),
  newCURSORpos(ROW,COL),
  chain_terms(ibisdb,ibisch,ibis,IBIS,_),
  msg_attr(Wattr,Fattr),
  nodename(ROW,COL,Wattr,Fattr,IBIS,"",NodeName,NODEref),!,
  getNODE(NODEref,NODE),
  NODE = node(_,_,_,_,STR),
  update(currentREF(NODEref)),
  update(currentNstr(STR)),
  update(currentCpos(1)),
  writeMSG(stay,["\nLoading ",NodeName," node."]),
  refreshNODE,
  writeMSG(go,["\n",NodeName," is loaded"]), !.

pdwaction(2,1):-
  dbSTATUS(closed),
  writeMSG(go,["\nIBIS database file is not open"]).

pdwaction(2,1):- refreshSCR.

%  ****** 2.2 Save the node currently in the editor

pdwaction(2,2):-
  dbSTATUS(opened),
  currentNstr(STR),
  currentREF(REF),
  getNODE(REF,NODE),
```

(**Fig. 13-6.** continued)

```
    NODE=node(N,K,A,D,_),
    term_replace(ibisdb,node,REF,node(N,K,A,D,STR)), !.

  pdwaction(2,2):-
    dbSTATUS(closed),
    writeMSG(go,["\n IBIS database file is not open"]).

  pdwaction(2,2):- refreshSCR.

  %  ****** 2.3 Erase a node and remove its links

  pdwaction(2,3):-
    currentREF(REF),
    cursor(R,C), RR=R+1, CC=C+1,
    msg_attr(Wattr,Fattr),
    lineinput(RR,CC,30,Wattr,Fattr,"Are you sure (y/n)? ","",ANS),
    upper_lower(ANS1,ANS),
    ANS1="Y",
    chain_terms(ibisdb,ibisch,ibis,IBIS,IBISref),
    deleteIBIS(REF,IBIS,NEWibis,DELibis),
    term_replace(ibisdb,ibis,IBISref,NEWibis),
    nodesINibis(DELibis,[],REFlist),
    deleteNODES(REFlist),
    clearCURRENT.

  pdwaction(2,3).

  %  ****** 2.4 Display and accept changes in node information.

  pdwaction(2,4):-
    currentREF(REF),
    getNODE(REF,NODE),
    NODE = node(Ntype,Ktype,A,D,STR),
    displayINFO(Ntype,Ktype,A,D,Ktype1,A1,D1),
    updateNattr(REF,STR,Ntype,Ktype,A,D,Ktype1,A1,D1).


  pdwaction(2,4).

  %  ****** 2.5 Directory of nodes in current file.

  pdwaction(2,5):- writeMSG(go,["option is inactive"]).

  /* ******************************************************** */
```

As you can see, the predicate branches to many other predicates. Because I have a limited space in this book, I will talk about the programming of one option. I will take the first option, loading the text of a node in the editor. In "pdwaction(2,1)" I load an ibis node. To do that I must first have a list of all the nodes in the IBIS structure. To get this list, I use "nodename." The input to this predicate is the IBIS structure which I retrieved with "chain_terms" subgoal. Before I continue, here's the code for "nodename":

```
nodename(ROW,COL,WATTR,FATTR,IBIS,OLD,NODEname,REF):-
  getTREE(keys(0,0,0,0),_,IBIS,TREE),
  getIDlist(TREE,IDLIST),
  TXT = "Node name:",
  lineinput_repeat(ROW,COL,40,WATTR,FATTR,TXT,OLD,NAME),
```

```
nodename1(ROW,COL,WATTR,FATTR,IDLIST,NAME,NODEname,REF),!,
write(NODEname), readln(_),
removewindow, !.
```

The first thing "nodename" does is to name all the nodes in a uniform way. To do this it uses two predicates, "getTREE" and "getIDlist." I list both of these predicates in FIG. 9-1i. The node names these predicates generate are called "chain-names." For example, the name of the root issue will always be "I1," while the first position responding to the root issue will have the name "I1P1." If I have an argument opposing this position, its name would be "P1A1." To get a better idea on this "chain-naming" process, take a look at FIG. 13-7.

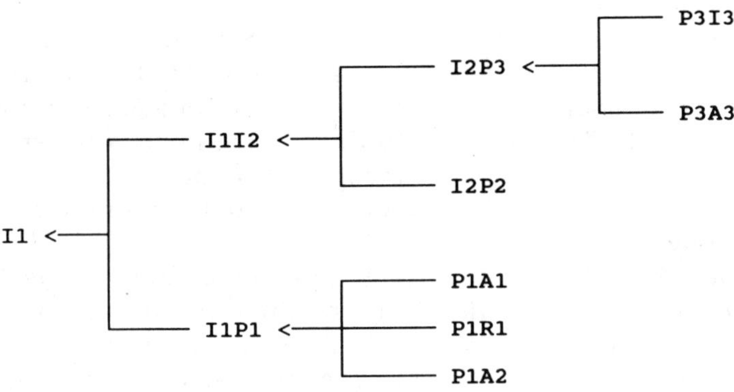

Fig. 13-7. Explaining the naming convention in MicroIBIS.

The effect of "nodename" is a box-menu of node names. After you select a node, "nodename" will succeed and return a node name and its database reference number (NodeName and NODEref). The next few subgoals will make the new node the current node ("update" predicates). In the end, "refreshNODE" will load the node text in the editor window. Now that you have loaded a new node in the editor, all you need is to edit it. To edit a node is straightforward. You just choose the Edit option from the pull-down menu.

The Edit Option

To start the editor, MicroIBIS uses the pull-down predicate "pdwaction(3,0)." The code for this predicate is in "main-mod.pro" in FIG. 9-1b. This predicate has three clauses. The first clause is the one which starts the editor. In this clause, the first subgoal makes sure that you have an opened IBIS file. If not, the whole clause will fail and the second "pdwaction(3,0)" will succeed. The next three subgoals will retrieve the current settings from the knowledgebase. These settings are the current node string, its reference number, and the current cursor position in the editor window. After that, you change the contents of the status line. To do that you use the TOOLBOX "changestatus" predicate. The contents of the status line are those commands which you need most when using the editor. What else! Oh yes, you need to shift to the editor window to make sure that you interact with the right window. Now start the editor. The predicate used to start the editor is "ibisEDITOR." It is in "ibis-ed.pro" in FIG. 9-1m, and here:

```
ibisEDITOR(Nname,Ntype,_,INstr,INpos,OUTstr,OUTpos):-
    MSG = "End editing with ESC or F10",
    edit(INstr,OUTstr,Ntype,Nname,MSG,INpos,"",1,1, 1,1,OUTpos,_).
```

A very short predicate, isn't it? All it does is to fire Turbo Prolog's built-in editor. I talked about "edit" in PART TWO, so I will not talk about it here.

The Relations Menu

When you want to respond to the current IBIS node, you choose the Relations option from the pull-down menu. As a result you will get a menu of relation names. Each relation name represents a link. Your current node will be the target of this link. Your response to the current node is the source node. MicroIBIS will create the source node for you, after you have made your selection from the Relations menu. Even more, it will put you in the editor so you can edit this node.

This is fine. The Relations option displays a menu of relations, but is this menu the same one whether or not the current node is an issue, a position, an argument, or a reference? What do you think? Well, the answer is NO because, the response to a current node might not be applicable to some other current node. For example, the response to a position might not be appropriate as a response to an issue. You can support a position, but there is no point in supporting an issue. You must answer issues, not recommend or support them. So what you need is four different menus: One menu for a current issue node, one menu for a current position node, one menu for a current argument node, and one menu for a current reference node. This is exactly what I did in MicroIBIS. You can see these four menus in FIG. 13-8.

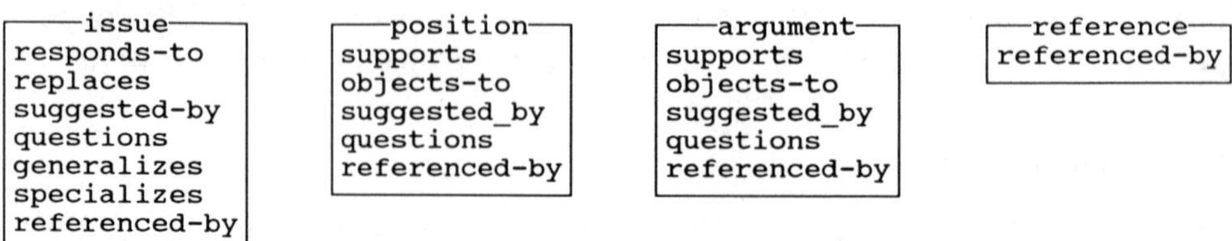

Fig. 13-8. The four "relations" menus of MicroIBIS.

Now turn to the programming part of the Relations menu. As you know by now, you use "pdwaction(4,0)" to execute each option on the pull-down menu (see FIG. 9-1b. There are three clauses for "pdwaction(4,0)":

```
pdwaction(4,0):-
  dbSTATUS(opened),
  currentREF(REF),
```

```
  currentNstr(Str),
  getNODE(REF,Tnode),          % in ibis-db.pro
  Tnode=node(N,K,A,D,Str1),
  saveCURRENT(REF,Str,N,K,A,D,Str1),
  relates_to(REF,_,_,_,Tnode), !.
pdwaction(4,0):-
  dbSTATUS(closed),
  writeMSG(go,["IBIS file is not open"]).
pdwaction(4,0):-
  refreshNODE.
```

The important clause, for now, is the first one. The last subgoal, "relates_to," does all the work of relating two nodes, but before you get to this subgoal, look at the one before it. What "saveCURRENT" does is to update the current node in the database. This will pave the road to create and edit a new node in the editor. Now you are ready for "relates_to." This predicate is a little bit complex. To appreciate its complexity, take a look at FIG. 13-9.

Fig. 13-9. Creating new links and nodes with relates_to

```
/* *********************** relates_to ******************** */

relates_to(Tref,Sref,Rel,node(Stype,Ktype,A,D,OUTstr),
                         node(Ttype,_,_,_,_)):-
  relationLIST(Ttype,RELlist,NtypeLIST),!,
  pulldown_attr(Attr),
  menu(2,43,Attr,Attr,RELlist,Ttype,1,Choice),
  matchRELATION(Choice,1,RELlist,NtypeLIST,Rel,Stype),
  getNattr(Ktype,A,D),
  concat_list1(["Edit this node as an <",Stype," ",Rel," ",
             Ttype,">."],"",MSG),
  shiftwindow(OLD),
  windowNUM("editwindow",NUM),
  shiftwindow(NUM), clearwindow,
  edit("",OUTstr,"<NODE EDITOR>",Stype,MSG,
       1,"",1,1,1,1,_,_), !,
  chain_inserta(ibisdb,nodech,node,
              node(Stype,Ktype,A,D,OUTstr),Sref),
  chain_terms(ibisdb,ibisch,ibis,IBIS,REF),!,
  insertIBIS(Tref,Sref,Rel,Stype,IBIS,NewIBIS),
  term_replace(ibisdb,ibis,REF,NewIBIS),
  update(currentIBIS(NewIBIS)),
  update(currentREF(Sref)),
  update(currentCpos(1)),
  update(currentNstr(OUTstr)),
  shiftwindow(OLD).
```

I'll start with its flow pattern: (i,o,o,o,i), which means you must supply the external database reference number for the target node, Tref, and the target node object, node(Ttype,_,_,_,_), while it returns the source node reference number, Sref, its relation with the target node, Rel, and its object, node (Stype,Ktype,A,D,OUTstr). So, take it step by step. The corner stone of "relates_to" is the "relationLIST" subgoal.

The "relationLIST(Ttype,RELlist,NtypeLIST)" subgoal, with a flow pattern (i,o,o), takes a target node-type, Ttype (issue) position, and so on. It returns two things: first, a list of all possible relations with the target node, RELlist; second, a list of node-types of source nodes, NtypeLIST. For each relation in RELlist there is a node-type in NtypeLIST. So as you can see it all depends upon the Ttype you enter. If it is an issue, you get one relations menu—if it is a position you get another. Which brings me to the point that there should be four "relationLIST" clauses in the program. FIGURE 13-10 shows these four clauses as they appear in MicroIBIS's "ibis-rel.pro" file in FIG. 9-1i.

In FIG. 13-10 there are more than "relationLIST" facts. You have a sample Turbo Prolog program which you can run to see how to generate a context dependent menu. Take your time to study the program to see how it works. This example should give you a good idea how "relates_to" works. The rest of "relates_to" is for creating the new node, editing it, and saving it in the database. Well, that's all there is to it folks.

Fig. 13-10. How to generate a context-dependent menu.

```
include "tdoms.pro"    % from TOOLBOX
include "tpreds.pro"   % from TOOLBOX
include "menu.pro"     % from TOOLBOX

PREDICATES
  relates_to(STRING,STRING,STRING)
  relationLIST(STRING,STRINGLIST,STRINGLIST)
     matchRELATION(INTEGER,INTEGER,STRINGLIST,STRINGLIST,STRING,STRING)

  test

GOAL
  makewindow(1,112,15,"a context dependent menu",0,0,25,80),
  repeat,
  test, !.

CLAUSES

test:-
  write("\n enter the node-type of your current node: "),
  readln(Ttype),
  relates_to(Ttype,Rel,Stype),
  write("\nThe current node (target node) is: ",Ttype),
  write("\nThe new node (source node) is: ",Stype),
  write("\nThe Relation (link) between source and target is: ",Rel).

test:-
  write("\n You should enter one of these node types:"),
  write("\n\t issue"),
  write("\n\t position"),
  write("\n\t argument"),
  write("\n\t reference"),
  write("\n\n so try again."),
  fail.

/* ********************** relates_to ******************** */

relates_to(Ttype,Rel,Stype):-
  relationLIST(Ttype,RELlist,NtypeLIST),
```

(**Fig. 13-10.** continued)

```
   menu(2,43,15,112,RELlist,Ttype,1,Choice),
   matchRELATION(Choice,1,RELlist,NtypeLIST,Rel,Stype).

/* ********************** matchRELATION **************** */

matchRELATION(NUM,NUM,[H1|_],[H2|_],H1,H2):-!.
matchRELATION(NUM,Count,[_|T],[_|T1],H1,H2):-
   Count1=Count+1,
   matchRELATION(NUM,Count1,T,T1,H1,H2).

/* *************************************************** */
/* ****************** default relationLIST ************* */

relationLIST("issue",
            ["responds-to","replaces","suggested-by",
             "questions","generalizes","specializes",
             "referenced-by"],
            ["position","issue","issue","issue","issue",
             "issue","reference"]).

relationLIST("position",
            ["supports","objects-to","suggested_by",
             "questions","referenced-by"],
            ["argument","argument","issue","issue",
             "reference"]).

relationLIST("argument",
            ["supports","objects-to","suggested_by",
             "questions","referenced-by"],
            ["argument","argument","issue","issue",
             "reference"]).

relationLIST("reference",
            ["referenced-by"],["reference"]).
```

The Map Option

When you choose this option, Turbo will execute it using "pdwaction(5,0)." There are three "pdwaction(5,0)" clauses, which are in FIG. 13-11.

In the first clause, dbSTATUS checks if a current IBIS file is open. If this is so, the second subgoal, map(REF), will draw the map in the IBIS-MAP window. When you are in the IBIS-MAP window you have three options:

1) select a node by moving the cursor to that node and pressing the ENTER key. MicroIBIS will load the node you select in the IBIS-EDITOR window.
2) operate on a node by moving the cursor to that node and pressing F10. MicroIBIS will display a hypertext menu of operations. This menu is somewhat similar to the Nodes menu.
3) cancel and go back to the pull-down menu by pressing the ESC key.

When you select a node, "map(REF)" will succeed and return the REF number of that node. The next subgoal, "ifNODEdeleted," will also succeed because you didn't delete a node. The last subgoal, "loadIBISnode" will load the node in the IBIS-EDITOR window. If you delete a node while in IBIS-MAP, "ifNODEdeleted" will fail. Then Turbo will execute the third "pdwaction(5,0)" clause. This clause doesn't do much, it just changes the status line and succeeds.

Fig. 13-11. Executing the Map option.

```
pdwaction(5,0):-
  dbSTATUS(opened),
  map(REF),                 % in ibis-map.pro
  ifNODEdeleted(REF),       % in ibis-db.pro
  loadIBISnode(REF), !.     % in ibis-db.pro

pdwaction(5,0):-
  dbSTATUS(closed),
  writeMSG(go,["IBIS file is not open"]).

pdwaction(5,0):-
  changestatus(
R 75,T 5

" >>>>>>>>>>>>>>>>>>>>>>> Select from pulldown menu <<<<<<<<<<<<<<<<<<<<<<<"
              ).
```

The "map" predicate itself is a complete story by itself. It is in a file by itself (see "ibis-map.pro" in FIG. 9-1i). I will not go into the details of how it works. Rather, you can load and run this file by itself. Just follow the instructions at the top of the file. It will tell you how to do that. Two things to notice when running "map" are the predicates "getTREE" and "treemenu." In "getTREE" you enter the ibis-structure object to get a tree object. This tree object is then passed to "treemenu" for display. In "treemenu," in FIG. 9-1j, you can see how to capture the keyboard input with the "treekeyact" predicate. One of the clauses for this predicate is:

```
treekeyact(fkey(10)):-
  treechoice(CHOICE), !,
  f10action(CHOICE).        % f10action is hypertext action
```

which Turbo executes when you press F10. In this clause you have "f10action" which displays the hypertext menu. Here is the code for "f10action":

```
f10action(NODEref):-
  cursor(R,C),
  pulldown_attr(Attr),
  menu(R,C,Attr,Attr,
       ["Relations","Delete","Attr","Contract","Expand"],
       map,1,Choice),
       mapCHOICE(NODEref,Choice).
```

Notice the hypertext menu options in "menu." I will stop here, but you can follow f10action through "mapCHOICE" to see how it works. I would like to stop discussing the programming part of IBIS-MAP and talk a little bit about the hypertext factor.

The Hypertext Factor. In an issue system, most of the time you need to move at random between different nodes. One way to do that is by writing a command interpreter which accepts a "Go TO <nodename>," or "FIND <nodename>" command, but this method is not compatible with the argumentative approach for problem-solving. In argumentation you tend to build a structure (tree, cascade, or network) of related issues, positions, arguments and references. I need a way to visualize this structure. I need a way to represent the knowledge-base of nodes and relations in an abstract visual form. This visual abstraction should act as a user-interface to the knowledge-base. Hypertext is the natural answer to such requirements.

With the hypertext ideas from PART ONE in mind, you can think of many hypertext features in an issue system. Some of these features could be:

1) a graphical representation of the IBIS structure as a tree, a cascade, or a network of nodes. In this structure, you label the inter-node links with the names of the relationship between these nodes. You can use this representation to edit, add, or delete nodes and links.
2) hypertext points in issues, positions, arguments and references: this feature allows you to link part of one node to another part of the same or different node.
3) executable points: These are textual chunks that you can execute while in a node. For example, you can have a complete C program acting as a hypertext point. When executed, the program could generate and display its output in a different window. These executable points are called command-points. For example, assume that the issue is "what should be the design of a house for. . ." The position could include a drawing of a possible design. To do this you can add a command-point as part of the position. The command line would execute a CAD package to draw the design alternative.
4) procedural attachment to links: A procedural attachment is a program that you can execute by selecting the link. There can be more than one procedure attached to the same link. Execution of procedural attachments can be conditional. A certain procedure attached to a link would execute only if certain conditions are satisfied. You can use constraints on the contents of the source and target nodes of a link as your conditions.

This of course is not a complete list of hypertext features. Nonetheless, it should give you a good idea of the possibilities in hypertext systems. In the current version of MicroIBIS you only have the first feature (the graphical representation of the IBIS structure, which we called "IBIS-MAP"). Now, I'll go back and talk about the last option on the pull-down menu—the Setup menu.

The Setup Menu

You might not like the way I used colors in MicroIBIS. You might like to have a larger window for the IBIS-MAP. You might like to suppress the node-attribute dialogue box so it doesn't show up every time you create a new link. If you like to change the way the system looks and acts, you can use the Setup option from the pull-down menu. When you do this you get the main setup menu (see FIG. 13-12).

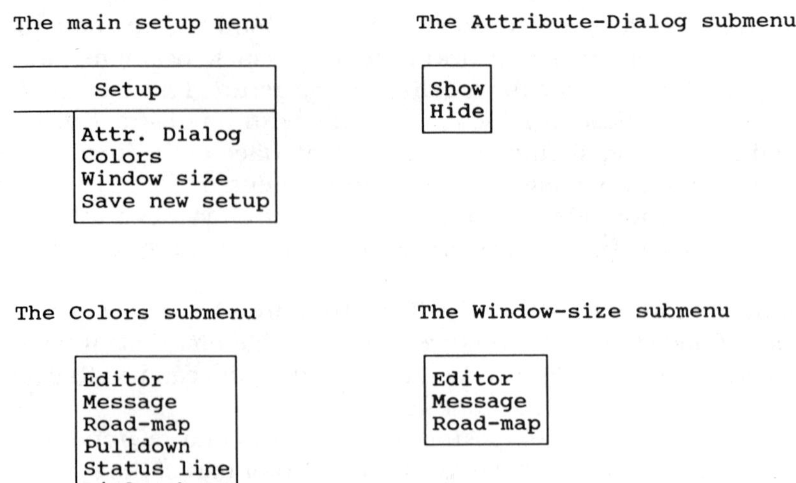

Fig. 13-12. The Setup menu and its three submenus.

Now see how you get to this menu first. As you know by now, to execute an option from the pull-down menu you have to have a "pdwaction" clause for it. For the setup main menu you have four options. For each option you have two "pdwaction" clauses. Take a look at these clauses in FIG. 13-13.

The first three options of the main setup menu have their own submenu (see FIG. 13-12). So if you look at the code in FIG. 13-13 you will see how to execute these submenus using "menu." When you choose from a submenu, the subgoal after "menu" will execute your choice. For executing the dialogue-box status change, use "attrCHOICE." For changing colors use "window_color." For changing the sizes of windows use "window_size."

Fig. 13-13. Executing the Setup main menu options.

```
/* ****************************************************** */
% change node-attribute dialogue-box status (show or hide).

pdwaction(6,1):-
  pulldown_attr(Attr),
  menu(3,67,Attr,Attr,["Show",
                       "Hide"],"",1,Choice),
  attrCHOICE(Choice).  % in ibis-db.pro

pdwaction(6,1).

% Change the window colors attributes

pdwaction(6,2):-
  pulldown_attr(Attr),
  menu(4,67,Attr,Attr, ["Editor",
                        "Message",
                        "Road-map",
                        "Pulldown",
                        "Status line",
                        "Dialog box"],"",1,Choice),
```

(**Fig. 13-13.** continued)

```
    window_color(Choice).  % in ibis-use.pro

  pdwaction(6,2).

  % Change window sizes

  pdwaction(6,3):-
    pulldown_attr(Attr),
    menu(5,67,Attr,Attr, ["Editor",
                          "Message",
                          "Road-map"],"",1,Choice),
    window_size(Choice),   % in ibis-use.pro
    refreshstatus.

  pdwaction(6,3):- refreshstatus.

  % Save current setup

  pdwaction(6,4):-
    save("ibis.sys",setupdb), !.

  pdwaction(6,4):-
    writeMSG(go,["Can't save to ibis.sys"]).

  /* ****************************************************** */
```

To save the new setup you use "Save new setup" option from the main Setup menu. MicroIBIS uses "pdwaction(6,4)" to save the new setup to a special file, which I call "ibis.sys"—the ibis system setting file. This file contains the knowledge-base of all the current system settings. Here is an example of the contents of one possible "ibis.sys" file.

```
pulldown_attr(48)
edit_attr(79,48)
msg_attr(95,48)
map_attr(30,48,79)
status_attr(48)
aux_edit_attr(15,79)
dialog_attr(15,31)
edit_size(3,36,21,44)
msg_size(20,0,4,36)
map_size(3,0,17,36)
```

The extension "attr" refers to the window color attribute, and "size" refers to the window size attribute. By this I have, more or less, covered all the options on the pull-down menu. It's time to move to a new topic. In the next section I talk about the modular programming approach I used in MicroIBIS.

MODULAR PROGRAMMING IN TURBO PROLOG

It is true that a Prolog program is more descriptive and understandable than, say, a LISP or a C program. The main reason for this, of course, is that Prolog is a descriptive language, while LISP is a functional language and C is a prescriptive language; but with large Prolog programs, such as MicroIBIS, you have a different situation. The program becomes a hard one to follow and understand. This is why you need to partition large programs into modules.

Another reason is the time saving in treating modules as building blocks for different applications. For many programmers, it makes a lot of sense to treat programs as parts which they can use to build different products.

The third reason has to do with memory management and interface to other languages. For large programs, the size of source code can be critical. In this case you need modules that you can compile separately. Later you can link the compiled portions into a complete and executable application. Also, sometimes you find it better to write parts of the program in a different language, such as Turbo C or assembly language. Then at run time you can link these parts into the application.

You can satisfy the first two reasons by partitioning MircoIBIS into several Prolog source code files. You select one of these files to be the main file. In the main file, I include all the other files, using the "include" directive. This approach is fine, as long as the size of the source code is still within limits. Also, this approach will not work if I want to use Turbo C or assembly language programs in the applications. To remedy this problem, you should use "projects."

With projects, you can write, edit, and compile the modules separately, and then link them together to create a single executable program. To change some part of the program, you only need to edit and re-compile individual modules, not the entire program. So I'll talk about the making of the MicroIBIS project.

The MicroIBIS Project

When programming with projects, the first thing you should do is to define the project. To do that you create a text file and give it the name of your project. How do you do that? For experienced Turbo Prolog programs the answer is probably an easy one. For all the others, you only need to follow these steps:

1) From the integrated environment of Turbo Prolog, choose the "Options/ Edit PRJ File" option from the pull-down menu. MicroIBIS will prompt for the name of your project file. In MicroIBIS, simply use "ibis" as the project name. Turbo Prolog will invoke the editor and create the file. A project filename must have ".prj" as its extension. If you entered a filename without the ".prj" extension, Turbo will add it for you.
2) The project definition file should contain the names of its modules. You must specify each module by its first name only (no extension) followed by a plus (+) or a new-line, or both. For example, MicroIBIS's project definition file, ibis.prj, contents are (also, see FIG. 9-1a):

```
tool-mod+
main-mod
```

3) When you are through editing the project file, press F10 to save the file and return to the main menu. You must place the project definition file on the current directory, along with the projects ".pro" files.
4) At link time, Turbo Prolog enters the names of the modules in a .prj file into the link command.
5) During compilation, the compiler must identify a symbol table shared by all the modules in that project. For this to happen, you must have the project name in each module. To do this you use the "project" compiler directive. An important thing to remember here is that the "project" directive should be at the very top of the module. Look at the top of two modules in MicroIBIS, main-mod.pro in FIG. 9-1b and tool-mod.pro in FIG. 9-1c. You will find this line at the very top of these two modules:

```
project "ibis"
```

By this you have finished defining the MicroIBIS project, but there is still the issue of communication between predicates across the module boundaries. For example, the pull-down menu which you use in "main-mod.pro" is part of the second module, tool-mod.pro. The declarations in these modules are local. The predicates in the "tool-mod.pro" don't know about these declarations. What you need is to make the shared predicate declarations global. To do this you use Turbo Prolog's "global declarations." Global declarations include: global domains, global predicates and global database sections. All the modules of a project must know exactly the same global declarations. An easy way to do this is by putting all global declarations in a single file. Then, you use the "include" directive to include this file in every related module. In MicroIBIS, I do exactly that. I put all the global declarations in a "ibis-glb.pro" file (see FIG. 9-1d). Then I include this file at the top of "main-mod.pro and "tool-mod.pro" (see FIG. 9-1b and FIG. 9-1c), which both have this line:

```
include "ibis-glb.pro"
```

Notice that I include "ibis-glb.pro" before any local declarations. This is a must for modular programming. To know more about projects and modular programming, refer to your Turbo Prolog's User and Reference Guides. Now that you are done with the project level of MicroIBIS, how about the module level? Each module is made of one or more parts. I put each part in a file by itself. For example, all the user-interface related predicates are in "ibis-use-.pro." So anyway, to put the whole thing together, I include these parts in one place. For the "main-mod.pro" module I have these include directives:

```
include "ibis-ut.pro"
include "ibis-gsc.pro
include "ibis-use.pro
include "ibis-db.pro
include "ibis-map.pro"
include "ibis-prt.pro"
include "ibis-ed.pro"
include "ibis-rel.pro"
```

and for the "tool-mod.pro" module I have these include directives:

```
include "tpreds.pro"
include "lineinp.pro"
include "filename.pro"
include "status.pro"
include "scrhnd.pro"
include "menu.pro"
include "pulldown.pro"
include "boxmenu.pro"
include "tree2.pro"
include "ibis-dia.pro"
```

Notice that, except for ibis-dia.pro, all these files are Turbo Prolog TOOLBOX files. What I did here is to put all the TOOLBOX files in one module, and all IBIS files in another module. I find this to be a very effective technique. I recommend that you use this technique whenever you need to use the TOOLBOX in one of your applications.

COPYING THE IBIS KNOWLEDGE-BASE TO AN EXTERNAL FILE

MicroIBIS is a Turbo Prolog program. As any Prolog program, MicroIBIS is a collection of facts and rules. In Prolog, I call these facts and rules "knowledge-base." As a stand-alone knowledge-based system, MicroIBIS's knowledge-base is in two parts:

1) Facts and rules to operate the integrated environment of MicroIBIS. Part of the integrated environment deals with user-interface items to display windows, pull-down menus, box menus, tree menus, status lines, and so on. Also, part of the integrated environment deals with reading and writing to external IBIS database structures. This part of MicroIBIS's knowledge-base constitutes a shell, similar to that of an expert system shell. I can use this shell to solve many problems. The knowledge-base making the shell will always be the same, unless you modify it yourself. The main point is that users of MicroIBIS need not worry about the knowledge-base making the shell. When you use this shell to solve a problem, you will have to fill it with domain knowledge. The domain knowledge is knowledge about the problem you are trying to solve. This knowledge forms the second part of MicroIBIS's knowledge-base.
2) Facts and rules representing domain knowledge about the problem. The domain knowledge in MicroIBIS contains nodes, the links between these nodes, and the general IBIS structure of a problem. The domain knowledge is not a static thing, it changes with the problem at hand. When you deal with a particular problem you create new nodes, delete old ones, change existing ones, and so on. This means you will need to add, delete, and update the knowledge-base at run time.

In Turbo Prolog, you can only assert and retract facts. This doesn't mean that you can't assert or retract rules. You can assert and retract rules by writing them as a special kind of fact. You can read more about writing rules as database facts in two places: in "Turbo Prolog: Advanced Programming Technique" by Safaa Hashim and Philip Seyer. Also, in "Metalogical Programming in Turbo Prolog" by Safaa Hashim (see references in Appendix A).

In MicroIBIS, it turns out that you only need facts to represent nodes, links, and their general IBIS structure. In Chapter 12, I talked about building a domain knowledge-base of a particular IBIS using these facts. For those interested in knowing the internal domain knowledge representation of MicroIBIS, I included the "Files/ Write KB to ext. file" option. As a pull-down menu option, you need a "pdwaction" clause to execute it. Here is the single "pdwaction" to execute this option:

```
pdwaction(1,8):- dumpIBIS.       % in IBIS-prt
```

which doesn't say much. It only redirects the work to "dumpIBIS" in "ibis-prt.pro" in FIG. 9-1g. You don't need to turn the pages to Chapter 9. I extracted "dumpIBIS" and its sub-predicates in FIG. 13-14.

Fig. 13-14. Writing IBIS KB to an external text file.

```
/* ****************************************************** */
/* DUMPING AN IBIS EXTERNAL DATABASE FILE TO A TEXT FILE  */
/* ****************************************************** */

PREDICATES
   dumpIBIS
     dumpDba
       wrIBIS(IBIS)
       wrNODE

CLAUSES

/* *********************** dumpIBIS ********************* */
dumpIBIS:-
  dbSTATUS(opened),
  newCURSORpos(Row,Col),
  readfilename(Row,Col,15,112,txt,"",FileName),
  writeMSG(stay,["Writing IBIS KB to ",FileName]),
  openwrite(ibistxt,FileName),
  writedevice(ibistxt),
  dumpDba,
  writedevice(screen),
  closefile(ibistxt),
  refreshSCR, !.

dumpIBIS:- writeMSG(go,["IBIS DB file is not open"]).

/* *********************** dumpDba ********************* */
dumpDba:-
  chain_terms(ibisdb, ibisch, ibis, IBIS, _),
  write("\n\n\n ******** THE IBIS TREE ********\n\n"),
  wrIBIS(IBIS),
  write("\n\n\n ******** THE NODES ********\n\n"),
  wrNODE,
  write("\n\n\n ******** END OF KB ********\n\n").
```

(**Fig. 13-14.** continued)

```
/* ************************ wrIBIS ********************** */
wrIBIS(X) :- write(X), nl.

/* ************************ wrNODE ********************** */
wrNODE:-
  chain_terms(ibisdb, nodech, node, Term, _),
  write(Term), nl, fail.
wrNODE.

/* ***************************************************** */
```

In the first clause of "dumpIBIS," I first check that there is a database file open—dbSTATUS(opened). Next I prompt the user to enter the filename where he wants to dump the knowledge-base. Before writing to the file, I need to tell the user to wait until it is done. The "writeMSG" subgoal displays the waiting message in the message window. The next two subgoals—"openwrite(ibistxt, Filename)" and "writedevice(ibistxt)"—create and open a text file on the specified disk and directory. All you need now is to write to this file. For writing to the external database file you use "dumpDba." After you are done writing to the file, you need to shift the control back to the screen and close the file, "writedevice(screen)" and "closefile(ibistxt)." The last subgoal of "dumpIBIS" refreshes the system windows and returns control to the "pull-down" menu predicate.

In "dumpDba," I divide the writing of the knowledge-base into two parts: (a) writing the IBIS structure (compound object), and (b) writing the node objects. The "wrIBIS" subgoal writes the ibis structure, and the "wrNODE" subgoal writes the node objects. The "chain_terms" subgoal of "dumpDba" retrieves the IBIS structure and passes it to "wrIBIS," so it can write it to the file. As for the nodes part, "wrNODE" uses backtracking to retrieve and write the "node" terms. The way it works is this: "chain_terms" retrieves a node term, then "write" writes the term to the file. The "fail" subgoal causes backtracking to "chain_terms" which retrieves the next term, and so on. This continues until there are no more node terms for "chain_terms" to retrieve. Here "fail" will fail the first clause of "wrNODE." Turbo will try the second clause, which succeeds instantly. By this I have finished writing the whole knowledge-base (the general structure and individual nodes) of a particular IBIS. Also, by this you come to the end of the book.

Appendices

A

References

Akscyn, R. M. and D. L. McCracken, ZOG and the USS CARL VINSON: lessons in Systems Development, Technical Report CMU-CS-84-127, Department of Computer Science, Carnegie-Mellon University, Pittsburgh, PA, March 1984.

Akscyn, Robert, Donald L. McCracken, and Elise Yoder, A Distributed Hypertext System for Sharing Knowledge in Organizations, in: Hypertext '87 Papers, Chapel Hill, NC, November 13 – 15, 1987.

Akscyn, Robert M., Donald L. McCracken, and Elise A. Yoder; KMS: A Distributed Hypermedia System for Managing Knowledge in Organizations. I Communication of the ACM, V. 31, No. 7, July 1988, pp. 820 – 835.

Allen, Todd, Robert Nix, and Alan Perlis, PEN: A hierarchical document editor, in: Proceedings of the ACM SIGPLAN Notices/SIGOA Conference on Text Manipulation, Portland, Oregon, June, 1981.

Backer, D. and S. Gano, Dynamically Alterable Videodisk Displays, Proceedings Graphics Interface 82, Toronto, Canada, May 1982.

Baskin, A. B., Logic Nets: Variable-valued Logic Plus Semantic Networks, International Journal on Policy Analysis and Information Systems, 4: 269, 1980.

Beeman, William O., Kenneth T. Anderson, Gail Bader, James Larkin, Anne P. McClard, Patrick J. McQuillan, and Mark Shields, Hypertext and Pluralism: From Lineal to Non-lineal Thinking, in: Hypertext '87 Papers, Chapel Hill, NC, November 13 – 15, 1987.

Begeman, Michael L., P. Cook, C. Ellis, M. Graf, G. Rein, and T. Smith, PROJECT NICK: Meetings Augmentation and Analysis, in: Computer-Supported Cooperative Work (CSCW '86) Proceedings, Austin, TX, December 3–5, 1986.

Begeman, Michael L., and Jeff Conklin; The Right Tool for the Job: Even the systems design process falls within the realm of hypertext. BYTE, October 1988, pp. 255–268.

Bender, W., Imaging and Interactivity, Fifteenth Joint Conference on Image Technology, Tokyo, Japan, November 1984.

Bigelow, James and Victor Riley, Manipulating Source Code in DynamicDesign, in: Hypertext '87 Papers, Chapel Hill, NC, November 13–15, 1987.

Biggerstaff, T., C. Ellis, F. G. Halasz, C. Kellog, C. Richter, and D. Webster, Information Management Challenges in the Software Design Process, MCC Technical Report STP-039-87, January, 1987.

Bolt, R. A., Put-that-there: Voice and Gesture at the Graphics Interface, Computer Graphics, 15(3): 262–270, August 1980.

Bolt, R. A., Spatial Data-Management, DARPA Report, MIT Architecture Machine Group, Cambridge, MA, 1979.

Bolter, Jay David, Hypertext and Creative Writing, in: Hypertext '87 Papers, Chapel Hill, NC, November 13–15, 1987.

Borning, A., D. B. Lenat, D. McDonald, C. Taylor, and S. Weyer, Knoesphere: Toward a Searcher's Guide to Encyclopedic Knowledge, paper submitted to IJCAI-83, Sunnyvale, CA, January 1983.

Brooks, Fred; The Mythical Man-Month. Boston: Addison-Wesley, 1975.

Brookes, B. C., Intelligent Information Systems for the Information Society, Elsevier Science Publishers, Amsterdam, 1986.

Brown, J. S., Process versus Product: A Perspective on Tools for Communal and Informal Electronic Learning, Education in the Electronic Age: A report from the Learning Lab, WNET/Thirteen Learning Lab, New York, 1983.

Brown, J. S., Notes Concerning Designed Functionality, Issues and Philosophy for an AuthoringLand, Xerox PARC CIS Working Paper, Xerox Palo Alto Center, Palo Alto, CA, February 1982.

Bush, V., As We May Think, Atlantic Monthly, 176(1): 101–108, July 1945.

Bush, V., Memex Revisited, in: Science is Not Enough, V. Bush, ed., pp. 75–101, William Morrow, 1967.

Bush, Vannevar, As We May Think, HyperAge: The Journal of HyperThinking, pp.14–20, HyperAge Communication, Inc., February–March, 1988.

Bush, Vannevar; As We May Think. The Atlantic Monthly, 1945. Also in Hyperage, February–March, pp. 16–20, 1988.

Brown, Peter J., Turning Ideas into Products: the Guide System, in: Hypertext '87 Papers, Chapel Hill, NC, November 13–15, 1987.

Buchert, R. F., K. H. Evers, and P. R. Santucci, SADT/SAINT Simulation Technique, in: National Aerospace and Electronics Conference Proceedings, 1981.

Bulick, Stephen, A Network Information Retrieval System, in: Bellcore Database Symposium, Bell Communications Research, September, 1987.

Campbell, Brad and Joseph M. Goodman, HAM: A General Purpose Hypertext Abstract Machine, in: Hypertext '87 Papers, Chapel Hill, NC, November

13 – 15, 1987.

Campbell, Brad and Joseph M. Goodman; HAM: A General Purpose Hypertext Abstract Machine. The Journal of the Communication of the ACM, Vol. 31, No.7 July 1988, pp. 856 – 861.

Carmody, S. and et al., A Hypertext Editing System for the 360, in: Pertinent Concepts in Computer Graphics, M. Faiman and J. Nievergelt, eds., pp. 63 – 88, University of Illinois Press, 1969.

Cashin, P., M. Robinson, and D. Yates, Experience with SCRAPBOOK, A Non-formatted Data Base System, Proceedings Proc. IFIPS Congress, 1973.

Catano, J., Poetry and Computers: Experimenting with Communal Text, Computers and the Humanities, pp. 269 – 275, 1979.

Cattell, R. G. G., An Entity-Based Database Interface, Technical Report CSL-79-9, Xerox Palo Alto Research Center, Palo Alto, CA, August 1979.

Charney, Davida, Comprehending Non-Linear Text: The Role of Discourse Cues and Reading Strategies, in: Hypertext '87 Papers, Chapel Hill, NC, November 13 – 15, 1987.

Charney, Davida and L. Reder, Designing interactive tutorials for computer users, Human-Computer Interaction, 2:297 – 317.

Charniak, E. and Drew McDermott; "Introduction to Artificial Intelligence," see "Abstract Representations," page 317, and "Abstraction Mapping," page 621. Addison-Wesley, 1986.

Churchman, C. West; The Systems Approach; Dell Publishing Co., Inc., New York, 1979.

Clocksin, W.F. and C.S. Mellish; Programming in Prolog. Springer-Verlag, New York, 1984.

Collier, George H., Thoth-II: Hypertext with Explicit Semantics, in: Hypertext '87 Papers, Chapel Hill, NC, November 13 – 15, 1987.

Collier, George H., Thoth-II: A Hypertext Browser, Technical Report, Artificial Intelligence and Information Science Research, Bell Communications Research, Morristown, NJ.

Combelic, D., User Experience with New Software Methods (SADT), in: Proceedings of the National Computer Conference, 1978.

Conklin, J., A Survey of Hypertext, MCC Technical Report STO-356-86, MCC Software Technology Program, Austin, TX, October, 1986.

Conklin, Jeff, Hypertext: a Survey and Introduction, IEEE Computer, 20(9): 17 – 41, September, 1987.

Conklin, Jeff and Michael L. Begeman, gIBIS: A Hypertext Tool for Team Design Deliberation, in: Hypertext '87 Papers PLM: Chapel Hill, NC DMT:November 13 – 15 DAT:1987.

Crane, Gregory, From the Old to the New: Integrating Hypertexts into Traditional Scholarship, in: Hypertext '87 Papers, Chapel Hill, NC, November 13 – 15, 1987.

Dehlinger, H., J. P. Protzen; Some Considerations for the Design of Issue Based Information System (IBIS). DMG-DRS Journal: Design Research and Method, V. 6, #2, April – June, 1972.

Delisle, N. and M. Schwartz, Context - A Partitioning Concept for Hypertext, Conference on Computer-Supported Cooperative Work Proceedings, Austin, Texas, December, 1986.

Delisle, N., Neptune: A Hypertext System for CAD Applications, Technical Report CR-85-50, Tektronix Computer Research laboratory, Beaverton, OR, January 1986.

Dershowitz, Nachum: "Programming by Analogy." Includes discussion on "program abstraction," in "MACHINE LEARNING: AN ARTIFICIAL INTELLIGENCE APPROACH, Vol. II, "Ryszard S. Michalski, Jamie G. Carbonell, and Tom M. Mitchell (editors), pp. 395 – 423, Morgan Kaufmann Publishers, Inc., California, 1936.

diSessa, Andrea, A Principled Design for an Integrated Computational Environment, Human-Computer Interaction, 1(1): 1 – 47, 1985.

diSessa, Andrea and Harold Abelson, Boxer: A Reconstructable Computational Medium, Communications of the ACM, 29(9): 859 – 868, September, 1986.

Einstein, Albert; Ideas and Opinions, based on Mein Weltbild, edited by Carl Seelig, new translations and revisions by Sonia Bargmann. Dell Publishing Co., Inc. New York, 1981.

Engelbart, D. C. and W. K. English, A Research Center for Augmenting Human Intellect, in: AFIPS Proceedings, Fall Joint Computer Conference, vol. 33, pp. 395 – 410, AFIPS Press, Montvale, NJ, Fall 1968.

Engelbart, D. C., A Conceptual Framework for the Augmentation of Man's Intellect, in: Vistas in Information Handling, Vol 1, P. D. Howerton and D. C. Weeks, eds., pp. 1 – 29, Spartan Books, Washington, D. C., 1963.

Engelbart, D. C., Authorship Provisions in Augment, IEEE 1984 COMPCON Proceedings, Spring 1984.

Engelbart, D. C., R. W. Watson, and J. C. Norton, The Augmented Knowledge Workshop, in: Proceedings of the National Computer Conference, vol. 42, pp. 9 – 21, AFIPS Press, Arlington, VA, 1973.

Engelbart, D. C., Toward Integrated Evolutionary Office Automation Systems, in: Proc. Int. Engineering management Conf., pp. 63 – 68, IEEE, New York, (Denver, CO) October 16 – 18, 1978.

Engelbart, D. C., Design Considerations for Knowledge Workshop Terminals, in: Conference Proceedings, pp. 9 – 21, NCC, 1973.

Engelbart, D. C., Coordinations Information Services for a Discipline or Mission-Oriented Community, Second Annual Computer Communications Conference, San Jose, CA, January, 1973.

Engelbart, Douglas C., Collaboration Support Provisions in Augment, in: AFIPS Office Automation Conference, 1984.

English, W. K., D. C. Engelbart, and M. L. Berman, Display-Selection Techniques for Text Manipulation, in: IEEE Trans. on Hum. Fact. Electron., pp. 5 – 15, HFE-8, March 1967.

Fahnestock, J. and M. Secor, Teaching Argument: A Theory of Types, College Composition and Communication, 34: 20 – 30.

Feiner, S., S. Nagy, and A. Van Dam, An Experiment System for Creating and

Presenting Interactive Graphical Documents, in: ACM Transactions on Graphics, vol. 1, pp. 59 – 77, January 1982.

Feiner, S., S. Nagy, and A. Van Dam, An Integrated System for Creating and Presenting Complex Computer-Based Documents, Computer Graphics, 15(3): 181 – 189, August 1981.

Feiner, S., S. Nagy, and A. Van Dam, Online Documents Combining Pictures and Text, in: Proc. Int. Conf. Research Trends in Document Preparation Systems, pp. 1 – 4, Swiss Institutes of Technology, Lausanne and Zurich.

Fischer, G. and H. Nieper, High Functionality, Information Retrieval, and the Document Examiner, Personalized Intelligent Information Systems, Report on a Workshop (Breckenridge, CO), K. Ehrlich and Janet H. Walker, eds., 1987.

Forbus, Kenneth D. and Dedre Gentner; "Learning and Physical Domains: Toward a Theoretical Framework." Includes discussion on "abstraction mapping" in section titled "Comparisons and Structure Mapping," in "MACHINE LEARNING: AN ARTIFICIAL INTELLIGENCE APPROACH," Vol. II," Ryszard S. Michalski, Jamie G. Carbonell, and Tom M. Mitchell (editors), pp. 311 – 348, Morgan, Kaufmann Publishers, Inc. California, 1986.

Foster, G. and M. Stefik, Cognoter, Theory and Practice of a Collaborative Tool, Conference on Computer-supported Cooperative Work Proceedings, Austin, Texas, December, 1986.

Frisse, Mark E., Searching for Information in a Hypertext Medical Handbook, in: Hypertext '87 Papers, Chapel Hill, NC, November 13 – 15, 1987.

Frisse, Mark E., Searching for Information in a Hypertext Medical Therapeutics Manual, Medical Information Group, Stanford University School of Medicine, 1987.

Garrett, L. N., K. E. Smith, and N. Meyrowitz, Issues, Strategies, and Tactics in the Design of a Hypermedia Document System, Conference on Computer-Supported Cooperative Work Proceedings, Austin, Texas, December, 1986.

Garrett, L. N. and Karen E, Smith, Building a Timeline Editor from Prefab Parts: The Architecture of an Object-oriented Application, in: Proceedings of the Conference on Object-oriented Programming Systems, Languages and Applications (OOPSLA '86), Portland, Oregon, September 29 – October 2, 1986.

Godfrey, D. and E. Chang, Alternative Database Facilities for Videotex, in: The Telidon Book, Frank Wm Tompa, Jan Gecsei, and Gregor V. Bochmann, eds., Press Porcepic, 1981.

Goldstein, I.P. and D.G. Bobrow; "A Layered Approach to Software Design," in Interactive Programming Environments, D. Barstow, H. Shrobe, and E. Sandewall, Eds., McGraw-Hill, pp. 387 – 413, 1984.

Goldstein, I.P. and D.G. Bobrow, An Experimental Description-Based Programming Environment: Four Reports, Technical Report CSL-81-3, Xerox Palo Alto Research Center, Palo Alto, CA, March 1981.

Goldstein, I.P. and D.G. Bobrow, Descriptions of a Programming Environment, in: Proceedings of the First Conference on AAAI, August 1980.

Goldstein, I.P. and D.G. Bobrow, A Layered Approach to Software Design, in: Interactive Programming Environments, D. Barstow, H. Shrobe, and E. Sanderwall, eds., pp. 387 – 413, McGraw-Hill, 1984.

Gonnet, Gaston H. and Frank Wm Tompa, Mind Your Grammar: A New Approach to Modelling Text, OED-87-01, Waterloo, Ontario, June 1986.

Goodman, Danny, The Complete HyperCard Handbook, Bantam Books, New York, 1987.

Grag, Pankaj K., Abstraction Mechanisms in Hypertext, in: Hypertext '87 Papers, Chapel Hill, NC, November 13 – 15, 1987.

Grag, Pankaj K. and Walt Scacchi, A Hypertext System to Manage Software Life Cycle Documents, in: The 21st Hawaii International Conference on Systems, Honolulu HI, 1987.

Grag, Pankaj K., and Walt Scacchi, On Designing Intelligent Hypertext Systems for Information Management in Software Engineering, in: Hypertext '87 Papers, Chapel Hill, NC, November 13 – 15, 1987.

Gregory, R., Xanadu-Hypertext from the Future, Dr. Dobb's Journal, pp. 28 – 35, January, 1983.

Guide User's Manual, Owl International, Inc., 14218 NE 21st Street Bellevue, WA 98007.

Guindon, R., SemNet: Three-dimensional Graphic Representations of Large Knowledge Bases, in: Cognitive Science and its Applications for Human-Computer Interaction, K. F. Fairchild, S. E. Poltrock, and G. W. Furnas, eds., Lawrence Erlbaum Associates, Hillsdale, NJ, in press.

Gullichsen, E., D. D'Souza, P. Lincoln, and T. Casey, The PlaneTextBook, MCC Technical Report STP-333-86(P), MCC Software Technology Program, Austin, Texas, 1986.

Halasz, F., T. Moran, and R. Trigg, NoteCards in a Nutshell, submitted to CHI+GI 1987, (Xerox PARC, 3333 Coyote Hill Road, Palo Alto, CA 94304), Toronto, Canada, April 1987.

Halasz, Frank, Reflections on NoteCards: Seven Issues for the Next Generation of Hypermedia Systems, in: Hypertext '87 Papers, Chapel Hill, NC, November 13 – 15, 1987.

Hammwohner, Rainer and Ulrich Thiel, Content Oriented Relations Between Text Units – A Structural Model for Hypertexts, in: Hypertext '87 Papers, Chapel Hill, NC, November 13 – 15, 1987.

Hashim, H. Safaa and Philip Seyer; Turbo Prolog, Advanced Programming Techniques. TAB Books, 1988.

Hashim, H. Safaa; Meta-Logical Programming in Turbo Prolog. Turbo Technix: The Borland Language Journal; March/April 1988, pp. 89 – 97.

Heckel, Paul; The Elements of Friendly Software design. Warner Books, 1984.

Hempel, Carl G.; Philosophy of Natural Science. Prentice-Hall, Inc., 1966.

Herot, C., R. Carling, M. Friedell M., and D. Kramlich, A Prototype Spatial Data Management System, Computer Graphics, 14(3): 63 – 70, July 1980.

Hershey, W., Idea Processors, BYTE, June, 1985.

Hiltz, Starr Roxanne, The 'Virtual Classroom': Using Computer-Mediated Communication for University Teaching, Journal of Communication, pp. 95 – 104, Spring, 1968.

Hiltz, Starr Roxanne and Murry Turoff, The Network Nation: Human Communication via Computer, Addison-Weseley, 1978.

Howard, V.A. and J.H. Barton; Thinking on Paper: refine, express, and actually generate ideas by understanding the processes of the Mind. William Morrow and Company, Inc. New York, 1982.

Howerton, P. D. and D. C. Weeks, Conceptual Framework for the Augmentation of Man's Intellect, in: Vistas in Information Handling, Volume 1, D. C. Engelbart, ed., pp. 1 – 29, Spartan Books, Washington, D.C., 1963.

Irby, C.H., Display techniques for Interactive Text Manipulation, in: AFIPS Conference Proceedings, pp. 247 – 255, MCC.

Jacobs, M.A. and D.J. Murray, FileVision, Telos Software Products, Santa Monica, CA, 1984.

Jonassen, D. H., Hypertext principles for text and courseware design, Educational Psychologist, 21: pp. 269 – 292, 1986.

Kay, Alan C., Computer Software, Scientific American, 251(3): 53 – 59, September, 1984.

Kay, A. and A. Goldberg, Personal Dynamic Media, Computer, 10(3): 31 – 43, March 1977.

Keen, Jack, HyperText in Corporate America, HyperAge: The Journal of HyperThinking, pp. 49 – 52, HyperAge Communication, Inc., February-March, 1988.

Kerr, Elaine and Starr Roxanne Hiltz, Computer-Mediated Communication Systems, Academic Press, New York, 1982.

Kochen, M., WISE: A World Information Synthesis and Encyclopedia, Journal of Documentation, 28: 322 – 343, 1972.

Koved, Larry, Restructuring Textual Information for Online Retrieval, 11278 (#50830), IBM T.J. Watson Research Center, Yorktown Heights, NY, July 23, 1985.

Kunz, Werner and Horst Rittel; Issues as Elements of Information Systems (IBIS). Working Paper 131, Institute of Urban and Regional Development, CED-UCBerkeley, 1970.

Lair, D.C. and M.E. Maron, An Evaluation of Retrieval Effectiveness for Full-test Document-Retrieval System, Comm. ACM, 28(3): 289 – 299, March 1985.

Lambert, Steve and Suzanne Ropiequet, CD ROM: The New Papyrus, Microsoft Press, Redmond WA, 1986.

Landow, George P., Context32: Using Hypermedia to Teach Literature, in: Proceedings of the 1987 IBM Academic Information Systems University AEP Conference, 1987.

Larson, J., A Visual Approach To Browsing in a Database Environment, IEEE Computer, June, 1986.

Learning Research Group, Personal Dynamic Media, Technical Report SSL-76-1, Xerox Palo Alto Research Center, Palo Alto, CA, March 1976.

Lenat, D.B., A. Borning, D. McDonald, C. Taylor, and S. Weyer, Knoesphere: Building Expert Systems with Encyclopedic Knowledge, in: IJCAI-83, Corporate Research, Atari, Inc., Sunnyvale, CA., January 1983.

Levy, A. H. and B. T. Williams, The Knowledge Access, Management, and Extension System in Pathology, in: Proceedings of the AAMSI Congress, D. Thursh, F. Mabry, and A. H. Levy, eds., 1985.

Liskov, B.H. and J.V. Guttag; Abstraction and Specification in Program Development, MIT Press, Cambridge, MA, 1986.

Lowe, David G., Co-operative Structuring of Information: The Representation of Reasoning and Debate, International Journal of Man-Machine Studies, 23: 97 – 111, 1985.

Lowe, David G., SYNVIEW: The Design of a System for Cooperative Structuring of Information, in: Computer-Supported Cooperative Work (CSCW '86) Proceedings, Austin, TX, December 3 – 5, 1986.

Malone, T., K. Grant, F. Turbak, S. Brobst, and M. Cohen, Intelligent Information-Sharing Systems, Communications of the ACM, 30(5), May, 1987.

Mantei, M.M. and D.L. McCracken, Issue Analysis with ZOG, A Highly Interactive Man-Machine Interface, in: Proceedings of the First International Symposium on Policy Analysis and Information Systems, 1979.

Marshall, Catherine C., Exploring Representation Problems Using Hypertext, in: Hypertext '87 Papers, Chapel Hill, NC, November 13 – 15, 1986.

Maxemchuck, N. F. and H. A. Wilder, Virtual Editing: I. The Concept, in: Proceedings of the Second International Workshop on Office Information Systems, Couvent Royal de St. Maximin, October 13 – 15, 1982.

McCracken, Donald L. and Robert Akscyn, Experience with the ZOG Human-Computer Interface System, International Journal of Man-Machine Studies, 21(2): 293 – 310, 1984.

McCracken, Donald L. and Robert Akscyn, The ZOG Approach to Database Management, CS-34-113, Carnegie-Mellon University, Pittsburgh, PA.

McQuillan, Patrick J., Computers and Pedagogy: The Invisible Presence, Journal of Computer-Based Educational Research, 1987.

Meyrowitz, N., Networks of Scholar's Workstations: End-User Computing in a University Community, IRIS Technical Report 85-3, Institute for Research in Information and Scholarship, Brown University, June 1985.

Meyrowitz, N., Intermedia: The Architecture and Construction of an Object-Oriented Hypertext/Hypermedia System and Applications Framework, in: Proc. OOPSLA '86, Portland, Oregon, Sept. 29 – Oct. 2, 1986.

Meyrowitz, N. and A. Van Dam, Interactive Editing Systems: Parts I and II, Computer Surveys, 14(3), ACM, Sept. 1982.

Michel, Stephen, Guide-A Hypertext Solution, CD-ROM Review, pp. 22 – 24, July/August 1987.

Mohl, R. F., Cognitive Space in the Interactive Movie Map: An Investigation of Spatial Learning in Virtual Environments, in: Ph.D. Dissertation, Department of Architecture, MIT, 1982.

Monty, M. L., Temporal Context and Memory for Notes Stored in the Computer, ACM SIGCHI Bulletin, 18(2): 50 – 51, October, 1986.

Monty, M. L. and T. P. Moran, A Longitudinal Study of Authoring Using NoteCards, ACM SIGCHI Bulletin, 18(2): 59 – 60, October, 1986.

Negroponte, N., An Idiosynchratic Systems Approach to Interactive Graphics, in: Paper presented at ACM/SIGGRAPH Workshop on User-Oriented Design of Interactive Graphics Systems, Pittsburgh, PA, Oct. 1976.

Negroponte, N., Books without Pages, IEEE International Conference on Communications IV, 1979.

Nelson, T.H., Literary Machines, T.H. Nelson, Swarthmore, PA, 1981.

Nelson, T.H., Replacing the Printed Word: A Complete Literary System, in: Information Processing 80, S.H. Lavington, ed., pp. 1013 – 1023, North-Holland Publishing Co., IFIO 1980.

Nelson, T.H., A File Structure for the Complex, the Changing and the Indeterminate, in: ACM, the 20th National Conference Proceedings, pp. 84 – 100, New York, 1965.

Nelson, T.H., Getting it Out of our System, in: Information Retrieval: A Critical View, G. Schecter, ed., pp. 191 – 210, Thompson Book Co., Washington, D.C., 1967.

Nelson, T.H., As We Will Think, in: Online 72: Conf. Proc. ... Int. Conf. on Online Interactive Computing, Brunel University, Uxbridge, England, vol. 1 D Sept. 1972, pp. 439 – 454, Online Computer Ltd., Uxbridge, England, 1973.

Nelson, T.H., A Conceptual Framework for Man-Machine Everything, in: The Proc. of the AFIPS National Computer Conference and Exposition, vol. 42, pp. M21 – M26, AFIPS Press, Montvale, New Jersey, 1973.

Nelson, T.H., Dream Machines: New Freedoms through Computer Screens - A Minority Report, in: Issued with Computer Lib: You Can and Must Understand Computers Now, Hugo's Book Service, Chicago, IL, 1974.

Nelson, Theodor H., The Hypertext, in: Proceedings International Documentation Federation Annual Conference, 1965.

Nelson, Theodor H., A New Home for the Mind, Datamation, pp. 169 – 180, March, 1982.

Newell, A., Donald McCracken, G. Robertson, and R. Akscyn, ZOG and the USS CARL VINSON, Computer Science Research Review, pp. 95 – 118, 1981.

Oddy, R. N., et al., Browsing through databases, in: Information Retrieval Research, Andrew J. Palay and Mark S. Fox, eds., Butterworths, London, 1981.

Oren, Tim, The Architecture of Hypertexts, in: Hypertext '87 Papers, Chapel Hill, NC, November 13 – 15, 1987.

Pasquier, Jacques, The Method and Model Base of the Electronic Book: Markov Chains and Reliability Modelling, Technical Report, Institute for Automation and Operations Research, University of Fribourg (Switzerland), June 1986.

Pereira, Fernando C.N., and Stuart M. Shieber; Prolog and Natural-Language Analysis. Center for the Study of Language and Information, CSLI, Lecture Notes No. 10. Stanford, 1987. (see pp. 27 – 28).

Pontecorvo, Michael S., A Hypermedia Multiple Perspective Mechanism, in: Hypertext '87 Papers, Chapel Hill, NC, November 13 – 15, 1987.

Psotka, J., L. D. Massey, and S. A. Mutter, The Instructional Design Environment, in: Intelligent Tutoring Systems: Lessons Learned, D. M. Russell, T. P. Moran, and D. S. Jordan, eds., Lawrence Erlbaum Associates, Hillsdale, NJ, in press.

Ragland, Craig, Hypertext, Hypermedia, and the Macintosh, in: MacA.P.P.L.E., August, 1987.

Ramakrishna, K., Schematization as an Aid to Organizing ZOG Information Nets, in: Ph.D. dissertation, Computer Science Department, Carnegie-Mellon University, 1981.

Raskin, Jef, The Hype in Hypertext: A Critique, in: Hypertext '87 Papers, Chapel Hill, NC, November 13 – 15, 1987.

Raymond, Darrell R., Personal Data Structuring in Videotex, in: Hypertext '87 Papers, University of Waterloo, Department of Computer Science Technology, Chapel Hill, NC, November 13 – 15, 1987.

Reese, W.L. Dictionary of Philosophy and Religion: eastern and western thought. [see Reification: From the Latin res ("things") and facere ("to make"). The fallacy of regarding a mental entity as though it were a thing], p . 485. Humanities Press, New Jersey, 1980.

Reitman, W., R. Roberts, R. Sauvain, D. Wheeler, and W. Lynn, AUTONOTE - A Personal Information Storage and Retrieval System, in: Proc. of the 24th National Conf. of the ACM, 1969.

Rich, Elaine; "Artificial Intelligence." See section on ABSTRIPS (ABstract STRIPS) in "8.1.5 Hierarchical Planning," on page 270. McGraw-Hill, Inc. Series in Artificial Intelligence, 1983.

Rittel, Horst; Some Principles on the Design of an Educational System for Design. DMG Newsletter, V.4, #12, Dec. 1970. V.5, #1, Jan. 1971. Sage Pubs. Inc. Cal., USA DMG-DRS Journal: Design Research and Methods, V.7., #2, Apr – Jun. 1973.

Rittel, H. & Webber, Melvin; Dilemmas in The General Theory of Planning. Modification of a paper presented to the panel on policy Sciences, American Association for the Advancement of Science, Boston, Dec. 1969. Reprint # 86, Inst. of Urban and Regional Development, UCBerkeley, 1972. Policy Sciences 4 (1973), pp. 155 – 169, Elsevier Scientific Pub, Co. Amsterdam.

Rittel, Horst, On the Planning Crisis: Systems Analysis of the First and Second Generation. BEDRIFTOKONOMEN # 8., pp. 390 – 396.

Rittel, Horst W. J.; APIS: a concept for an argumentative planning information system. Working paper # 324, Institute of Urban and Regional Development, CED-UCBerkeley, 1980.

Rittel, Horst W. J.; Lecture Notes, Architecture 130: Introduction to Design Theories and Methods. Department of Architecture, College of Environmental Design, University of California, Berkeley, Spring 1987.

Robertson, C., D. McCracken, and A. Newell, The ZOG Approach to Man-Machine Communication, Technical Report CMU-CS-79-148, Department of Computer Science, Carnegie-Mellon University, Pittsburgh, PA, Oct. 1979.

Robertson, C., A. Newell, and Ramakrishna, ZOG: A Man-Machine Communication Philosophy, Technical Report, Department of Computer Science, Carnegie-Mellon University, Pittsburgh, PA, 1977.

Robertson, C., D. McCracken, and A. Newell, Experimental Evaluation of the ZOG Frame Editor, Technical Report CMU-CS-81-112, Department of Computer Science, Carnegie-Mellon University, Pittsburgh, PA, April, 1981.

Russell, Bertrand, (1872 – 1970); An inquiry into meaning and truth Baltimore: Penguin Books, 1965.

Salamon, R., B. Blum, and M. Jorgensen, A Framework for the Use of Computed Links in the EXPLORER-1 Knowledge Management System, in: MEDINFO 86, IFIP-IMIA, L. T. Nguyen and R. A. Greenes, eds., pp. 891 – 894, Elsevier Science Publishers B.V., North-Holland, 1986.

Schank, Roger, with Peter Childers; The Creative Attitude: learning to ask and answer the right questions. Macmillan Publishing Company, New York, 1988.

Schatz, B. R., Telesophy, Bell Laboratories, August 1984.

Schneiderman, B. and J. Morariu, The Interactive Encyclopedia System (TIES), Department of Computer Science, University of Maryland, College Park, MD, June 1986.

Schneiderman, Ben, User Interface Design for the Hyperties Electronic Encyclopedia, in: Hypertext '87 Papers, Chapel Hill, NC, November 13 – 15, 1987.

Schneiderman, Ben, User interface design and evaluation for an electronic encyclopedia, CS-Tech. Rep.-1819, Department of Computer Science, University of Maryland, College Park, MD, March, 1987.

Schneiderman, Ben, Philip Shafer, Roland Simon, and Linda Weldon, Display Strategies for Program Browsing: Concepts and an Experiment, CAR-Tech. Rep.-192, CS-Tech. Rep.-1635, Department of Computer Science, University of Maryland, College Park, MD, 1986.

Schneiderman, Ben; Designing the User Interface: Strategies for Effective Human-Computer Interaction. Addison-Wesley, 1987.

Seybold, P. B., Tymshare's Augment: Heralding a New Era, in: Seybold Report on Word Processing, vol. 1, pp. 1 – 16, Oct., 1978.

Shapiro, E., A First Look at Dayflo, Byte, 9(3): 81 – 86, March 1984.

Shasha, Dennis, NetBook-A Data Model to Support Knowledge Exploration, in: Proceedings of the Eleventh International Conference on Very Large Data Bases, Stockholm, August, 1985.

Smith, John B., Stephen P. Weiss, and Gordon J. Ferguson, A Hypertext Writing Environment and its Cognitive Basis, in: Hypertext '87 Papers, Chapel Hill, NC, November 13 – 15, 1987.

Smith, John B. and Stephen F. Weiss; An Overview of Hypertext, The Journal of the Communication of the ACM, Vol. 31, No. 7, July 1988, pp. 816 – 819.

Smith, John B., Stephen F. Weiss, Gordon J. Ferguson, Jay David Bolter, M. Lansam, and D. V. Beard, WE: A Writing Environment for Professionals, 86-025, University of North Carolina, Department of Computer Science, Chapel Hill, NC, August, 1986.

Smith, Karen E. and Stanley B. Zdonik, Intermedia: A Case Study of the Differences Between Relational and Object-Oriented Database Systems, in: Proceedings of the Conference on Object-Oriented Programming Systems, Languages, and Applications (OOPSLA '87), Orlando, FL, October 4–8, 1987.

Smith, L. C., Memex' as an Image Potentiality in Information Retrieval Research and Development, in: Information Retrieval Research, R. N. Oddy, et al., ed., pp. 345–369, Butterworths, London, 1981.

Smolensky, Paul, Brigham Bell, Barbara Fox, Roger King, and Clayton Lewis, Constraint-based Hypertext for Argumentation, in: Hypertext '87 Papers, Chapel Hill, NC, November 13–15, 1987.

Stefik, M., G. Foster, D. G. Bobrow, K. M. Oahn, S. Lanning, and Lucy Suchman, Beyond the Chalkboard: Using Computers to Support Collaboration and Problem Solving in Meetings, Communications of the ACM, 30(1), 1986.

Sterling, Leon and Ehud Shapiro; "The Art of Prolog: Advanced Programming Techniques." See section titled "Structured data and data abstraction," pp. 25–28. MIT Press Series in Logic Programming, MIT Press, Cambridge, MA, 1986.

Svibely, J. R. and J. W. Smith, A Prototypic Hypertext Information System for Pathologist, Informatics in Pathology, 1: 133–142, 1986.

Tanguay, David A., A General System for Managing Videotex Information Structures, CS-86-23, University of Waterloo, Department of Computer Science Technology, June 1986.

Tanimoto, Steven L.; "Hierarchical Planning" in "The Elements of Artificial Intelligence: An Introduction Using Lisp," pp. 167–168, Computer Science Press, Maryland, 1987.

Tanimoto, Steven L.; The Elements of Artificial Intelligence: An Introduction Using LISP. Computer Science Press, Inc., 1987.

Tennent, R. D.; "Chapter 7: Procedural Abstraction" in "Principles of Programming Languages." Prentice-Hall International Series in Computer Science, series editor C.A.R. Hoare, London, 1981.

Thompson, Bev and Bill Thompson, Hyping Text: Hypertext and Knowledge Representation, AI Expert, pp. 25–28, August, 1987.

Thorsen, Linda J. and Mark Bernstein, Developing Dynamic Documents: Special Challenges for Technical Communicators, in: Proceedings of the 34th International Technical Communications Conference, Denver, CO.

Thursh, D., F. Mabry, and A. H. Levy, Computers and Videodiscs in Pathology Education: ECLIPS as an Example of One Approach, Human Pathology, 17: 216–218, 1986.

Thursh, D. R. and F. Mabry, A Knowledge-Based System for Pathology Education, Bull. Pathology Education, 6(2): 36–45, Fall 1980.

Tompa, Frank Wm, Retrieving data through Telidon, in: Proceedings CIPS, 1982.

Tou, F., M. Williams, R. Fikes, D. A. Henderson, and T. Malone, RABBIT: An Intelligent Database Assistant, in: Proceedings of the American Association for Artificial Intelligence, Pittsburgh, August 16–20, 1982.

Trigg, R., A Network-based Approach to Text Handling for the On-line Scientific Community, in: Ph.D. Thesis (University Microfilms #8429934), University of Maryland, College Park, MD, 1983.

Trigg, R., L. Suchman, and F. Halasz, Supporting Collaboration in NoteCards, Conference on Computer-supported Cooperative Work Proceedings, Austin, Texas, December, 1986.

Trigg, Randall H. and Peggy M. Irish, Hypertext Habitats: Experiences of Writers in NoteCards, in: Hypertext '87 Papers, Chapel Hill, NC, November 13 – 15, 1987.

Trigg, Randall H., T. P. Moran, and Frank G. Halasz, Adaptability and Tailorability in NoteCards, in: Proceedings of INTERACT '87, Stuttgart, West Germany, 1987.

Trigg, Randall H. and M. Weiser, TEXTNET: A Network-Based Approach to Text Handling, ACM Transactions on Office Information Systems, 4(1): 1 – 23, January, 1986.

Trigg, Randall H.; A Network-based Approach to Text Handling for the Online Scientific Community, Ph.D. Thesis, University of Maryland, (University Micro-films # 8429934), 1983.

Turbo Prolog TOOLBOX: User Guide and Reference Manual. Borland International, Inc. 1987.

Van Dam, A., FRESS (File Retrieval and Editing System), in: Text Systems, Barrington, RI, July, 1971. Van Dam, A. and D. E. Rice, On-Line Text Editing: A Survey, Computing Surveys, 3(3): 93 – 114, Sept. 1971.

Van Dam, A. and D. E. Rice, Computers and Publishing: Writing, Editing and Printing, in: Advances in Computers, Academic Press, New York, 1970.

VanLehn, K., Theory Reform Caused by an Argumentation Tool, ISL-11, Xerox Palo Alto Research Center, 1985.

Vliet, J. C. von, A Simple Mechanism for Authorship of Dynamic Documents, in: Text Processing and Document Manipulation: Proceedings of the International Conference, Peter Brown, ed., pp. 34 – 42, Cambridge University Press, 1986.

Vliet, J. C. von, Concept Browser: A System for Interactive Creation of Dynamic Documentation, in: Text Processing and Document Manipulation: Proceedings of the International Conference, U. Corda and G. Facchetti, eds., Cambridge University Press, 1986.

Walker, D., Knowledge Resource Tools for Accessing Large Text Files, 85-21233-25, Bell Communications Research, 1985.

Walker, Janet H., Document Examiner: Delivery Interface for Hypertext Documents, in: Hypertext '87 Papers, Chapel Hill, NC, November 13 – 15, 1987.

Walker, Janet H., The Document Editor: A Support Environment for Preparing Technical Documents, in: Proceedings of the ACM SIGPLAN Notices/SIGOA Conference on Text Manipulation, June 1981.

Walker, Janet H., Symbolics Sage: A Documentation Support System, in: Intellectual Leverage: The Driving Technologies, IEEE Spring Compcon84, 1984.

Walker, Janet H. and R. L. Bryan, An Editor for Structured Technical Documents, in: Protext IV.

Weyer, Steven A., As We May Learn, in: Multimedia in Education: Interfaces to Knowledge—Education Advisory Council Conference Proceedings, April 1987.

Weyer, S. A., The Design of a Dynamic Book for Information Search, International Journal of Man-Machine Studies, pp. 87 – 107, 1982.

Weyer, S. A., Searching for Information in a Dynamic Book, Report SCG-1, Xerox Palo Alto Research Center, Palo Alto, CA, February 1982.

Weyer, S. A. and A. H. Borning, A Prototype Electronic Encyclopedia, ACM Transactions on Office Information Systems, 3(1): pp. 66 – 88, Jan. 1985.

White, J. E., A High-Level Framework for Network-based Resource Sharing, AFIPS Proceedings, National Computer Conference, New York, 1976.

Whitney, P. and C. Kent, Interactive Documents, in: Design in the Information Environment, S. Feiner, ed., pp. 118 – 132, Alfred Knopf, New York, 1985.

Wilder, H.A. and N.F. Maxemchuck, Virtual Editing: II. The User Interface, in: Proc. SIGOA chConf. Office Automation Systems, pp. 41 – 46, ACM, Philadelphia, PA, June 21 – 23, 1982.

Wilson, K. S., Palenque: An Interactive Multimedia Optical Disk Prototype for Children, Technical Report, Bank Street College of Education, Center for Children and Technology, New York, 1987.

Woods, W. A., What's in a Link: Foundations for Semantic Networks, in: Representation and Understanding: Studies in Cognitive Science, D. G. Bobrow and A. Collins, eds., Academic Press, New York, 1975.

Yankelovich, N., G. P. Landow, and D. Cody, Creating Hypermedia Materials for English Literature Students, Institute for Research in Information and Scholarship, and department of English, Brown University, Providence, RI, October, 1986.

Yankelovich, N., N. Meyrowitz, and A. Van Dam, Reading and Writing the Electronic Book, Computer, 18(10): 15 – 30, Oct. 1985.

Yankelovich, N., INTERMEDIA: System for Linking Multimedia Documents, IRIS Technical Report 86-2, Institute for Research in Information and Scholarship, Brown University, Providence, RI, 1986.

Yankelovich, Nicole and et al., The Sampler Companion: Four Educational Software Samples, in: Proceedings of Frontiers in Education Fifth Annual Conference, Golden, CO, October 19 – 22, 1985.

Yankelovich, Nicole, Bernard Hann, and Noeman Meyrowitz, Intermedia: The Concept and the Construction of a Seamless Information Environment, IEEE Computer, January 1988.

Yankelovich, Nicole, George P. Landow, and Peter Heywood, Designing Hypermedia 'Ideabases'-The Intermedia Experience, IRIS Technical Report, Institute for Research in Information and Scholarship, Brown University, Providence, RI, 1987.

Yankelovich, Nicole and Andries van Dam, Spinning Scholarly Webs: The Annenberg/CPB Project Report to Higher Education, The Annenberg/CPB Project, Washington, D.C., 1987.

Young, J. S., Hypermedia, MacWorld, 3(3): 116 – 121, March 1986.

B

MicroIBIS: A User Guide

Whether you run MicroIBIS from a directory on a hard disk, or on a floppy disk, you should have the following files in the same directory:

ibis.exe	
ndialog.scr	
nodeinfo.scr	
ibis.sys	(if any)
prolog.err	(if any)
$++++++++.ibs	(if any)

The first three files are basic to all MicroIBIS operations. The file "ibis.sys" contains the knowledge-base for the system setup attributes. MicroIBIS generates "ibis.sys" when it executes the "Setup/Save new setup" option from the main menu. Version 1.0 of MicroIBIS is a prototype, not a final product. The system is not fully debugged. For this reason you might get some unexpected problems. To report on these problems, the system will need the "prolog.err" file.

The "prolog.err" file comes with your Turbo Prolog system. The "++++++++.ibs" file refers to any of your IBIS database files. In the current version of MicroIBIS, your IBIS database files should be in the same directory with "nodeinfo.scr" and "ndialog.scr." That's all there is to it folks! You are all set up to solve your problems with MicroIBIS. If you have any comment or suggestion, you may write to me at the following address:

Reader Inquiry Branch
Windcrest Books
Imprint of TAB BOOKS
Blue Ridge Summit, PA 17294-0850

I hope to hear from you. Have fun with MicroIBIS! In the rest of this guide, I give a general overview of the basic functions in MicroIBIS. I start with Files menu.

Note on the Notation for Selecting Menu Options. In this book, when you want to execute a menu option you use a special notation to indicate the command sequence to do that. For example, to create a new IBIS file, you write:

```
(Files/New)
```

which means that you should choose the "New" option from the "Files" submenu.

The Files Menu (Files)

All your operations on IBIS database files must go through this menu, so take these operations one by one.

Creating a New IBIS File (Files/New). To create a new IBIS file, you choose the "New" option. MicroIBIS issues a message to inform you that it has successfully created the file. It will wait for you to hit any key before it continues. After you hit a key, it will prompt you with a dialogue box. In this dialogue box you should enter the attributes for the main (root) issue.

The node attributes dialogue box has three fields:

Name: (enter here name of person raising the issue)
Date: (enter here date, for example 12-23-1988)
Knowledge Type: (i.e., factual, conceptual, and so on.)

You will notice that MicroIBIS has entered a date for you in the "Date" field. This is the system's date—you can change this if you want to. To move around in the dialogue box you can use these command keys:

Move left one col	left arrow or spacebar
Move right one col	right arrow
Erase one character to the left	spacebar
Erase one character to the right	BACKSPACE or CTRL-H
Move one field up	up arrow
Move one field down	down arrow
Move to first field	HOME
Move to last field	END
End and accept attributes	ESC or F10

After you exit the dialogue box, MicroIBIS puts you in the IBIS-EDITOR to enter your main issue. When entering the text for the main issue, try to be brief. If you have extra reference material that should go with the main issue, use the "Relations" menu to create a link to a reference node.

Loading an Existing IBIS File (Files/Load file). When you load an existing IBIS file, MicroIBIS opens the file and puts you in the IBIS-MAP mode. The cursor will be in the upper left corner of the IBIS-MAP window. Refer to the "viewing the IBIS road map: the Map option" section, for operating in the IBIS-MAP mode.

When you load an IBIS file, MicroIBIS automatically opens the database file for reading and writing. Also, MicroIBIS allows you only to work on one file at a time. So, when you load a new file while working on a current one, MicroIBIS will automatically close the current file before it opens the new one.

Saving an IBIS File (Files/Save and Files/sAve as). Generally you don't need to use the Files/Save command. MicroIBIS automatically updates the database file for you. Whenever you create or delete nodes and links, the system will record these changes directly. So, when you load a new file, or quit MicroIBIS, the file will have all the changes you made in the session.

With the "File/sAve as" option, you can save the current state of your IBIS file to another file. You can use this option to create backup copies of your IBIS files.

IMPORTANT NOTICE! I recommend using the "File/sAve as" option on a regular basis to safeguard against any unexpected system breakdown.

Directory of IBIS Files (Files/Directory). This is similar to the DOS directory command, except that it only lists the files with the "ibs" extension.

Exit Temporarily to DOS (Files/Operating system). You use this option when you need to give DOS commands, or execute other programs. To go back to MicroIBIS you should type "exit" at the DOS prompt.

Writing the Knowledge-Base to a Text File (Files/Write KB to Xfile). With this option you can view the actual knowledge-base for a particular IBIS problem. The system will prompt you to enter a name for the text file to which it will write the knowledge-base. After it finishes writing the knowledge-base to your file, you can exit to DOS to view that file. You will notice that the knowledge-base has two sections. The first section has one object—the "ibis" object. Following the "ibis" object section is the nodes section. In this section there will be a list of all the "node" objects in your IBIS file.

Print the IBIS File (Files/Print). To get a hardcopy or a text file of your current IBIS, you choose this option. When you do, you will see another menu with two options: Printer (Files/Print/Printer) and File (Files/Print/File). Use the Printer option to send the output directly to the printer. Use the File option to get a text file of your current IBIS database file. Later you can enter this text file in your favorite word processor to edit and print your final IBIS report.

Quit MicroIBIS (Files/Quit). You use this option to end MicroIBIS and exit to DOS.

Operations on Nodes: The Nodes Option

Once you create or load an IBIS file, you can use this menu to operate on a single node.

Loading a Node in the IBIS-EDITOR Window (Nodes/Load node). This option prompts you for the name of a node to load in the IBIS-EDITOR. If you hit the ENTER key, MicroIBIS will display a menu of names for the nodes in the IBIS file. When you choose a node, the system will load this node in the IBIS-EDITOR. To edit the node, you choose the Edit option from the main menu.

Saving a Node (Nodes/Save node). You use this option to save the changes you made to a node before loading a new node.

Deleting a Node and its IBIS Sub-tree (Nodes/Delete node). When you choose this option, MicroIBIS will delete the current node and all the nodes linked to it.

Viewing the Node Attributes (Files/Attributes). You use this option to know the author, date, node-type and knowledge-type of the current node. MicroIBIS displays a dialogue box at the top of your screen with four fields: node-type, knowledge-type, author's name, and date. You can change attribute values in these fields. When you exit the attributes dialogue box, MicroIBIS saves the changes you made to the IBIS file. To move around in the attributes dialogue box, use the following command keys:

Move left one col	left arrow or spacebar
Move right one col	right arrow
Erase one character to the left	spacebar
Erase one character to the right	BACKSPACE or CTRL-H
Move one field up	up arrow
Move one field down	down arrow
Move to first field	HOME
Move to last field	END
End and accept attributes	ESC or F10

Directory of Nodes in an IBIS File (Nodes/Nodes dir). This option is currently inactive. I use this option as an exercise for programming menu options in Turbo Prolog. If you are interested in adding this option, you can still view the directory of nodes by using the "Nodes/Load new" option. When the system prompts you for a node name, just press ENTER. As a result you will get a menu of all the node names in your IBIS file. To exit this menu without loading a node press ESC.

The IBIS-Editor: The Edit Option

You choose this option to edit the text of a node in the IBIS-EDITOR window. The IBIS-EDITOR uses Turbo Prolog's built-in editor. This editor is a WordStar-compatible editor. The status line at the top of the IBIS-EDITOR window informs you about the text you are editing. It tells you the position of your cursor, the editing mode you are in, and the name of the IBIS node you are editing. See FIG. B-1 for the top-of-window status line. Also in the same figure you can read about the meaning of each indicator on that line.

There is another status line at the bottom of the screen. I will refer to this status line as the system's status line. In the editor mode, the system's status line reminds you of those editor command keys that you need most (see FIG. B-2).

Here is a brief description of the commands appearing in the system's status line:

F1-Help	get help on the editor commands

Node-type	Line	Col	Node-ID	Insert	Indent	Text-mode

Status	Description
Node-type	Indicate the type of node you are editing, which could be one of these types: issue, position, argument, and reference.
Line	Shows which line number of your cursor.
Col	Shows which column number of your cursor.
Node-ID	This is the label of the node as it appears in the nodes directory or the IBIS-MAP window. For example, the root issue ID will be I1, the first position from the root issue would be I1P1, and so on.
Insert	Tells you that the editor is in Insert mode; your keyboard input will be inserted at the current cursor position. Use Ins key or Ctrl-V to toggle the editor between Insert mode and Overwrite mode. In Overwrite mode, your keyboard input will overwrite characters currently at your cursor position, your input will not be inserted before the existing text.
Indent	This indicator tells you that the autoindent feature is set On. You toggle it off and on with the command Ctrl-Q-I.
Text mode	This tells you whether text mode (word-wrap mode) is on. You toggle it off and on with the command Ctrl-Q-W.

Fig. B-1. The top-of-window status line in IBIS-EDITOR.

F2-Xsave	save text of a node to an external file
F3-Load	load an external text file in the current node
F4-Replace	replace text
F5-Zoom	zoom the IBIS-EDITOR window to full screen
F7-Xcopy	copy a block of text from an external file
F8-Xedit	call the auxiliary editor
(F10 or ESC)-End	end editing and return to the main menu

As I said earlier, IBIS-EDITOR uses WordStar-like commands. If you are not familiar with WordStar commands, you can use F1 to get help on which command does what. For your reference I list all the function commands keys in TABLE B-1. For a complete set of commands, refer to TABLE B-2.

Auxiliary Editor. When you are in the IBIS-EDITOR window, you can invoke the Auxiliary editor in one of two modes: In Xcopy mode, to copy blocks from an external file, which you invoke by pressing F7; in Xedit mode, to edit a

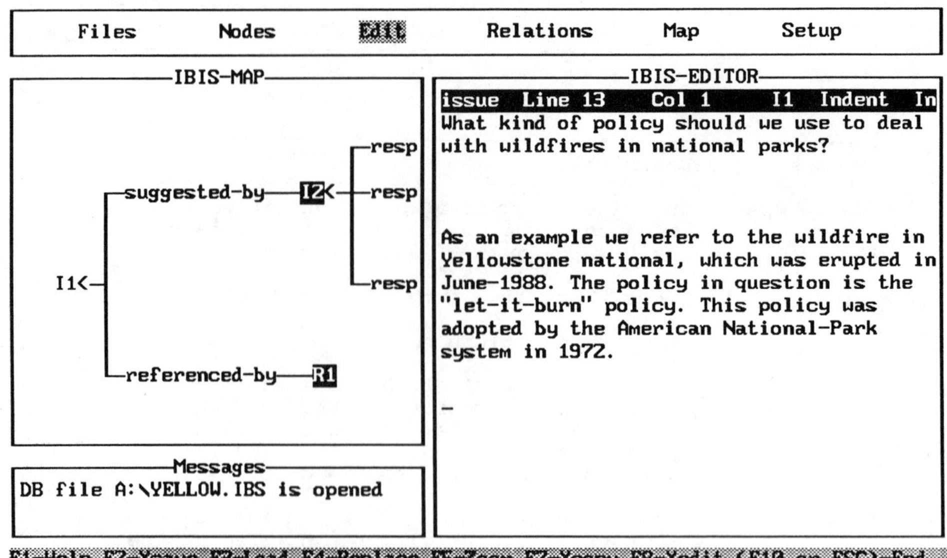

Fig. B-2. The system's status line in IBIS-EDITOR mode.

Table B-1. The Editor (Function) Command Keys.

Key	Function
F1	Call up online Help
F2	Save node in IBIS-EDITOR window to Xfile
F3	Load an external text file in the current node
F4	Replace text
F5	Zoom the IBIS-EDITOR Window
F6	No effect
F7	Copy from the Auxiliary Editor (Xcopy)
F8	Invoke the Auxiliary editor (Xedit)
F9	No effect
F10	End IBIS-EDITOR and return to main menu

Table B-2. A Complete List of IBIS-Editor Commands.

Basic Cursor Movement Commands			
Character left	Ctrl-S	or	Left arrow
Character right	Ctrl-D	or	Right arrow
Word left	Ctrl-A		
Word right	Ctrl-F		
Line up	Ctrl-E	or	Up
Line down	Ctrl-X	or	Down
Scroll up	Ctrl-W		
Scroll down	Ctrl-Z		
Page up	Ctrl-R	or	PgUp
Page down	Ctrl-C	or	PgDn

(**Table B-2.** continued)

Quick Cursor Movement Commands			
Beginning of line	Ctrl-Q-S	or	Home
End of line	Ctrl-Q-D	or	End
Top of window	Ctrl-Home		
Bottom of window	Ctrl-End		
Top of file	Ctrl-Q-R	or	K<Ctrl-PgUp>
End of file	Ctrl-Q-C	or	K<Ctrl-PgDn>
Beginning of block	Ctrl-Q-B		
End of block	Ctrl-Q-K		
Last cursor postion	Ctrl-Q-P		
Go to line …	Ctrl-Q-L		
Go to position …			Shift-F2

Insert and Delete Commands			
Insert mode on/off	Ctrl-V	or	Ins
Insert line	Ctrl-N		
Delete line	Ctrl-Y		
Delete to end of line	Ctrl-Q-Y		
Delete character left of cursor	Ctrl-H	or	Backspace
Delete character under cursor	Ctrl-G	or	Del
Delete word right of cursor	Ctrl-T		

Block Commands			
Mark block-being	Ctrl-K-B		
Mark block-end	Ctrl-K-K		
Copy block	Ctrl-K-C	or	Ctrl-F5
Copy to printer	Ctrl-K-P		
Delete block	Ctrl-K-Y		
Undo delete block	K<Ctrl-K-U>	or	K<Ctrl-F7>
Hide/display block	Ctrl-K-H	or	Alt-F7
Move block	Ctrl-K-V	or	Alt-F6
Read block from file	Ctrl-K-R	or	F7
Write block to file	Ctrl-K-W	or	Alt-F5
case change	Ctrl-K-E	or	Ctrl-F6

Miscellaneous Commands			
Autoindent on/off	Ctrl-Q-I	or	Alt-I
Control character prefix	Ctrl-P		
Find	Ctrl-Q-F	or	Ctrl-F3
Find and replace	Ctrl-Q-A	or	F4
Find and replace again	Ctrl-O	or	Shift-F4
Find place marker	Ctrl-Q-N		
Insert mode	Ctrl-V	or	Ins
Return to main menu	Ctrl-K-D	or	F10
Load file			F3
Lowercase word	Ctrl-B-L		
Quit edit, no save	Ctrl-K-D		
Repeat last find	Ctrl-L, Ctrl-Q-L	or	Shift-F3
Reverse case of word	Ctrl-B-R		
Save and continue editing	Ctrl-K-N		F2
Tab insert	Ctrl-I Ctrl-O	or	Tab
Text mode	Ctrl-Q-W		
uppercase word	Ctrl-B-U		

Table B-3. Commands for the Auxiliary Editor's Modes.

Hot Key	Xcopy	Xedit
F1	No effect	Online Help
F2	No effect	Save text in Xedit window
F3	No effect	Load a file into Xedit
F4	No effect	Replace text
F5	Zoom Xcopy window	Zoom Xedit window
F6	No effect	No effect
F7	Mark block begin/end	Invoke Xcopy window
F8	No effect	Invoke another Xedit window
F10	Mark block end; End Xcopy	Save text to a file

secondary text file while in the IBIS-EDITOR window. In TABLE B-3, I give a summary of the hotkeys available for the Auxiliary editor's two modes.

Extending the IBIS Tree: The Relations Option

You use this option to respond to the current node. The Relations menu lists all possible links that you can have with the current node. In MicroIBIS, I assume that the current node is the target node and the newly created node is the source node. For example, if your current node is an issue and you want to take a position from that issue, you can pick the "responds-to" link. In this case, the issue node will be the target node and the position node is the source node. Here is a sketch of this process:

issue(I) <——— responds-to ——— position(P)

Actually, this graphical representation is what you will see when you choose the Map option from the main menu.

The Relations menu is context-dependent. In other words, The contents of the Relations menu depends on the type of your current node. So, for each node-type (issue, position, argument, or reference) you will see a different Relations menu. Take a look at FIG. B-3, you will see the four relation menus.

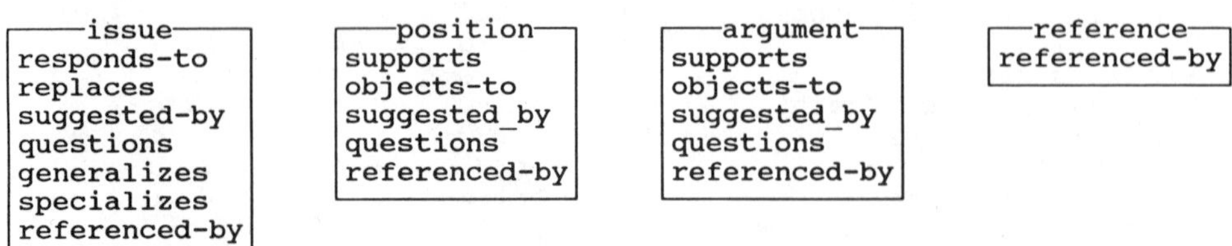

Fig. B-3. The four "relations" menus of MicroIBIS

Viewing the IBIS Road Map: The Map Option

You enter the IBIS-MAP mode by choosing the Map option from the main menu. When you do so, MicroIBIS puts you in the IBIS-MAP window, with the cursor at the upper-left corner. Also, at the bottom of the screen the system's status line changes to reflect the new mode. The status line reminds you of those command keys active in the IBIS-MAP mode. FIGURE B-4 shows the system's status line (shaded) in the IBIS-MAP mode. Oh! One last thing about the status line: Currently, the F1 command in the status line has no effect.

Also, you can refer to TABLE B-4 for a complete list of all command keys active in the IBIS-MAP mode.

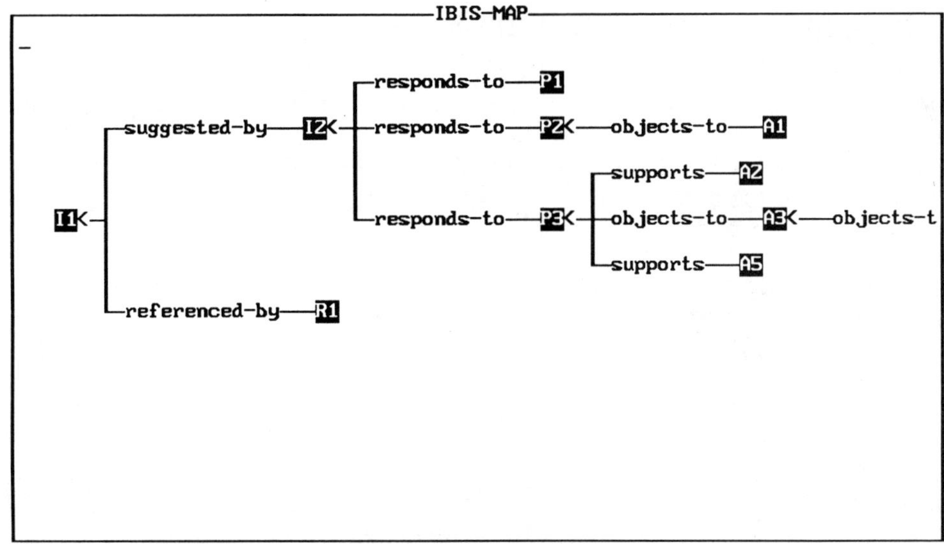

Fig. B-4. The system's status line in the IBIS-MAP mode.

Table B-4. Summary of Commands Active in IBIS-MAP Window.

Description	Command Key
Move up one row	Up
Move down one row	Down
Move left one column	Left
Move one column	Right
Move up fast	PgUp
Move down fast	PgDn
Move left fast	Ctrl-Left
Move right fast	Ctrl-Right
Select/Load node (node under cursor)	Return
Invoke hypertext menu (node under cursor)	F10
Zoom window	F5
End IBIS-MAP	ESC

There are two important things you need to know about the IBIS-MAP mode:

1) selecting a node: to select a node, you move the cursor to that node and press ENTER. When you do so, MicroIBIS will load the text for that node in the IBIS-EDITOR window.

2) Operating on a node: to add, delete, or view attributes of a node, you move the cursor to that node and press F10. When you do so, MicroIBIS will display the hypertext menu. The options on this menu are similar to those on the Nodes submenu on the main menu. The hypertext menu is a more convenient way to interact with your IBIS while in the IBIS-MAP. You don't need to go out to the main menu to add or delete nodes.

Configuring IBIS: The Setup Option

Part of the user-interface design in MicroIBIS is the ability to customize it. The first time you bring up MicroIBIS, you will notice the default setup. You can change the default setup by choosing the Setup option from the main menu. As you can see in FIG. B-5, there are things that you can change: The attributes dialogue box switch, colors, and window sizes. So look now at each one of these separately.

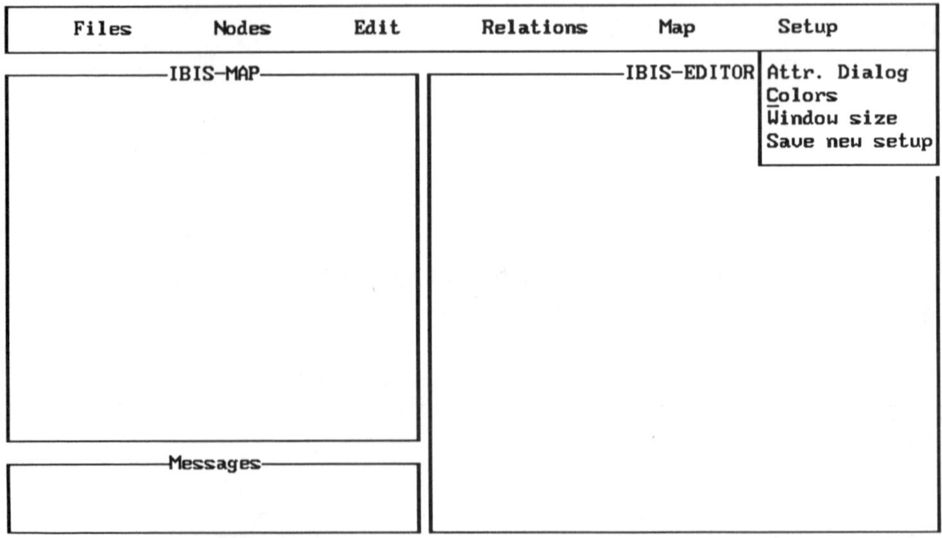

Fig. B-5. The Setup menu of MicroIBIS.

The Attributes Dialogue Box Toggle Switch. Part of MicroIBIS's default setup is the manual calling of the attributes dialogue box. Remember that when you create a new IBIS file, the system will automatically bring up the attribute dialogue box for you. Then, all you need to do is fill in the node attributes—but, other than that, every time you create a new node, you have to bring up the attributes dialogue box manually. Of course, you do that by choosing the "Nodes/Attributes" option from the main menu, or you can use the Attributes option from the hypertext menu while in the IBIS-MAP mode.

You can make the system bring the attributes dialogue box automatically for you every time you create a new node. To do that you choose the "Setup/Attr Dialog" option. What you will get is a submenu with two options: "Show" and "Hide." What you have here is actually a toggle switch. To make the attributes dialogue box come up automatically, choose the "Show" option. On the other hand, to suppress the attributes dialogue box choose the "Hide" option. To try the switch, change it to "Show." Then, go to the "Relations" menu and create a new node and see what happens. The attributes dialogue box will come up automatically. Fill in the fields and exit by pressing ESC or F10. Next, go back to the "Setup" menu once more. This time change the "Attr Dialog" switch to "Hide." Now create a new node, and notice what happens. Well, there is no attributes dialogue box up there—you suppressed it. Got it? Move now to the next option on the Setup menu.

Changing Colors. In the default setup of MicroIBIS, you only use two colors (black and white) for all the windows, menus and status lines. If you want to change this, you choose the "Setup/Colors" option from the main menu. As a result, you will get the Colors submenu. From this menu, you can choose to change the colors of one of these items:

Editor window
Message window
Road-map window
Pull-down menu
Status line
Dialogue box window

Now say that you wanted to change the colors of the editor window. So, you choose "Editor." Next, MicroIBIS will ask you if you want to change the screen colors or the window frame colors. After you make your choice, you will see a color chart with a box-shaped cursor. Use the arrow keys to move the cursor around the color chart. The Status line at the bottom of the screen will explain how to select a color from the chart (use the arrow keys). It will also tell you how to end the selection process (press F10). The colors in the IBIS-EDITOR will change to reflect the changes you made in the color chart. Fun, isn't it! Have fun coloring your MicroIBIS.

Resizing Windows. In MicroIBIS there are three system windows—these are: the IBIS-EDITOR window, the IBIS-MAP window, and the Message window. In the default setup these windows are *tiled*—i.e., placed next to each other. To move and resize any one of the three system windows, you choose the "Setup/Window size" option. When you do so, you will get another submenu. From this submenu, you can choose a particular window to move or resize. When you are resizing a window, the status line at the bottom of the screen tells you which key(s) do what. I include a complete list of these keys and their function in TABLE B-5.

Saving the Configuration to "ibis.sys". Once you are satisfied with the new setup, you can save this setup by choosing the "Setup/Save new setup" option. When you do so, MicroIBIS saves the new setup in the "ibis.sys" file. After you have saved your setup, exit temporarily to DOS and see for yourself. Remember, you exit temporarily to DOS by choosing the "Files/Operating Sys-

Table B-5. The Command Key(s) for Resizing a System Window.

Key(s) Function	Command key
contract/expand the chosen window at normal speed	Arrow keys
contract/expand the chosen window at fast speed	Ctrl_Arrow keys
reposition the window left, right, up, or down	Shift-Arrow keys
expand the window to the right screen edge	End
expand the window to the left screen edge	Home
move the window to the right screen edge	Shift-End
move the window to the left screen edge	Shift-Home
move the window to the top right screen corner	Ctrl-End
move the window to the top left screen corner	Ctrl-Home
end the resizing session for that window	F10

tem" option. Next time you run MicroIBIS, it will use "ibis.sys" to initialize the system instead of the default setup. An important thing to remember here, "ibis.sys" must always be in the same directory with the "ibis.exe" file.

C

Glossary of Terms

abstractions—In the Webster's New Collegiate Dictionary the word "abstract" means "1 a: disassociated from any specific instance, not an entity. 2: expressing a quality apart from an object <the word poem is concrete, poetry is not>." In hypertext we use abstractions to structure and give meaning to the textual, visual, and audible data. Abstractions transform data into information. Without the ability to generate, store, and retrieve abstractions, wouldn't be able to make sense of the data stored in the computer. Abstractions are the building blocks of recognition, understanding, and thinking.

anonymous variable—There are two kinds of variables in Prolog: regular and anonymous variables. A *regular variable* is a name with the first character being an uppercase letter or an underscore ("_"). You use regular variables in goals and subgoals to return atom and compound-objects matched by these variables. An *anonymous variable*, on the other hand, is a lone underscore ("_"). You use "_" in goals and subgoals to tell Turbo Prolog that you are not interested in returning any matching atoms or compound-objects.

arguments—The elements of a Prolog relationship. An argument can be a variable, a compound-object, a number, or an atom (a string, symbol, or a char).

argument (in Prolog)—In Turbo Prolog, an argument is just an element of a Prolog relation (see definition of arguments above).

argument (in Issue Based Information Systems theory)—An argument is a statement (made up of a number of propositions) which you can use either to support, or object to, a position (answer) from an issue (question).

argumentation—A process that uses formal (logical) and informal (rhetorical) reasoning to answer controversial questions. In this book I use hypertext to support the argumentation process to help resolve issues that are hard to solve using the traditional systems approach.

atom—There are four kinds of constants in Turbo Prolog: numbers, compound-objects, characters, and atoms. An atom can either be a STRING or a SYMBOL. In general, Prolog atoms are groups of characters that are treated as a single entity. A disadvantage of atoms is that memory for the characters is allocated precisely once, and never freed. This makes it faster to compare the numbers to which the atoms are mapped than it would be to compare the atoms.

attribute—From the Latin ad ("to") and tribuere ("ascribe"). Thus attribute is that which is ascribed to a thing. Aristotle, the Greek philosopher (384-322 B.C.), first used attribute as part of his concept of the world of things. For Aristotle, the world divides into individual substances and attributes of those substances. The attributes of something could be properties, differences, and similarities that distinguish one thing from another. In Prolog, to represent attributes of objects you can use the relationship "attribute(OBJname,ATTRname,ATTRvalue)."

backtracking—A built-in mechanism of Prolog such that when successfully executing a subgoal and returning an answer, Prolog returns to a previous subgoal and tries to resolve it in a different way.

blackboard systems—A knowledge representation approach in which several representations are used in a single knowledge system.

bound variable—A variable which Prolog assigns a known value.

browser—A display window in which hypertext systems show all items that make a hypertext document. The items in the browser could be in the form of a hierarchical list of item names. In graphical browsers the items are nodes, represented by icons, and linked together in a network structure. The main interaction with browser is by Mouse. Using the mouse, the user can inspect, edit, move, add, or delete items.

built-in predicate—A predicate defined internally in Prolog.

clauses section—Turbo Prolog's part of the program containing facts and rules. To signal the start of the clauses section you put the keyword "CLAUSES" at the beginning of the section.

computer-supported cooperative work—Field of research which deals with the development of computer tools that support the style of working in groups.

Computer-Aided Software Engineering (CASE)—This is the field of developing tools to support the software development activities such as requirements analysis, specifications, design, assessment, coding, building, testing, quality assurance, maintenance, project management, and project communication.

domains section—Turbo Prolog's object-types declarations section. The keyword "DOMAINS" signals the start of the domain section.

Decision Support System (DSS)—A program that helps the decision maker collect and analyze information according to a certain problem solving approach. For example, IBIS is a decision support system which gives the decision maker an idea of the major issues involved, the positions from these issues and pros and cons of those positions. Decision Support Systems often use knowledge representation techniques in their operation. For example, MicroIBIS uses Logic Programming in Turbo Prolog for its knowledge representation. Another example of knowledge representation suitable for DSS is blackboard systems.

decision theory—Originally it was started as a branch of probability theory concerned with methods of making optimal decisions in a state of incomplete information. Currently there are new approaches in decision theory that include not only incomplete information but also inexact or fuzzy information, this is the approach based on the theory of fuzzy sets and fuzzy logic developed by Lotfi Zadeh at the University of California, Berkeley. A third approach to decision theory emphasizes on the consequential nature of information in making decisions. The third approach is developed by Horst Rittel at the University of California at Berkeley.

declarative languages—Programming style in which you state (declare) what is computed rather than prescribe how to compute something. Prolog is a declarative programming language, but C is a procedural (prescriptive) language.

delimiters—In hypertext, delimiters are symbols that you use to signal the start and end of hyper-words and hyper-regions. In this book I used braces "{" and "}" as the hypertext delimiters.

design—According to Horst Rittel "design is an activity aiming at the production of a plan which, if implemented, is expected to lead to a situation with certain desired characteristics and without unforeseen, undesirable side effects.

expert systems—A program that uses rules of thumb to capture the knowledge of human experts in particular domains. An example of expert systems is MYCIN, a knowledge system developed at Stanford University in the mid-70s for the diagnosis and treatment of meningitis and bacteremia infections.

fact—A ground relation between objects representing something that exists or a relation that is true. The relation is a fact.

fail—A built-in Prolog predicate which as a subgoal causes Prolog failure and possibly backtracking to a previous subgoal.

flow pattern—A descriptive form showing whether the predicate parameters are only input, only output, or both input and output parameters. For example, the predicate member(ELEMENT,LIST) has these valid flow patterns: (o,i) and (i,i).

free variable—A variable that currently doesn't have a value assigned to it by Prolog.

functor—The name of a compound object, e.g., attribute (john, profession, actor), the word "attribute" is a functor.

GUIDE—OWL International hypertext system for Macintosh and IBM personal computers. In contrast to Apple's HyperCard (which has been available to users only since August, 1987), GUIDE has been used since 1985.

gIBIS—A graphical hypertext-based implementation of the IBIS methodology developed at Microelectronics and Computer technology Corporartion (MCC) by Jeff Conklin and Michael Begeman.

goal—A Prolog query that could be made of one or more subgoals.

groupware—Programs that support the problem solving process in groups. Groupware must deal with communication problems arising from different members of the group interacting with each other at the same time. Also there is the problem of who has the ground.

Horn clauses—A special form of logical clauses in which there is at most one conclusion (the Head of the clause) and zero or more conditions (subgoals) in the body of the clause. They are called Horn clauses, because they were first studied by the logician Alfred Horn in 1951.

Houdini—MaxThink Inc.'s hypertext system.

hypothesis—From the Greek hypo ("under") and tithenai ("to put")—in English this means "a foundation or supposition." The word Hypothesis is often used to refer to an explanation which, based on the degree of our confidence and confirmation, could become an accepted theory or law.

HyperCard—Apple Computers Inc. hypertext system for the Macintosh, developed by Bill Atkinson and modeled after XEROX PARC's NoteCard.

HyperLink—The built-in scripting language of HyperCard.

hypermedia—This is a more general concept than hypertext. In hypermedia the contents of nodes need not only be text. Nodes can contain graphics, audio recordings, pictures, digitized speech, slides, animation films, and so on.

hypertext—Also called "linked text" and "extended text" often refers to multiple pieces of text saved either in separate files or database records, and linked together to reflect certain structure and meaning of information. On the computer screen the different pieces of text are displayed each in its own window. To show the relationship between the different items most hypertext systems use browsers. Some hypertext systems use graphical browsers to represent the structure of hypertext as a network of nodes and links (MCC's gIBIS, MCC's PlaneText). Other simpler systems use indented text (outline processors) or tables of text or images (XEROX's NoteCard and Apple's HyperCard). Hypertext systems allow the user to select their own path through very complex, highly interrelated items of information.

hypertext authoring system—A hypertext system that allows the user to both create as well as view hypertext documents. HyperCard on the Macintosh, and GUIDE for the IBM personal computer, both are hypertext authoring systems.

hypertext browsing systems—A read-only hypertext system with which the user can only view hypertext documents. In this category fall many reference and public information systems such as those in public libraries and airports. Another example of a hypertext browsing system is the Symbolics Document Examiner for the on-line help system for the Symbolics LISP machine.

HyperWare—The finished hypertext documents for instruction, training, or entertainment purposes. HyperWare is a kind of software for which, in order to run, you need a special hypertext system such as GUIDE, NoteCards, or HyperCard. For HyperCard, user's HyperWare is also known as StackWare, from "Stack" the term used for a single HyperCard document. Many publishers now publish HyperWare documents to be used with popular hypertext systems.

Hypothesis—From the Greek hypo-tithenai which means "a foundation or supposition." Hypothesis often refers to an explanation with a certain degree of confirmation. A hypothesis with a high degree of confirmation could become an accepted theory or law. While a hypothesis with a low degree of confirmation is easily discarded.

infix notation—This is the style of writing arithmetic expressions with the operators between the two values or expressions on which they operate. Also, in Turbo Prolog you write predicates in prefix notation with the predicate name coming before the arguments "studies (john,art)." In Micro-Prolog from Logic Associates of London, an interpreted version of Prolog for the PC, you can use both infix and prefix notations in writing predicates.

issue—A controversial question which doesn't have a definite answer or solution, only resolutions. The resolution of an issue almost always has an unanticipated consequence with side effects. You can deal with issues by using deliberation to show the pros and cons of every position (answer) you take from the issue. It is impossible to anticipate all the side effects of positions from issues. The best bet is to deliberate as much as you can until you run out of time, money, or people that support the deliberation process.

IBIS—The term stands for "Issue Based Information Systems." It is a method for using deliberation and argumentation to explore and analyze problems using issues, positions, and arguments. The method uses a question-and-answer process which starts by raising the main issue (also called the root issue). The method could be used by a single person or a group of people. In response to the main issue, participants suggest positions, which could be argued for or against by others. IBIS was developed by W. Kunz and H. W. J. Rittel with the purpose of supporting and coordinating debate over planning and environmental design decisions in environmental design and planning.

knowledge-base—The set of facts and rules in a Prolog program. In Turbo Prolog, the knowledge-base is placed in the "clauses" section of the program.

knowledge-based systems—Programs that use knowledge and inference mechanisms to solve problems.

knowledge representation—A method for encoding facts and relationships about the objects and concepts of the world, in the computer.

link—A relationship between the nodes in a hypertext system. In Prolog you can represent links using the predicate "link(SOURCE_NODE,TARGET_NODE)", "link(RELATION_NAME, SOURCE_NODE,TARGET_NODE)," "link (RELATION_NAME, LINK_ATTRIBUTES_LIST, SOURCE_NODE, TARGET_NODE)," and so on.

name—In Prolog, names are basically atoms. Name is also a string type that can be both stored efficiently and operated on quickly.

natural language understanding—An artificial intelligence approach that deals with the development of programs that through the analysis of natural language, can communicate with humans.

node—The basic component of hypertext systems. HyperMedia nodes could contain text, graphics, video, and audio information. Physically nodes could be saved in the computer as separate files, or separate data records in a single database file.

NoteCard—A hypertext system developed at XEROX Palo Alto Research Center by Frank Halasz, Tom Moran, and Randy Trigg. NoteCard was created as a support tool to help engineers and information analysts collect, organize, and analyze information about a particular topic and produce reports on the topic on a regular basis.

parameters—Object and variable names in a Prolog relation.

PlainText—A hypertext system developed at Microelectronics and Computer technology Corporation (MCC) and used for software design development and research.

point—A piece of text (a word, sentence, paragraph, and so on) or graphics (a line, a geometrical shape, or part of a drawing) which is linked to other points or nodes.

position—In IBIS, issues are questions. To answer, or respond to, these issues you post positions. For a question to be an issue, it must have at least two competing positions.

predicate—What is affirmed or denied of a subject. In Prolog, every fact or rule is a predicate. Another name for Prolog predicates is the word "relation." I write predicates by specifying the name and the type of objects involved in the relation.

predication—The act of affirming or denying a predicate of a subject. In modern logic you deal with classes, sets and relations, while in Aristotelian logic you deal with predication.

predicate calculus—A particular form of logic in which objects are represented as terms. In this form of logic, terms are of three kinds: (1) Constant symbols, symbols standing for individual concepts. In Prolog such terms are called *atoms.* (2) Variable symbols, symbols standing for different individuals at different times. (3) Compound terms, each compound term consists of a function symbol (functor) and an ordered set of terms as its arguments. The compound term uses constant and variable symbols to construct more complex concepts of individuals. To represent relationships between objects, predicate calculus uses predicates. A predicate is an atomic proposition that consists of a "predicate symbol" and an ordered set of terms as its arguments.

prefix notation—See infix notation.

problem solving—In the narrow sense of the term it is defined in AI literature as the process of achieving a desired goal after starting from an initial state. The solution involves moving through a problem space in a sequence of operations. In a more general sense—in the design theory and methods literature—it is defined as the process of resolving the inconsistencies and conflicts between the desired state (ought-to-be state) and existing state. Unlike the AI approach, design theoreticians believe that problem solving is an open-ended process and there is no termination rule. According to Horst Rittel, there are two kinds of problems: tame problems, such as those in Engineering and Scientific fields, and wicked problems, such as those in environmental and social fields (W. Kunz and W. J. Rittel, 1970).

problem space—This is a representation of all the possible alternative solutions to a problem and the different states and interactions of these solutions.

procedural programming—See *declarative programming.*

Prolog—This is the first logic programming system, first developed by Alain Colmerauer in 1972. The name stands for "PROgramming in LOGic." The design of Prolog is based on the procedural interpretation of Horn clauses. The early Prolog systems were interpreters. The first Prolog compiler was written for the PDP10 at the University of Edinburgh by D. H. D. Warren, L. M. Pereira, and F. Pereira in 1977. They built a Prolog compiler that executes LISP-like logic programs as efficiently as compiled LISP.

recursion—A programming technique in which a function, procedure, or predicate calls itself. In Prolog there are two kinds of recursion: in-body recursion and tail recursion. In tail recursion the recursive call is the last subgoal of a rule or query. Tail recursion is more efficient because it uses less stack space. In-body recursion, if not carefully managed, could easily cause a memory overflow error.

reification—When constructing a network of nodes and links you are basically building an entity-relationship model with nodes being entities, and links being the relationships between these entities. For example, the relationship "generalizes(NODEA,NODEB)" is a link. To search and Unify Variables with relationship names you can treat relationships or predicates as entities. In predicate logic, this treatment of relationships as objects is known as reification. In this book I gave one example of using reification when I used the predicate relation (RELATION_NAME, LIST_OF_ARGUMENTS).

relation or relationship—Prolog predicates are also called relationships. The predicate `color(red)` is a unary (one place) relationship, `is-a(john,doctor)` is a binary (two place) relationship, and `name(rosalia,redil,roy)` is a ternary (three place) relationship.

rule—This is a logical form with one or more conditions and at least one conclusion. Prolog rules that have at most one conclusion are also known as Horn clauses.

rule firing—This is a Prolog internal process for selecting the next rule to execute after matching the head of the rule with the subgoal at hand.

scientific method—Also known as the "hypothetico-deductive method," normally associated with the procedures of mathematics and physics, uses logical deduction to extract new facts from existing and unrelated sets of facts and rules about the world.

semantic networks—A type of knowledge representation in which facts and rules are represented as a network of nodes and links.

subgoal—Part of a Prolog goal, or a condition in the body of a rule. In the rule "wealthy(X):- own(X,bmw), own(X, house)," the conditions "own(X,bmw)" and "own(X,house)" are subgoals.

systems approach—The traditional definition of the systems approach is that "the style of attacking problems in a well-defined, rational, straightforward, and systematic way that results in an optimal and least expensive solution." Horst Rittel found that the methods of the traditional systems approach are not adequate for solving wicked problems (see definition of wicked problems). He suggested a new definition for the systems approach that uses argumentation as its method. He calls the traditional systems approach "the systems analysis of the first generation," while his approach is "the systems approach of the second generation." Another definition of the systems approach is that of C. West Churchman. In his book "the systems approach," Churchman suggested these characteristics: (1) The systems approach begins when first you see the world through the eyes of another. (2) The systems approach goes on to discovering that the every-world view is terribly restricted. (3) There are no experts in the systems approach.

tame problems—These are the well-defined problems we often find in mathematics, science, and some class of engineering problems (see also wicked problems).

term—In Turbo Prolog terms are either objects defined by one of the standard domain types (symbol, string, char, integer, real, file, and so on) or a compound term (a functor followed by a list of terms enclosed in parentheses and separated by commas).

Turbo Prolog—This is a popular compiler version of Prolog for IBM-PC and compatibles. Turbo Prolog has an extensive library of built-in predicates. Also, Turbo Prolog has built-in predicates for building efficient external databases, and built-in predicates for writing sophisticated graphics using Borland's Graphical Interface (BGI).

textual region—A string of characters between any two positions in a node. Textual region need not be a single word, sentence, paragraph, or section of text.

unification—The mechanism by which Prolog solves its queries. In unification, Prolog tries to match a subgoal against facts and the left hand side of rules to either satisfy that subgoal, or determine one or more further subgoals necessary to evaluate the original subgoal.

wicked problems—These are the not-so-well defined problems that you often find in mathematics, science, and some class of engineering problems. According to Horst Rittel, wicked problems have these characteristics: (1) Every WP is essentially unique. (2) Every WP can be considered to be a symptom of another WP. (3) Every formulation of a WP corresponds to a formulation of the solution, and vice versa. (4) There is no definitive formulation of a WP. (5) A WP can be explained in many different ways. (6) WPs have no stopping rule. (7) The set of all permissible solutions to a WP cannot be enumerated. (8) There is no trial-and-error in a WP. (9) The problem solver of a WP has no right to be wrong. (10) The solutions of a WP are "good/bad" not "true/false." (11) There is no immediate, or even ultimate, test of a solution of a WP.

D

Utility Predicates

```
DOMAINS
  SYMBOLLIST = SYMBOL*
  STRINGLIST = STRING*

/* ****************************************************** */
/* *********************** ifEXIST ********************** */
/* ****************************************************** */

PREDICATES
  ifEXIST(STRING)


% flow pattern: (i)

% if the file exists return doing nothing.

ifEXIST(FileName):-
  existfile(FileName), !.

% if the file doesn't exist, ask if user wants to create it.

ifEXIST(FileName):-
  makewindow(11,15,112,"",5,7,3,45),
  write("\File doesn't exist, create it (y/n): "),
  readln(Ans),
  upper_lower(Ans1,Ans),
  frontchar(Ans1,CHAR,_), CHAR = 'Y',
  file_str(FileName,""), removewindow, !.

ifEXIST(_):- removewindow, fail.      % remove window 11

/* ****************************************************** */
/* *************** revision of a list ***************** */
/* ****************************************************** */
```

```
PREDICATES
  rev(SYMBOLLIST,SYMBOLLIST,SYMBOLLIST)
  member_out(SYMBOL,SYMBOLLIST,SYMBOLLIST)

CLAUSES

/* Given a list of elements X, and a list of additions and
   deletions in X,we call Z, "rev" derives Y, the  revised
   list of X such that: rev(X,Y,Z) is true.

    where the relation between the three lists X, Y and Z
    is such that:

    if A exists in X as well as in Z, it is not in Y.
       (in other words when we revised X into Y we deleted
        A from X)

    if A exists in X but not in Z, then A continues to be in Y.
       (in other words when we revised X into Y we kept A.)

    if A exists in Z but not in X, then A must be in Y.
       (in other words when we revised X into Y we added a new
        member A that was not there in X).
*/




/* ********************* rev **************************** */
/* Given a list X, and list of differences between X and a
   version of X, we call Y, revise returns Y. such that:

/* 1. if the list of differences is empty, X and its version
      are identical
   2. if the original list, X, is empty, then the new
      version of X, Y, is identical to the list of
      differences between X and Y.
   3. if the first member of X is also in Z, then it should
      not be in Y.
   4. if the first element of X is not in Z it should be in Y. */

  rev(X,X,[]).
  rev([],Y,Y).
  rev([A|X],Y,Z):- member_out(A,Z,Z1), !, rev(X,Y,Z1).
  rev([A|X],[A|Y],Z):- rev(X,Y,Z).

/* ********************** member_out ******************* */

/* For a given element A and a list Z, this predicate checks
   if A is a member of Z then it returns all of Z, except
   A. Otherwise, it fails.

  member_out(A,[A|Z],Z).
  member_out(A,[B|Z],[B|Z1]):- member_out(A,Z,Z1).

/* **************************************************** */
/* ********************* findHyperText ****************** */
/* **************************************************** */
% flow pattern: (i,i,o)

PREDICATES
   findHyperText(STRING,INTEGER,STRING)
      findStart(STRING,INTEGER,INTEGER)
         findStart1(STRING,INTEGER,INTEGER)
      findHyperText1(STRING,STRING,STRING)
```

```
CLAUSES
/* Given a string "String" and a position (integer) in
   that string "Pos", "findHyperText" finds the hypertext
   region pointed at by the user.

   A hypertext region has a starting and ending label:
   Starting label = "{"
   Ending label   = "}"
*/


findHyperText(String,Pos,HyperStr):-
   findStart(String,Pos,Spos),
   frontstr(Spos,String,_,String1),
   findHyperText1(String1,"",HyperStr).

/* ******************* findStart & findStart1 *********** */

findStart(String,Pos,StartPos):-
   frontstr(Pos,String,String1,_),
   findStart1(String1,Pos,StartPos).

findStart1(String,Pos,Pos):-
   StartLabelPos=Pos-1,
   frontstr(StartLabelPos,String,_,StartLabel),
   StartLabel="{", !.

findStart1(String,Pos,StartPos):-
   NewPos=Pos-1,
   frontstr(NewPos,String,FrontString,_),
   findStart1(FrontString,NewPos,StartPos).

/* ***************** findHyperText1 ********************* */

findHyperText1(Str,HyperStr,HyperStr):-
   fronttoken(Str,"}",_), !.

findHyperText1(Str,Hstr,HyperStr):-
   frontchar(Str,' ',Rest),
   concat(Hstr," ",Htemp),
   findHyperText1(Rest,Htemp,HyperStr), !.

findHyperText1(Str,Hstr,HyperStr):-
   frontchar(Str,'\n',Rest),
   concat(Hstr,"\n",Htemp),
   findHyperText1(Rest,Htemp,HyperStr), !.

findHyperText1(Str,Hstr,HyperStr):-
   fronttoken(Str,Htoken,Rest),
concat(Hstr,Htoken,Htemp),
   findHyperText1(Rest,Htemp,HyperStr).


/* ***************************************************** */
/* ********************** searchPOINT **************** */
/* ***************************************************** */
% flow pattern: (i,i,i,o)
/* given the text for a target point HTXT (region of text
between "{" & "}") and the text for the whole node NTXT,
find the position POS of HTXT in NTXT. The third argument
to search POINT must always be the empty string "". */
PREDICATES
  searchPOINT(STRING,STRING,STRING,INTEGER)
    searchPOINT1(STRING,STRING,STRING,INTEGER)

CLAUSES
```

```
searchPOINT(Hstr,Str,Nstr,Pos):-
  fronttoken(Hstr,Tok,Hstr1),
  fronttoken(Str,Tok,Str1),
  concat(Nstr,Tok,Nstr1),
  searchPOINT1(Hstr1,Str1,Nstr1,Pos), !.

searchPOINT(Hstr,Str,Nstr,Pos):-
  fronttoken(Str,Tok,Str1),
  concat(Nstr,Tok,Nstr1),
  searchPOINT(Hstr,Str1,Nstr1,Pos).

searchPOINT1("",_,Nstr,Pos):-
  str_len(Nstr,Pos), !.

searchPOINT1(Hstr,Str,Nstr,Pos):-
  fronttoken(Hstr,Tok,Hstr1),
  fronttoken(Str,Tok,Str1),
  concat(Nstr,Tok,Nstr1),
  searchPOINT1(Hstr1,Str1,Nstr1,Pos).

/* ****************************************************** */
/* ************* GENERAL UTILITY PREDICATES ************* */
/* ****************************************************** */

PREDICATES
  nth_member(STRINGLIST,INTEGER,STRING)
  msg(INTEGER,INTEGER,STRING)

CLAUSES

/* ********************** nth_member ******************** */
% flow pattern: (i,i,o)

  nth_member([],_,""):-!.
  nth_member([H|_],1,H):- !.
  nth_member([_|T],N,MEMBER):-
    M=N-1,
    nth_member(T,M,MEMBER).

/* ********************** msg ************************** */
% flow pattern: (i,i,i)
/* given a row R, a column C and a string Str, display Str
in a window at the row R and column C. */

msg(R,C,Str):-
   makewindow(10,22,112,"Message",R,C,3,40),
   window_str(Str),
   repeat,
      inkey(_),  % repeat waiting for a key to be pressed.
   !,
   removewindow.

/* ****************************************************** */
/* ******************** changeDIR *********************** */
/* ****************************************************** */
% flow pattern: (i,i,i,i)
/* given a row ROW, a column COL, a window attribute WATTR,
and a frame attribute FATTR, prompt the user with an input
line to request the new path and directory names.  */

/* this program requires TOOLBOX utilities              */

/* ************** Turbo Prolog TOOLBOX programs *********
   ********** Copyright 1986, Borland International****** */

include "tdoms.pro"      % TOOLBOX text domains declarations
```

```
include "tpreds.pro"      % TOOLBOX text predicates declaration

DATABASE
  insmode
  lineinpstate(STRING,COL)
  lineinpflag

% required Turbo Prolog TOOLBOX modules

include "lineinp.pro"     % TOOLBOX line input predicate

PREDICATES
  changeDIR(INTEGER,INTEGER,INTEGER,INTEGER)
  changeDISK(STRING)
  pathNAME(STRING)

CLAUSES

changeDIR(ROW,COL,WATTR,FATTR):-
  disk(DISK),
  lineinput_repeat(ROW,COL,45,WATTR,FATTR,"Directory: ",DISK,NEWDISK),
  changeDISK(NEWDISK),!,
  removewindow.
changeDIR(_,_,_,_).

changeDISK(DISK):-
  pathNAME(DISK),
  disk(DISK),!.
changeDISK(_):-
  msg(17,1,"error in directory name."), % in "user-h.pro"
  fail.

pathNAME(DISK):-
  fronttoken(DISK,_,Str),
  fronttoken(Str,":",Str1),
  fronttoken(Str1,"\\",_).

/* ****************************************************** */
/* *********************** treemenu ******************** */
/* ****************************************************** */
% an example on using treemenu follows this section
/*
                   Treemenu (V.2)

(treemenu is copyright of Borland International, 1987.)

(modified version of the TURBO PROLOG TOOLBOX TREE MENU)
(Based on treemenu in "tree.pro" from the TOOLBOX, parts of
 tree.pro was used by permission from BORLAND INTERNATIONAL)

modifications are in:

1. predicate "listsum" is now tail recursive (more efficient).
2. Arrows pointing to parent nodes are added.
3. the arcs between nodes are labeled with relation names
   to facilitate this tree definition.
4. predicate draw_right is now tail recursive, the
   draw_rightlist appears at the end of draw_right, not in
   the middle.
5. a new predicate "writetext1" was added for writing labels.

*/
/* ****************************************************** */
/*
include "tdoms.pro"
```

```
DOMAINS
  SELECTOR=INTEGER
  TREE = tree(STRING,STRING,SELECTOR,TREELIST)
  TREELIST = TREE*

DATABASE
  treewindow(ROW,COL)
  treechoice(SELECTOR)
*/

DOMAINS
  ROWLIST=ROW*
  COLLIST=COL*

PREDICATES
  treemenu(SYMBOL,TREE,SELECTOR)
  treeaction(SELECTOR)
  f10action(SELECTOR)

  draw(symbol,TREE)

  writetext(ROW,COL,INTEGER,STRING,SELECTOR)
  writetext1(ROW,COL,STRING,COL)
  treeline_ver(ROW,ROW,COL)
  treeline_ver1(ROW,ROW,COL)
  treeline_hor(COL,COL,ROW)
  treeline_hor1(COL,COL,ROW)
  scr_ch(ROW,COL,CHAR)

  lastinlist(ROW,ROWLIST)
  lastinlist(COL,COLLIST)
  listsum(ROWLIST,ROW,ROW)
  listsum(COLLIST,COL,COL)
  treekeyact(KEY)
  just(ROW,COL)
  just1(ROW,COL,ROW,COL)
  just2(ROW,COL)
  nodelistlen(ROWLIST,INTEGER)
  nodelistlen(COLLIST,INTEGER)
  remove_treechoice
  newupdate(DBASEDOM)
  treedrop(INTEGER,STRING,STRING)

CLAUSES

/* ********************** treeline_ver ******************* */

/* draw vertical lines connecting elements in the tree */
  treeline_ver(R1,R2,C):-
        treewindow(STROW,STCOL),           /* find the starting position */
        makewindow(_,_,_,_,_,_,ROWS,COLS), /* returns the tree windows size */
        C>=STCOL, C<STCOL+COLS-2, R1<STROW+ROWS-2,
        R2>=STROW, SLROW=STROW+ROWS-2,
        max(STROW,R1,STROW1), min(R2,SLROW,SLROW1),
        CC=C-STCOL, RR1=STROW1-STROW, RR2=SLROW1-STROW,
        treeline_ver1(RR1,RR2,CC),fail.
  treeline_ver(_,_,_).

/* ********************* treeline_ver1 ******************* */

  treeline_ver1(R1,R2,C):-
        R2>R1, R=R1+1,
        scr_char(R1,C,'°'),
        treeline_ver1(R,R2,C).

/* ********************** treeline_hor ***************** */
```

```
/* draw horizontal lines connecting elements in the tree */
  treeline_hor(C1,C2,R):-
        treewindow(STROW,STCOL), makewindow(_,_,_,_,_,_,ROWS,COLS),
        SLCOL=STCOL+COLS-2,
        R>=STROW, R<STROW+ROWS-2, C1<SLCOL, C2>STCOL,
        max(STCOL,C1,STCOL1), min(C2,SLCOL,SLCOL1),
        RR=R-STROW, CC1=STCOL1-STCOL, CC2=SLCOL1-STCOL,
        treeline_hor1(CC1,CC2,RR),fail.
  treeline_hor(_,_,_).

/* ********************** treeline_hor1 **************** */

  treeline_hor1(C1,C2,R):-
        C2>C1, C=C1+1,
        scr_char(R,C1,'á'),
        treeline_hor1(C,C2,R).

/* ************************* scr_ch ******************** */

/* write a character in a tree window  */
  scr_ch(R,C,CH):-
        treewindow(STROW,STCOL), makewindow(_,_,_,_,_,_,ROWS,COLS),
        R>=STROW, R<STROW+ROWS-2, C>=STCOL, C<STCOL+COLS-2, !,
        RR=R-STROW, CC=C-STCOL,
        scr_char(RR,CC,CH).
  scr_ch(_,_,_).

/* ************************* treedrop ****************** */

  treedrop(0,TEXT,TEXT):-!.
  treedrop(N,TEXT,TEXT1):-frontstr(N,TEXT,_,TEXT1).

/* ************************* writetext ***************** */

  writetext(ROW,COL,ATTR,TEXT,SELECT):-
        str_len(TEXT,LEN),
        treewindow(STROW,STCOL), makewindow(_,_,_,_,_,_,ROWS,COLS),
        ROW>=STROW, ROW<STROW+ROWS-2, COL<STCOL+COLS-2, COL+LEN>STCOL,
        REALROW=ROW-STROW,
        RSTART=COL-STCOL,
        REND=RSTART+LEN,
        VST=STCOL-STCOL, VEND=VST+COLS-2,
        max(RSTART,VST,RSTART1), min(REND,VEND,REND1),
        REALLEN=REND1-RSTART1,
        DROP=RSTART1-RSTART,
        treedrop(DROP,TEXT,TEXT1),
        field_str(REALROW,RSTART1,REALLEN,TEXT1),
        field_attr(REALROW,RSTART1,REALLEN,ATTR),
        cursor(R,C),
        R=REALROW,
        C>=RSTART1, C<RSTART1+REALLEN,     !,
        field_attr(R,RSTART1,REALLEN,31),
        assert(treechoice(SELECT)).
  writetext(_,_,_,_,_).

/* ************************* writetext1 *************** */

writetext1(ROW,COL,TEXT,COLAFTERTEXT):-
  str_len(TEXT,LEN),
  COLAFTERTEXT=COL+LEN,
  treewindow(STROW,STCOL), makewindow(_,_,_,_,_,_,ROWS,COLS),
  ROW>=STROW, ROW<STROW+ROWS-2, COL<STCOL+COLS-2, COL+LEN>STCOL,
  REALROW=ROW-STROW,
  RSTART=COL-STCOL,
  REND=RSTART+LEN,
```

```
  VEND=COLS-2,
  max(RSTART,0,RSTART1), min(REND,VEND,REND1),
  REALLEN=REND1-RSTART1,
  DROP=RSTART1-RSTART,
  treedrop(DROP,TEXT,TEXT1),
  field_str(REALROW,RSTART1,REALLEN,TEXT1), !.

writetext1(_,C,_,C).

/* **************************** listsum ****************** */

  listsum([],S,S):-!.
  listsum([H|T],OS,NS):-TS=OS+H,listsum(T,TS,NS).

/* ********************** lastinlist ******************** */

  lastinlist(RMAX,[RMAX]) :- !.
  lastinlist(RMAX,[_|T]) :- lastinlist(RMAX,T).

/* ********************* nodelistlen ******************** */

  nodelistlen([],0):-!.
  nodelistlen([_|T],N):-
        nodelistlen(T,X),
        N=X+1.

/* ********************** newupdate ********************* */

  newupdate(_):-retract(treewindow(_,_)),fail.
  newupdate(X):-assert(X).

/* ************************* just *********************** */

/* Cursor window control */
  just(R,C):-
        cursor(ROW,COL),       /* current cursor pos */
        RR=ROW+R, CC=COL+C,
        makewindow(_,_,_,_,_,_,ROWS,COLS),
        ROWSS=ROWS-3, COLSS=COLS-3,
        just1(RR,CC,ROWSS,COLSS).

/* ************************ just1 *********************** */

/* move cursor and control windows */
  just1(R,C,_,_):-R<0,!,cursor(0,C),just2(R,0).
  just1(R,C,_,_):-C<0,!,cursor(R,0),just2(0,C).
  just1(R,C,ROWS,_):-R>ROWS,!,cursor(ROWS,C),DR=R-ROWS,just2(DR,0).
  just1(R,C,_,COLS):-C>COLS,!,cursor(R,COLS),DC=C-COLS,just2(0,DC).
  just1(R,C,_,_):-cursor(R,C),fail.

/* ************************* just2 ********************* */

/* scroll tree in window with cursor and update tree position */
  just2(DR,DC):-
        scroll(DR,DC),  /* scroll is a Turbo Prolog standard predicate */
        treewindow(R,C),!,
        CC=C+DC, RR=R+DR,
        newupdate(treewindow(RR,CC)),
        fail.

/* *********************** treekeyact ****************** */

/* Tree input key action */
  treekeyact(right)     :-just(0,1).
  treekeyact(ctrlright) :-just(0,5).
  treekeyact(left)      :-just(0,-1).
```

```
  treekeyact(ctrlleft)  :-just(0,-5).
  treekeyact(up)        :-just(-1,0).
  treekeyact(pgup)      :-just(-5,0).
  treekeyact(down)      :-just(1,0).
  treekeyact(pgdn)      :-just(5,0).
  treekeyact(ctrlhome)  :-treewindow(R,C),!,RR=-R,CC=-C,just2(RR,CC).
  treekeyact(end)       :-cursor(_,C),makewindow(_,_,_,_,_,_,COLS),
                          DC=COLS-3-C,just(0,DC).
  treekeyact(home)      :-cursor(_,C),DC=-C,just(0,DC).
  treekeyact(cr)        :-treechoice(CHOICE), !, treeaction(CHOICE).
  treekeyact(esc).

/* *******************************************************
@@@ F10 is a hypertext hotkey that displays hypertext
   operations menu
****************************************************** */
  treekeyact(fkey(10))  :-
    treechoice(CHOICE), !,
    f10action(CHOICE). % f10action is a hotkey action


/*treekeyact(fkey(1)):-help.  If helpsystem is used */

/*treekeyact(fkey(5)):- resizing the tree-window */

/* ******************** remove_treechoice *************** */

  remove_treechoice:- retract(treechoice(_)), fail.
  remove_treechoice.

/* ****************************************************** */
/* ***********************draw_right ******************* */
/* ****************************************************** */
/* @@@ This is a modified version of draw_right */

PREDICATES
  draw_right(TREE,ROW,ROW,COL,COL,COL,COL,ROW)
  draw_rightlist(STRING,STRING,SELECTOR,TREELIST,
                 STRINGLIST,STRINGLIST,
                 ROWLIST,ROWLIST,
                 ROW,ROW,
                 COL,COL,COL,COL,ROW)
  connect_nodesright(STRINGLIST,ROW,COL,INTEGER,COL,COL,ROWLIST)
  con_nodesright(STRINGLIST,ROW,COL,ROW,ROW,COL,COL,ROWLIST)
  cornerright(ROW,ROW,ROW,ROW,CHAR)
  check_lastright(ROW,COL,ROWLIST)

CLAUSES
draw_right(_,_,_,_,_,_,_,_):-
  keypressed, !,
  readkey(KEY),
  treekeyact(KEY),
  fail.

draw_right(tree("root",NAME,SELECT,[]),
           CURROW,NEWCURROW,
           _,CURCOL,CURCOL,_,RESROW):- !,
  NEWCURROW=CURROW+2,
  RESROW=NEWCURROW,
  writetext(RESROW,CURCOL,112,NAME,SELECT).

draw_right(tree(RELATION,NAME,SELECT,[]),
           CURROW,NEWCURROW,
           _,CURCOL,CURCOL,COLSTEP,RESROW):- !,
  NEWCURROW=CURROW+2,
  str_len(RELATION,LEN),
```

```
  CURCOL1=CURCOL+LEN+COLSTEP,
  RESROW=NEWCURROW,
  writetext(RESROW,CURCOL1,112,NAME,SELECT).

draw_right(tree("root",NAME,SELECT,TREELIST),
           CURROW,NEWCURROW,
           LASTNAMECOL,NEXTNAMECOL,CURCOL,COLSTEP,RESROW):- !,
  draw_rightlist("",NAME,SELECT,TREELIST,
                 [],_,
                 [],_,
                 CURROW,NEWCURROW,
                 LASTNAMECOL,NEXTNAMECOL,CURCOL,COLSTEP,RESROW).

draw_right(tree(RELATION,NAME,SELECT,TREELIST),
           CURROW,NEWCURROW,
           LASTNAMECOL,NEXTNAMECOL,CURCOL,COLSTEP,RESROW):-
  draw_rightlist(RELATION,NAME,SELECT,TREELIST,
                 [],_,
                 [],_,
                 CURROW,NEWCURROW,
                 LASTNAMECOL,NEXTNAMECOL,CURCOL,COLSTEP,RESROW).

/* ************************ draw_rightlist ************** */

draw_rightlist(RELATION,NAME,SELECT,[],
               RELlist,RELlist,
               NodeRowList,NodeRowList,
               CurRow,CurRow,
               NEXTNAMECOL,NEXTNAMECOL,CURCOL,COLSTEP,RESROW):-
  str_len(NAME,NAMELEN),
  str_len(RELATION,RELLEN),
  CURCOL1=CURCOL+1+NAMELEN+COLSTEP+COLSTEP+RELLEN,
  CURCOL2=CURCOL+COLSTEP+RELLEN,
  nodelistlen(NODEROWLIST,LEN),
  listsum(NODEROWLIST,0,SUM),
  RESROW=SUM div LEN,
  COLAFTERarrow=1+CURCOL2+NAMELEN,
  COLAFTERdash=2+CURCOL2+NAMELEN,
  COLAFTERname=CURCOL2+NAMELEN,
  connect_nodesright(RELlist,RESROW,COLAFTERdash,
                     LEN,CURCOL1,COLSTEP,NODEROWLIST),
  writetext(RESROW,CURCOL2,112,NAME,SELECT),
  scr_ch(RESROW,COLAFTERname,'<'),
  scr_ch(RESROW,COLAFTERarrow,'á'),
  check_lastright(RESROW,COLAFTERdash,NODEROWLIST), !.

draw_rightlist(RELATION,NAME,SELECT,[H|T],
               RELlist,ResRELlist,
               NodeRowList,ResNodeRowList,
               CurRow,CurRow2,
               LNCOL,LNCOL2,CURCOL,COLSTEP,RESROW):-
  H=tree(Rel,_,_,_),
  str_len(NAME,NAMELEN),
  str_len(RELATION,RELLEN),
  CURCOL1=CURCOL+1+NAMELEN+COLSTEP+COLSTEP+RELLEN,
  draw_right(H,CurRow,CurRow1,LNCOL,LNCOL1,CURCOL1,COLSTEP,Noderow),
  draw_rightlist(RELATION,NAME,SELECT,T,
                 [Rel|RELlist],ResRELlist,
                 [Noderow|NodeRowList],ResNodeRowList,
                 CurRow1,CurRow2,
                 LNCOL1,LNCOL2,CURCOL,COLSTEP,RESROW).

/* ******************** check_lastright *************** */

check_lastright(ROW,_,[ROW|_]):-!.
```

```
check_lastright(ROW,COL,[_|LIST]):-!,
  check_lastright(ROW,COL,LIST).

check_lastright(ROW,COL,_):-
  scr_ch(ROW,COL,'Ç').

/* ****************** connect_nodesright **************** */

connect_nodesright([REL],ROW,COL,1,COL1,COLSTEP,_) :-!,
  treeline_hor(COL,COL1,ROW),
  writetext1(ROW,COL1,REL,COL2),
  COL3=COL2+COLSTEP,
  treeline_hor(COL2,COL3,ROW).

connect_nodesright(Rlist,ROW,COL,_,COL1,COLSTEP,[RMAX|L]):-
  lastinlist(RMIN,[RMAX|L]),
  con_nodesright(Rlist,ROW,COL,RMIN,RMAX,COL1,COLSTEP,[RMAX|L]).

con_nodesright(_,_,_,_,_,_,_,[]).

con_nodesright(_,_,COL,_,_,_,_,[R1,R2|_]):-
  R22=R2+1,
  treeline_ver(R22,R1,COL), fail.

con_nodesright([Hrel|Trel],ROW,COL,RMIN,RMAX,COL1,COLSTEP,[ROW1|T]):-
  CC=COL+1,
  treeline_hor(CC,COL1,ROW1),
  writetext1(ROW1,COL1,Hrel,COL2),
  COL3=COL2+COLSTEP,
  treeline_hor(COL2,COL3,ROW1),
  cornerright(ROW,RMIN,RMAX,ROW1,CORNCHAR),
  scr_ch(ROW1,COL,CORNCHAR),
  con_nodesright(Trel,ROW,COL,RMIN,RMAX,COL1,COLSTEP,T).

/* *********************** cornerright ******************* */

cornerright(RMIN,RMIN,_,RMIN,'ô') :- !.

cornerright(RMAX,_,RMAX,RMAX,'ê') :- !.

cornerright(_,RMIN,_,RMIN,'Ö') :- !.

cornerright(_,_,RMAX,RMAX,'â') :- !.

cornerright(RMIDT,_,_,RMIDT,'é') :- !.

cornerright(_,_,_,_,'û').


/* *************************** draw ********************** */

/* draw a tree in the selected direction */

  draw(right,TREE):-
    draw_right(TREE,0,_,0,_,0,3,_).

/* ************************* treemenu ******************* */

/* @@@@@ modified version @@@@@ */
/* treemenu construct and display a box diagram of a tree structure */

treemenu(DIRECTION,TREE,CHOICE) :-
/* if this makewindow is commented out the tree will be
drawn in the currently active window */
  makewindow(81,66,23,"",0,0,24,80),
  makestatus(112,"F1:Help  F10:Select  Retrn:Select  Arrows:move around  Ctrl
```

```
arrows: move fast"),
  newupdate(treewindow(0,0)),
  repeat,
    remove_treechoice,
    draw(DIRECTION,TREE),
    readkey(KEY),
    treekeyact(KEY), !,
  removestatus,
  not(KEY=esc),
  treechoice(CHOICE),!.

/* ****************************************************** */
/* ****** using the new treemenu in an example ********** */
/* ****************************************************** */
include "c:\\toolbox\\tdoms.pro"

DOMAINS
  SELECTOR=INTEGER
  TREE = tree(STRING,STRING,SELECTOR,TREELIST)
  TREELIST = TREE*

DATABASE
  treewindow(ROW,COL)
  treechoice(SELECTOR)

include "c:\\toolbox\\tpreds.pro"
include "c:\\toolbox\\status.pro"
include "c:\\toolbox\\tree2.pro"  % tree2.pro is in Fig. 4-6

CLAUSES
  treeaction(_). % clauses matched by Turbo when you press ENTER
  f10action(_).  % clauses matched by Turbo when you press F10

% to run the example uncomment the following GOAL section
/*
GOAL

  treemenu(right,
           tree("root","Francis",1,
                 [tree("wife_of","Josie",2,
                        [tree("working_address_of","Martinez",3,[]),
                         tree("car_of","Dodge-Colt",4,[])
                                ]),
                  tree("working_address_of","San Francisco",5,[]),
                  tree("home_address_of","Antoich",6,[]),
                  tree("car_of","Honda",7,[]),
                  tree("son_of","Allen",8,
                       [tree("age_of","12",9,[])])
                 ]),Choice).
*/

/* ****************************************************** */
/* **** a logical hypertext revision system ************* */
/* ****************************************************** */
/* In this system hypertext is represented as a list of
   items. An item is a compound object with two arguments:

         item(POS,hypertext-ITEM)

   POS is an INTEGER number representing the relative
   position of a hypertext-ITEM in the hypertext.
   A hypertext-ITEM could be:

         1. a chunk of text,
         2. an expansion button,
         3. a replacement button,
```

```
        4. a note button,
        5. a reference button,
        6. a command button,
        7. a keyword (index) button

    For now, we don't need to worry about the details of
    the hypertext-ITEM.  So, we will assume that a hypertext-ITEM
    is just a Turbo Prolog symbol.

To try the system, load and run the program and give this goal:

Goal: revision([item(1,a),item(2,b),item(4,f)],
               REVISION,
               [item(3,c),item(4,d)]).

...and Turbo will return this answer:

REVISION = [item(1,a),item(2,b),item(3,c),item(4,d)]
1 Solution.

*/

DOMAINS
  item = item(INTEGER,SYMBOL)
  itemlist = item*

PREDICATES
  revision(itemlist,itemlist,itemlist)
  rel(SYMBOL,itemlist,itemlist,itemlist)  % more general version

CLAUSES

/* ******************** revision *********************** */
revision(X,X,[]):-!.
revision([],Y,Y).
revision([item(Pos,A)|X],Y,[item(Pos,A)|Z]):- !,
  revision(X,Y,Z).
revision([item(Pos,A)|X],[item(Pos,B)|Y],[item(Pos,B)|Z]):-
   A <> B, !,
   revision(X,Y,Z).
revision([item(Pos,A)|X],[item(Pos1,B)|Y],[item(Pos1,B)|Z]):-
  Pos > Pos1, !,
  revision([item(Pos,A)|X],Y,Z).
revision([A|X],[A|Y],Z):-
  revision(X,Y,Z).

/* ****************** rel ****************************** */
rel(revision,X,X,[]):-!.
rel(revision,[],Y,Y).
rel(revision,[item(Pos,A)|X],Y,[item(Pos,A)|Z]):- !,
  rel(revision,X,Y,Z).
rel(revision,[item(Pos,_)|X], [item(Pos,B)|Y],[item(Pos,B)|Z]):-
   !,
   rel(revision,X,Y,Z).
rel(revision,[item(Pos,A)|X],[item(Pos1,B)|Y],[item(Pos1,B)|Z]):-
  Pos > Pos1, !,
  rel(revision,[item(Pos,A)|X],Y,Z).
rel(revision,[A|X],[A|Y],Z):-
  rel(revision,X,Y,Z).

/* ***************************************************** */
/* ************** END OF UTILITY PREDICATES ************* */
/* ***************************************************** */
```

Index

E

F

Q

R

S

T

U

V

W

X

Y

Exploring Hypertext Programming: Writing Knowledge Representation and Problem Solving Programs

If you are intrigued with the possibilities of the programs included in *Exploring Hypertext Programming* (TAB Book No. 3208), you should definitely consider having the disk containing the software applications. This software is guaranteed free of manufacturer's defects. (If you have any problems, return the disk within 30 days, and we'll send you a new one.) Not only will you save the time and effort of typing the programs, but also the disk eliminates the possibility of errors that can prevent the programs from functioning. Interested?

Available on disk for the IBM PC at $24.95 for each disk plus $2.50 shipping and handling (requires DOS 3.1 or later).

Yes, I'm interested. Send me:

____ copies 5 1/4" disk requiring 360K (#6734S), $24.95 .... $ ________

____ copies 3 1/2" disk requiring 360K (#6735S), $24.95 .... $ ________

____ TAB BOOKS catalog (free with purchase; otherwise send $1.00) in check or money order (credited to your first purchase) .... $ ________

Shipping & Handling: $2.50 per disk in U.S. ($5.00 per disk outside U.S.) $ ________

Please add appropriate local and state sales tax. $ ________

TOTAL $ ________

☐ Check or money order enclosed made payable to TAB BOOKS

Charge my ☐ VISA ☐ MasterCard ☐ American Express

Acct No. ________________ Exp. Date ________

Signature ________________

Name ________________

Address ________________

City ________________ State ________ Zip ________

TOLL-FREE ORDERING: 1-800-822-8158

(in PA and AK call 1-717-794-2191)

or write to TAB BOOKS, Blue Ridge Summit, PA, 17294-0850

Prices subject to change. Orders outside the U.S. must be paid in international money order in U.S. dollars.

**If you need 340K disks, write us at 17294-0214.

TAB 3208